A SELECTIVE GUIDE TO ENGLAND

By the same author

SOUTHEY
PARISH AND EMPIRE
LIVINGSTONE AND AFRICA
NEW UNIVERSITY
THE RAILWAYS OF BRITAIN
TRANSPORT
BRITAIN AND THE WORLD
ST PANCRAS STATION
TRANSPORT MUSEUMS
LIFE IN VICTORIAN LEICESTER
LEICESTER PAST AND PRESENT
THE RAILWAY IN ENGLAND AND WALES
(Volume I)

Anthologies

AFRICAN DISCOVERY
(with Margery Perham)
JOURNEYS IN ENGLAND
A DEVON ANTHOLOGY

A SELECTIVE GUIDE TO ENGLAND

Jack Simmons

John Bartholomew & Son Limited
Edinburgh and London

British Library Cataloguing in Publication Data

Simmons, Jack
A selective guide to England.
1. England – Description and travel – 1971–
– Guide-books
I. Title
914.2'04'857 DA650

ISBN 0-7028-1098-3

First published in Great Britain 1979 by
JOHN BARTHOLOMEW & SON LIMITED
12 Duncan Street, Edinburgh EH9 1TA
And 216 High Street, Bromley BR1 1PW

ISBN 0 7028 1098 3

Cathedral plans based on those used in Alec Clifton-Taylor's *Cathedrals of England* (Thames & Hudson, 1967)

Book and jacket design: Susan Waywell
10/11pt Monophoto Baskerville (169)

Printed in Great Britain by
Hazell Watson & Viney Ltd, Aylesbury, Bucks

TO
DAVID JEFFREYS
OBSERVANT TRAVELLER

CONTENTS

CONTENTS

CONTENTS

CONTENTS

PREFACE

This is a book I have long wished to write. I have been travelling throughout England for well over 40 years, since my eyes were first opened as a schoolboy to what was to be seen in Liverpool and Norwich and Lincoln. This book attempts to record and analyse some of the pleasure my travelling has brought me. The ideas on which it is based are indicated in the Note that follows.

Here I should like to express my thanks to the many friends who have travelled with me, driven me, introduced me to things I might otherwise not have known about. Wyndham Ketton-Cremer showed me the splendour of Sall; Philip Larkin took me to South Dalton, Michael Robbins to Lytes Cary, Norman Scarfe to Mildenhall and Heveningham, David Treffry to Molland and Stourhead. I owe more than I can express to A. L. Rowse, who has guided and accompanied me all over the country, from Lanercost and Burton Agnes to Castle Drogo, to Cotehele and St Mawes in the Tudor Cornwall that is peculiarly his own. A number of younger friends have driven me to places that I should not have visited easily without their help, and I am greatly obliged to them: Steve Bowen, Colin Jennings, Stephen Johnson, Alan Payne, Nigel Pittard.

I am grateful to the photographers whose work is reproduced here – particularly to A. F. Kersting, who has furnished half the pictures in the book.

I owe other debts of different kinds: to Alec Clifton-Taylor for his writings – indispensable to anyone who tries to look at England intelligently – and his conversation; to Richard Newnham; to Anthony Adams; to the British Railways Board and its former Controller of Public Relations, Eric Merrill; and especially to Christopher Wheeler, for the energy and untiring hard work he has given to the book's production.

3 July 1978 J.S.

A NOTE TO THE READER

Most guidebooks set out to be comprehensive: to describe, or at least mention, the largest possible number of objects within the territory they deal with. They try to indicate all those that are "important" and (what may not be the same) those that are best worth seeing. Good guidebooks of this kind are priceless companions, indispensable in visiting a new place or a foreign country. My own gratitude to them is beyond acknowledgment.

But I think there is room for another sort of guidebook too: one that proceeds on a highly selective principle, choosing for discussion a limited number of things only, and describing them at greater length than the comprehensive guidebook can afford. I have been led to this belief by my own experience of travelling, in Europe and elsewhere – always for a very limited time, and anxious to spend none of that on seeing what is uncongenial to me, however important it may be, or liked by other people. The guidebooks I have referred to often fail me here. They list faithfully; they hardly convey quality or character.

This book attempts what I think is desirable, for one small country. I have taken about 130 places in England, widely assorted, from prehistoric forts and medieval cathedrals to canals and a newly-built bridge. They are spread over the whole country, from Berwick to Dover and Falmouth. But the maps show that they are not spread evenly. Here and there little clusters appear, of several places close together; elsewhere, over many miles, there may be few or none. What explains this unevenness, and this choice?

A few principles have influenced the selection:

1. *Every place included is accessible to the public. Every house described is open, at times that are fixed (see p. 498) – though of course that does not apply to houses referred to in passing, as part of the architecture of a town.*

2. *Every place here has been visited, or revisited, by me within the last five years. Changes come suddenly and drastically; I have tried to keep the information up to date.*
3. *Some indication is always given of the reason why the place or building described is worth going to see, of its particular appeal to the eye or the mind. The reader should therefore be able to decide, from the description, if it is likely to interest him.*
4. *The photographs are designed to help here too. There is one at least for every entry.*
5. *Many of the most famous things in the country are omitted, like Canterbury and York; Oxford and Cambridge and Stratford-upon-Avon; Windsor, Blenheim, Chatsworth, Hardwick, Castle Howard; St Paul's, Westminster Abbey, the Tower of London. Their fame is assured, and they figure in every guidebook to England. There is no need to draw attention to them.*
6. *The places selected range from great cities like Leeds and Liverpool to small pieces of landscape (Clunbury, Great Amwell). Each appears to me to have some memorable quality of its own. Perhaps few can be reckoned perfect; but all have, in my opinion, at least an element of perfection about them.*
7. *Finally, all the things chosen are, I think, highly characteristic of England: in design or in shape or in some way reflecting its history. Many of them – a timbered house like Speke, a Holland or Wyatt interior (Berrington, Heveningham), the stone circles of Avebury, a late-Gothic church (Sall), the man-made landscape at Sledmere or Stourhead – are to be seen, in this form, nowhere else. They are surely some of the best things that England has to show.*

"I", "me", "in my opinion": those words recur, here and throughout. They have to. This is not an objective book, it is subjective. Nobody else's choice would have been the same as mine. But I believe that anyone who reads what is written here about some individual place or object, is interested by that and goes to see it for himself, will find the trouble worth taking. In the laconic phrase familiar in the French Michelin guides: it is "worth the journey", or at least "merits a detour".

THE STRUCTURE OF ENGLAND

England is a small country: less than a quarter the size of France, slightly bigger than the State of New York. It shares an island with Wales and Scotland, whose peoples have separate languages and long histories of their own. It is crowded – too crowded surely for welfare and happiness, crowded with inhabitants, with motor vehicles and all the complex apparatus of modern life. It is crowded too with history, with traditions and memories. They have played a great part in the imagination of Englishmen, expressed at its highest in their literature, as well as in their sentiment – and the English are famed for their sentiment, often their sentimentality. Historical tradition, moreover, has shaped to an unusual extent the institutions, the customs and behaviour of the country. It has nearly 2,000 years of recorded history, besides an immemorial past before that began, which the archaeologists are doing much to reveal. That history is quite exceptionally well documented. The 11th century furnishes, in Domesday Book, a record that is unique. English manorial history demonstrates a continuity of landowning to which there are few parallels anywhere else.

Continuity is indeed one of the outstanding characteristics of English history. The country has been through great upheavals. It had its Civil War and revolutions in the 17th century, but they ended in compromise. There is no date here that has the same significance as 1789 in France or 1917 in Russia; no date, that is, marking the permanent overthrow of an old-established political system and its replacement by a wholly new one.

And finally, England is crowded with the memorials of her history. It is the business of this book to explore them: landscape and streets and towns, churches and the monuments they contain, all so much evidence of the life of the past, recent and remote. Only a few of these things are discussed here; but enough, it is hoped, to indicate both the tightly-packed wealth of the whole inheritance and something of its individuality, the differences it displays from habits and practices favoured on the Continent of Europe and in other parts of the world.

★

The country can be divided in many respects into two, by a diagonal line stretching from the estuary of the River Severn to the Humber. About two-fifths of England, in area, lie to the north and west of this line, three-fifths to the south and east. The population is divided in almost exactly the same proportions. Moreover, the number of people living in the area of the Greater London Council is much the same as that in the four largest conurbations, the West Midlands, Merseyside, Greater Manchester, and West Yorkshire, put together.

The line is a divider in other ways too. Nearly all the coal, for example, which was the chief foundation of England's greatness in the 19th century, lies to the north of it, in the East Midlands, in Lancashire and the North-East. Partly in consequence, most of the older heavy industry in the country falls into the northern division too.

Roughly parallel to this line, and a little to the south of it, runs a series of oolite limestone hills: from Somerset and the Cotswolds through the Oxfordshire and Northamptonshire uplands to Lincoln Edge. These hills have furnished a large part of the finest building stone in England, displayed in churches, houses, towns, and villages. A large part, but by no means all: for London owes much of its distinction to the white jurassic limestone, from Portland on the south coast, shipped up in great quantities since the 17th century by sea; and in the North another limestone, the white magnesian associated particularly with Tadcaster, gives a peculiar, sometimes an unearthly beauty to the country churches perched up above the lower end of the Plain of York. There are other stones too, not far behind these, inferior chiefly in that they are too soft or too hard for satisfactory use in decoration: the sandstone of the North-West, for example, East Midlands ironstone, the granite of Cornwall. And here and there very small deposits of stone are found, used only in a confined district and making a delightful discovery when one comes upon them: like the green Hurdwick stone of Tavistock in South Devon.

The materials used in old roofs are a study in themselves. Perhaps the best, once again, are those of limestone: from Stonesfield in Oxfordshire or Collyweston in Northamptonshire. But there are excellent English slates, notably in Cumbria, Leicestershire, and Cornwall, which come in a whole range of colours, from green through blue and grey to purple. Alas, these slates are not now often used: the Leicestershire quarries have been shut down for nearly 100 years. Railways made it economic to convey to every part of the country the much less interesting slates of North Wales – a uniform purple in colour and cut by machine to a small range of uniform sizes.

In the same way the railways helped to destroy the old local variations in English brick, by transporting rapidly and cheaply the machine-made bricks of Bedford and Huntingdon, mass-produced on a vast scale. The heyday of elegant brick building in England was from the 16th century to the 19th. Here too a whole range of local varieties can be found: the "London stocks" made in North Kent, yellow with a strong admixture of purple, the delicate reds used for example at *Farnham** and *Rye*, the exquisite silver-greys seen round Newbury in Berkshire.

And then timber: a building material quite as important as stone down to the 16th century, when it began to become dear with the increasing consumption of trees for the making of ships and for industrial purposes. (That scarcity continues: so that England today is much less heavily afforested than France or Germany.) What we now see is only a tiny fragment of the timber building that once existed. Much of that was

* Places described in the main body of the book are printed here in italics.

consumed by fire, or by vermin; much deliberately replaced by brick or stone. What still remains, however, is impressive, especially in the central part of England, from East Anglia to Hereford and northwards to Cheshire and Lancashire. Timber-framed buildings, with plaster or brick infilling, were often intended to be covered with some kind of uniform outer skin, which might be decorated with patterns or more elaborate "pargetting". But on many of them these timbers have always been exposed, as we can see from the rich ornamentation they bear – barbaric perhaps, but striking and at its extreme fantastical, as at *Little Moreton Hall* in Cheshire.

Perhaps here, at Little Moreton, we are furthest in spirit from the world we know today. We have our own follies and fantasies; but in building they take entirely different forms, just as they use different materials. The dizzy height here, the crazed elaboration, the bizarre angles, the curves (made more curvaceous still by the behaviour of the timber) – we reject all these things totally; and we laugh at "stockbrokers' Tudor", the pale debased reflection of it fashionable for a time in the early 20th century. Instead, we have the unrelenting and ponderous geometry of concrete. The English have not adapted themselves well to the use of this material, or seized such opportunities as it offers. They have allowed their towns to be submerged, instead, in a wilderness of ill-disposed, ill-proportioned, and ill-shaped "office blocks" (at least the language has supplied a suitably crude term for the things), executed almost invariably in concrete of a hideous dun colour. There are, happily, exceptions; but nobody's list of them could be long.

All these things appear at their most depressing in London: a wonderful city, but also a very strange one. It sometimes seems to cultivate ugliness with passion. Look, for a single example, at the bridges over the Thames: where can a more repulsive collection be found? The best of them, Waterloo Bridge, is a replacement for one that was still finer, the Rennies' masterpiece. The new London Bridge insists on asymmetry. For the rest, the ugliness, the sheer coarseness of the shapes into which stone and iron have been hewn and twisted, staggers the mind. One looks on to the Continent – at the Marshal Juin Bridge in Lyon, for example, erected not long ago – and one despairs; despairs all the more because there is so fine a tradition of bridge-building elsewhere in England, higher up the same river for instance at *Maidenhead*; and in our own time the country has produced in the *Severn Bridge* a triumph, generally acknowledged as such throughout the world.

★

London has dominated the whole country, distorted its growth, and also enriched it – in all senses of that word – beyond measure. Rather less than seven million people live under the Greater London Council. There is nothing unique in that, among capital cities: Dublin, Copenhagen, and Athens contain a higher proportion of their countries' people, Vienna and Stockholm almost exactly the same. Two things set London apart here: the length of time during which it has dominated England, and the agglomeration built up around it. It was the largest town in Roman Britain, and has remained much the largest ever since. The "Outer Metropolitan Region" is now reckoned to include some 13 million people. And in the 1960s the planners began to familiarise us with a new entity. They called it "The South-East". Into this region they swept the whole of East Anglia; to the north-west it stretched as far as Northamptonshire; westwards it took in the whole of Dorset. This tract of country included – as it always had since the first census was taken in 1801 – rather more than a third of the people of England. But Victorian Norfolk, Oxfordshire, and Dorset knew little of London; they led a self-contained life of their own. Today they are all, in some measure, becoming dependent on London. Vast new towns are already being built on their borders – for instance at Milton Keynes in north Buckinghamshire. Peterborough, Northampton, and Swindon, which all lie beyond the line we are considering, are engaged in turning themselves deliberately into big cities: cities in their own right no doubt according to their ambition, but, to speak the truth, in large measure satellites of London.

London is, for many people, a malign influence. There is nothing new in that opinion. In 1684 Evelyn thought it "by far too disproportionate already to the nation"; Cobbett's diatribes against the capital, "the Great Wen", met with much applause from his contemporaries. The place that London should occupy in the economy and society of the whole country is an ancient, and open, question in England.

From what has just been said it might be supposed that the whole of this South-East is suburban. That is far from true. There are places within 20 miles of Charing Cross that have not changed essentially over the past 200 years; many more in Kent and Sussex that are well within reach of the commuters' electric trains, and yet "undeveloped". The South-East is full of rich rewards for the traveller – the geologist and the botanist, no less than the student of history and archaeology, of the visual arts, of social organisation and change. And, taking the region as defined by the planners, it should be said at once that the outer parts of it, in Norfolk and Suffolk and that tract of Dorset which is beyond the influence of Bournemouth, contain large stretches of rural England touched by the 20th century very lightly indeed. To those who travel for pleasure, to see whatever may be worth the journey, the South-East remains as rewarding as any part of the country.

★

The historic South-East is, like the planners', dominated by London. It is to be thought of in terms of the Thames Estuary and the shores of the English Channel, with their hinterland: corresponding roughly therefore to the modern counties of Essex, Kent, Surrey, and East Sussex. This has always been the classic approach to England from the Continent: of invaders who succeeded, like Julius Caesar and William the Conqueror, and of Napoleon and Hitler, who failed. Equally it was here that Augustine, the spiritual invader, established his base at Canterbury, a town on the Roman road from the Kent ports to London; and that has been the capital of the religious life of the country ever since. *Dover* was always a main port of entry, close to the narrowest part of the

Straits. The Channel Tunnel, if and when it is built, will be no more than an up-to-date expression, in new terms, of this old pattern. For the same reason, Kent abounds in fortifications: the Roman Richborough, the magnificent castles erected by the Normans at Dover and Rochester, by Henry VIII at Deal and Walmer; the Martello towers of the early 19th century; and behind them, across Romney Marsh, the Royal Military Canal.

This corner of the island has naturally been susceptible to influences coming from the Continent: in Gothic architecture, initiated in England by William of Sens at Canterbury; as a home for refugees – for Protestants from the Netherlands, for example, in the 16th century, importing Flemish ways of building to Colchester and Sandwich. As we should expect, from this cause and from the proximity of London, there is much sophistication here. From the Middle Ages, perhaps the finest surviving flintwork in England is at St Osyth's in Essex. In the same county is the tallest ancient brick building we have, at Layer Marney – in which there appear some of the earliest signs of the Italian Renaissance to be seen anywhere in England outside the capital. Some of the best brickwork the country can show is here on a large scale in the castles at *Farnham*, for example, and Hurstmonceux.

The clay for making this brick and the tiles that cover roofs and often walls so beautifully, was largely dug out of the Weald, the undulating plain lying between the North Downs and the sea. The Weald in Kent, and still more in Sussex, also provided oaks, needed for building ships and making iron (which was smelted with charcoal): so that in the 16th century it was one of the chief industrial districts of England. Thereafter its importance in this respect declined, as its trees became too few and too small to supply the demands of the fleet built up by England when she rose to maritime greatness, and as iron began to be made more efficiently, in Shropshire and then in the North.

The central part of southern England – West Sussex, Hampshire and the Isle of Wight, and Dorset, with Wiltshire and Berkshire inland – is bonded together by one physical element that runs through the whole of it, the chalk; the chalk of the Downland in Sussex and Berkshire (see *Slindon*, *Uffington*), of Salisbury Plain, of the spine of the Isle of Wight and the splendid cliffs of Dorset (see *Golden Cap*). It contains the big maritime towns of Southampton and Portsmouth, which the Island guards, with the historic city of Winchester behind them. Again, it lay open to unwelcome attack: hence the walls of Southampton and the historic fortress of *Portchester*.

Some of the richest parts of rural England lie here, in the valleys of the *Test* and the Hampshire Avon, the big cornlands of Wiltshire; appropriately too some of the finest of all English country houses, like *The Vyne* and Wilton and Longleat, with the Hoares' paradise at *Stourhead*. But again, much of this southern landscape is of a different sort: the heaths of East Berkshire and the New Forest, Hardy's country in Dorset.

Further west, in Somerset, Devon, and Cornwall, most things are on a smaller scale – smallest of all in Cornwall. That is true chiefly of man-made things. There are no grander, more awesome cliffs in England than those between *Hartland* and Boscastle; and Dartmoor has, in parts, a wildness, a sense of the infinity of space, that is otherwise to be found only in the far North-East, in Yorkshire and Northumberland. But the trees are small here too, kept down by the gales off the sea; the Cornish elm is a special variety, smaller than its fellows, with a delicacy all its own. The roads are narrow and tortuous, as the car-driver finds when he starts negotiating the lanes, say, round *Totnes* or in the valley of the Lynher, north of Liskeard.

This is the most strongly Celtic part of England, though not the sole part in which there is a Celtic infusion, for that appears constantly along the Welsh border from the Severn to the Mersey and again, far north, in Cumberland. The Celtic influence is present in Somerset and Devon; but Cornwall is a full part of the Celtic world, with Galicia and Brittany, with Wales and Ireland and the Hebrides. There is a Cornish language, now being laboriously revived after having been dead for more than 200 years. There are

Cornish inflections in the use of the English language, as there are in every other element in the relationship with England. The River Tamar, which divides Cornwall from Devon, is in many respects a true frontier.

There is much that is different in Cornwall: the people themselves – very many of them, though by no means all, short and dark; their indirect approach to question and answer; the food (including, when you can get it properly made, an admirable creation, the Cornish pasty); the landscape, much of it dominated by the mining for tin and copper in earlier days and by the flourishing china-clay workings of our own time; the powerful presence of Nonconformity, with its physical manifestations, often very unpleasant. Indeed Nonconformity, political and cultural as well as religious, has played a large part in the history of Cornwall; and history is here, as in other Celtic countries, always significant, perhaps to the point of exaggeration. It is part of the charm cast by Cornwall – the fascination that the county has exercised over so many Englishmen, like Tennyson from Lincolnshire – that the remote past is here so immediately present: in standing stone monuments from prehistory, in place-names commemorating the Celtic Saints, in the traditions and legends of King Arthur. But Arthur is to be encountered elsewhere in England too, notably in Somerset at Cadbury Castle and Glastonbury.

In this long western peninsula – and here one must speak of Cornwall and Devon together – the most dominant force has been the sea. It gave the peninsula its greatest town, Plymouth; and nearly all its important smaller towns are, or once were, ports. The two counties together have provided a disproportionate number of the outstanding English seamen, above all in the reign of Elizabeth I. Their fisheries, of Brixham and Looe, Newlyn and Padstow, are famous. And, by an odd quirk of fate, when the maritime business of the western ports was declining, in favour of London and the giants like *Liverpool*, Southampton, and Hull, they began to find a new life, first as genteel watering-places and then in our own age as hosts to an invading swarm of summer visitors:

so that today many people in these two counties have come to depend for their livelihood on the holiday industry.

To the east of Devon lies Somerset. In certain respects it is the richest county in England: not in terms of material wealth, but visually. Its landscape is exceptionally varied, ranging from wide marshes and levels to the Mendips and Quantocks – ridges of hills less than 20 miles apart yet wholly different in geology, economy, and form – to wild Exmoor and its dizzy seaward termination in the cliffs of Minehead and Porlock. It enjoys some of the most beautiful of all English building stones, displayed to perfection in its cathedral of *Wells*, in houses like *Montacute* and *Brympton d'Evercy*, and in its church towers (see *Ile Abbots*), which form a series that truly has no rival in the world.

★

The majority of those who use this book may be expected to set off from London, or to be making their way up to London from the great centres of population in the Midlands and the North. That brings one advantage: for most of these journeys will have to cross the grain of the country, the diagonal line drawn in economic and physical terms from the Severn to the Humber. No one with a pair of eyes can fail to see what this means; though it is more easily appreciated if one travels by train or by secondary roads than it is from the insulated, self-contained motorway. If you are making your way north, to Birmingham or Manchester or Sheffield, you climb out of London to cross the chalk escarpment of the Chilterns; you traverse the low-lying valley of the Bedford Ouse and then cut through the great limestone belt to reach the midland plain, watered by the River Trent. In 100 miles, 80 minutes' journey by electric train, you have sawn through a cross-section of the country.

The southern end of the limestone belt, loosely called the Cotswolds, stretches down into the valley of the Severn, the longest of English rivers. The great city here is *Bristol*, the historic entrepôt for so much of England's trade with southern Europe and America. Down the Severn, with the tributary rivers and canals that fed it, poured the produce of mid-western England, wool from the sheep pastured on the Cotswolds, hardware from Birmingham and the Black Country. The limestone is everywhere, in dry walls by the road-side or running across fields, in farmhouses and their barns. Whole villages are built of it, with scarcely one intrusion of brick; even small towns, like *Chipping Campden.* Bath, a much bigger one, might be called a city of limestone. The stone is used wonderfully in the churches: at Campden again, at Burford and Northleach and a score of others.

The availability of this stone, and the wealth concentrated here so lavishly, helped to produce distinctive ideas in architecture in the 14th and 15th centuries, first in *Bristol* cathedral and then at *Gloucester.* The eastern parts of Gloucester cathedral provide our earliest surviving monument of the new style, developed in this Vale of Severn and eventually over all England for the next 200 years: the style we call, not very happily, Perpendicular. Here was something peculiarly English, rendering the churches and larger houses erected in this country between about 1360 and 1540 markedly different from those of the same time on the Continent. At its highest, in the royal chapels of Cambridge and Windsor and in many parish churches (of which a dozen figure in this book), the style attains great dignity, a noble self-assurance: here and there too an elegance, a lightness of decoration through the use of the fan vault, the earliest example of which now surviving is also at Gloucester.

So in the Cotswolds and in the lower valley of the Severn one thinks perhaps first of the emergence of this major English achievement in architecture. But the landscape is as notable, and just as English: in the steep escarpment itself, in the valleys of the little rivers that run off it, Churn and Coln and Windrush, and their villages, like Bibury and Eastleach. All this springs too from the limestone, no less than *Hidcote* and the other lovely Cotswold gardens.

★

Englishmen have often been inclined to treat the Midlands harshly. They chuckled, they did not protest, when Hilaire Belloc called them "sodden and unkind". Sodden they could hardly fail to be, for they absorb much of the water from the hills to the south and north. That is mere fact: the unkindness is a matter of opinion. What Belloc thought of, no doubt, was the grim industrial development imposed on the country: vast brickworks, with the chasms they open up in the clay; textile and hardware towns, their streets of dull brick, reaching out into endless suburbs; the shapeless sprawl of Birmingham; the pungent ugliness (which may yet be engaging) of the Black Country and the Potteries. This tract, stretching from the Chilterns to the Humber and the Mersey, falls into two parts, which have long been called the West and the East Midlands. Beyond, reaching down to the sea, lies Lincolnshire, whose affinities are in many ways closer with East Anglia to the south.

The country between Trent and Severn, and south-eastwards as far as Coventry, is one of England's chief industrial regions. It has a special place in the development of English trade and technology. In *Coalbrookdale* the Darby family first developed the smelting of iron from coal; the Staffordshire Potteries sent out their wares all over Europe and North America; in Birmingham the partnership of Matthew Boulton and the Scotsman James Watt was established; in the 20th century the manufacture of motor vehicles on a large scale came to be located pre-eminently in Birmingham and Coventry. It is a district especially interesting for its small manufactures: the guns of Birmingham, locks in Wolverhampton, needles in Redditch. These metal-workers could rise to beauty in their crafts. At their highest, one thinks of the work that Boulton supplied to Robert Adam, for example at *Syon*. Birmingham can still show most handsome iron street name-plates. And it was there that the great English printer John Baskerville spent the whole of his working life, devising the types so much admired in France – and used in the printing of this book.

Here then is a region dominated by industry. Yet it comprehends other things too. Shakespeare's country is hardly more than 20 miles from the middle of Birmingham. A little of the Forest of Arden remains; in Stratford-upon-Avon itself, for all the tourist invasion, Shakespeare's presence can be felt. Then to the west, between the Severn and the borders of Wales, comes the country that Housman finely called "the quietest under the sun". It is just that. The Welsh border, from the Wye and the Malvern Hills to the Long Mynd and – most remote of all – Clun Forest (see *Clunbury*), is the very antitype of what we have just been considering in and around Birmingham. Here, within much less than 50 miles, you can pass completely from one world into another.

There is no obvious border between the West and the East Midlands. Let us take the East Midlands as comprising the present counties of Derby, Nottingham, Leicester, and Northampton. Here too is the same contrast between our own world and a much older one. Though the industrial belt is very extensive – some 50 miles long from Chesterfield through Derby and Nottingham to Leicester – it is nowhere more than 20 miles broad. The scale of much of the industry is again relatively small. In the south it is textiles and footwear, dispersed through an industrialised countryside; in the north, in bigger units, coal and iron. At its northern extremity, in Derbyshire, there is one of the sharpest contrasts to be found anywhere in England: between the wild hills of the Peak, desolate, wind-blown, austere, and the cluster of splendid houses that lie just below, one of the fine fruits of English civilisation from the 16th century to the 18th. Hardwick and Bolsover, Chatsworth and Haddon, *Sudbury* and *Kedleston* – they form a circuit as notable as that of the *châteaux* on the Loire.

At the southern end of the East Midlands, in Leicestershire and Northamptonshire, you are again in limestone country. If the small towns and villages of the Cotswolds have a more perfect beauty, that arises in part from uniformity: it is limestone there alone. Here however there is something more, the rich orange-tawny ironstone, to provide variety; and it is often used with care to that end (as at the churches of Whiston and Melton Mowbray) in alternating bands of colour, with striking effect. Here too are some of the best quarries, still being worked, at Weldon, Clipsham, and Ketton.

Like Derbyshire, this is a country of the aristocracy. There are striking assemblies of their monuments at Exton, *Stapleford*, and *Stanford-on-Avon*.

That brings one by a natural transition into Lincolnshire, where there are assemblies equally noble (both relating to the same family) at Edenham and Spilsby. This is the second largest of the historic English counties. It has been said that Yorkshire could have formed a whole kingdom on its own. If so, then Lincolnshire would make a handsome principality – a more considerable one than many of the old Imperial States in Germany. Of all the English counties, this is the Great Unknown. It contains no large city; it is still unravished by motorways; its coastal resorts are small, and not very inviting. It keeps itself to itself.

At the southern end it shares with Norfolk an outstanding group of English parish churches, in the triangle of country between Spalding, Wisbech, and King's Lynn. And besides them it has *Boston*, the spires of Grantham and Louth, *Lincoln* cathedral, and the noble Romanesque church of *Stow*. If a student of English church architecture had to be confined to one county, Lincolnshire might well be his best choice.

Its landscape is remarkable too, though some of it may be an acquired taste. The flat country in the south has no romantic beauty, but it has the same appeal as Holland (with which it shares its name); and where it gives place to the limestone uplands to the west, for instance round Bourne, the transition has an interest, even a mild drama, of its own. The coast is flat; but the vast stretches of sand, sea, and unbroken sky are not equalled in scale anywhere else in England. The thousands who may visit Skegness or Mablethorpe on a fine Bank Holiday or in July form hardly more than a speck on the total expanse of this shore. And inland the Wolds contain villages as secluded as those of the Welsh Border. More than any other county, Lincolnshire seems a place of surprises, of discovery. It has two admirable modern guidebooks, and Sir Francis Hill's history of Lincoln is the best we have of any English city. All the same, one constantly says to oneself when one is in Lincolnshire: why has nobody ever told me of *this*?

★

It is curious that whilst "the West Country" is a phrase used commonly, to mean the western peninsula (sometimes with the Vale of Severn thrown in), people never talk of an "East Country". Yet there is one, almost as marked as the West, comprising Lincolnshire, Cambridgeshire, Norfolk, and Suffolk, pivoting on the Wash and the rivers that run into it. The central part comprises the two flat districts known as the Marshland (drained by the sea) and the Fenland (drained by the rivers). Most of it has been reclaimed laboriously from the water over the centuries, to form as it does today some of the most productive arable land in the country. The rich dark earth stretches far away in every direction, with its thick crops of potatoes and grain. Its ancient prosperity is reflected in the wealth of the parish churches, in the cathedrals of *Ely* and Peterborough, in Cambridge, and in King's Lynn, which was, with *Boston*, its principal port in the Middle Ages.

The Wash and its river basins form a broad and shallow trough. Moving eastwards across Norfolk you climb with surprising abruptness up to a low chalk plateau, most of it about 200 ft above the sea. It affords wide sweeping views to a far distance. The coast is low-lying, much beloved by bird-watchers and sailing men, until one comes to the point at which the chalk reaches the sea round Sheringham and Cromer. There for a moment there are cliffs.

The two East Anglian counties, Norfolk and Suffolk, are large. Of the pre-1974 counties, Norfolk stood fourth in size, Suffolk tenth: these two alone occupied one-fourteenth of the whole country. Driving across say from King's Lynn to *Norwich*, the amplitude strikes one everywhere: an amplitude expressed in the enormous, noble churches of the two counties – of which *Walpole St Peter* and *Sall* and *Mildenhall* are a sample – and their great country houses, like Oxburgh and Blickling, *Houghton* and *Heveningham*. These buildings bespeak an exceptional wealth, and East Anglia was indeed one of the wealthiest parts of England until the great shift of economic life came in the 18th century, with the development of steam power, based on coal, which attracted away the textile manufactures.

The capital of East Anglia is *Norwich*, a city that displays this past wealth lavishly. In the Middle Ages, it was a big town; it is by no means small now. It was a port and had relatively easy access to the sea, though like most inland ports – like *Gloucester* and Chester too – it eventually lost out to others on the coast; in this case to Yarmouth and Lowestoft.

Ipswich, the county town of Suffolk, on the other hand, has kept its position as a port, with Harwich near by briskly fulfilling its old rôle as a passenger packet station for the Netherlands and Germany, as well as developing the new container traffic. Ipswich has begun to display some of the characteristics of a satellite town of London: we are back again here well within the planners' South-East. Yet – to remind us how artificial that entity still is – on the London side of Ipswich lies the Stour valley, where Suffolk marches with Essex, the country of Gainsborough and Constable. If those painters returned to life now, they would still be able to find some things they could recognise from the world they knew.

★

It is a lengthy journey in spirit, but only a short one in time, from East Anglia to the North. Where does the North begin? At a line drawn from the Humber to the Mersey? But that would put Sheffield into the Midlands, though it is in essence a thoroughly northern town. Perhaps it is best to accept the boundary of the new county of South Yorkshire and to say that we move into the North directly we leave Derbyshire.

The southern part of this north country is largely industrial. Here are seven of the largest English cities – *Liverpool* and Manchester, *Leeds* and Bradford, Sheffield, Hull, Newcastle; together with many others high in the second rank, *Stockport*,

Bolton, and Preston in the west, for example, Halifax and Middlesbrough in the east. There is a great physical barrier in the Pennine range of hills, running north and south: the barrier between the ancient rivals Lancashire and Yorkshire. It might seem as if there were no North at all, only a North-West and a North-East. There is indeed a North: a North that feels itself different from the rest of England, the whole of which it lumps together, sometimes superciliously, as the South; a North that is above all suspicious, often apprehensive, of London. These feelings express themselves equally in Manchester or Bradford or Newcastle. Their recent history has helped to unite these northerners: their common experience, marking those who lived through it indelibly, in the depression of the 1930s, alike at Barrow-in-Furness and on Tyneside; the difficult adjustments called for lately in the Lancashire cotton towns and in Hull. These parts of the North are linked by their outlook as industrial communities. They are still the large-scale producers of modern England – where the Midlands deal, by comparison, in small things; as for London, many northerners would argue that it only consumes. And a Yorkshireman has a pride in size, in quantity, like that of a Texan in the United States.

These cities have indeed much to be proud of. Many of them have battled through against heavy odds to industrial and commercial achievement, and that finds memorable expression in the dock buildings of *Liverpool*, the Italianate warehouses of Manchester, the mills of Bradford and the towns around it. Their triumphs have not been in material things alone. Manchester can boast of three great libraries and the Hallé Orchestra; the Huddersfield Choral Society is famous; the scientific institutions of Newcastle have a long and distinguished history; two of the earliest towns that established museums of their own in England were Sunderland and Warrington.

The common character of the North is wholly evident in the landscape. For here are most of England's wide spaces. Small country though it is in reality, you can get on the Pennines or *Cheviot* the illusion of unlimited distance, of standing alone above the world. And sometimes, when you feel that most strongly, you will also have an eerie awareness, in this bare land, of the people who have been here before you long ago. Most of all of the ubiquitous Romans – at the fort on the Hardknott Pass above Eskdale in Cumbria, in the sequence of camps along Dere Street through High Rochester, and on the famous Wall they built from coast to coast (see *Housesteads*). But you come upon the Romans' predecessors too, in the Cumbrian stone circles – the Keswick Carles, Long Meg and her Daughters not far from Penrith. And powerfully, brilliantly, upon their successors of the 7th century, when Northumbria was the most highly civilised part of Europe, in the age of Aidan and Bede. They confront you at *Holy Island*, but not in such remote places alone. You find them in industrial towns, still grim with the memory of the 1930s, at Monkwearmouth and Jarrow.

Three-quarters of the people in the North live in urban communities. But large as those communities are, they occupy only a small fraction of the land. Much the greater part of that is open, a good deal of it wild and spacious. The Pennines are again the divider. To the west of them lie the English Lakes; to the east the dales and moors of Yorkshire. This is country to be seen, above all, on foot, though the car and the bus provide ready access to it. There is one railway line that strides up almost its whole length and furnishes an incomparable introduction to the country. It is beyond doubt the grandest scenic railway in England. The line runs up Airedale, crosses to follow the Ribble in its hollow between Penyghent and Whernside, almost to its source, rides very high over viaducts and through tunnels, with long sweeping looks down into Dentdale and Garsdale to the west, reaches its summit on Mallerstang Common and then drops steeply down to *Appleby*, to bring a final surprise: the last 30 miles into Carlisle along the valley of the Eden, through an exquisite pastoral landscape. In two and a half hours you have taken a sample of England at its emptiest and most desolate, and then at its gentlest, most controlled and civilised.

As you slip along from Appleby, you see a distant range of hills to the west. They are in the Lake District: a strikingly compact territory – you could easily drive round the whole of it, should you have a mind to, in a day – which has been accounted, for well over 100 years now, one of the principal delights of England. It owes its repute to its own merits; but also to the inspired interpretation of Wordsworth. Many writers have written well, especially perhaps in English, of the country they loved – Thomas Hardy of Dorset, Crabbe of Suffolk, the Brontës of the wild Yorkshire moors. But Wordsworth goes further than any of them, in the extent and minuteness of his description, the analytical power that underlies the scenes and stories transfigured in his poetry. He wrote a little prose guide to the Lakes; no visitor today can want a better companion to them. Along with that, try the Fourth Book of *The Prelude*.

Towards the close of his life Wordsworth saw a steadily-growing stream of summer visitors coming to this country, brought there in large measure by their reading of his own work; and he came to fear for its seclusion, which he knew was part of the essence of its beauty. The battle he started has been rumbling or raging ever since. The campaign against extending railways into the heart of the mountains – above all, the proposed line from Buttermere to Braithwaite in 1883 – was successful; and one of those who did most to prevent that particular outrage was H. D. Rawnsley, who went on, partly in consequence, to become a founder of the National Trust. In our own time the battle has centred on road-building, a motorway over Dunmail Raise. We have yet to see how that will end.

Meanwhile, it cannot be denied that much of the older seclusion has gone. Still, much survives. If the chief centres – Windermere, Bowness, Ambleside, and Keswick – are packed tight in summer, and the narrow roads are brutally over-crowded, there is yet a great deal of room up above on the hills; some of the smaller lakes are almost as quiet as ever (see *Esthwaite*); and if one does find the overcrowding oppressive there is delectable country, almost unvisited, on the edge of the District, especially to the south and east.

The dales and moors of Yorkshire are, in this respect, somewhat more fortunate. The Lake District is one concentrated unit; these Yorkshire hills and valleys are dispersed, and much larger, taken all together, in extent. They include notable things that are man-made: above all, the ruins of the Cistercian monasteries (see *Rievaulx*), the great castles like *Richmond*, some houses with superbly-landscaped gardens and parks. The hills are not so high as they are in the Lake District, and their nature is well indicated by the term "moors". They are less easily accessible; no motorway runs as close to them as the M6 does to the Lakes. Geologically they are different. The slates and sandstones further west give place here to the millstone grit, coarse, resistant to the fierce northern winters, immensely durable. The northern end of the Pennines, drained by the upper Wear and Tees, is surely the wildest country in the whole of England: wildest of all in upper Weardale, where deserted industrial communities make the desolation more emphatic.

And so we are led on to the Scottish border. The landscape and settlement here can never be understood unless they are thought of in terms of that frontier, whether we are looking at Hadrian's Wall or *Durham* cathedral ("half church of God, half fortress 'gainst the Scot") or the ultimate citadels of Carlisle and *Berwick-on-Tweed*. The country remains empty in part because so much of man's works was destroyed in the fighting between Englishmen and Scots, which did not die down until the 17th century. The Wall is one of the most astonishing monuments of Imperial Rome. It has been long held in veneration, constantly investigated and interpreted afresh in the light of new knowledge. To stand on it now and look away towards Scotland puts one back, as few other things in the north of Europe can, into the minds of the defenders of the Roman Empire.

This far county of Northumberland has a very long story, almost continuous from the Bronze Age to our own time: the strange "cup-and-ring" carvings that appear round Rothbury and on Dod Law; the Wall; the 7th century, dimly revealed to us now at Yeavering and brightly on *Holy Island*; the Normans' iron grip on the country they had conquered, displayed, in church as well as state, at Norham; the high Middle Ages, at Hexham and in the elegant castle of *Warkworth*; the Elizabethan walls of *Berwick*; Vanbrugh's house at *Seaton Delaval* – and that, in its weird setting, introducing coal into the story, with all that it has meant for England; George Stephenson's birthplace at Wylam, and the scenes of his early experiments with the locomotive; the town-planning of Newcastle under Grainger and Dobson; then in the 20th century a cluster of late country houses, throwbacks to the romantic past – like Cragside, built for Lord Armstrong, whose vast Elswick Works are still today one of the largest employers on the Tyne. This one county affords in itself a miniature history of England.

★

There is a view of the different parts of the country. How should one travel about it? With a car available, it is a simple matter; every place described in this book lies on a motor road, or close to one. But many people have no car, or if they have one prefer not to use it for travelling of this kind. For all the growth of cross-Channel car ferries, many foreign visitors – and that also includes Americans – rely on public transport.

That, in England, is still fairly good. Most of the extensive travelling required in the preparation of this book was undertaken quite easily by train and bus. The English railway system is very much alive: in some parts of the country, particularly in the North, now sparse, but dense in the South-East. Bus and motor-coach services too are numerous. They are very imperfectly integrated with the railways. The worst drawback to using the buses is the difficulty of getting accurate information about them, except on the spot in the places from which they run. Some suggestions are made to help with journeys on p. 498.

There is another word to be said on this matter. Use car or train or bus to get to a place; but when you arrive there, walk. Settle down, if you can, for a few days on a major town described here, and go round it on foot. In an old street filled with modern shops, keep your eye above the level of the shop fronts: you will be astonished by the charm of brick and stonework to be discovered like that, say in Northbrook Street in Newbury or Whitefriargate in Hull. And where you can penetrate to the backs of old houses, they often reveal something quite different from the fronts. If the town stands on a considerable river, that probably provides one of the chief keys to its history. English towns are nearly always laid out as if they were ashamed of their rivers (but see *Bedford*). Much poking about, on foot, is therefore needed to get a proper sense of what the river has meant to the place. That is most strikingly exemplified in London; but it is equally true of *Bristol* or *Lincoln*.

Again, in the countryside, this book tries to provide an object for each journey, something undoubtedly worth while travelling to see. It often goes a little further, to refer to other things near by, which there is not space to describe but are also worth visiting. In a country so closely-packed as England, it will seldom be true to say that a single thing, a landscape or a garden or an antiquity, stands alone. There will nearly always be something else to be brought into consideration at the same time. For the fullest enjoyment of the country you need other guidebooks besides this one; not less important, you need good maps. About those things I have something to say on pp. 496–7.

A book like this can be used in several different ways: as an introduction, to help the visitor to decide where he wishes to go; as a guide to be taken and used in the places it describes; as an aid to recollection after the travelling is done. However it is used it will do its job best if it leads to more reading – and equally to more looking, with sharper, more inquisitive eyes. The purpose of the book is to suggest, to indicate some of the things that are worth seeing in this small and richly-endowed country; no more.

Places that are the subject of entries in this book are indicated on the following maps by black triangles and italic type. Each entry has a grid reference to one of these maps.

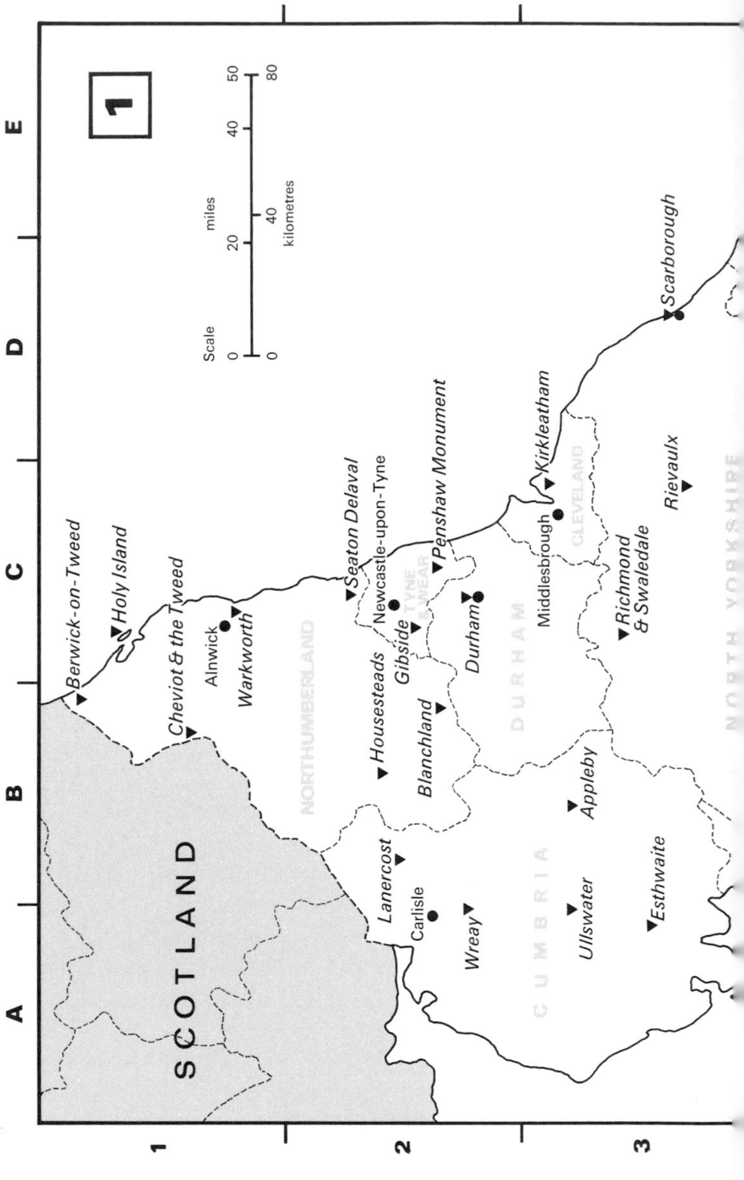
1
A
B
C
D
E
1
2
3
Scale
miles
kilometres
0
20
40
50
0
40
80
SCOTLAND
NORTHUMBERLAND
TYNE & WEAR
DURHAM
CLEVELAND
CUMBRIA
NORTH YORKSHIRE
Berwick-on-Tweed
Holy Island
Cheviot & the Tweed
Alnwick
Warkworth
Seaton Delaval
Newcastle-upon-Tyne
Housesteads
Gibside
Penshaw Monument
Blanchland
Durham
Middlesbrough
Kirkleatham
Scarborough
Rievaulx
Richmond & Swaledale
Appleby
Lanercost
Carlisle
Wreay
Ullswater
Esthwaite

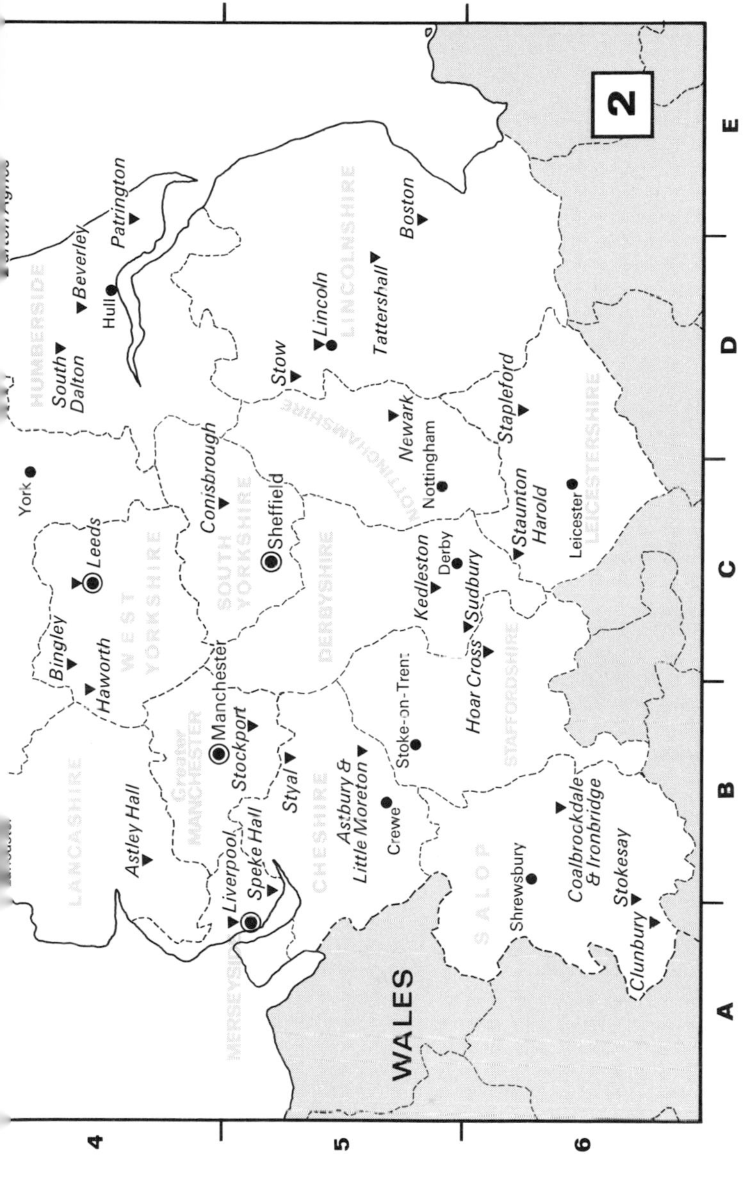

2
HUMBERSIDE
South Dalton
Beverley
Patrington
Hull
York
LINCOLNSHIRE
Lincoln
Stow
Tattershall
Boston
NOTTINGHAMSHIRE
Newark
Nottingham
LEICESTERSHIRE
Stapleford
Staunton Harold
Leicester
WEST YORKSHIRE
Leeds
Bingley
Haworth
SOUTH YORKSHIRE
Conisbrough
Sheffield
DERBYSHIRE
Kedleston
Derby
Sudbury
Hoar Cross
STAFFORDSHIRE
Stoke-on-Trent
LANCASHIRE
Astley Hall
Greater MANCHESTER
Manchester
Stockport
MERSEYSIDE
Liverpool
Speke Hall
CHESHIRE
Styal
Astbury & Little Moreton
Crewe
SALOP
Shrewsbury
Coalbrockdale & Ironbridge
Stokesay
Clunbury
WALES
A
B
C
D
E
4
5
6

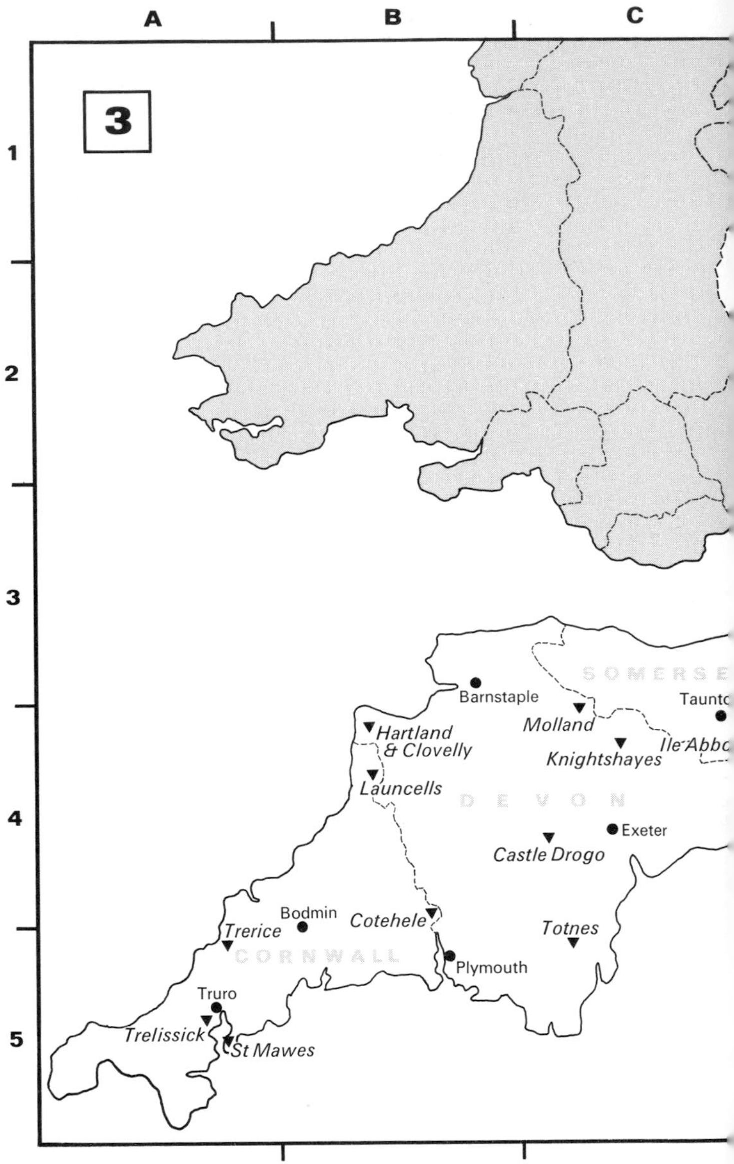
A
B
C
3
1
2
3
4
5
SOMERSE
DEVON
CORNWALL
Barnstaple
Taunto
Molland
Hartland
& Clovelly
Knightshayes
Ile Abbo
Launcells
Exeter
Castle Drogo
Bodmin
Cotehele
Trerice
Totnes
Plymouth
Truro
Trelissick
St Mawes

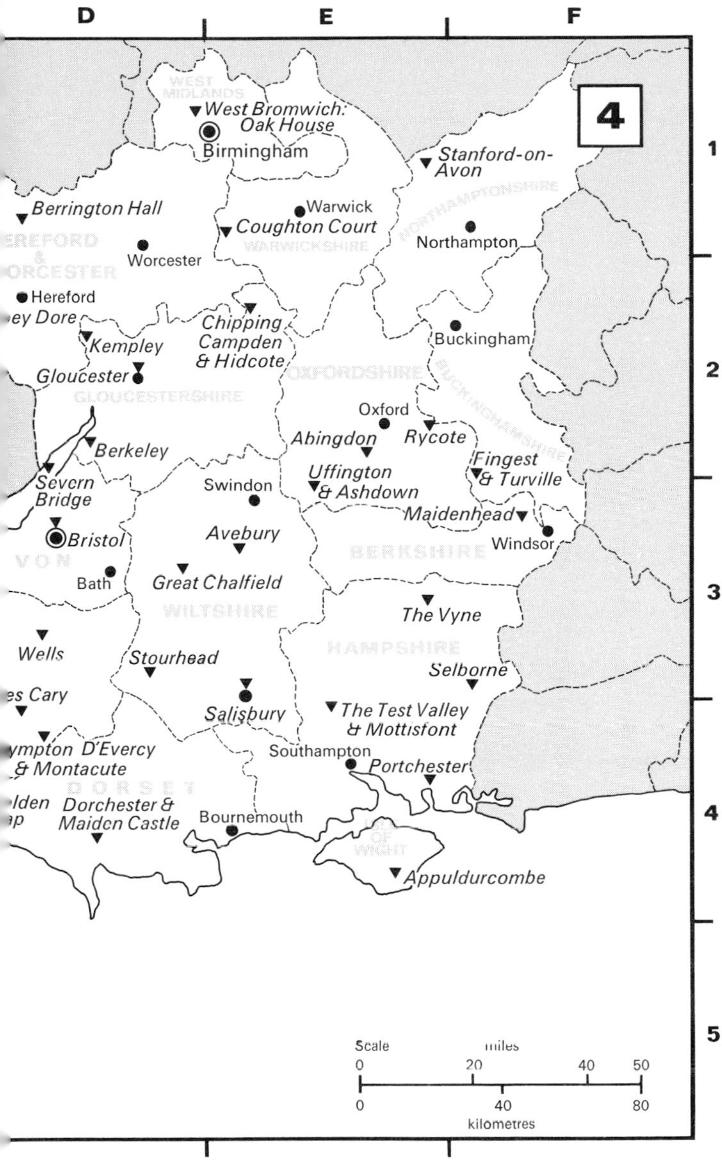

D

E

F

4

WEST MIDLANDS

▼ West Bromwich: Oak House
◉ Birmingham

▼ Berrington Hall

Warwick ●
▼ Coughton Court
WARWICKSHIRE

▼ Stanford-on-Avon

NORTHAMPTONSHIRE

Northampton ●

HEREFORD & WORCESTER

Worcester ●

● Hereford

ey Dore

▼ Kempley

▼ Chipping Campden & Hidcote

OXFORDSHIRE

BUCKINGHAMSHIRE

Buckingham ●

Gloucester ▼

GLOUCESTERSHIRE

Oxford ●

▼ Berkeley

▼ Abingdon ● Rycote

▼ Fingest & Turville

Severn Bridge

Swindon ●

Uffington & Ashdown ▼

Maidenhead ▼

● Windsor

◉ Bristol

▼ Avebury

BERKSHIRE

Bath ●

▼ Great Chalfield

WILTSHIRE

The Vyne ▼

▼ Wells

▼ Stourhead

HAMPSHIRE

Selborne ▼

es Cary
▼

● Salisbury

▼ The Test Valley & Mottisfont

mpton D'Evercy & Montacute

Southampton ● ▼ Portchester

DORSET

lden
p

Dorchester & Maiden Castle ▼

Bournemouth ●

ISLE OF WIGHT

▼ Appuldurcombe

Scale miles
0 20 40 50

0 40 80
 kilometres

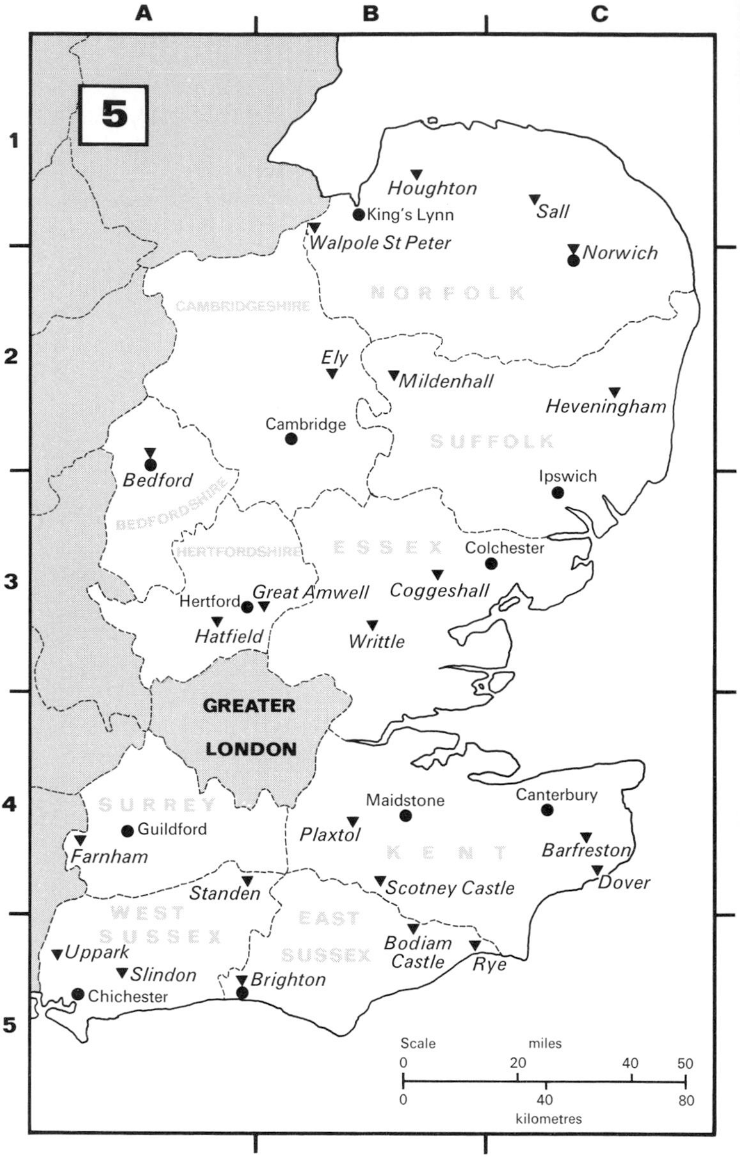
A
B
C
5
1
2
3
4
5
Houghton
Sall
King's Lynn
Walpole St Peter
Norwich
NORFOLK
CAMBRIDGESHIRE
Ely
Mildenhall
Heveningham
Cambridge
SUFFOLK
Bedford
Ipswich
BEDFORDSHIRE
HERTFORDSHIRE
ESSEX
Colchester
Great Amwell
Coggeshall
Hertford
Hatfield
Writtle
GREATER
LONDON
Maidstone
Canterbury
SURREY
Guildford
Plaxtol
KENT
Barfreston
Farnham
Dover
Standen
Scotney Castle
WEST
SUSSEX
EAST
SUSSEX
Bodiam
Castle
Rye
Uppark
Slindon
Brighton
Chichester
Scale
miles
0
20
40
50
0
40
80
kilometres

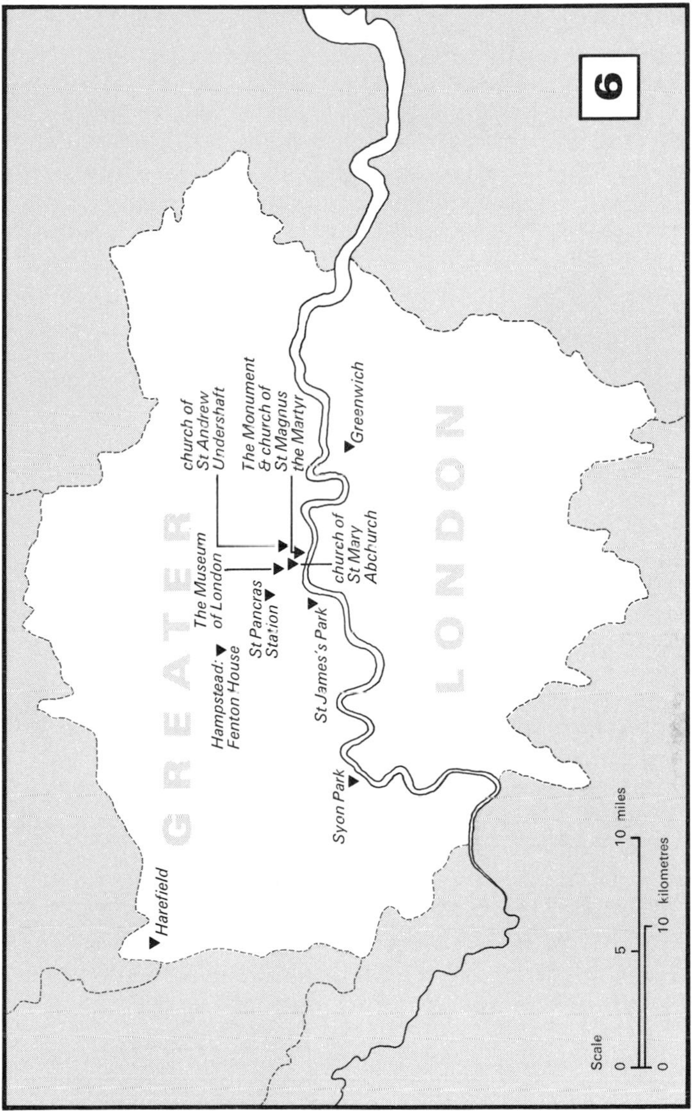
6
GREATER LONDON
Harefield
Syon Park
Hampstead: Fenton House
St Pancras Station
The Museum of London
St James's Park
church of St Andrew Undershaft
The Monument & church of St Magnus the Martyr
church of St Mary Abchurch
Greenwich
Scale
0
5
10 miles
0
10 kilometres

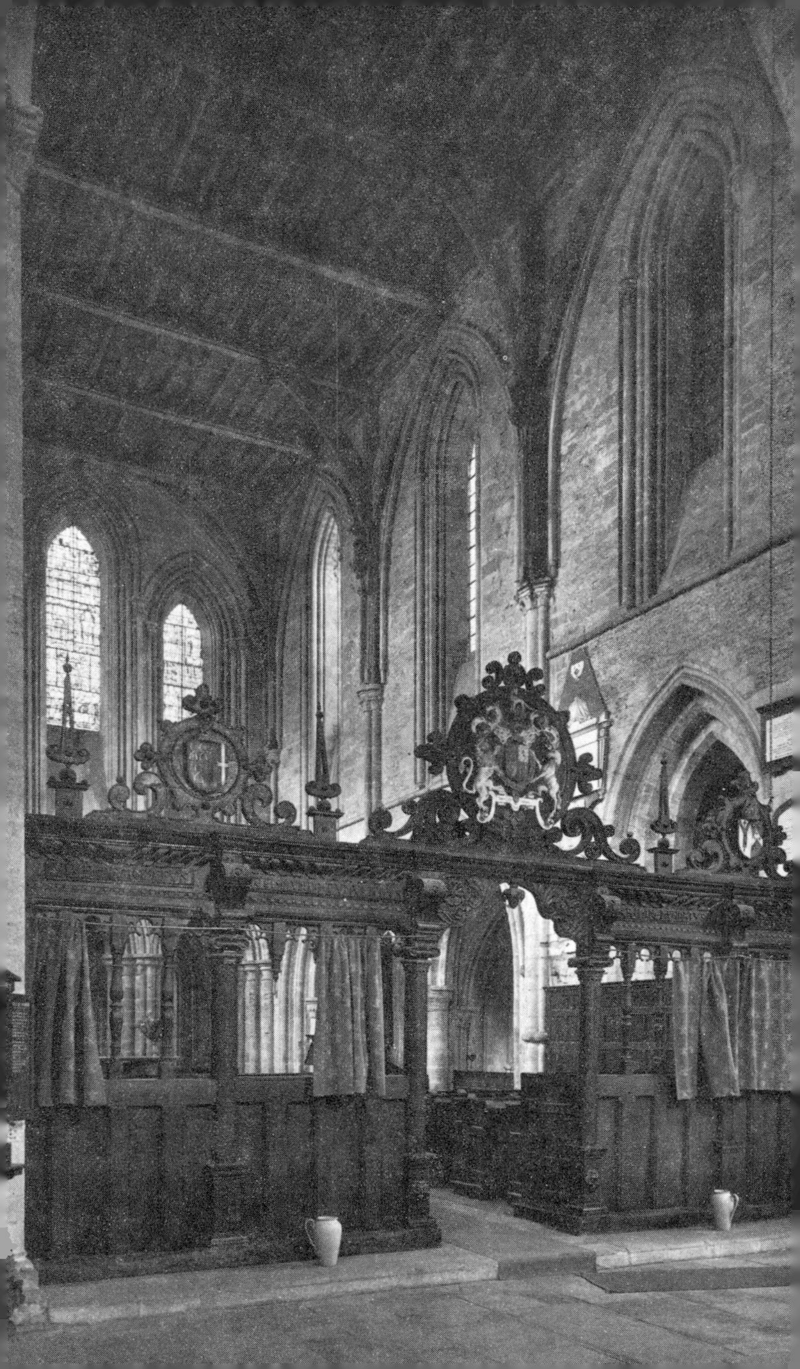

Abbey Dore: church of St Mary Hereford and Worcester 4D2

Abbey Dore is a secluded village, hidden in the deep untravelled country between Hereford and the Black Mountains of Wales. A Cistercian abbey was founded here – remote places were always favoured by that Order (see *Rievaulx*) – in 1147. The present church was built chiefly between 1180 and 1220, though money was still being raised to complete it in 1260, and the final consecration took place some 20 years after that. The abbey was dissolved in 1536, and its property passed to the Scudamore family. The church was allowed to decay, until it was rescued and repaired by the first Lord Scudamore about 100 years later. When he had finished his work in 1634 he left the church very much as we see it now. It was sensitively restored by R. W. Paul in 1902–3.

The building was originally a large one, about 250 ft in length, but the whole of its nave of ten bays has gone, with all the structure of the monastery. What we are left with is the eastern part of the church: transepts, choir, and ambulatory, with a tower oddly placed in the angle between the choir and the south transept. The original Cistercian church had no tower. There was no need of one, for bells were condemned by the Order as frivolous. The tower here, a very homely affair, was added in the 17th century.

"Homely" is not a suitable description of any part of the medieval building. The transepts, by which you now enter, belong to the earliest phase of the work at the close of the 12th century: lofty, majestic, austere, the austerity heightened by their present emptiness of furniture. One alteration has been made to the fabric, and it is a sad one. In the wreck of the church after the Reformation the stone vaults fell in, and in the 17th century they were replaced by flat wooden ceilings. When the pointed vaults were there, the sense of height would have been greater still.

Abbey Dore: the chancel, through the Jacobean screen

(A. F. Kersting)

Move into the choir through the big 17th-century screen, and you are in another world. The bay nearest you is part of the original church and has the same severity as the transepts; but the rest belongs to the next generation, to the early 13th century, and its character is quite different. Facing you, behind the altar, is an arcade of three bays, not high but sturdy, and indescribably delicate in their mouldings and their carved capitals. Through this arcade, and diagonally through the other arches of the choir, you can see more pillars, more arcades beyond. They belong to the ambulatory, the processional path that was added, with a series of chapels, at the same time. The whole of this part of the church represents the perfection of English Gothic building, at the moment of balance between its first severity and the elaboration that was shortly to come. The effect of richness is not absent here; but it is attained by a deft spareness of touch, as in the mouldings that move up the walls and frame the windows. The ambulatory behind the altar is as striking, through the concentration of the clustered columns into a small space. The side aisles, needed to complete the processional path, are an extension of the chapels that opened out of the eastern walls of the original transepts.

All this beauty must have fallen into dismal dilapidation in the 16th century. Lord Scudamore was a High Churchman, a friend of Laud's, and he determined to make what remained of the church seemly for Anglican worship. He used timber for his work throughout, and a carpenter celebrated in Herefordshire, John Abel, roofed the building in and gave it the screen that spans the entrance to the choir. The screen has been called ponderous; but it was intended quite deliberately to shut off the choir from the remainder of the church. Under Lord Scudamore the transepts, now so bare, were used for the ordinary parochial services – hence the gallery on the west wall, which survives in isolation: the pews, now moved into the choir, were then here. All this represents the application of Laud's ideas of the peculiar sacredness of the choir, worked out in the special conditions of Abbey Dore.

The whole of the woodwork is of the 17th century, except

Mr Paul's lectern. The plain screens that shut off the choir on the north and south sides do much to produce the sense of enclosure that is so enjoyable here; it is as if one were in a large room. The altar is railed in on all sides, as Laud liked. It is the medieval stone altar, 12 ft long, rescued from base uses on a farm and set up by Lord Scudamore's orders in 1633. Though scandalised Protestants may have murmured, the arrangement has never been undone. The glass in the east window is a work of the same age, rare in England, depicting the Ascension, the Apostles, and other saints.

All this survived, undisturbed by the subsequent changes of religious fashion; the Scudamores were powerful landlords and able, in this remote place, to keep a jealous eye on it. The church shows us the strength of the Anglicanism of the 1630s (see also *Astbury* and *Leeds*), a harking back in some senses to the medieval world, before the Reformation. That world it displays in its loveliest form.

Abingdon: County Hall Oxfordshire 4E2

"The finest town hall in England", said Celia Fiennes in 1698. Her judgment would not be absurd today, though the building is not, strictly speaking, a town hall, and it must be allowed that handsome competitors for the title have appeared since her time (see *Leeds* and *Newark*). It is the product of one of those small local jealousies which have often been an incitement to handsome building. Some English counties, like Hertfordshire and Cheshire, had always one recognised capital. In many others two or more claimed the primacy. Berkshire fell into this class. Under the Tudors and Stuarts there was rivalry in this matter between Reading and Abingdon, concentrated chiefly on the holding of the assizes. In 1677 the Corporation of Abingdon resolved to stake its claim in the most public way by building a new assize court, to be erected in conjunction with a market house. This is what resulted.

Building started early in 1678 and took about five years to complete. The "undertaker" of the work was Christopher

(Roy Nash)

Kempster of Burford, a mason who worked for Wren in London. Whether the design was his, or whether Wren had any hand in it, we cannot tell.

The fabric is of limestone throughout, from Kempster's own quarry at Burford and from Headington, patched subsequently with other stone from Clipsham and Box. It is perfectly simple in plan. The Market Hall is on the ground floor (with cellarage below it), enclosed by an open arcade and covered with a fine timber ceiling. The first floor (reached by a staircase enclosed in the tower at the back of the building) is the Court Room, for the assizes. It is lighted by lofty round-headed windows. The judges occupied a raised dais at the east end, below the royal arms. Above is a set of small rooms with dormer windows. They project through the hipped roof, which is crowned by a cupola, surrounded with a wooden balustrade.

The proportions of the building are majestic. It is splendidly tall, decorated strongly yet with just moderation. The interplay of glass and stone and white paint, especially on a day of sunshine and fleecy cloud, is something to remember.

It did not serve, however, to win the prize that Abingdon coveted. In the long run Reading emerged as the county town of Berkshire, beyond dispute. Since 1974, indeed, Abingdon has been transferred out of Berkshire altogether, into Oxfordshire. But in one sense it is still the victor. Reading has become today a far bigger and more important place. But it has no building within two classes of the County Hall at Abingdon.

Appleby Cumbria 1B3

Appleby is a very small town. But it returned two Members to Parliament from 1298 to 1832; it was the capital of Westmorland, until the administration was moved to Kendal; and it remained a borough, first chartered in the 12th century, until 1974. It had a very ancient market, and that continues weekly still – together with a horse fair on two days in June. These things give the little town its character: the market and fair, in particular, must account for the large number of its pubs.

Moreover, diminutive as it may seem in the scale of towns today, it is really two towns. The older is Bongate, on the right bank of the River Eden, with its church of St Michael, which was certainly there before the Norman Conquest. It is today hardly more than a thoroughfare, a racing ground for cars and lorries, tearing along A66.

The newer grew up below the castle, which crowns the hill on the opposite bank of the river and has always been associated with it. This new town, with its own church of St Lawrence, had emerged by the beginning of the 12th century. More than once in that century Appleby passed into the hands of the Scots. It became English for good only in 1175. In 1199 the townspeople secured a charter from King John that made them legally independent of the owners of the castle. "Old Appleby where the bondmen dwell" – that is, Bongate – remained however under their jurisdiction. The town then prospered for over 150 years. Both churches were rebuilt or extended, a Carmelite friary, a hospital, and several chantries established. In the 14th century it had a population (both boroughs together) of about 3,000 – which made it a big town then; but it suffered from the Black Death in 1349, and from Scottish attacks. The last and worst of those was in 1388, when the place was devastated. It never recovered its former prosperity. In Henry VIII's time Leland could describe it as "a shire town but a poor village, having a ruinous castle where the prisoners be kept". Camden said the same about 40 years later. When in 1598–9 the town was again attacked by the plague, 128 people are recorded to have died, out of a total population that was probably not much above 500. Appleby had become a "poor village" indeed.

It did not begin to grow again for a long time. Wesley described it in 1766 as "a county town worthy of Ireland". In the 19th century it had recovered its position a little, but it remained one of the smallest boroughs in the country, with Winchelsea, Woodstock, Southwold, and Eye.

What constitutes a town in England? No legal definition of a town exists in this country. One distinction used to be between those places that were boroughs – having valid proofs of their status, and exercising in consequence of it certain powers – and those that were not. But that has long ceased to be useful, for though Basildon, Thurrock, and Havant had each a population of over 100,000 they yet were not boroughs; and anyway boroughs, in the old

Appleby: looking down Boroughgate to the church (A. F. Kersting)

sense, ceased to exist in 1974. All one can say is that there are certain qualities, impalpable and eluding definition, that give a place an "urban" character and make it a solecism to refer to it as a village.

Appleby is a good example. Small as it is, nobody with any feeling in these matters, if he had seen it, could describe it as anything but a town. Bongate, straggling along the Sands on the right bank of the river, could be a village street. But Boroughgate, the chief street of the newer borough, is a shapely piece of townscape, of the same family as Castle Street in *Farnham* and Sheep Street in the still smaller town of Burford. It has indeed a more pleasing symmetry than either of those others: for the Castle lies at the top of the street, and as one looks down it is terminated by the little old Moot Hall on the left and St Lawrence's church, screened off by a stone arcade of 1811, directly in the centre. Moreover, the axis of the street is emphasised by two stone pillars, the one at the top bearing the enigmatic inscription "Retain your loyalty. Preserve your rights". Who put it there?

The answer to that question takes us back into feudal history. The lordship of Appleby came into the hands of the Clifford family from the Veteriponts late in the 13th century. The last of that violent line was the Lady Anne Clifford (1590–1676), a superb *grande dame.* Her two marriages, to the Earl of Dorset and the Earl of Pembroke and Montgomery, were both unhappy. From her second husband she was estranged not only by personal antipathies but also by politics. He supported the Parliament in the Civil War, she – trenchantly and without swerving – the King. It was to her orders that Appleby Castle was garrisoned, and it held out until October 1648, when it was one of the last Royalist strongholds remaining. Her uncongenial husband died in 1650. Under the Republican government that followed she set herself deliberately to rebuild the castles of her ancestors – Skipton, Pendragon, Brough, Brougham, Barden Tower, as well as Appleby: a gesture of defiance remarked by the government but allowed to pass unresisted. She spent her later years in a constant series of progresses between these dispersed possessions, rebuilding and repairing churches, keeping everything under close surveillance. Appleby benefited from her generous charities. She founded an almshouse there for 12 poor women, completed in 1653, which she named – challenging the dreary Puritanism then triumphant – St Anne's Hospital. It is still there, unaltered as she would have wished, at the top of Boroughgate. And it was she who erected the pillar at the top of the street and ordered its inscription: plain-spoken, like everything she uttered. After she died her estates descended to the Tufton family, Earls of Thanet. The sixth Earl, within 10 years of her death, dismantled the castles of Brougham and Brough and, partly using the stone from them, added a spacious new house to the keep at Appleby, which remains little changed today.

So you stand at the top of the hill by the pillar and the entrance to the Castle (to which there is no admission), looking down Boroughgate. There are green banks on both sides of the street, planted with lime trees. The houses are in general low and modest, built of the local sandstone, a soft pink. One or two bolder accents occur towards the foot: the handsome tall White House, 18th-century Gothic and plastered; Barclay's Bank, an agreeable Victorian building. And at the very foot do not miss Capstick's, drapers, with a nice iron-framed Gothic shopfront.

St Lawrence's church is low and a little rustic, the lines of its lead roofs irregular. It contains an interesting organ; but here too it is Lady Anne's spirit that prevails. She repaired the church in 1654–5 and had the fact recorded on a rafter of the roof. On the north side of the altar is the tomb she erected to the memory of her beloved mother: the effigy very grand indeed, not rustic at all but metropolitan. And behind it is her own monument. It could not possibly be more characteristic. No effigy. Nothing but a black table tomb, and above it an heraldic record, in gilt and colours, of her descent through the Cliffords from the Veteriponts, back to the Norman Conquest.

Appuldurcombe Isle of Wight 4E4

The Isle of Wight is still something of a world of its own. For all the narrowness of the straits and the rowdy helicopters, the car-ferries and the frequent passenger steamers that cross them, it remains detached and separate. For three months in the summer it is invaded with visitors, and the little towns and narrow roads become choked; for the other nine it is quiet, turned in on itself, a late-surviving fragment of the Victorian age.

The scale of everything here is small, with only one exception: the splendid chalk cliffs east of the Needles and between Blackgang and Ventnor. No church on the Island has ever been grand; no house either – not even its royal palace,

Osborne. Among the older houses, Appuldurcombe is the biggest. Since 1943, when a land-mine exploded near by, it has been a roofless shell.

There was a religious house on the site in the Middle Ages. At the Dissolution the Worsley family secured the estate, adapting the conventual buildings and extending them. They took their place among the leading gentry of the Island and acquired a baronetcy in 1611. Sir Robert Worsley, who succeeded in 1690, made a grand marriage, with a Thynne of Longleat. He determined to replace the medieval house. The work was under way by 1701 and continued until 1713. The house was enlarged and remodelled by his third successor, Sir Richard, in 1773–82. Some alterations were made in the 1830s. Then in 1855 it was sold, becoming in succession a school and a monastery, and occupied by troops in both wars.

The architect of the house, beyond much doubt, was John James, a Londoner whose best-known work is St George's, Hanover Square. His fine east front survives, essentially unaltered, ennobled by good carving in the capitals of the pilasters and round the main doorway (notice particularly the grotesque head immediately above it). The whole of his work was executed in stone, whereas the inner walls of the later parts were of brick. Sir Richard Worsley's changes of the 1770s were made to accommodate his remarkable collection of paintings and antique sculpture, some of it today in museums, a fair proportion in the hands of his family at Brocklesby (Humberside).

The plan of James's house provided for a tall centre with four slightly lower wings attached to it. The later alterations were mainly internal, though the colonnade on the south side (with its iron balustrade above) and the big *porte-cochère* on the west are additions of the 1830s. The use of the several rooms, as they were in 1780, is indicated by notices on their walls.

It is slightly eerie to need such notices for a house of the 18th century, one that was still lived in 40 years ago. Sir Nikolaus Pevsner observes that Appuldurcombe "does not make as good a ruin as one might hope to find". I do not agree with him. Let me say why.

As a building, the house is certainly not in the first rank. Its present condition makes it sadly gaunt, above all the unfilled rectangles of its windows. Here a Gothic ruin, with fragments of its stone tracery, must always be more appealing. Then again, it is a house – not a church or a temple, nor a castle testifying to ideas of warfare that are now quite gone; a house that could well be lived in, as many of its kind are today, and yet remains desolate. It might be called a matter-of-fact ruin. But, for all that, it has a poetry of its own. The colour and texture of its outer walls are lovely. They are mainly built of local sandstone, quarried on Worsley property at St Lawrence and known as "Green Ventnor". For dressings and the carved work Portland limestone was used, shipped conveniently along the south coast. Today the house can show almost a rainbow of colours, green, lemon,

Appuldurcombe House: the east front (D.o.E.)

lavender, pink, grey. It is surrounded with noble trees, oaks and Spanish chestnuts and a cedar. Its place in the landscape is delightful: looking down to Wroxall in a cleft of the hills and up to the high St Martin's Down beyond. At the back, to the west, on another high point stands the far-seen obelisk erected by Sir Richard Worsley to the memory of his predecessor Sir Robert. And then, two miles away to the north by a gentle by-road, is Godshill, the parish church, with the family's monuments. Appuldurcombe represents a way of life that has vanished here, never to return. The fabric is admirably cared for, but the house is – it must be – petrified. Nevertheless, to anyone who will take the whole place in, landscape and house and history all together, this is a sight worth some trouble to see.

Ashdown see **Uffington**

Astbury and Little Moreton Hall Cheshire 2B5

It is desirable to approach Astbury from the main road (A 34) that leads from Congleton, two miles to the north, to Newcastle-under-Lyme. Congleton is a busy and interesting little town, proud enough of its past to have produced not long ago a good history of itself; but historically it is an offshoot of Astbury, within which parish it lay.

Taking this route, you see the centre of Astbury village for what it is: a distinguished composition, carefully controlled. It lies at a right angle to the road, comprising a broad green centring on a shapely sycamore and lined with two rows of houses, not all of one time or sort but chiefly of brick and similar in size. This is not a model village, set out to a design imposed by a single landlord, like *Blanchland* or *Houghton* – though the Egertons may have had something to do with moulding it to its present form. It exemplifies what may be achieved by harmony of scale, sensitive planting, and a quiet variety of colour.

The village rises up a gentle slope, and at the top of

Astbury church from the west (A. F. Kersting)

it stands the church (St Mary), behind an arched gateway that provides a formal approach to it. The plan of the building is unusual, and best taken in from the outside first. You see at once from the village green that it comprises a tall nave, lighted with a big clerestory, with a tower and spire standing almost detached from it at the north-west corner. The west front looks strange: a porch with a superstructure rising the whole height of the building. It is too small to be the basis of a second tower, never completed. Might it have been intended to carry a spirelet or a cupola, answering to the tall spire close by? There is no telling. It remains a puzzling element in the design of the western *façade*.

Moving round the church, on the north side of the churchyard, you see that the fabric is not all of one piece. The north aisle is older than the nave, in architectural language Decorated, not Perpendicular. Moreover the eastern end of the aisle is simpler and older still; it was built as the chapel of the Moreton family (we shall come on them again in a moment) and subsequently merged into the rest of the aisle. If you walk further to the east you will get a splendid view of the church, quite different from the one with which you began.

Inside, you find yourself in what seems a parallelogram but is not in fact so, for the nave is 8 ft wider at the west end than at the east, so that you get a fuller view than is commonly possible of the arcades on both sides. There is no mystery here. Strong sunlight comes in through the huge windows of the clerestory; they are uncoloured now, and one must rejoice in that, looking at some of the fearsome glass below, e.g. O'Connor's in the two westernmost windows of the south aisle. The east end is a blunt termination, a flat wall. Structurally, chancel and nave are one.

The church is filled with woodwork, of varying kinds and high quality, appropriate to a county that has always been rich in good timber and has known very well how to use it. The three roofs are all excellent, divided into square panels with bosses at the points of intersection. In the south aisle, over the screen, is a singularly beautiful piece of wood-carving, a pendent to contain the pyx or possibly a lamp. The chancel screen is delicately traceried, though the upper part has been a good deal restored. All this belongs to the late 15th century, when the nave was built; but there is other woodwork, almost as good, dating from 200 years later. The box pews and pulpit are of a simple Jacobean design; the altar-rails more elaborate, using different timbers in a bold strapwork pattern.

In strictly architectural terms, Astbury cannot be called the finest church in Cheshire. There it is beaten by Nantwich, whose chancel contains, in addition, some of the loveliest medieval wood-carving in England. But then Nantwich is a town church, filled with ugly Victorian clutter: a curse from which Astbury is entirely free, unless one brings the glass into account, and that does not dominate the building. The Jacobean age gave Astbury the furniture it needed as an Anglican parish church, and did the job so competently that no one has attempted to do it again. There it is: a noble monument of the later Middle Ages and the 17th century.

★

Little Moreton Hall (two miles away to the south) is surely the most celebrated half-timbered house in England, overtopping all its rivals. "Overtopping" is the right word here: for what makes Little Moreton unique among houses of its kind is the Long Gallery superimposed on the whole of the south front. Imagine that removed, and you would have something that would, except in one or two respects, be a house recognisably of the same family as Bramall or *Speke* or such a town house as Churche's Mansion in Nantwich. But that would indeed be imagination: for the Long Gallery is there, and it stamps its presence upon everything else.

The house is moated all round: something that is seldom made clear in the conventional photographs. One has to think of Little Moreton first as a medieval building, probably H-shaped, with the present Great Hall as its centrepiece, enclosed within the moat. We have only one date in the whole history of the creation of the house: the 1559 that is carved on the north face of the courtyard. The Great Hall clearly belongs to the end of the 15th century or the very beginning of the 16th; the whole work cannot have been finished much before 1575. The Moretons who built it were gentry of the middle rank, who had been established here since the 13th century.

You pass through the gatehouse into a cobbled courtyard. All that faces you is of two storeys only; the tall part of the building is above. One thing is evidently odd: the pair of semi-octagonal projections in the north-east corner of the

Little Moreton Hall from the south-west (A. F. Kersting)

court. They serve as oriels to the Hall and the Withdrawing-Room. They are placed very close together, one might say in a jumble: for the windows in their inner faces mask one another to such an extent that one set of them was left unglazed.

The Hall is a broad room, somewhat altered at its west end. Out of it to the east lead the Parlour and the Withdrawing-Room, which is the most handsome room in the house, enriched with oak panelling of unusual thickness and depth and with a deeply-moulded timber ceiling.

The Chapel, in the south-east corner of the courtyard,

comprises no more than a small square room, on to which has been added a tiny chancel, projecting out towards the moat; the two divided from each other by a simple wooden screen. The chancel walls carry a faded painting of Biblical texts, divided into panels by vertical strips decorated in a crudely Renaissance manner. This was a not uncommon practice in Elizabethan parish churches. The east window is similar in its design to that at *Speke*.

Above, on the first floor, there is a Guests' Hall (now divided into two) with a couple of roughly-carved brackets and some more plain moulded beams in the ceiling; together with a number of small rooms and closets. And then, on top, the Long Gallery. Apartments of this kind came into fashion in the 1560s. One can scarcely believe that a family like the Moretons – not grand people at all in their society, and evidently conservative in their tastes – can have been among the pioneers in adopting this mode; that the south wing of the house, which seems to have been under construction in the opening years of Elizabeth's reign, can have been originally designed to carry a Long Gallery in this bold, indeed hazardous fashion. Rather it seems likely that they decided to add it while the wing was being built, or perhaps after it was finished.

The Gallery is 68 ft long, extending the whole width of the front, with a room opening out of it, standing above the gatehouse. It is lighted almost continuously with windows on both sides. The timbers have warped, giving the tipsily curvaceous character to the exterior of the house, and inside the Gallery a very marked dip at the eastern end. In between the main beams of the roof there is a pattern of timbers, curved and cusped. At each end the gable has plaster decoration derived from *The Castle of Knowledge*, a book of maxims and allegories published in 1556. The effect of the whole room has been impaired by the horizontal cross beams inserted, in the 17th century or the 18th, to carry a flat ceiling. One must try to think these insertions away if one is to do justice to the idea of those who conceived it.

The unfortunate change just mentioned is the only one

of importance that has been made in the Moretons' house. When Cotman drew it in 1806, it had evidently declined into a farmhouse; but the fabric was kept in repair, and fortunately it never fell into the hands of a romantic Victorian, determined to "improve" it by restoration. A little black painting was undertaken on the white plaster below the eaves on the south front (could not that now be removed?), one or two brick buttresses were added, and some tie-pins inserted into the roof of the Long Gallery. That was all. We thus see the house almost exactly as it was when the Moretons completed it towards the end of the 16th century.

There is an agreeable little garden to the north-west of the house, within the moat, including two artificial mounds designed to serve as viewing-points. A summer house may possibly have stood on one of them. Their view was of course intended to be over the garden and back to the house. We today take a wider and less confined one, of the house and garden in their landscape: the unemphatic pastoral landscape of Cheshire (no wonder it produces a justly famous cheese), dominated on the eastern side by the range of hills, partly across the border in Staffordshire, capped by the tower (an 18th-century folly) on Mow Cop. The Elizabethans did not go in for follies, of that kind; but they took delight in extravagance. In that line none of their buildings can outdo Little Moreton.

Astley Hall Chorley Lancashire 2B4

Chorley is a small industrial town with some character, injured physically by the busy A6 road, which passes through its centre. It has one splendid asset: the park of this house, lying immediately to the north-west. The park is extremely large, hilly and diversified with some noble beeches and a small lake. In the distance to the east is the line of the moors. It became the property of the borough of Chorley and was opened to the public in 1925. No town could have a more agreeable place for its pleasure, on its doorstep.

Astley Hall is a strange building, which seems almost to

throw out a challenge to anyone arriving before it. What he sees there is entirely of the 17th century, but it is a front to something older: a small house of the 1570s, built around a stone-flagged courtyard, which survives in large measure at the back.

The estate belonged to the Charnock family in the Middle Ages. The last of their male line, Richard Charnock, died in 1653, and it seems to have been his son-in-law, Sir Richard Brooke, who gave the house its present front. It exemplifies the change of ideas and practice from those of James I's time to Charles II's, not through any change of design but as a mixture deliberately chosen. We can see here a medley of the feelings of two generations, of the old-fashioned and the up-to-date.

Some of it is rustic: the entrance doorway, for instance, is simply crude. But the *façade* as a whole compels attention. It has the rather box-like character of many Jacobean houses, but relieved by two bold projecting bays. Perhaps originally

(A. F. Kersting)

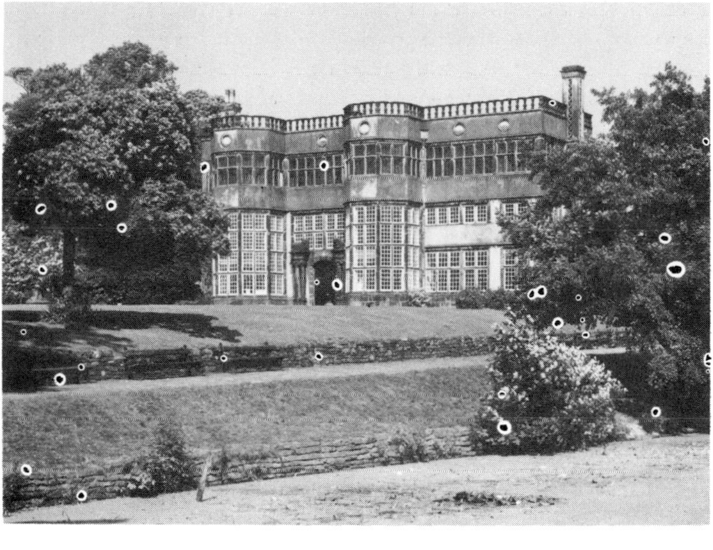

its red brick was exposed, which would have made it more cheerful. Now it is rendered, and though the colour itself, a warmish buff, is not disagreeable, the effect is undoubtedly austere.

Inside, the architectural character of the house is Jacobean, but the decoration is of the 1650s, and remarkably skilful. The ceilings in the Great Hall and the Drawing Room, to the right of it, show plasterwork, deeply undercut, of astonishing virtuosity. The figures are no works of art; but the technical skill they display is outstanding.

The Hall is panelled all round, and 15 portraits are set into the wainscoting. They depict figures in military and political history, going back as far as Tamerlane but for the most part of the 16th century, and they seem to have been installed here in the 1640s. The choice of subjects is curious and has not been explained. It is worth noting, however, that they are nearly all pairs of opponents: Tamerlane and Bajazet, for example, Parma and William the Silent, Elizabeth and Philip II. Can this reflect the thoughts of a man just living through the English Civil War?

The Morning Room to the left of the Hall is dark and quiet, again in the Jacobean manner. But the staircase leading out of the Hall is another piece of exuberant carving of the later age: a primitive ancestor of such splendid pieces as were to come shortly afterwards in houses like *Sudbury*.

The rooms upstairs are simpler, with little elaborate decoration anywhere; the Long Gallery at the top (again, by the 1650s, something that was going out of fashion) quite plain. Its south front is glazed almost continuously from one end to the other. A noble shovelboard is here, 23 ft long, on 20 legs elaborately carved.

Below, in the Oak Room, there is a truly magnificent four-poster bed, one of the finest pieces of Jacobean oak furniture to be seen anywhere. The carving is not only technically accomplished; it has refinement too, notably in the bases of the corner-posts and at the top in the rich cornice.

For the rest, the house contains some other interesting pieces of oak furniture and a number of miscellaneous exhibits, mostly relating to Chorley and its neighbourhood. Like Oak House, *West Bromwich*, it is a municipal possession, rightly prized.

Avebury Wiltshire 4E3

It would be an exaggeration to say that human life has continued at Avebury for 6,000 years: an exaggeration, but only a slight one. The earliest evidence of settlement that we have here goes back, it is now thought, to about 3700 B.C. Silbury Hill, the huge prehistoric mound, can be dated at about 2500 B.C. The stone circles and avenues were erected, for some formal religious purpose, not long after that. When the Romans laid out their road from Bath to Mildenhall (outside Marlborough) they skirted the base of Silbury, rather than cross or slice through it. The present village emerged in the Saxon period. Parish church and manor house and cottages and pub all lie close to the prehistoric circles. No place in England gives so strong a sense as Avebury of the total time-scale of human life.

Its merits as a place of settlement are clear. It stands just below the western edge of the Marlborough Downs, sheltered from the east wind. Water is readily available from two rivers, Kennet and Winterbourne. The Ridgeway, a great prehistoric route (see *Uffington*), passed close by, with other tracks leading eastwards into Surrey and Sussex.

There are four principal monuments, or groups of monuments, to be seen now: Windmill Hill, north of the village; West Kennet and Silbury Hill, close together, to the south; and the circles in and around the village itself.

Windmill Hill is reached by a footpath leading west from the Swindon road: low, broad, and comprising three concentric circles of banks and ditches, covering an area of 21 acres. It was one of the first Neolithic sites to be scientifically investigated (in 1925–9 and 1957) and it has given its name to certain types of pottery found there. The site seems to have been used continuously for well over 1,000 years. It has provided a great deal of evidence about Neolithic agriculture, as well as some indications of trade: stone axes made in Cornwall, Wales, and Westmorland, for example. There is no proof that the enclosure was ever a settlement. It may have been used for defence, or as a central meeting-place for the people of the surrounding district. Further excavation, in areas not yet investigated, may show.

At West Kennet, on the other side of Avebury village, is an enormous long barrow, a tomb containing five chambers under a mound that is roughly rectangular and flanked by two ditches, of a type found also in Gloucestershire and in France. The chambers open out of a central passage. They are constructed of sarsens (the grey sandstone boulders lying on the surface of the Downs, used also in the circles here and at Stonehenge). The remains of 46 human beings, of all ages, were found inside them. That is no great number, for so elaborate a tomb. Were these people of some special distinction?

Here is only one of many questions the barrow raises. It was first described by John Aubrey 300 years ago, partially excavated in 1859 and fully in 1955–6. It has suffered much damage from farmers, digging into it casually for flints and rubble. It was the second monument in the country to be protected under the Ancient Monuments Act of 1882.

The first was its neighbour Silbury Hill. This conical grass-covered mound represents one of the most remarkable feats of construction, of any kind or age, in England. Its base covers five and a half acres; it is 100 ft high; it is entirely man-made. There is nothing to compare with it anywhere in Europe. For a parallel one must turn to the Pyramids of Egypt. It was built up in six huge steps, each about 16 ft high, the steps being filled in subsequently to make a smooth outline; and enclosed by a ditch, crossed by two causeways.

The labour involved here staggers the mind. The hill contains nearly nine million cubic feet of quarried material. The task would have taken 700 men 10 years, requiring organisation, planning, and technical skill of a very high order. The whole work has remained completely stable since

Silbury Hill (A. F. Kersting)

its erection. Silbury must rank among the principal monuments of European engineering.

Again, what was its purpose? Nobody knows. Shafts have been sunk into the hill three times – in 1776–7, 1849, and 1967–70 – and its centre has now been carefully explored. These operations have revealed the hill's wonderful construction but nothing of its contents, supposing it ever contained anything. If it was used for burial, not a single human bone has been found.

So finally to the stone circles. They comprise the Sanctuary, one and a half miles south-east of the village, and the circles at the village itself. These were linked by the West Kennet Avenue of standing stones, the northern part of which is still extant. The Sanctuary contained a succession of circular timber buildings, the latest and largest of them 66 ft in diameter, ranging in time from about 2500 to 2000 B.C. The great circle at Avebury itself comprises a bank with a ditch inside, lined with nearly 100 standing stones. About a quarter of these remain today, almost all on the western side. Within

(Aerofilms Ltd)

Avebury: air view of the village from the west. In the foreground, Avebury Manor and church. Behind, the great Circle; inside it, on the right, five standing stones in the Southern Inner Circle

the big circle were two smaller ones, not concentric but lying north and south (the eastern end of the main street runs between them). The ditch is now only half its original depth. To get the full scale of the stones it must be remembered that they were sunk 3–4 ft into the ground. The largest of them weighs nearly 60 tons.

The religious purpose of these monuments, and their relationship with one another, cannot at present be explained. Some astronomical significance may attach to them. What is clear to anyone is that they are relics of a vanished system of beliefs, most powerfully embodied. The same feeling fills one's mind at Stonehenge (25 miles away to the south).

These two great works are linked in some ways and yet different. They belong to a group, generally called henge monuments, that are, so far as we know, found only in the British Isles.

The village of Avebury demands attention too. The church (St James) is full of interest (it has even kept the loft of its rood-screen, a rarity in England), and the Elizabethan Manor House that adjoins it is charming. So the succession of life has continued; and with it the succession of inquiry too. The examination of the Avebury monuments, begun three centuries ago, has been taken long stages further during the past 50 years, to form a substantial contribution to archaeology – a science and art that has developed very notably in that time.

Barfreston: church of St Mary Kent 5C4

Barfreston is easily seen on the way from *Dover* to Canterbury. Driving, you take the A2 and turn right for Shepherdswell just beyond Lydden Hill, where the road rises steeply on leaving Dover. You can also get there by the train to Shepherdswell station, from which it is a walk of one and a half miles by the same by-road. This runs along the side of a valley. Presently you see Barfreston ahead to the left, the little red-tiled church scarcely distinguishable from the houses. Very many churches, like this one, originally lacked towers and were not larger in scale than the buildings around them. What made them different was the quality of their design and workmanship. So it is here. Barfreston stands with Kilpeck (Hereford and Worcester) high in the top class of small Romanesque village churches in England.

The building is no more than 50 ft long, comprising a nave, a chancel, lower and smaller, and nothing else – not even a bell-cote. One of the pair of Norman windows at the west end was replaced by a larger one in the 15th century. Otherwise the church has remained essentially unchanged since 1200. It was restored with sensibility and care in 1839–41.

It stands in a tiny churchyard, perched up above a steep

little slope. For so small a building, the east end is spectacular, with a wheel window, the spokes formed by little columns, flanked by the symbols of the Evangelists. The design is French in character, matched by two surviving examples, at Beauvais (St Etienne) and Trie-Château. Barfreston church is indeed, like its magnificent neighbour at Canterbury, compounded of French and English elements. The very fabric shows it: for the lower part of the walls is constructed of flints from the surrounding chalk, the upper part of limestone imported from Caen.

Neither Kent nor the whole of south-east England could furnish stone capable of being carved with the refinement shown here. A cornice of heads, less brilliantly grotesque than those at Kilpeck, runs below the eaves. The most striking displays of sculpture are at the east end and in the two doors set in the south wall. There is a certain confusion of motifs – beasts interspersed irregularly with leaf carvings, with sacred figures somewhat oddly disposed among them. One or two of the carvings are curiously off-centre – e.g. the bishop, above the Christ in Majesty, over the main south door. There is no evidence that this figure alludes to Thomas Becket, martyred at Canterbury a few years before it was carved.

Such little irregularities are merely piquant. They do not affect one's appreciation of the quality of the work. Norman sculpture is more often powerful than delicate – though in the crypt at Canterbury it is both. Here at Barfreston, especially on the main south door, it is incised rather lightly: gentle, almost dreamlike, different in spirit from the ferocity displayed at Kilpeck. The contrast arises in part from the nature of the materials the sculptors had to work in. The red sandstone at Kilpeck is as good as it can be, but still it *is* a sandstone: the delicacy of the roundels here, with their foliage and winged beasts, could be attained only in limestone.

The interior of the church is simple, severely plain. Its walls were originally covered with paintings (see *Kempley*), which survived in the chancel until the restoration. The nave

Barfreston church: the south porch (A. F. Kersting)

is high in proportion to its length; the chancel arch surprisingly lofty, flanked by two lower ones, now blocked up.

As you leave the village, take the road to Frogham; then turn right for Aylesham, and so for Canterbury. The road from Frogham onwards, Nightingale Lane, forms a strange frontier. To the right is a countryside of farms and a little parkland; to the left, the huge spoil-heap of Snowdown Colliery. The coalfield is an improbable feature of East Kent. It is still in active production. So here, across Nightingale Lane, two elements in the economy of England confront each other sharply – as at *Conisbrough*; one that has developed recently, the other immemorially old.

Bedford Bedfordshire 5A2

Most old towns in Europe lie on rivers, still navigable or once so. That often explains their origin. On the Continent, especially during the last 200 years, the town was commonly orientated towards the river, laid out along it – as one sees in France with the quays and streets of Lyon or Besançon, with the tree-shaded grass at Châlons-sur-Marne. But in England nearly all towns turn away from their rivers as if ashamed of them. With this nation of shopkeepers, commercial considerations were paramount. Factories and warehouses were allowed to occupy the banks of the river, for the ease of communication that it brought them; the river was scarcely ever treated as an amenity (though see *Durham*). A few signs of repentance appeared in the later Victorian age. The grandest of these is the Victoria Embankment in London. The most charming is at Bedford.

Bedford grew up at a crossing of the River Ouse: at first by a ford (from which it took its name) and then later by a bridge. The handsome stone bridge we see now was completed in 1813 and widened sympathetically in 1940. The Swan Hotel, erected by the Duke of Bedford to the designs of Henry Holland in 1794, stands immediately east of the bridge. Beside it and for half a mile beyond, the north bank of the river was laid out with great care in the 1880s, to provide a walk along by the water with gardens and a road for vehicles. Behind that, villas sprang up for the comfortable citizens of the town, most of them in a dark brownish-red brick, peculiar to the locality. The whole was shaded by big trees, now full-grown. The south bank was left altogether without building, almost in its natural state

(Eric J. Chalker)

Bedford: the River Ouse, with the bridge of 1813; St Paul's church behind; the Swan Hotel on the right

– a foil to the trim development opposite. The river is spanned by a gracefully-curved suspension bridge (engineer, John J. Webster, 1888). At the end of the half-mile continuous building stops; the road and walk pass into parkland and glades of trees. All this is terminated by a new road (1974), for carrying the traffic round the town away from its centre; sadly impairing the former quiet of the place, though necessary enough. The road crosses the river on an excellent concrete bridge, lithe and admirably detailed.

There are other things to think of and see in Bedford. It is Bunyan's town – he was born at Elstow, just outside. John Howard, the prison reformer, also lived close by, at Cardington: he is commemorated by a fine statue on a splendidly-enriched pedestal, by Alfred Gilbert (1890). The Cecil Higgins Museum (housed by the site of the Castle) is distinguished, and has just been enlarged to accommodate the important Handley-Read collection of Victorian art. But it is, most of all, the river that makes the town memorable, lively with eights and fours and solitary oarsmen, and an old-established regatta in July. The municipality regards it with a proper pride: the Embankment gardens are tended delightfully, and the lay-out is gradually being extended, on the opposite side of the stone bridge. Here, for once in England, water comes into its own.

Berkeley Gloucestershire 4D2

Berkeley is a small town, which grew up as a dependency of a castle and remains that, in large measure, today.

A castle was erected here soon after the Norman Conquest, but the earliest part of the present structure is the circular Keep, begun in 1153. A hall was added later in the 12th century. The whole building was reconstructed in the 1340s, the present Great Hall then displacing its predecessor. As it now stands, the fabric of Berkeley Castle, apart from the Keep, is almost entirely of that time. Most of the outer defences on the west, or entrance, side were removed and the entrance itself patched up after the Castle had been captured by the forces of the Parliament in the Civil War in 1645. Otherwise, it has been adapted gradually and unobtrusively to the peaceful purposes of a country house. There were no large-scale alterations in the 19th century, like those at Alnwick and Warwick. The Castle is still in the hands of the Berkeley family, who trace their ownership of it back to 1153.

The Keep divides the Outer Ward from the Inner. The Inner Ward has become the centre of the whole house. You enter it by a stone staircase in the "fore-building" – a rare survival of an appendage often attached to castle keeps, providing a narrow entrance that could be closely guarded. This brings you on the first floor to the King's Gallery, named in commemoration of the imprisonment here and subsequent fearful murder of Edward II in 1327 (see *Gloucester*). The Guard Room over the entrance is now called King Edward's Room; but the exact locality of the crime is uncertain.

The tour of the house now goes through a series of rooms making three-quarters of the circuit of the whole complex of buildings. The Picture Gallery and the Drawing Room lie together and contain some paintings that reflect the Berkeley family's long-maintained passion for foxhunting. They include a Stubbs and a Ben Marshall, and a number of portraits depicting the heads of the family in the canary-yellow coats of the Berkeley Hunt. In the Drawing Room there is also an interesting 17th-century painting of the Castle. A series of smaller rooms follows, and then the Great Hall, splendid and nobly furnished: essentially as it was built about 1340, except that the timber roof seems to have been lowered, to make a flatter arch, in 1497. One of the Hall's chief distinctions is the fine stone arcade framing the windows on the courtyard side, with a version of the "Berkeley arch": a four- or five-sided arch framing another, usually with double-curved foils. The screen is covered with crude 16th-century painting. Over the fireplace – brought here from Wanswell Court, another Gloucestershire house – hangs Gainsborough's portrait of Admiral Sir George Cranfield Berkeley. The Grand Staircase leads to what is now the Morning Room, but was formerly the Chapel. It has a flat panelled ceiling, with beams and brackets painted in red and green. This bears (high up, and not easily visible) a series of texts from the Book of Revelation, translated into Norman-French by John Trevisa, perhaps a follower of Wyclif, who became chaplain at the Castle and vicar of Berkeley; he was buried in the parish church when he died in 1412. The subdued colouring here is delightful. The Long Drawing Room also has a striking formal beauty of its own, with a notable carpet and mirrors – two of them made for the house and incorporating the Berkeley arms. The King's Pew by the entrance was brought here from the Chapel. The Small Drawing Room ends the sequence, with a plain 15th-century timber roof and walls hung with Brussels tapestries.

Now descending into the Inner Ward, one can appreciate the subtlety with which the Castle has been brought to serve its successive and different purposes. The elegant polygonal turret projecting on the south side of the courtyard provides an entrance substituted for the original one, which led to the Keep.

The terraced gardens outside the main gateway afford a view of the Castle as a whole. Berkeley Castle is the only large building in England that is built of tufa, a porous material originally precipitated by spring water out of limestone. Since it is very rough and coarse-grained, it cannot be dressed smooth. Its colour is lovely. Tufa is usually grey, but here iron has percolated into it, giving it a strong infusion of pink; a whole range of tints is the result in these walls and terraces.

Immediately behind is the church (St Mary), a complement to the Castle, with some of the Berkeley lords, from the 14th century to the 17th, commemorated by monuments in the south aisles of the chancel and nave. The church had no tower, conventionally placed as part of the fabric of the building, for that would have overlooked the Castle and impaired its security. So the tower stood at a distance away

Berkeley Castle from the south (Roy Nash)

to the north. The present one replaced a medieval predecessor, which had become ruinous, in 1753.

The core of the church dates from the 13th century, seen in the tall lancet windows at the west end and in the arcades of the nave. The aisles are of the 14th century, the rest of the building – including the flat timber roof, replacing a high gabled one – of the 15th. It is notable for its bold stone screen, a rarity in a parish church (see *Totnes*). There are fragmentary wall-paintings at the west end and in the chancel.

The little town stands at a cross-roads, north-east of the Castle and church. It has a modest coaching inn and some pleasant houses of the 18th century. Though the community was always dominated by the Berkeleys, it threw up in the Georgian age a figure who achieved fame far beyond England. Edward Jenner was born in the town in 1749, spent nearly all his life in it and died there in 1823. It was at Berkeley that he began vaccination against smallpox in 1796. The wooden hut in which he made his experiments is preserved. Within 10 years his practice had come to be widely accepted, abroad as well as at home. Already before he died vaccination had been made compulsory in several European states. Jenner was a simple and agreeable man, of complete integrity. The disease he attacked was one of the principal killers of his time. By his methods, and the subsequent further refinement of them, it was conquered. Few discoveries of greater importance to human life and happiness have been made in the past 200 years. Fewer still, of any time, have been developed so completely in one place as Jenner's were here in Berkeley.

Berrington Hall Hereford and Worcester 4D1
Henry Holland is among the most refined of English architects. He has been unfortunate, in that so many of his principal works have been destroyed, or altered beyond recognition: Carlton House and the East India House in London, for example, the Royal Pavilion at *Brighton*, Wimbledon Park House in Surrey, Wenvoe Castle in South Wales.

As a young man, things came to him easily. He learnt the trade under his father, a London master-builder, through whom he was introduced to "Capability" Brown (see *Heveningham*), the most famous English landscape gardener of his time. Holland married Brown's daughter and became his partner, taking over from him most of his strictly architectural work. This is well exemplified at Berrington, where Brown was called in soon after 1775 to lay out the grounds and Holland prepared designs for the house in 1778.

The estate had then just been bought by Thomas Harley, brother of the first Earl of Oxford. (The Harleys were a Herefordshire family, who originated at Brampton Bryan on the Welsh border.) Thomas Harley was a successful man of business, who had been Lord Mayor of London, able to afford the highest quality and to be content with nothing else. Moreover, while the house was being built, his daughter Anne became engaged to marry the heir of Lord Rodney, one of the most prominent naval commanders of his time. This enlarged Harley's ideas. When he died in 1804 the Rodneys succeeded him at Berrington, and they remained there until 1900. The estate was then sold to a politician, Frederick Cawley (who became a peer in 1918). The present Lord Cawley made over the house and park to the Treasury in 1957, whereupon it was transferred to the National Trust.

The structure is of brick, cased in sandstone quarried only a mile away – a dark red, veering in some lights towards purple. The richness of colour is counteracted by the restraint of Holland's design. Apart from the frieze on the portico, its coffered ceiling and Ionic columns, there is no decoration on the front of the house at all. But the plainness is deliberate, springing from no poverty of purse or spirit. Look at the delicacy of the glazing bars of the windows, as thin as they well could be. The back, facing on to a courtyard, is even plainer. It was disfigured by a vile Victorian tower, asymmetrically placed. That has recently been removed, to the National Trust's credit, apart from the steps leading up to it, giving access to the right-hand side of the house.

The entrance hall immediately announces an interior different from the outside. It is extremely rich, yet never opulent. Here, as at every other point in the house, the decoration is kept under the firmest control. The prevailing tones are buff, picked out here and there with gold, and a greyish green; the marble floor is a quiet reflection of the rest. The ceiling appears to be gently domed, but that is an illusion, imparted by the shallow segments and the curved triangle they necessitate at each corner.

The ceiling of the Drawing Room is exquisite – no other word will do: pale blue, lavender, gold, and white. It has circular paintings, and it is enlivened with seahorses and cherubs in low relief on the plaster. The windows are cased in magnificent curtain-boxes. The carving of the chimney-piece is outstanding, and the superb steel grate (imported by the first Lord Cawley) carries a set of Wedgwood medallions of Roman emperors.

The staircase, in the centre of the house, is a triumph: rectangular, and lighted by a dome. The balustrade is patterned with lyres, the plasterwork again delectable, and the glass of the dome carried in a metal frame, designed and cast with extreme delicacy.

The Drawing Room has been somewhat altered. It has another very fine chimney-piece, though originally it was finer still, with a central medallion in silver. Three pictures of naval battles hang here (a fourth is in the Business Room at the back of the house), all recording the victories of Rodney. Throughout the house there are small references to the navy, in the plasterwork for instance; in this chimney-piece there is a battleship to be seen, and a naval fort.

In the Library, on the other hand, the references are as they should be literary, with a series of eight medallion portraits of writers in the ceiling. Throughout this sequence of rooms, the doors are notable for their mahogany nobly treated and their endlessly varied brass-work.

But the pleasures of Berrington do not end here. A charming garden is to be seen close to the house, and a memorable landscape beyond. The house looks southward over an amphitheatre, bounded by the Black Mountains, Brecon Beacons,

Berrington Hall: the Library (Country Life)

and Radnor Forest. To the left is a lake, natural but improved by the planting of Capability Brown; at the extreme right Croft Ambrey, crowned by an Iron-Age hill-fort. In the nearer foreground are the trees of the park, disposed with Brown's careful informality. Again, as at *Clunbury* further north, an extreme quietness prevails, surviving from an older England.

Berwick-on-Tweed Northumberland 1B1

Berwick* is the sole example in England of a kind of town not uncommon on the Continent: a frontier post, heavily fortified, retaining its fortifications complete. Carlisle was once another, the counterpart of Berwick at the western end of the Scottish border. But its fortifications were less sophisticated

* Pronounced "Berrick".

than Berwick's; they decayed in the 17th and 18th centuries and were almost wholly demolished early in the 19th as the city became a centre of industry and communications. Berwick, on the other hand, continued little changed. No factories or mills were established there. When the railways arrived, they made a junction at Tweedmouth, on the opposite bank of the river. And so Berwick remained a small place. Its population is about 12,000.

The town seems to be of English foundation, established by the kings of Northumbria in the 7th century. But in 880 it was seized by the Scots, and it then remained with them until 1174, when they lost it to England. Thereafter, for the next three centuries, it shuttled between the two kingdoms. It did not pass finally to England until 1482. In 1551 it was agreed between the English and Scots that it should be neutralised, with a small district around it. Hence the famous phrase "the kingdoms of England, Scotland, and Berwick-upon-Tweed". The town was at length quietly incorporated into Northumberland in 1844.

This story of Berwick's movement back and forth between England and Scotland is a story of shifting power. It was a naturally important place, a key to the security of both kingdoms. The outcome of the struggle was illogical. As early as 1237 it was accepted that the frontier lay on the Tweed. Berwick was on the north bank of the river and therefore clearly in Scotland. Only superior military strength caused it to become English. Even so, Berwick*shire* always remained a Scottish county.

For one brief moment, in 1296–7, Berwick looked like becoming more than a frontier post. At the height of his attempt to bring Scotland under English control, Edward I, having sacked the town, determined to rebuild it and to make it the financial capital of a Scottish kingdom reorganised under him. If England and Scotland had become virtually one state, Berwick would have been a central point in it. Edward had created new towns (*bastides*) elsewhere, Flint for instance and Winchelsea; this was the last of the series he planned. It was not a wholly new foundation. Rather, as he had done at Hull, he took an existing town and sought to give it a fresh direction and importance. But as the King's difficulties and preoccupations elsewhere increased in the last 10 years of his life the project was dropped.

If Edward I did not make Berwick into an administrative capital, he did begin to turn it from a roughly-fortified place into a fortress. A castle already stood there; in its hall he had pronounced his judgment in favour of John Baliol as King of Scotland in 1292. He began to strengthen it and to rebuild the town walls in stone. What he began, his grandson Edward III continued, until the walls included 19 towers. But they were still not strong enough; Berwick continued to be taken and retaken. In 1405 their inadequacy was demonstrated in a new way when Henry IV captured the town using artillery.

The medieval walls then were elaborate, yet did not render Berwick secure. Fresh attempts were made early in the 16th century to improve them. In Henry VIII's reign they began to follow new patterns, under the influence of Italian military engineering. Something bigger was then attempted: a citadel on the eastern side of the town, worked on intermittently between 1550 and 1557 but left unfinished. Finally, in 1558–69, an ambitious effort was made to turn Berwick into a complete fortress: a precaution against the military alliance between the French and the Scots. But with the flight of Mary Queen of Scots into England in 1568 that danger ceased to be pressing, and the work was abandoned.

The Elizabethan walls survive largely intact. There is only one set, of the same date and kind, more complete than Berwick's; and that is at Lucca.

The medieval fortifications enclosed a larger area than those of the 16th century, for they included the Castle and the northern part of the modern town. In the later development the line of the defences was drastically shortened, and the Castle abandoned altogether. It quietly disintegrated, and its ruin was completed by the railway, which fixed its station firmly where the historic great hall had stood. The wall along the shore of the estuary and up the Tweed is medieval;

(John Dewer Studios)

Berwick-on-Tweed: air view from the north. Left to right in the foreground: Windmill, Brass, and Cumberland Bastions

the 16th-century work begins at Meg's Mount and completes the circuit, eastward to Brass Bastion and then south to King's Mount.

Virtually the whole of this circuit can be walked today. The pleasure has been recently enhanced by the work undertaken in conserving the structures and investigating what lies below the surface of the ground. The Citadel, for instance, entirely overlaid by the Elizabethan fortifications, was revealed only in 1960.

Five main structures are to be seen, erected between 1558 and 1566. They are all bastions – forts that have two faces meeting at an angle. Only two of them were finished: Windmill Bastion on the east and Cumberland Bastion on the north. But Brass Bastion fell not far short of completion, and the whole complex can be appreciated best today by looking at this north-eastern part of it. Cumberland Bastion stands now cleaned and fully revealed, with a sizeable open space in front. The range includes Scotsgate, somewhat altered in the 19th century. Only one of the gateways still stands as it was when the Elizabethan fortifications were built; that is Cowport, between Brass and Windmill Bastions on the eastern side. Windmill Bastion replaced the Citadel, on whose site, within the rampart, now stands the small but massive Magazine, erected in 1749. King's Mount marks the point at which the 16th-century fortifications stopped. They are continued by the medieval walls along the waterfront; on the quay there are houses built against them at the back. The line goes on northward along the Tweed to Meg's Mount and then beyond to the shore below the Castle, ending in a spectacular piece, the 13th-century White Wall, which descends in a stepped cascade from the Castle to the river.

Looked at as a whole from a distance today, the town builds itself up around an elegant 18th-century steeple. This does not belong to a church but to the handsome Town Hall (1760), which neatly closes the lower end of Mary Gate. It is a good building; unlike many of its kind, which are interesting only in their *façades*, this one is not surprised if one comes upon it from the rear, from Hide Hill. The parish church (Holy Trinity), which is without any tower or spire, is one of the very few churches erected under the Republican government of 1649–60 (see *Staunton Harold*), and the only one in a town of any importance. Its predecessor was destroyed when Cromwell captured Berwick in 1648. This one was put up in replacement, and finished in 1652. It is a simple rectangle, with small turrets at the corners. Inside it is distinguished chiefly by its military memorials, including several to the town's Lieutenant-Governors. For Berwick remained a garrison, and its Barracks are almost opposite the church across a little square. They are the oldest purpose-built barracks in England today, planned in 1717: a competent design in the manner of Vanbrugh, though probably not by him. They contain the Regimental Museum of the King's Own Scottish Borderers.

Berwick stands on the north bank of the river. Tweedmouth opposite, now in effect a suburb, is a separate parish. The three bridges crossing the river are the lowest in the series, of exceptional variety and interest, that span the Tweed (see under *Cheviot*). The oldest of the three – a stout 15-arched structure with massive cutwaters – was completed in 1624. It is a visible monument of the union of the crowns of England and Scotland. There was never a bridge here in the Middle Ages. It would have provided dangerous assistance to an invader, of either kingdom. But when James VI of Scotland succeeded to the English throne in 1603 it was hoped that the ancient warfare would cease; and so, apart from one brief revival in 1639–51, it proved. That it was safe to build a bridge at Berwick, and that it was never taken down in subsequent warfare, showed that peace had now at last descended upon the Lothians and Northumberland.

The bridge was narrow: adequate, in normal conditions, for the first three centuries of its life but obviously unable to carry heavy motor traffic. It became a most troublesome bottleneck, which had to be removed. The result was the building of the Royal Tweed Bridge, opened in 1928.

It could scarcely be more different. The English had little confidence then in the special properties of reinforced concrete: so that while Maillart was building in Switzerland some of the most elegant of all bridges in that material, they timidly employed it as if it had been stone. Here, for instance, the bridge is able to spring over the Tweed in three gigantic leaps, the northernmost 361 ft wide. But in doing so the bridge draws attention to itself much too loudly. It is in truth a ponderous structure, the effect of its long smooth arches marred by the clumsy vertical struts supporting the roadway. It has the spring of a tiger – wearing a hobbled skirt.

The third bridge, upstream, the Royal Border Bridge, is a masterpiece: one of the longest and loftiest stone viaducts in England, carrying the main East Coast railway line. It was designed by Robert Stephenson and opened in 1850. Standing on 28 arches, which rise from tapering piers, it is gracefully curved at the south end as it rides high above Tweedmouth. The bridge is well seen from the north bank of the river, close to the point where the White Wall of the Castle comes down. As you cross it slowly, the whole town of Berwick is spread out below, brown and grey but enlivened by red pantiled roofs, crowned by the spire of the Town Hall and girdled still by the walls built to defend it. Here is a compendious reminder of the long and stormy relationship of England and Scotland, within the small island of Great Britain.

Beverley Humberside 2D4
There are two good ways of approaching Beverley, each with its own merit. If you are going there chiefly to see the Minster, then you should try to come in from the south, by train from Hull. There, sitting on the left-hand side, you will see the great building first in the distance behind a screen of pylons and cables; then you get the best view of it, from the south-east. It is a moment to remember. If you arrive from the north, from Driffield, that will bring you in by the New Walk and North Bar Without, which make a delightful street line.

The New Walk was laid out in 1782, as a continuation of North Bar Without. It is planted with big trees, mostly chestnuts, and fenced in with white posts and chains. The houses are all of the 18th and 19th centuries. The whole range on the left-hand or east side, from No. 62 North Bar Without to No. 48, are good Georgian, in a variety of modes and sizes; No. 62, trim and secluded, is outstanding. On the opposite side two black-and-white houses take the eye – unfavourably at first: whatever can these importations from Cheshire be doing here? – picked up by another such building at the far end of the street. They are all due to a local architect, James Elwell, and date from 1880–94. Though aggressively alien in spirit, they are curiosities, entertaining from the carved figures and panels in wood that decorate them, including scenes from *Punch* and *The Cloister and the Hearth*.

The street is closed by the North Bar itself, a gateway of 1409 built of brick – a material much used in east Yorkshire in the later Middle Ages, particularly in the parish church of Hull. Beverley once had five gates; this is the only one that survives. Beyond it is North Bar Within, showing a handsome brick terrace of five tall houses on the right (notice the doorcases and the end bays), then the Beverley Arms Hotel, and facing it – emphatically not in brick, but in gleaming white Tadcaster stone – St Mary's church.

Beverley resembles *Wells* in having two outstanding churches: a collegiate church (at Wells a cathedral) and a fine parish church at the other end of the town. The tower of St Mary's, built after the collapse of an earlier one in 1520, stands up handsomely, and the building presents a carefully-composed front to North Bar Within.

The interior is glorious, though less than it once was through injuries suffered in the Civil War, and especially through Puritan vandalism after the King's forces gave up the town in 1643. The whole of the medieval glass was then destroyed and 25 brasses were ripped out, leaving only their sockets behind. The building was heavily refurbished in the 19th century, and on the whole well. Look for example at the west window (designed by A. W. N. Pugin), with its glowing blues, and the chancel screen by John Bilson, who is remembered with gratitude as a scholarly investigator of architectural history.

The church is best looked at from east to west. An earlier church was rebuilt from about 1280 onwards. The oldest part is the large north-west chapel of the chancel. Then the chancel itself was taken in hand early in the 14th century, with its aisles and the transepts. The most distinguished part of all this is the small north-eastern chapel; on the south side of its vault the ribs cross one another as they often do in the Flamboyant building of France.

The nave is chiefly of the 16th century, rebuilt after the

collapse of the tower, which evidently fell westward, though without damaging the west front. Inscriptions on the north side tell us who paid for the work: John Crossley and Joan his wife, the Good Wives of Beverley, and the Minstrels, who appear in person on the easternmost capital.

The flat timber ceilings are of interest. The one in the chancel depicts a series of 40 of the kings of England. It dates from 1445, but it has been so completely repainted that it is no more than a brave attempt to reproduce the original. The chancel also has an excellent series of carved stalls.

Coming out of the church, turn left. The streets then fork, and the left-hand one brings you into the Saturday Market Place, with the broad Market Cross of 1714 at the top, and pricking up beyond it the twin towers of the Minster.

The Saturday Market Place still busily fulfils the function implied in its name. It runs on a shallow curve and comprises two parts: the northern one relatively narrow – not much more than a wide street – with the Cross in the centre, the southern an open square. It is lined with modest houses built of brick and often stuccoed. This Market Place has suffered in several ways: by the opening-up of roads to through traffic, especially at the north-east corner; by the erection of a vile jazz-modern shop, conspicuous on the critical site at the south end; and by the replacement of the pantiles on the roofs of so many of the houses by dull Welsh slates. These orange-red pantiles help to give Beverley its prevailing character, like *Newark*. They need to be jealously preserved.

At the south end is Toll Gavel, a bottleneck for modern traffic but not to be enlarged, one hopes, on that account. At the fork beyond bear left (noticing, if you are on foot, the fierce green snakes intertwined round the pillars at the entrance to a shop close by) into Walkergate. You then arrive in the Wednesday Market, smaller than its counterpart and triangular. Out of it runs Highgate, which leads straight to the Minster.

Moving up it, you might be approaching one of the great churches of France. On this side it rises abruptly from the houses, and the illusion is heightened by the presence of some intrusive wires, a curse from which in general Beverley has kept itself commendably free. If you pass on round the west end of the church, by St John Street into Long Lane, and look back you get a view of a quite different sort. From this side, the south-west, the Minster rises up, like few other churches of its size anywhere, apparently from an open meadow.

The Minster (*monasterium*) was the church of a religious house, founded first for monks by St John of Beverley in the 8th century, refounded as a college of secular canons by King Athelstan in the 10th, and dissolved in 1548, when the canons' domestic buildings were pulled down and the church became a parish church, as it is still. The Romanesque church was almost completely destroyed by fire and the collapse of its tower. The work of rebuilding it began about

Beverley Minster from the south-west (B.T.A.)

1230; and to this phase belongs the whole of the eastern part – seen from this point across the meadow in the pure Early English work of the south transept. The nave was reconstructed from 1308 onwards, its flowing Decorated tracery seen clearly here too. Then came the west front with its towers, finished by 1450: an outstanding piece of the late English Gothic, or Perpendicular. A hint of one other building phase can also be picked up here. The central tower is no more than a flat square cap, with what look like 18th-century Gothic patterns on its base. It formerly bore a cupola, which was indeed erected early in that century, when much work was done on the Minster under the direction of Hawksmoor. The cupola was taken off in 1824. To see what the Minster was like just before it was demolished, go to the town Art Gallery and look at J. C. Buckler's big watercolour drawing of it on the first-floor landing. You may, or may not, share my regret that it was removed.

The building is very large, with a double set of transepts, as at *Salisbury* and *Wells*, a plan favoured by the English but not often found on the Continent. It is vaulted in stone throughout – no timber masquerading as stone here, as there is at York. Inside it appears entirely homogeneous, for the western part of the church, built in the 14th century, deliberately follows the fashion of the eastern part, two generations older: something unusual in the Middle Ages, though found also in a more famous example, at Westminster Abbey. The only exception occurs at the west end, in the bay under the towers, which dates from the 15th century and is fully in the manner of that time.

Though the canons' buildings have gone, one relic of their life remains inside, in the north choir aisle: the beautiful double staircase to the destroyed chapter house, a pair of arcaded flights with slender Purbeck marble shafts that support the vault standing out in front of them. The 16th-century choir stalls are good, with the most numerous series of misericords to be found in any English church.

In the sanctuary, on the left of the altar, stands one of the grandest medieval tombs in the country, commemorating either Lady Eleanor Percy or her daughter. It was completed some time after 1339. The carving is sumptuous, but disciplined; and admirable in the management of the curved elements, the cusps and ogees and the little figures in the spandrels. The screen adjoining the tomb, behind the high altar, which carried the shrine of St John before the Reformation, is of the same kind; the two must have been intended to make a single composition. But unlike the tomb the screen has lost its medieval figures; the statues and mosaic portraits added to it in the 1890s are vapid beside their medieval counterparts near by. And finally, on the right of the sanctuary, are the priests' seats, of the same quality as the tomb but executed in wood.

All the medieval glass that survives has been assembled in the east window. There is some pleasing 19th-century glass, for example in the south window of the main south transept.

Both the west and the east fronts of Beverley Minster are good. The west front is well organised, soaring and taut. Perhaps one may take leave of this splendid building by going down Flemingate, on the way out to Hull. Looking back from there, the east end stands now immensely broad-shouldered behind its double transepts, but brought to an elegant point in the big ogee arch over the window. Here, as everywhere else in the church, the effect has been thought through to a successful conclusion.

From this side, as from all others, the Minster rises up to preside over the town. But it shows no arrogant domination. If its graceful towers rise higher than anything else in the place, the tower of St Mary's stands up to them nevertheless, respectfully but firmly; and the red-roofed houses form the domestic counterpoint to them both. The harmony of the whole has been gravely threatened in recent years by two big road-building projects. The people of Beverley have resisted them to good purpose, and so far have stopped them. Should anything of the kind be proposed again, they will deserve the support of every lover of English towns in fighting it; for this is a town far too precious to be dismembered.

Bingley West Yorkshire 2C4
The Leeds & Liverpool Canal was nearly 50 years in construction. It was planned, with advice from Brindley, by an engineer from Halifax named Longbotham, under whom it was begun in 1770. The first section on the Yorkshire side, from Leeds through Bingley to a point near Gargrave, was opened in 1777; the whole work was finished only in 1816. A straight route intersecting the Pennines was out of the question. Instead, it made its way through them in a great arc, and this meant that although the direct distance was about 70 miles, the canal took 127. It was designed to connect the two biggest manufacturing districts of the north, affording the means for the woollens and other goods of Yorkshire to be taken direct to Liverpool, for export overseas. But the long delay in completing it weakened the canal financially, and even when it was opened (with "a grand aquatic procession") it had already been caught up with, and passed, by competitors. It cost in the end £1,200,000, nearly five times what was originally estimated, and its heyday, when it came into full use, was short. By 1841 Leeds and Liverpool were joined by railway, which conveyed goods much more rapidly. In winter moreover the canal was frequently made impassable with ice, when the railway kept open.

The canal, then, was no more than a qualified success. But that was hardly its own fault: it was overtaken by developments not anticipated when it was planned. It remains a major work of engineering: one of the few large English canals to traverse really high country. The ascents of the Pennines are of special interest, and here at Bingley is the steepest of them. At this point the canal is lifted 89 ft by eight locks, one set of five and one of three. The higher set is "Bingley Five-Rise", also called "Bingley Great Lock". It makes not merely a "flight" but a "staircase", in which the top gates of one lock form the bottom gates of the next. A well-informed critic condemned it as an "unfortunate arrangement", on the ground that it required five locks full of water to pass one boat up the whole staircase. Nevertheless it was a bold device, economical in capital cost, for overcoming

"Bingley Five-Rise" (British Waterways Board)

an exceptionally steep climb, and it impresses one powerfully still with the logical directness of the canal-builders of the 18th century. At the summit the canal widens out into a little basin, now filled with pleasure craft.

There is a fine view down from the head of the staircase into Bingley, with a notable group of mill chimneys, and across the River Aire to the hills beyond.

Blanchland Northumberland 1B2
A very small village, lying in a secret hollow of the hills. However you approach it, from Hexham, from Consett, or

Blanchland village from the south (Eric G. Meadows)

from Weardale, you drop down on it from above, to a great surprise. You have come over high moorlands, bare in summer and stark in winter, and you suddenly reach a settlement utterly unlike anything around it: shapely and trim, compact, planned. What can explain it?

The place takes its origin from the foundation of an abbey of Premonstratensian canons in 1165, its name transferred from Blanchelande in Normandy. It was only a small house, never rich, and it had troubles to meet in the wars between England and Scotland under Edward III. After the Dissolution its property passed through the hands of a series of purchasers until 1704, when it was bought by Nathaniel Lord Crewe, Bishop of Durham. After his death the trustees of his extensive estates (bequeathed to charity) built the village of Blanchland as we see it now, partly in the ruins of the monastery. It is therefore an 18th-century "model" village, arising out of – though not actually following – a medieval plan. Part of the church of the monastery survives, and its gatehouse; fragments of it have been incorporated in later buildings.

The church (St Mary) is now L-shaped, comprising the chancel and the north transept, at the end of which is the tower. The nave has gone, though the lower part of its south wall remains as the boundary of the churchyard on that side. What survives is chiefly of the 13th and 14th centuries, though the aisle of the transept and the east end of the chancel were rebuilt in the Victorian age. Lord Crewe's trustees repaired the church, adding two windows at the west end in line with the original windows of the transept and imitating them well, to make a seemly front. There are three little panels of 15th-century glass in the eastern windows of the chancel, and a range of interesting medieval grave-slabs showing weapons and other symbols, rudely incised, on the floor of the transept.

The village is in two parts. First a group of four lanes comprising simple stone-built cottages and converging by the churchyard, with the little Victorian school (Gothic, and also stone-built) at the meeting-place. Below the school is the gatehouse of the monastery, a plain 15th-century structure. Beyond that, towards the river, comes the second set of houses, the nucleated group built by the Crewe trustees about 1753. This is L-shaped (reflecting the church – consciously?) and comprises two open spaces, nearly rectangular, lined with houses and terminated at the south end by the bridge. At the top, immediately by the gateway, is the largest house, what is now the Lord Crewe Arms Hotel. This is thought to have been originally the Abbot's Lodging. The monastic buildings lay on the south side of the church, and foundations of some of them have been excavated in the hotel garden.

None of the houses is distinguished individually. It is the whole that is memorable: the brown stone buildings (of millstone grit streaked with iron) pleasingly disposed, set in the green valley of the Derwent, surrounded by trees, its only tall accent the church tower. The stonework is everywhere undressed; with one exception, the roofs are of stone slabs, not of slates. Here is a work of the Georgian age that is neither formal nor imposing: a medieval settlement refashioned with economy and skill.

Bodiam Castle East Sussex 5B5

Bodiam Castle is a building erected all at one time, to meet a national emergency. In the first phase of the Hundred Years War the English had invaded France with brilliant success, crowned by the triumphs of Crecy and Poitiers. After 1369, however, they suffered almost nothing but defeat, and there was a serious danger that the French might invade England in return. In 1377 they attacked and burnt *Rye*, Winchelsea, and Hastings. Before long it seemed as if they might go further than that, to land an army.

Some measures were then taken for the defence of Sussex and Kent. The towns of *Dover* and Sandwich were protected with fortifications; so were private houses, from the Archbishop of Canterbury's at Saltwood to Roger Ashburnham's at *Scotney*; and at least one wholly new castle was built – this one at Bodiam, by Sir Edward Dallingridge, in 1385–8.

The River Rother was then navigable from its mouth at Rye up to this point, where there was a bridge and a small harbour. That determined the position of the castle. It was designed to meet invasion from the river and to control the bridge that crossed it; protected not only by a broad moat but also by the undrained marshes that filled the shallow valley.

The plan of the building is regular and simple, deriving perhaps from a French origin and exemplified elsewhere in England at the same time, as at Nunney in Somerset. It is square, with a circular tower at each corner, rectangular towers in the centre of three of the walls, and a much heavier gatehouse on the fourth, guarding the main entrance to the castle, which is approached today by a causeway and two little bridges. Half-way over, there is a fragment of masonry: all that remains of the barbican, a detached outer gateway

Bodiam Castle from the north-east (Eric J. Chalker)

that itself stood on an island. The original bridge was over the western arm of the moat, the path making a right angle at the barbican. (The three-sided stone base from which the bridge sprang can still be seen.) This arrangement exposed the whole flank of an attacking force – on its weaker side, unprotected by shields – to the defenders of the castle and their missiles.

The shell of the fabric is quite complete, splendidly constructed in the durable sandstone of the Weald. Inside the walls, however, the buildings are almost wholly ruinous. The

Great Hall lay on the south side; it is still divided from the buttery by its stone screen of three arches. The owner's living quarters lay along the east wall, with the chapel at its northern end; the servants occupied the west side, the garrison of the castle the rooms immediately west of the gatehouse.

The castle never confronted a French army. It was attacked only once in its life – a swift affair in 1483. It continued in occupation at least until the following century. Then in the Civil War it was heavily plundered, and afterwards allowed to fall into decay. In the 20th century it had the good fortune to attract the notice of Lord Curzon, who bought it and restored it with the same care and attention as he gave to *Tattershall*. On his death he bequeathed it to the National Trust.

No castle in England gives a clearer idea of late-medieval fortification than Bodiam, whether approached from the river and its bridge or seen in the whole context of its valley from Ewhurst, away to the south.

Boston Lincolnshire 2E5

Boston was a notable port in the Middle Ages. In the 13th century its tax assessment once reached almost as high as London's, and was higher than that of any other port in the country. Later it became a staple town for the export of wool, and the Hansa merchants from north Germany were permitted to establish a trading post there. It lay up the River Witham, some distance from the sea, in the same kind of situation as *Bristol*: secure against the raids of pirates or foreign enemies, but always liable to interruption of its trade through flooding or silting in the river. In 1500 strong measures were taken to improve the flow of the water, under the direction of a Flemish engineer. They were effective for a time, but the fight proved a losing one, and over the next two generations the town declined. It enjoyed a modest prosperity in the 18th century, and a serious attempt was made to enable it to regain something of its old position when docks were constructed in the 1880s. In our own time it has grown substantially, the population doubling in the last 20 years, to stand now at 50,000. So although it is no longer a great port, it is a thriving town of moderate size: a centre of agriculture, with some light industries and a steady maritime trade.

Boston has always pivoted on its big market place, and there any visitor should start. On market days – especially on Saturdays in summer – it is crowded with stalls and threaded by a ceaseless string of slow-moving traffic. At night and on Sundays it stands quite clear. Over it all at the north end rises the vast church of St Botolph; the largest unaltered medieval parish church in England.* To do it justice, one should begin near the top of the market place on the right. From there, and there alone, the building can be seen as a whole, in its relationship to the town of which it has always been the heart. The most famous piece of it is the tower at the west end, long nicknamed the Stump – perhaps indicating that its dizzy height was intended to be surmounted by a still dizzier spire, which was never erected. This celebrated tower is far too often photographed from across the river, where it seems to rise up alone. From the market place however it appears in its context, as the superb climax of an exceptionally large building. From here too the varying pitch of the roofs can be enjoyed, behind their decorated parapets. They are covered in silver-grey lead, which admirably sets off the darker limestone of the walls below.

The present church replaced an earlier one. It was begun in 1309 but went forward slowly. Most of the building is probably of the second half of the 14th century; the topmost stage of the tower was added late in the 15th.

* St Michael's, Coventry, was bigger, but it was burnt out by bombing in 1941 and is now only an incomplete shell; St Nicholas, Yarmouth, the biggest of all, was similarly wrecked and has been much altered in its reconstruction.

Boston church from the east (Janet & Colin Bord)

Inside, the scale is overpowering. This is a parish church, conceived as nothing else, and its design is perfectly simple: a nave with a pair of aisles and a chancel – no transepts, the only extensions to the rectangular plan a big south porch and the tower. The font stands as it should, in an ample cleared space, disencumbered of seating. The nave is 60 ft high. Fifty years ago it, and the aisles, were given flat-pitched roofs, replacing pointed ones of the 18th century similar to that which still covers the chancel. This was a pity, for it diminishes the sense of height. The east window was put in by Sir Gilbert Scott, who restored the church with respect twice in 1843–56; it is based on the larger east window of Carlisle cathedral. Some of the fittings of the chancel are notable: the gilded iron altar rails (*c.* 1740) and the misericords of the stalls, dating from the end of the 14th century. They can all be studied easily with the aid of the brief and simple descriptions provided. Some are very graphic and amusing: look for Sir Yvaine's horse, sliced in two by a portcullis, or St George thrusting his spear in triumph down the dragon's mouth, or the mermaid singing to the sailors. The pulpit in the nave is a splendid one of 1612. At the north-west corner in the floor is the incised monument of Wessel Smalenburgh, merchant of Münster in Germany, who must have been trading in Boston when he died in 1340.

And now for the tower. It is open to a height of 137 ft from the ground, lighted by tall windows, and sumptuously vaulted. It was built in four separate stages, and on that account it has been criticised, for they do not make a perfect whole. Indeed it must be allowed that the third stage (the highest but one) is a little mechanical. But the octagon at the top is lovely, and gives the tower a felicitous crown.

There are other things worth seeing in Boston: the medieval Guildhall, a brick structure of the late 15th century, now a pleasant museum of the town's history, and next to it Fydell House, an elegantly comfortable building of 1726. Along the river there are numerous old brick warehouses, many of them dilapidated today: the embodiment of Boston's former business on the water, now transferred to the docks.

No one would call this town picturesque. It is a busy, active place, not at all self-conscious; justly famed for its church, but also for something else. It gave its name to another Boston, a far greater city in Massachusetts, christened by Puritan emigrants who left this part of Lincolnshire in pursuit of a religious order acceptable to them. Perhaps as many as 8 per cent of the population of Boston itself crossed the Atlantic in 1630–3. Late in the 18th century the town and its neighbourhood made a large contribution to English enterprise in Australia. George Bass grew up in Boston; Sir Joseph Banks, Matthew Flinders, and John Franklin all lived near by. If the town was not the great port it had once been, it still played its part in expansion and settlement overseas; a leading movement in the history of England from the 16th century to the 19th.

Brighton East Sussex 5A5

The English seaside resort has a long history, stretching far back into the 18th century. It reached its great popularity in the Victorian age, largely owing to the development of the railways, and retained it until the second World War. In the 1950s it lost ground fast, through the growth of cheap air travel to resorts on the Continent. Brighton has felt all these fluctuations, of prosperity and decline. It has weathered them with notable success, chiefly because of the variety of pleasures and interest it has to offer. It affords a good range of lively entertainment; fine walking on the Sussex Downs; a brisk train service to and from London, only 50 miles away. It is a cheerful place, noisy and not nowadays elegant, but alive at every season of the year. Finally – and here it completely outdistances all its rivals – Brighton is a place of architectural note.

The sea-front has been gravely maltreated. Walk out on to the Palace Pier – a jolly experience anyway, not to be missed. Look back, and what do you see? A hotchpotch of buildings overshadowed by tall blocks of flats. The Victor-

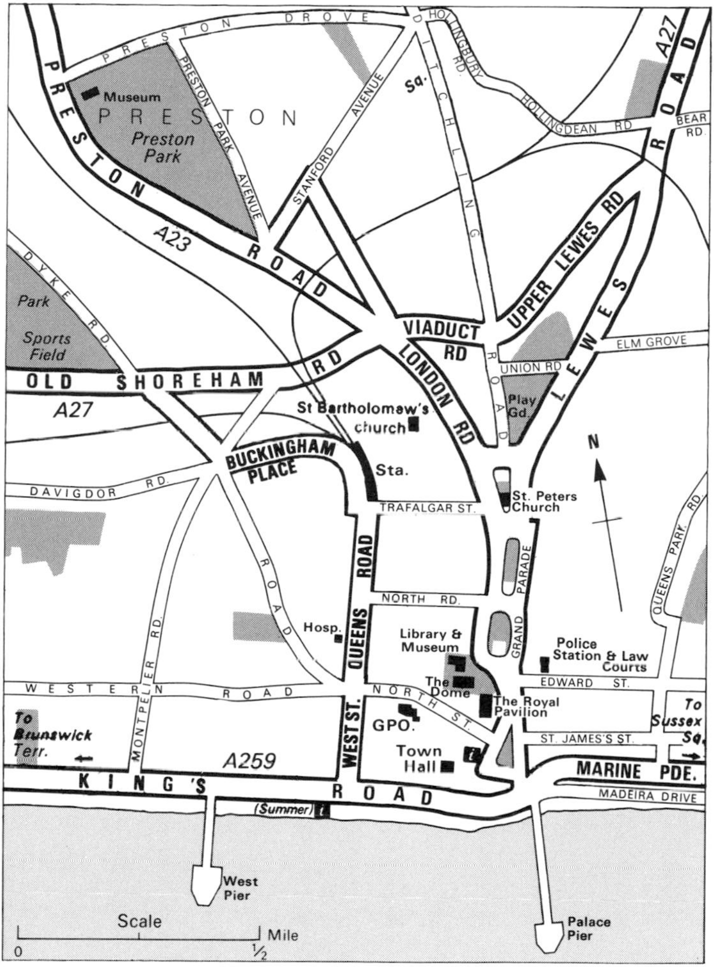

ians started the business. The Grand Hotel (1862–4) is unacceptably tall in relation to its earlier neighbours; but it carries off that dominance by its bay windows and swaggering ironwork. The Metropole (1888), a few paces west, was the real disaster, for it is much bigger and it lacks those virtues.

Its lines are horizontal, its details coarse and boring; above all it is built of the fierce red brick and terracotta favoured by its architect Waterhouse. It is a hideous Temple of Mammon. What the Victorians began, the 20th century has continued, during the past two decades at an increasing speed.

The centre of the town is the Old Steine, with the Pavilion and the Victoria Gardens to the north of it, a cool green valley bordered by tallish houses of the 18th century and the early 19th, characteristic of Brighton in their shape, with sets of bow windows, a few of them displaying the black glazed "mathematical tiles" that are a local speciality. The old fishing village lay immediately to the west, and though there is little of the village left about it now it has some of the flavour of a small pre-Victorian town, the narrow Lanes huddled closely together.

The great development of Brighton began in the mid 18th century, under the influence of the physician Dr Richard Russell. Presently it grew outwards from the original village both east and west. To the east the first memorial of that growth is the Royal Crescent (1798–1807). At the beginning of the 19th century part of the manor of Brighton belonged to Thomas Kemp. His son T. R. Kemp, an eccentric, decided to develop his property east of the Royal Crescent. He began work in 1823 on what came to be called Kemp Town. The architects he employed were Amon Wilds and his son, and C. R. Busby. They modelled themselves on Nash (though the detail and massing of their work are much inferior to his), and they had something of his interest in landscape. The most ambitious part of Kemp Town is Sussex Square – no square at all but a huge open space enclosed by two double-curved sides. In the centre is a green garden, with trees and shrubs clinging to its mound, contorted by the endless wind.

Sussex Square marks the eastward termination of the older Brighton. To the west there is a corresponding development beyond the borders of Brighton proper, in the parish of Hove. Here it begins with Brunswick Terrace (by the Wilds and Busby again), two sets of 13 houses facing straight on to the sea. It continues with Adelaide Crescent, again with double-curved wings and a garden, and Palmeira Square to the north of it. Sussex Square, though spectacular, is too vast to make a satisfactory composition. These are smaller, and in that respect better, but the architecture is fragmented and the decoration perfunctory. The impression is everything in these big sweeps of building at Brighton, the detail seldom refined.

At the centre of it all is the Royal Pavilion. George, Prince of Wales, first visited Brighton in 1783, at the age of 21. Shortly afterwards he leased a farmhouse on the Steine. Here he brought Mrs Fitzherbert, to whom he was secretly married in 1785. Henry Holland was commissioned to enlarge the house, in his own elegant way. The Prince used it frequently, so turning Brighton from an invalids' resort into a brilliant watering-place. In 1804–8 a riding-house and stables were added under a very large dome, in an Indian style, to the design of William Porden. The Prince then determined to transform Holland's house into something Oriental too. In 1815 John Nash began remodelling it. The work took seven years to complete.

It was a remodelling only. Most of Holland's building was preserved, with a new skin fitted tightly round it, and with the addition of large rooms at each end. The style is a blend of many. Though Hindu and Islamic ideas preponderate, the building is not wholly Oriental, for there are Gothic and Rococo elements in it too; and Holland's reticent classicism is not quite submerged. The result is tumultuous profusion, of line, shape, and colour, inside and out.

The Pavilion is charmingly set, facing the Steine over a lawn. It is gay with onion domes and minarets, and lace-like stonework. Inside the sense of profusion rises, through the Grand Corridor to the Banqueting Room, scarlet and gold; the prevailing mood here is Chinese. Yet the rich fantasies do not continue unbroken. The Saloon, facing on to the lawn, is quiet and cool. Then however comes what was one of the richest pieces of all, the Music Room, with a set of chandeliers in the shape of water-lilies and gilded serpents

(The Royal Pavilion)

Brighton: the Royal Pavilion, North Drawing Room

climbing up every pillar. Alas, it was recently set on fire and though it is now being patiently restored, that work will take a long time.

Before Nash's work was finished, the Prince became King George IV. His restless mind was soon preoccupied with the transformation of Buckingham Palace in London. He visited Brighton less frequently, last of all in 1827. His successor William IV came from time to time. Queen Victoria and the Prince Consort did not care for the Pavilion – they belonged to an entirely different world of taste and feeling. It was closed in 1845, and the furniture removed. It might have been demolished had not Brighton itself stepped in and purchased the building from the Crown for £50,000. For many years it was a sad place, much of it empty and shabby.

Since the second World War, however, it has been admirably restored, with the help of H.M. the Queen, who has returned more than 100 pieces of the furniture that belonged to it. Now it is a great sight: extravagant, weird, beautiful, tawdry, haunting, by turns – the Pavilion is indeed something unique.

Such were the grand compositions prepared for Brighton as it developed in the early 19th century. The Victorian town grew much faster, aided by the railway, which arrived from London in 1841. At this point the special interest of the town for today's visitor shifts, away from squares and crescents and streets and the Pavilion to churches. For some reason that is not altogether clear, Brighton became a town filled with the varieties of religious experience. As early as 1851 there were 38 churches and chapels in Brighton and Hove, 12 belonging to the Church of England, the rest representing various forms of Dissent. One of them, St Paul's by R. H. Carpenter (the architect subsequently of Lancing College Chapel, a few miles away to the west), became known as "the Puseyite church". The church is still a landmark in the centre of the town from its octagonal timber steeple. It was built through the efforts of the Rev. H. M. Wagner, vicar of Brighton from 1824 to 1870. His son Arthur became a very notable priest. He was an immense, almost Falstaffian presence, rich, saintly, determined, and fearless. As a high Tractarian he faced much obloquy; he was even beaten up in the Brighton streets. He built three churches out of his own pocket and a fourth, in conjunction with his family, to the memory of his father: all these in the poorer parts of the town, where his mission lay. One of them, St Bartholomew's, is among the outstanding English churches of the 19th century.

It lies a little below the railway station, in a quarter that has recently been much "re-developed". The building rears up, a dizzy cliff-like structure in red and yellow brick, a plain rectangle with a high pitched roof. No tower or spire: anything of the kind would be unthinkable here, even impertinent. You enter by a passage at the side. To get the full first impression, walk straight ahead to the back of the church

Brighton: St Bartholomew's church (A. F. Kersting)

and then – only then – turn round. No concession was made by Father Wagner or his architect – a local man little known otherwise, Edmund Scott – to conventional beauty. The walls are of brick, patterned and unplastered, now streaked with salt. There is a plain wagon roof with tie-beams, uniformly dark, a mysterious distant crown. Height and proportion are all. The height is tremendous – 135 ft, nearly a third as much again as Westminster Abbey, the highest medieval church in England; higher than Reims, not far short of Amiens.

In 1895–1910 the church was decorated and furnished, in accordance with the highest taste of those years, by Henry Wilson. He gave the altar a magnificent canopy, a ciborium, together with a pulpit and font, all made chiefly of red and green marble, very plainly treated; gargantuan candlesticks, communion rails, and a Lady altar showing sumptuous metalwork. (The mosaics on the east wall are later, and nothing to do with Wilson.) These things are a tribute to the continuance of devotion that Father Wagner inspired. That devotion is still palpable in St Bartholomew's today. If ever a building was numinous, this is.

There are many other churches worth seeing in Brighton too. It is fascinating to move from St Bartholomew's to St Peter's, five minutes' walk away, an early work (1824–8) by Barry (of the Houses of Parliament), still with an 18th-century flavour to its Gothic. Its external stonework is delightful, and its tower stands up charmingly amid the trees and gardens north of the Pavilion. Move across into Hove, and you see a splendid high-Victorian work in the parish church of All Saints, by J. L. Pearson, built in 1889–1901 but without the spire that should have crowned the south-west tower. Inside it is ample, harmonious, complete. Its rhythm is determined by the transverse stone arches, made more emphatic by the dark timber framing of the roof between them. The eye is led subtly from the nave into the short chancel by two successive narrowings of the space, to the climax of the sanctuary with a tall stone reredos and an enriched vault.

Brighton has an old parish church (St Nicholas), which

it would be ungracious to ignore; it contains one thing of note, a majestic 12th-century font. But it was restored to death by Carpenter, and it lacks savour by comparison with those wholly new works of the 19th century that have just been considered.

This can be no more than a brief anthology from the visual pleasures of Brighton. There are many more, of very various kinds, in the town and its immediate environs: from the 18th-century windmill at West Blatchington, high up on the Downs, to the old village of Rottingdean (the houses lived in by Kipling and Burne-Jones facing each other beside the green) and, from our own time, Sir Basil Spence's complex of buildings for the University of Sussex, at Falmer. The search for these and other things is well rewarded. One more element of Brighton remains to be mentioned, as delightful as any of the rest: the special atmospheric glitter of the place. The sea here seems to enjoy a sparkle all of its own. Many millions of tired town-dwellers have been refreshed by it, over the past 200 years, pouring down to "this London by the sea".

Bristol Avon 4D3

Among the 10 largest cities in the English provinces, Bristol is historically the most interesting. It also offers the richest and most varied visual pleasure. It can show good, and often distinguished, monuments of every age from the 12th century to the 20th. But it is by no means a city of art, a place of the past. With its suburbs, its population is well over half a million. It throbs with fast-moving traffic, does business with a large hinterland (stretching across the Severn into South Wales), and produces a wide range of goods, from cigarettes to aircraft. To understand Bristol, in history or today, one must always think first in terms of trade.

The pattern of its development differs from that of all the other chief English industrial towns. It emerges as a considerable port in the 11th century, eight miles from the open sea up a tortuous river, which could protect it well from attack. The Normans built a castle to secure and defend it, close to Bristol Bridge from which the place takes its name.* It became a European city from its trade: in slaves, in wine from Bordeaux, in Iceland fish. From their experience in that last, most dangerous commerce, Bristol seamen were fitted to undertake the crossing of the Atlantic, and under the Venetians John and Sebastian Cabot they initiated the exploration of the North American mainland in 1497–8. Bristol's prosperity continued with no major interruption until late in the 18th century, when it began to lose its pre-eminence among the western ports to *Liverpool* and Glasgow. Its situation, far from the sea, had now become a drawback: as ships grew larger they found it difficult to navigate the tidal Avon. For a moment, in 1833–45, Bristol made a spirited attempt to recover the ground it was losing, by means of the railway and the ocean-going steamship; but in the end the rival ports benefited most from these efforts. Bristol was heavily bombed in 1940–1, when much of the old city was destroyed. But it has suffered from other vandals too, besides Hitler, including the City Council and the University. Though it has now recovered in large measure from the effects of the war, it faces complex difficulties. Among European cities, Bristol shows an affinity in this respect with Amsterdam. Both are great cities still, with a splendid past; but both are engaged in an uphill struggle to maintain their position today and in the future.

★

Of the old town of Bristol, about a third was destroyed in the German air-raids. The historic centre, where the medieval Cross formerly stood (it is now at *Stourhead*), was at the junction of Corn Street, Broad Street, and High Street; the fourth limb, Wine Street, with almost everything else that lay to the east, has gone. The Exchange in Corn Street, by the elder John Wood (1740–3), is one of the best of

* Brig-stow, the place of the bridge. The "l" comes in from an ancient oddity of local dialect.

BRISTOL

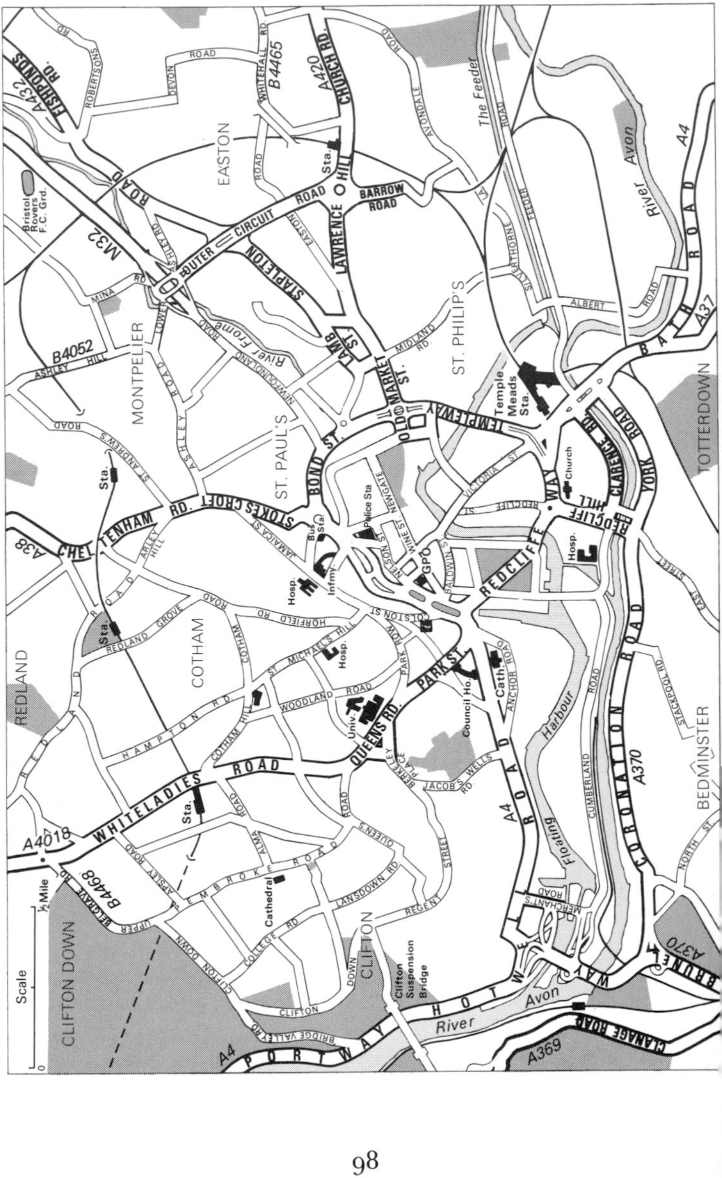

EASTON
ST. PHILIP'S
ST. PAUL'S
MONTPELIER
REDLAND
COTHAM
CLIFTON
CLIFTON DOWN
TOTTERDOWN
BEDMINSTER
FISHPONDS RD.
A432
ROBERTSONS RD
DEVON ROAD
WHITEHALL RD.
B4465
A420
CHURCH RD.
AVONDALE
The Feeder
FEEDER RD.
River Avon
A4
BATH ROAD
A37
Bristol Rovers F.C. Grd.
M32
OUTER CIRCUIT ROAD
LAWRENCE HILL
Sta.
BARROW ROAD
STAPLETON ROAD
EASTON RD.
ASHLEY RD.
MINA RD.
LOWER ASHLEY ROAD
River Frome
NEWFOUNDLAND ROAD
LAMB ST.
MIDLAND RD
SILVERTHORNE
ALBERT
B4052
ASHLEY HILL
OLD MARKET ST.
TEMPLE WAY
Temple Meads Sta.
ST. ANDREW'S ROAD
BOND ST.
Police Sta
NEWGATE
VICTORIA ST.
Church
CLARENCE RD.
YORK ROAD
REDCLIFF ST.
REDCLIFF HILL
REDCLIFFE WAY
STOKES CROFT
CHELTENHAM RD.
A38
ARLEY HILL
JAMAICA ST.
Bus Sta.
Infmy.
Hosp.
NELSON ST.
WINE ST.
GPO
BALDWIN ST.
EAST STREET
HORFIELD RD
COLSTON ST
REDLAND GROVE
ST. MICHAEL'S HILL
PARK ROW
PARK ST.
Council Ho.
Cath.
ANCHOR ROAD
STACKPOOL RD.
Harbour
CUMBERLAND ROAD
CORONATION ROAD
A370
WOODLAND ROAD
Univ.
HAMPTON RD
COTHAM HILL
QUEENS RD.
BERKELEY PLACE
JACOB'S WELLS RD.
WHITELADIES ROAD
A4018
ALMA ROAD
QUEEN'S RD.
A4 ROAD
Floating
NORTH ST.
ST. MERCHANT'S ROAD
APSLEY ROAD
PEMBROKE ROAD
Cathedral
LANSDOWN RD.
REGENT STREET
BELGRAVE RD.
B4468
UPPER BELGRAVE RD.
COLLEGE RD.
CLIFTON DOWN
Clifton Suspension Bridge
HOTWELL ROAD
Avon
River
BRIDGE VALLEY RD
CLIFTON
PORTWAY
CUMBERLAND ROAD
BRUNEL WAY
CLANAGE ROAD
A369
Scale
0
½ Mile

all Georgian public buildings; there is a courtyard behind its nobly-balanced *façade*. In front, on the pavement, stand the brass "nails", on which money was paid down to make a bargain ("paid on the nail"). Opposite is Lloyd's Bank (Gingell and Lysaght, 1854–8), a gorgeously-decorated temple of commerce. The pair, facing each other, summarise much of the difference in spirit between the Georgian and the Victorian age. Almost next to the Exchange is All Saints' church, Norman and 15th-century, with a Georgian tower. It contains the monument of Edward Colston, a notable philanthropist, by Gibbs and Rysbrack (1729); the effigy is filled with Colston's own compassion.

In spite of modern destruction and rebuilding, the old town of Bristol keeps a recognisable shape. The line of the wall is clear on the north side: St John's church stands on it, with a gateway below. It then curves round by St Stephen's Street to Baldwin Street and Bristol Bridge. Immediately above the bridge stands St Nicholas's church, recently made into a good museum of the history of Bristol. It is a double structure. The lower church, or crypt, is built into the city wall (15 ft thick). Above it is the upper church, good Gothic of 1763–9. To the west of the walled area, on an arm of the river, lay the principal quays of the town. They ceased to serve as such when the basin was filled in, to form the present City Centre; but the names Narrow Quay and Broad Quay survive on the east side. The water now stops abruptly at the south end of the Centre; when ships are tied up there, one can get some faint notion of what business was once like, in the city's greatest days.

In the 17th century the town extended southwards, on to the marshy land between the two arms of the river. Welsh Back here has all the character of a quay. Out of it opens King Street, a signal piece of townscape, still paved, presided over by three remarkable buildings: a dizzy timbered inn, the Llandoger Trow, dated 1669; Coopers' Hall, on the other side of the street (William Halfpenny, 1743–4); and the Theatre Royal (James Paty, jr, 1764–6). This is the oldest theatre in England still in continuous use. Inside, it was remodelled in 1800 and remains today much in that state. It has now been extended with two small additional theatres, and the entrance reconstructed; the work was sensitively designed by Peter Moro. At the top of the street on the same side is the former Public Library of 1739–40 (by Paty's father).

Just south of King Street is Queen Square. This is a sad spectacle. It was once among the amplest Georgian squares in England. But two sides of it were destroyed in the Reform Bill riots of 1831; and 100 years later the Corporation ravaged the still noble space by constructing a broad motor road diagonally across it, leaving William III, in a fine equestrian statue by Rysbrack, to preside serenely in the middle over the disgraceful ruin.

Now cross the river by the race-track of Redcliff Way. Redcliff was an ancient suburb of the city, distinguished by its spectacular parish church of St Mary. This is often called the finest parish church in the country; and certainly few competitors can challenge it. The hexagonal north porch, by which you enter, is unlike any other, its main door decorated in a way that recalls Spain, or even the East – certainly not England. The tower, in an uncommon position at the north-west corner of the church, did not receive its present spire until 1872. Inside, the church presents a splendid harmony. The earliest part is on the south: the porch, the aisle, and the transept on that side date from *c.* 1330–70, and the rest follows, built or rebuilt over the succeeding century. The design of the vaults is outstanding: diverse within the unity that characterises the building as a whole composition. The cost of completing them was borne largely by William Canynge the younger (?1399–1474), an exceptionally rich Bristol merchant and shipowner, one of the wealthiest Englishmen of his time. He is commemorated by two monuments in the south transept. At the west end of the church there are notable wrought-iron screens; the one under the tower was made by William Edney in 1710 to stand at the entrance to the chancel, whence it was later removed. Above it, on the north wall of the nave, stands the monument of Sir

William Penn, a Bristolian who became an Admiral under the Commonwealth and Charles II, with his armour and flags ranged about it. His elder son was the founder of Pennsylvania.

Temple Meads railway station lies within a few minutes' noisy walk to the east of the church. This was the terminus of I. K. Brunel's broad-gauge Great Western Railway from London, completed in 1841. The station he designed for it is on the left of the main approach road. It is now used as a car park, and very shabby: a remarkable Gothic hall with a timber hammerbeam roof 72 ft wide – a piece of the poetry of the Industrial Revolution.

Now drive or take the bus (from this point, in the station forecourt) back through the Centre to College Green. This is a large triangular open space, dominated on the west side by the Council House (W. Vincent Harris, 1935–55). On the south lies the Cathedral. It was built as an Augustinian abbey; Bristol did not become the seat of a bishop until the 16th century. The nave is Victorian, by Street: a modest and sensible continuation of the chancel and its aisles, which are of outstanding distinction. They were erected under Abbot Knowle (1298–1332), and they form one of the earliest of "hall churches": those, that is, in which the aisles and the central part are of the same height, and the lighting comes entirely from the aisle windows, to give the whole the unity of a single "hall". The design is rarely found in England or France, but it became general in Germany in the 14th and 15th centuries. The vaulting of the aisles, with its transverse horizontal members, is notable and without precedent. The lierne vaulting of the central roof is also of exceptional beauty – the inspiration of that in St Mary Redcliff and, in part at least, of a pattern that radiated during the next 200 years throughout Europe. The Berkeley chapel, to the right, has at its entrance another remarkable vault of equal merit, on a tiny scale; and inside a lovely brass chandelier of the 15th century. The Lady Chapel behind the altar was sumptuously redecorated, in accordance with the original colour scheme, in the 1930s. The star-shaped recesses containing

Bristol cathedral: vault of the south choir aisle (Reece Winstone)

the abbots' tombs are another peculiarity of Bristol. Taken all together, these things enable it to be said that "English design surpassed that of all other countries during the first third of the 14th century". (The words are Sir Nikolaus Pevsner's; his account of Bristol in *The Buildings of England* provides an exceptionally fine guide to the city's architecture.)

If the 14th-century work here is outstanding, there are other beauties too: the Elder Lady Chapel, dating from 100 years earlier; the Norman Chapter House, richly decorated with geometrical patterns; even a small reminder of the Anglo-Saxon world, in the sculpture of the Harrowing of Hell, found upside down in the floor of the Chapter House and now erected in the east wall of the south transept.

Coming out of the cathedral and turning to the left, you pass the Abbey Gateway, another rich piece of Norman work, and then arrive suddenly at the 20th century, with Charles Holden's City Library of 1906, one of the most chaste and satisfying *art nouveau* buildings in the country. The exterior remains untouched, apart from a modest extension of the 1960s. Inside, the entrance with its blue vault, the staircase, the tunnel-like gallery to which it leads, and then the reading room, provide a succession of pleasures rare in municipal buildings anywhere.

Now cross College Green to look at the Lord Mayor's Chapel, marked out by its charming pink tower. It was the chapel of the Hospital of St Mark, founded in 1220, was bought by the Corporation in 1541, and became early in the 18th century the civic church. Its fabric has suffered from restoration and enlargement, but it is crowded with monuments of Bristol citizens and contains Continental stained glass of some interest, much of it bought in 1823.

Coming out of the Lord Mayor's Chapel, turn to the right and ascend Park Street, dominated by the satisfactory bulk of the tower of the University, a late product of the Gothic Revival (Sir George Oatley, 1925). Two good houses are to be seen near by, both in the hands of the Bristol Art Galleries: the Red Lodge in Park Row, with a sequence of fine Elizabethan rooms on the first floor; and the Georgian House in Great George Street, with excellent 18th-century furniture and fittings.

Clifton, beyond, was developed as a spa and a high-class residential district, tentatively in the 18th century and then with a rush from 1810 onwards. It is not the equal of Bath. But then Clifton is a very different sort of place: essentially a suburb – and, as such, one of the most striking in the country – developed two generations afterwards. It must be said with regret that much of Clifton has, in recent years, become seedy, some of it squalid: so that at present it seems to be going downhill while Bath, through much tribulation, has been going up.

Nevertheless Clifton has one memorable thing to show: the gorge of the Avon bounding its west side, 250 ft deep, and the bridge that spans it. The gorge offers sharp contrasts: buildings rising tier upon tier on its eastern flank; opposite, the almost unbroken expanse of Leigh Woods; and far below to the south, where the valley opens out, the beginning of industrial Bristol, dominated by three huge red tobacco warehouses.

The iron suspension bridge springs from an open green on the Clifton side. Unless you suffer from vertigo, you should walk across it and back again. It was planned by Brunel and begun in 1836; then work stopped, and it was carried through to completion only in 1864. By that time it could be nothing but a memorial to the genius who designed it; he had died five years earlier. To appreciate the bridge and the ravine one should see it from below. The steep walk (or drive) down past the Grand Spa Hotel and then by Granby Hill and Hope Chapel Hill brings you to a piquant contrast. The roaring traffic of the A4, the road to Avonmouth, first hits you hard. But facing on to the road at the foot of the hill, its skirts discreetly withdrawn, is the three-sided Dowry Square, laid out in 1720 and completed over the next generation; and opposite a long terrace of handsome brick houses of the same date. You are now in the Hotwells, a spa that developed at much the same time as Bath and was visited especially by consumptive patients; the Bristol

(A. F. Kersting)

churches abound in their sad memorials. Brace yourself now for the stink and din of the Hotwell Road. You will be rewarded by seeing the ravine and the bridge from the river bank.

Brunel's spirit is constantly present in Bristol; now indeed, since 1970, more than ever. He saw his Great Western Railway as the first stage of steam communication between London and New York. The second was to be supplied by steamships. He designed two for this purpose, both to sail from Bristol: *Great Western* (1838) and *Great Britain* (1843). *Great Britain* was a major landmark: the first iron steamer to cross the Atlantic, and the first large ship to be propelled by a screw, rather than paddles. After many adventures she fetched up as a hulk in the Falkland Islands, whence in 1970 she was towed back to Bristol. She is now to be seen, in course of restoration, in the Great Western Dock (off Cumberland Road) in which she was built. Many "ancient monuments" have been restored, with refined care, in our time. No restoration has been more remarkable than this one. It is still in progress, carefully explained and documented as it moves on its way. When it is finished, it will itself be a notable monument to the skill and enthusiasm generated by the developing study of industrial archaeology.

A short bus-ride brings you back to Temple Meads station and the busy centre of Bristol. One other thing may be mentioned, which cannot be brought conveniently within this itinerary: Redland church, built at the expense of John Cossins, a retired London merchant, in 1741–3. The architect was William Halfpenny. It stands charmingly by Redland Green, a small rectangular structure with a cupola. There is delightful woodwork inside, especially in the chancel; the altar slab rests on a noble gilded eagle. Busts of Cossins and his wife by Rysbrack are in niches at the back of the church. Notice the interesting inscription to the memory of Colonel George Napier beneath.

★

The visit outlined here gives a sample of Bristol's riches, no more. It is a city worth visiting for several days, and a good base from which to see Gloucestershire, Wiltshire, and Somerset, three of the most rewarding counties in England.

Brympton d'Evercy and Montacute Somerset 4D4

I first went to Brympton d'Evercy more than 30 years ago and was fortunate enough to see the house under the guidance of the remarkable woman who then lived there, Mrs Clive. Its impact on me was indelible. When I went back, long afterwards, I found I had remembered it all and exaggerated the merit of nothing. It grips one from the moment one first sees it. At every turn there is a surprise. No part of it is a major work of architecture, and yet the whole that it composes is most distinctive, in the odd conjunction of the house and the adjoining buildings, in its setting on the slope between trees and water, and in the incomparable golden Ham Hill stone that is used everywhere, mellowing variously according to age and source.

Brympton is two or three miles west of Yeovil. The approach to it is by a narrow lane. It stands low and reveals itself only in a clearing in the trees. There, suddenly, it is: a 16th-century house at the end of a forecourt, with a church (St Andrew) beside it crowned by a bell-turret, slightly top-heavy. Though the church is very small it has transepts, and a chapel opening out of the chancel on the north side. The south transept is the oldest part, of the 13th century; the chapel the latest, of the 15th. The sense of crowding is made greater by the solid stone screen that firmly shuts off the nave from the rest of the church, and by the numerous monuments it contains, notably the priest's in the north transept and the grand one to John Sydenham (d. 1626) in the chancel. Adjoining the church stands what is known today as the Priest's House, a 15th-century building.

The estate came into the Sydenham family by marriage with one of the Stourtons (see *Stourhead*) in 1434, and it was they who gave the house, by successive stages, most of the form it wears today. Its west front, facing on to the courtyard, dates from about 1520, comprising the hall, with the staircase turret and the parlours on the north side. About 1690 a whole new front was added at right angles, facing south: a plain rectangle of 10 bays with six dormer windows opening out behind a parapet: entirely different in style from the earlier building, but unified with it by the continuing use of the same stone.

This extravagant addition seems to have broken the Sydenhams, who tried to sell the property in 1697 and finally mortgaged it to Thomas Penny, a member of a well-to-do family in Yeovil. He made his own little contribution to the ensemble, in the porch added on to the front of the house and in the Clock Tower on the north side of the forecourt: two romantic confections of old and new stonework, dating from 1722. He also fell into financial difficulty, and sold the estate in 1731 to Francis Fane, whose family and collateral descendants have been there ever since. They have not altered the house, but the surrounding gardens are their work. When the south wing was new, it looked out over a formal terrace to a sunken garden; the whole house was surrounded by trees, planted in serried rows. In the 19th century and since, all this has been simplified and the sunken garden replaced by a small lake, which provides a delightful counterpoint to the house. The slopes of the hill to the north are now partly planted with vines; beeches and other fine trees rise up above. The setting is, in our time, almost exactly right.

Inside, the house has one notable feature, and a number of charming little things to show. The hall was divided horizontally in the Elizabethan age to give it two storeys, where

Brympton d'Evercy: the south front (A. F. Kersting)

previously it had been open to the roof. Otherwise the chief rooms are all on the ground floor of the south wing, a series of five opening out of one another. One contains a nice collection of small sketches; notice the amusing American interior by S. Bidwell and the four little watercolours by Edward Lear. The dining room at the end presents a rich harmony of reds, in hangings and upholstery and mahogany, lighted up by the table silver. At the back, behind these rooms, an astonishing staircase, shallow and straight, runs up for almost the entire length of the building.

The house has only lately been opened to the public. The present owner has made a spirited attempt to enlarge the range of its interest, with an exhibition of glove-making from Yeovil and a substantial collection of agricultural equipment in the Priest's House. No effort can be too great to keep this complex of buildings and landscape in its present admirable order.

★

Brympton is a house of the early 16th century and the late 17th. A couple of miles away to the west is Montacute, entirely of the Elizabethan age that lies between. Like Brympton, Montacute is built wholly of Ham Hill stone, which was quarried little more than a mile west of Montacute itself. But whereas Brympton is essentially a two-storey building, lying low on the ground with no vertical emphasis at all, Montacute is on three or four storeys, and with the aid of its pinnacles and chimneys it shoots upwards. It is among the most beautiful Elizabethan houses in the country.

The village of Montacute began as a dependency of a castle erected on the top of the shapely pointed hill (*mons acutus*) above it. A small priory was established there, the gatehouse of which is still standing. It was dissolved in 1539, and over the span of the next generation much of its property passed to the Phelips family, as tenants. Sir Edward Phelips was able to purchase it and became lord of the manor in 1608. He was a prosperous and successful lawyer, who had been Speaker of the House of Commons in 1604. Seven years later he became Master of the Rolls. He was rich enough

Montacute: the east front (A. F. Kersting)

to have a town house in London and to rent Wanstead, a great estate in Essex, besides building this house at Montacute. Work was in progress here in 1598–9; building seems to have been completed in 1601. It is all of one time. With only one important addition, it stands almost exactly as Sir Edward Phelips left it.

The designer of the house seems to have been William Arnold, a Somerset stonemason who was also chiefly responsible for the building of Wadham College, Oxford. He was not an architect, in our sense of the word: the profession had not yet emerged, as such, in his time. But he was an experienced craftsman; he had pattern-books at his disposal; and clearly he was a man with eyes and ideas of his own.

The main entrance to the house was from the east, through a gatehouse that has now gone. The porch gives on to a screens passage – a little old-fashioned by 1600, still continuing the medieval tradition. The dark room on the left was built as the Buttery, linked to the kitchens behind. It became a parlour in the 18th century, and subsequently a dining room. The screen is of stone, with two arches, giving access to the Great Hall. This is panelled. The ceiling is plain, but a rich decorative effect comes from the carving on the screen and chimney-piece, the coloured glass, and the plasterwork, lively and rustic, on the far wall, depicting a scene from married life and the punishment of a hen-pecked husband. The Parlour and the Drawing Room lie beyond, each with a fine chimney-piece: in the first, one in its original position, of Ham Hill stone; in the Drawing Room, one rescued from Coleshill in Berkshire after it was wrecked by fire in 1952.

There are two staircases, both of stone, one in each corner of the house; the elaborately-carved wooden staircase was just coming in elsewhere when Montacute was built (see *Hatfield*). The principal room on the first floor is the Library, reached through an ante-room. Originally this was the Great Chamber, the principal reception-room of the house, used also for formal meals. It fell into disuse in the 18th century and was refurnished in the 1840s, when the present decorative plaster ceiling was put in. On the other side of the ante-room is Lord Curzon's Room. Its name brings us to a new figure in the history of the house. Lord Curzon, who much loved old buildings (see *Bodiam*, *Tattershall*), rented Montacute from 1915 to 1929. He made some changes in its arrangements, including the installation of a bath here, concealed inside a cupboard of Jacobean style. Next to the Library, also facing west, are two bedrooms, the Crimson Room (with its dressing room) and the Hall Chamber.

Above is the Long Gallery, occupying the whole central top storey of the south front; the longest now extant anywhere, unaltered. The Long Gallery was an Elizabethan innovation, and its popularity continued far into the 17th century (see *Little Moreton*, *Sudbury*). One of its uses was to provide a place for the ladies of the house to walk in, when the weather was cold or wet. One can visualise that particularly well here at Montacute, where the gallery is still sparsely furnished. It did not become a magnificent sitting-room, as it did for instance at *Hatfield*.

The fortunes of the Phelips family fluctuated. The Civil War hit them, and there were family disputes. However

Edward Phelips, who succeeded in 1750, husbanded the property well and benefited from large legacies. He did a good deal for the house, and one thing very notable. In 1785 he laid out a new approach, with a drive coming in from the west, to make the entrance on that side, and in the following year he embellished the west front with a splendid set of carvings removed from Clifton Maybank, a house of the mid 16th century on the other side of Yeovil, which was being demolished. As sculpture, these panels are finer than anything made for Montacute. They glorify the west front still. In the 19th century one misfortune followed another. The owners ceased to live in the house, and it was let. In 1929 it was put up for sale, unsuccessfully. Two years later it seemed likely to be pulled down for its materials, which were valued at under £6,000. It was saved by the Secretary of the Society for the Protection of Ancient Buildings, A. R. Powys, who persuaded Ernest Cook to buy the house and present it to the National Trust.

By this time Montacute was almost unfurnished, and when the Trust opened it to visitors it was very bare. Since that time, as the result of determined effort, it has been gradually provided with the furniture it needs. Some of the pieces come from other National Trust properties, like *Stourhead*, some have been given or lent, by private persons (including one member of the Phelips family) or by the Victoria and Albert Museum in London.

There was something even better to come. An agreement was reached between the Trust and the National Portrait Gallery, by which a considerable number of portraits of the 16th and 17th centuries from the Gallery were taken to Montacute and hung there. This was a brilliant imaginative stroke. The Portrait Gallery has long had many more pictures in its charge than it can show in London. Here is a means of displaying them, in a most appropriate setting, and at the same time of enriching a house that, through misfortune, has come to need adornment very badly. Most of the pictures are in the Long Gallery. They are displayed with great care and they have given it a delightful new life.

There is more pleasure to be had in the gardens outside the house. The Elizabethan garden on the east side is enclosed by a long stone wall, punctuated with ornaments and with two most charming little summer-houses, one at each corner away from the house. Other gardens extend to the south, and in the park beyond them are noble trees. The house is always visible between and above them, with its endearing touches of fantasy: golden even on the dullest day, brilliant in the sunshine of summer and autumn.

Burton Agnes Humberside 2D4
Burton Agnes Hall is a late Elizabethan house, built in 1601–10 by Sir Henry Griffith. Most unusually, its predecessor the Old Hall survives beside it, and it is best to begin there. From the outside this building is undistinguished: a red-brick rectangle it appears, no more. But in fact it is the stone house built by Roger de Stuteville about 1170, virtually intact. The normal plan was followed here, with the chief room not at ground level but on the first floor. The entrance is through an undercroft, stone-vaulted, the capitals of the pillars carved simply. In a corner is the spiral staircase leading to the hall upstairs, unfurnished now but impressive. Long afterwards the upper part was encased in brick outside, no doubt to harmonise with the 17th-century Hall near by. The wonder is that it was not demolished. Its survival shows us, in a single place, something of the change in domestic comfort and pretensions from the medieval to the modern world.

The Elizabethan house is imposing, yet it is also friendly, for two reasons. It is built of a rich warm red brick, sparingly dressed with stone. And at the corners it combines bay and bow windows, to the full height of three storeys, with a most happy effect. Bows were a rare feature at this date: they did not become at all common until the next generation. In this respect Burton Agnes is an oddity among the larger houses of its time.

Inside you arrive at one end of the Great Hall, which

Burton Agnes: the south front (A. F. Kersting)

has a ponderous wooden screen loaded with figure carving. The alabaster chimney-piece is equally opulent, though the quality of its carved figures is perhaps rather higher. The elaboration of all this is counteracted by the simple 18th-century ceiling and the portraits hung on the walls. No such relief is afforded in the Drawing Room, where the decoration, especially the grisly subject-matter of the chimney-piece, is restless and oppressive. But like all the corner rooms it enjoys the advantage of the cross-lighting that comes from the bow and bay windows adjoining one another.

The staircase is remarkable, tucked into the core of the

house, relatively narrow, with its central posts in pairs joined by arches, so that tiered arcades rise beside you as you ascend. The upstairs Drawing Room is calm and quiet, under the firm hand of the 18th century. But there is 18th-century sportiveness close by too, in the Chinese Room, with black lacquer screens brought here in the 1730s.

The whole of the top floor is occupied by the Long Gallery. Until recently this was divided into three rooms. Now it has been reopened as one, and the effect is admirable, with pleasant open views to the north over the garden and eastwards across flat country down to the sea.

Among Elizabethan houses Burton Agnes is of the second rank in size, a gentleman's house not a nobleman's. But Sir Henry Griffith was a powerful man in his native Staffordshire and up here in Yorkshire, a member of the Council of the North. All this is reflected in its character and scale. On the death of his son in 1654 the estate descended to the Boyntons, who have been here ever since.

The house has a strong personality of its own, and as one leaves it, looking back from under the Jacobean gatehouse, it lodges itself firmly in one's recollection, and for good.

Castle Drogo Devon 3C4

Castle Drogo can safely be described as the last big English country house: not only the last that has yet been built, but the last there will ever be. Here the long line, reaching back into the Middle Ages, comes to an end.

Many of these houses were designed by their owners, the men who paid for them, in collaboration with professional architects, or even sometimes, as at *Sudbury*, without any architect at all. By the 20th century, with the increased complication of the processes of building a large house, a professional architect was absolutely required. He was in a position of authority through his technical skill and the administrative resources supplied by his office. It was still possible, however, for a client to play a great part in the design and realisation of the building. But to achieve that successfully – without merely interfering, to frustrate or ruin the architect's intentions – he had to be at once intelligent, imaginative, and realistic; determined, though also flexible; and good-tempered. At Castle Drogo exactly those conditions were fulfilled.

Julius Drewe, for whom the house was built, made a fortune out of the Home & Colonial Stores, a grocery business he founded with a single partner in 1883. In 1889 he retired, in his early thirties, and set himself to lead the life of a country gentleman. He lived first in Sussex and then turned his eyes towards Devon, with which he had some family connections. Drewe was a romantic, who desired to build himself a castle. Such a thing could still be done at the opening of the 20th century, in a conventional way, in the tradition of the Gothic Revival. Drewe acquired a site of superlative splendour, a promontory at the junction between the gorge of the River Teign and the Vale of Chagford, nearly 1,000 ft above the sea and looking westwards to a huge tract of Dartmoor. Here he bought 450 acres of land in 1910. He quickly chose his architect: no medievalist but Edwin Lutyens, a romantic like himself and an original genius, one of the great Englishmen of the 20th century. It is likely that the choice was made on the advice of Edward Hudson, for whom Lutyens had fashioned the remarkable castle on *Holy Island*. Work began in 1911; the first wing was occupied in 1919; the whole was finished in 1931.

Drewe and Lutyens were both men of very strong will. They worked in close conjunction throughout, and neither got his own way entirely. Lutyens planned a frontal approach, up the steep side of the hill from the south-west; but Drewe had another idea, and a better one, of a drive from the village of Drewsteignton, level or gently descending to the platform on which the Castle was to stand.

Granite was used throughout, quarried in Whiddon Park on the opposite side of the Teign gorge. Drewe required the walls to be massive, more solid than Lutyens had intended. This additional expense helped to force a reduction in the scale of the building; a reduction also designed to make the house easier to live in.

What emerged was a house in two parts, set at an obtuse angle, one running north-east along the promontory, the other to the south. The storeys vary in number according to the levels, from three to six.

Over the front door is a lion carved in low relief, heraldic yet also unmistakably Assyrian. The entrance is narrow but

Castle Drogo: the entrance front (Country Life)

intriguing, especially in the vault with its little saucer domes, which recur throughout the Castle, usually at the turning of corners. The Hall, not big, is cheerful and opens straight into the Library. Here all the woodwork is of Lutyens's design, from the ceiling and bookcases to the screens that cover the radiators – the house was centrally heated from the beginning. Up a gentle flight of stairs is the Drawing Room, the gayest room of the series, lighted on three sides with windows in deep embrasures, which survey the whole scene below. The charm of the room is heightened by the Venetian glass chandeliers that adorn it. The furniture of the house, it must be said, is not of much distinction, but there are some good Spanish pieces and a number of the walls are hung with tapestries, chiefly Brussels.

The descent to the Dining Room is by a tall and narrow

staircase, with a window in six tiers of 48 lights, not of equal size. Here are amplitude and variety, achieved in a very confined space. The Dining Room is disappointing, with a ponderous low ceiling, which resulted from one of the changes of plan. The Kitchen quarters, reached along a handsome vaulted corridor, are remarkable for their equipment, designed by Lutyens himself – dresser and plate-racks, even pestle and mortar.

Four small rooms are on the ground floor, above. They were the first set in the Castle to be occupied and face down towards the Teign gorge. They are friendly, comfortable, pleasant to live in. Do not miss the bathroom and lavatory on the other side of the passage; Lutyens's hand is on them too.

The Chapel is reached by a flight of steps close to the main entrance. It is in effect a crypt, with a very low vault, the seating placed higher than the altar. Here Lutyens turned a change of plan to the best account. The foundations of a Great Hall had been laid when the work was reduced in scale in 1912. The Hall was then abandoned, and the Chapel built in the unused foundations.

Only half the house is open to visitors. The two top floors are still lived in by the Drewe family. There are many different pleasures to be picked up outside: in the varying treatment of the masonry and its colours, changing under the light, grey, silver, buff, with the occasional glitter of quartz; in the windows, different in size and in the thickness of their mullions; above all perhaps in the south end of the building, where the sides of the wall come out in blades, knife-sharp – a wonderful demonstration of the properties of granite. Nor is this all. The house is surrounded with alleys and walks, artfully contrived. Their climax comes in the circular lawn (designed as a tennis court), surrounded by a monumental yew hedge.

Castle Drogo is a most notable house, tightly enclosed in a frame designed for it but also set, more broadly, in a magnificent natural landscape. If this is the end of the line of country houses, the end is splendid indeed.

Cheviot and the Tweed Northumberland 1B1
The Cheviot itself – as distinct from the whole range of the Cheviot Hills – is dome-shaped and rises to 2,676 ft. It is wild, for all its smooth outline from a distance rather grim, and certainly very remote.

The best way to approach it is from Wooler, leaving the little town by Cheviot Street and making your way up to Langleeford. On the way you negotiate a very steep hump. Directly afterwards, there is Cheviot rising up nobly in front. But there is still a long way to go, up the deep gully of the Harthope Burn, before the road ends, and at Langleeford the ascent begins. It is one of those famed hills and mountains that are best seen from below. On top it is hardly more than a wide mossy moorland.

The Cheviot landscape, near Wooler (A. F. Kersting)

Nevertheless it dominates the whole of these Eastern Marches of the border between England and Scotland, a tract full of history and natural grandeur. East of Wooler is Chillingham, where there is a famous herd of wild white cattle in the park of the castle, and the sumptuous late-medieval tomb of Sir Ralph Grey in the church. To the west is Yeavering Bell, capped by a large Iron-Age hill fort. Below it in the valley was a palace of the Northumbrian kings in the 6th and 7th centuries. The site was excavated in 1953–7 and yielded striking new evidence of their might and its physical expression, in massive timber buildings and an amphitheatre 25 ft high, also constructed entirely of timber, for holding assemblies in the king's presence. The road by Yeavering runs on to Kirknewton and so to cross the Tweed into Scotland at Coldstream.

The Tweed is an outstanding river, one of the loveliest in Britain, running through Scott's country past Abbotsford, where he lived, and Dryburgh, the exquisite place where he is buried. Its last 20 miles form the frontier between England and Scotland. It is crossed in that space by two notable bridges, with a third spanning a tributary close by, and three more at its mouth at *Berwick*.

The highest of these is at Coldstream. It was erected to Smeaton's design in 1763–6: a solidly handsome stone structure of five main arches, with a smaller one at each end, and big triangular cutwaters projecting up and down stream. Some three miles below, the Tweed is joined by a substantial tributary, the Till. Not far from the confluence the Till is crossed, at Twizel, by a remarkable medieval bridge: of one wide high arch, hump-backed and ribbed underneath, all in pale-grey stone. The landscape here is delectable, the river making a sharp bend under a cliff just north of the bridge, whilst on the south side it flows through pastures shaded by big trees. And then, about eight miles lower down the Tweed, comes the Union Bridge, the oldest iron suspension bridge now extant in Europe. It dates from 1820 and was designed by (Sir) Samuel Brown, employing the wrought-iron links that he had patented three years before. The slim-looking

The Union Bridge (A. F. Kersting)

chains are suspended from pylons, built of pink stone, on each bank, the one on the English side standing alone against a cliff, the Scottish one having an arch and a toll-house. Taken together with the group at Berwick, these bridges form a fascinating sequence, and they are looked after meticulously, with a proper pride.

Chipping Campden and Hidcote Gloucestershire 4E2
The main street of Chipping Campden is one of the most completely harmonious in England; and being English, its harmony is composed of diversity. The buildings in it range from the 15th century to the 20th. There is not one formal terrace, no group of adjacent houses designed alike. No single building stands out as more important than the rest. The little town as a whole, and above all this street and the approach to the church, are more striking than any individual element in them.

The fronts of the houses are nearly all of limestone, interrupted only on one or two of them by pale-tinted smooth plasterwork. The colour of the stone cannot be described with precision. It comprises a spectrum of yellows and browns, varying greatly according to the weather and the light. Very few of these buildings have been cleaned, as so many have been in recent years elsewhere. The air here is pure, free of pollution except that arising from motor vehicles, and the stone is wonderfully durable. Its texture is as beautiful as its colour, and the masons' work a study in itself, in the dressing and handling of stone, the laying of tiles on roofs.

The unity is due to two other things as well. It is a matter of scale. Most of these buildings are of two storeys, none of more than three. Not one overtops the rest. And the whole town is bound together by strong threads of green. There is a broad grass verge along much of the north side of the street, planted with a few trees; a red chestnut punctuates the junction of the main street and its branch towards the church; there are glimpses everywhere of the surrounding trees and fields.

Chipping Campden was an important town in the Middle Ages. Its name indicates its character: "chipping" means "market", and it was as a point of sale for wool from the Cotswold sheep that the place developed. By the mid 13th century it had a weekly market and three annual fairs. Its prosperity is reflected in the elaborate reconstruction of the church in the 15th century. It then declined, though generously assisted by Sir Baptist Hicks, a very wealthy London merchant who bought the manor about 1608 and built himself a great house there, becoming Viscount Campden in 1628. By the Victorian age it was a backwater, with tiny textile industries and a railway station nearly two miles off. In the 20th century its exceptional beauty came to be appreciated; it grew into an interesting centre for a number of crafts, such as C. R. Ashbee's Guild of Handicrafts and the Golden Cockerel Press. A trust was formed in 1929, largely under the influence of F. L. Griggs, a fine artist who lived in the town, to guard and preserve it. The preservation has been intelligent, not stifling or obtrusive; but needless to say Chipping Campden is seen at its best early and late in the day, when there are fewest cars in it.

The town stands close to the northern face of the Cotswolds, nearly 500 ft above sea-level. The road from Evesham through Weston Subedge climbs steeply. Dover's Hill, to the left at the top, was the scene of sports, which flourished in the 17th century until they were put down by the Puritans. The road enters the town from the west and leads straight into the main street, which curves gently and gracefully, leading up to the climax of it all, the church at the east end. The street splits into two, with a pair of little public buildings on an island in the middle: the Town Hall, medieval but reconstructed early in the 19th century, and the Market Hall, a complete work of 1627, one of Hicks's gifts to the town.

Everyone will make his own choice among the individual houses in the street. Here is a selection of six. On the north side (the left, moving up towards the church) the King's Arms makes a good beginning, as it shows the nature of the street front. Its *façade* is Georgian, but that has been applied to an older building, more homely. This can be seen from the back of the hotel, in its garden. A range of irregular roofs appears there; no hint of them is visible in the street. Next door is the Cotswold House Hotel, a more sophisticated building, with a beautiful circular staircase. Then round the curve, nearly at the Y-junction, comes the late-14th-century Grevel House, rightly famous for its two-storeyed bay window, perfect in proportion and ornament.

Bedfont House, almost opposite, on the south side of the street, is a cause of sadness: a distinguished work of the 1740s by Thomas Woodward, delightfully decorated, and gravely injured by Victorian plate-glass windows, staring out like great blind eyes, destroying the whole articulation of the front. Woolstaplers' Hall is a contemporary of Grevel House, with a good timber roof inside. It houses a museum, with a remarkable collection: some local bygones and other relics, as one would expect, but also a great number of machines, typewriters, mantraps, sewing machines, the basket of a balloon, cameras, part of the equipment of a cinema of the 1920s. It is all carefully described and kept in admirable order: a fascinating assemblage, most improbable in a place of this sort. And lastly, further west, Dover House should not be missed, Georgian, reticent, well bred. A neat tablet above the door commemorates Griggs, who lived there.

The right-hand fork leads to an unforgettable group of buildings: the Almshouses, the gateway of the big house,

Chipping Campden: almshouses, church, Jacobean lodge and gateway
(A. F. Kersting)

and above them the tower of the church. The Almshouses were erected at Hicks's expense in 1612. There is surely no building of their time that is more delightful in England. Every detail – mullions, gables, finials, chimney-stacks – is crisp, and the stonework is as good as the design. The gateway with its lodges, demonstrative and curvaceous, belong to Hicks's great house. Built about 1613, it was destroyed in 1645, in the course of the Civil War. A few other fragments of it remain in the grassy enclosure beyond.

The church (St James) now appears almost entirely a work of the 15th century, though it incorporates a good deal of older building. The tower is elaborately decorated, yet the ornament is strong, never fussy. Inside, the proportions are characteristic of Gloucestershire; the building is short, and relatively high. The lofty piers of the nave, set close together, have concave sides; there is a window over the chancel arch. The pulpit and lectern are Jacobean, donations again from Hicks.

In the chancel there are four brasses, the biggest and most celebrated of them commemorating the wool merchant William Grevel (d. 1401) and his wife. The Gainsborough chapel, south of the chancel, contains the monuments of Sir Baptist Hicks and his family. He and his wife lie in the centre, a pair of white effigies enclosed in dark marble. Their daughter Juliana and son-in-law Edward Noel are near them: dramatic standing figures by Joshua Marshall. Two more Noel ladies look down, their busts in circular Caroline niches. It is all in black and white, with a little gold. This is a very impressive mortuary chapel.

The church possesses two exceptional treasures, kept behind glass under the tower: a set of late-15th-century altar hangings and a cope of about 1380. They are examples of the embroidery for which England was once famous throughout Europe: *opus anglicanum* it was called, simply "English work". The cope is of a rich red, the altar hangings of white sown with sprays of gold, green, and blue, with the Virgin in glory in the centre of the back cloth.

★

Chipping Campden is a good place to stay for an exploration of the Cotswolds. Three miles away to the north-west is Hidcote Manor, with a garden of outstanding distinction, belonging now to the National Trust. The road goes there by Hidcote House, a noble building of 1663, with curved gables. It faces west and glows in the evening sunlight. Hidcote Manor is a more modest house, though it has a tiny chapel of its own (long used as a barn) in its front courtyard. The estate was bought in 1907 by Lawrence Johnston, American by birth, who had a passionate feeling for gardens. There were then some beeches here, and a single cedar, and no other ingredient in what is to be seen now. Johnston's choice of the place might indeed seem a rather strange one. It lies high (600 ft above the sea), close to the western face of the Cotswolds. So it is cold and windy. The soil is heavy, and full of lime. Another man might have accepted these as limitations, and sought to turn them to account. Johnston did better. He saw them as a challenge, and overcame them. He began with almost nothing, and made it all.

Hidcote: the pavilions, with the Stilt Garden behind

(A. F. Kersting)

The house lies below the level of the escarpment. The garden rises towards it by two grass terraces, side by side and entirely different. The Theatre Lawn is very broad, enclosed by a yew hedge and crowned at the far end by a pair of old beeches. The terrace next to it is narrower and more complicated. You enter the Circle, formed by lilacs, and look away to a pretty pair of tiny pavilions with hipped roofs, flanking a short flight of steps. Beyond them is the Stilt Garden, with a quaintly formal arrangement of clipped hornbeams; and beyond that, on the skyline, a gate. Pass through it, and the whole Vale of Evesham unfolds below, with Bredon Hill in the distance.

This is the central axis of the garden, seen from the house. But it spreads out at greater length to left and right – that is, to north and south. To the north is the Kitchen Garden, with many old French roses and a bed rich with irises in late spring. To the south the Long Walk, enclosed in a tall hedge of hornbeam and presided over by a Monterey pine, leads to another open landscape: not a valley but a series of falling slopes. To the east of the Long Walk is a wooded tract called Westonbirt (after another famous Gloucestershire garden), planted especially for the autumn. Below Westonbirt is the Bathing Pool, with a stream running from it, forming the Stream Garden, in a number of small separate divisions. Close to the house the Old Garden is also in several parts, so small that they are almost like rooms. In the White Garden everything is white except in the late summer, when the Scotch Flame Flower throws scarlet all over the hedges.

The plan of the garden, in this outline, gives little idea of Johnston's achievement, or his art. It is all contained within about 10 acres: a tiny area to comprehend so much, without any overcrowding. There is a great sense of space here (including, of course, the wide distant sweeps beyond the garden to the west), and also most intimate enclosure. The hedges do more than separate one division of the garden from another. They provide the shelter, the wind-breaks, that this cold open space requires. Johnston brought plants from all over the world to Hidcote. He showed a lordly determination to overcome the difficulties that confronted him. There was too much lime here for some plants, rhododendrons and azaleas. Very well: a section of the Stream Garden was made with lime-free soil, brought in for the purpose. If someone attempted a similar task today, it would be with mechanised earth-moving equipment. But who would have the eye, the head and the mind, to evolve it all; the toughness and patience – the expectation of the future – to carry it through?

This garden is the work of a genius, comparable with that of the great masters of planting in the 18th century, who worked on a different scale and in an entirely different world (see for instance *Heveningham* and *Houghton*); the work of an American, realised in England. It is a great addition, made in the 20th century, to the historic riches of the Cotswolds.

Clovelly see **Hartland**

Clunbury Salop 2A6

In valleys of springs of rivers,
By Ony and Teme and Clun,
The country for easy livers,
The quietest under the sun.

Housman's words characterise this tract of Shropshire and Herefordshire perfectly, as we see it now. But it was not always so, for it lies in the Marches of Wales and was much harried in the fighting between the English and Welsh in the Middle Ages, as well as between the Marcher Lords themselves. The fragments of castles are witnesses to that still, Clun and Wigmore and Pembridge; so are the squat immensely solid church towers, planned with an eye to defence (see *Kempley*). The country is sparsely served by railways now, and traversed by only one road of any importance

(B.T.A.)

A44 from Worcester to Aberystwyth. So it is little visited. It lies in the deepest peace, remote from the modern world.

This is a good sample of it. Half-way between Clun and Craven Arms a narrow lane skirts the northern face of Clunbury Hill. From here you look down to Clunbury church, across to the gentle slope of Clundon, and then beyond that to the sharply-pointed Sunnyhill, whose thick woods conceal on the top the earthwork known as Bury Ditches, the scene in legend (though probably not in fact) of the last stand of the British chief Caractacus against the Romans. It is a country of mixed farming, with apple trees among the houses in the village and much honeysuckle in the hedgerows in late summer.

The towns of the region are tiny, markets as they have always been and hardly more: Bishop's Castle (shapely and charming), Clun, Kington, Presteign and Knighton just across the border in Wales. The nearest large town is Wolverhampton, 50 miles away to the east and much more distant than that in spirit and in time.

Coalbrookdale and Ironbridge Salop 2B6

The Coalbrookdale works figure in English economic history as the place at which a critically-important change in the technique of iron-production occurred in 1709. Here Abraham Darby began to use coke instead of charcoal in the smelting of iron; something never achieved successfully before, on a commercial scale. The change was vital. The supply of charcoal, a product of trees, was declining as the demand for timber for many purposes increased. Coke came from coal, and that in England was inexhaustible. Coal was already being used in the production of lead, copper, and tin. Darby first applied it effectively to making iron. He and his partners (all Quakers) kept the process secret. No details of it were published until 1747; at the end of the 18th century some big ironworks in the neighbourhood were still using charcoal. Nevertheless the change initiated at Coalbrookdale was decisive. It began to link the production of iron with coal; and that involved a move away from Sussex and the Forest of Dean to the large coalfields of the Midlands and the North. Darby relied wholly on water-power. The steam engine did not begin to be applied directly to iron-production until 75 years after his work began. When that happened, the full potential of England's iron-making, with coal as its indispensable fuel, came to be realised.

The Dale itself is a side-cut from a deep winding gorge of the Severn, the longest of English rivers. Iron ore was being worked in Coalbrookdale in the early 16th century, and a blast furnace was in use 100 years later. In 1708 Abraham Darby, a maker of full-bellied iron pots, took a lease of the works. He reconstructed the furnace and began smelting iron there with coke very early in the next year. He continued to turn out his pots, with kettles and other domestic utensils, successfully. The furnace was dependent on water-power, which usually failed in the summer months until the installation of a steam engine in 1743 enabled water to be circulated continuously from the Pool above the work and so allowed production to continue all the year round. The original furnace remained in use, altered and recon structed, until 1818. Thereafter the Coalbrookdale Company smelted its iron elsewhere, concentrating on manufacture in Coalbrookdale itself.

Although the chief products of the works were relatively small domestic articles, they entered the field of industry too. The first iron railway wheels that we know of were made here in 1729, the first iron track in 1767. In the next decade they became involved in something far more ambitious: the casting of members for the first substantial iron bridge to be built anywhere in the world. This was erected to span the Severn close to Coalbrookdale itself and brought into use in 1781. The Iron Bridge – known by that simple name ever since – was a spectacular demonstration of the capabilities of metal construction. It remains one of the outstanding monuments of the Industrial Revolution.

Before it was built there was no bridge over the Severn between Buildwas and Bridgnorth. There were ferries, but they were difficult to maintain owing to the strength and speed of the river. These deficiencies handicapped industrial development, and in 1775 a bridge was decided on, financed by private subscription. The third Abraham Darby was treasurer of the undertaking. The bridge had to avoid impeding traffic on the river, and the narrowness of the gorge precluded a long structure of stone. The proposal for a single-span bridge in iron was due to a Shrewsbury architect, Thomas Farnolls Pritchard; and though the bridge as built was somewhat different, and he died before that was completed, he must be regarded as its prime designer, aided by Darby and the other ironmasters interested in the project. Its construction entailed a realignment of the neighbouring road system. Soon a stage-coach was crossing it, on its way between Shrewsbury and London.

On the north bank of the river a township quickly developed, with a market, removed here from Madeley up above. It has kept its original name, Ironbridge, to the present day. The valley had long been served by horse-drawn railways. In 1862–4 steam-operated ones appeared, linking it with Wellington and Shrewsbury and Birmingham. But for all that the place remained withdrawn, inward-looking. Today it forms part of the fast-growing New Town of Telford; but the sense of its separateness is still marked.

The historic sites here are now all in the hands of the Ironbridge Gorge Museum Trust. There are three main centres, separated by a mile or two and some steep hills: first, the heart of it all, the gorge itself; second, the Coalport China Works; third, Blists Hill Open Air Museum. Cheap guides, well written and well produced, are on sale for each.

Let us begin at Ironbridge, with the bridge itself. It stands very much as it has always done, lacking only the iron lamp-posts that originally decorated the centre of the parapet. The bridge is still a thing of wonder today, with the property of changing its character according to one's point of view. From a distance it looks fine-drawn, like a cobweb; from the river-bank below – what it really is – lithe and strong.

(A. F. Kersting)

In 1973–4 the whole structure (which had been settling) was strengthened by massive concrete work in the bed of the river: a remarkable operation, excellently portrayed in a film shown at the Trust's Information Office, which is in the former toll-house at the south end of the bridge. For a long time the bridge has been used by pedestrians only. It is now structurally safe. The ironwork still needs treatment and painting, which is due to be put in hand shortly – in time, we may hope, for the bicentenary of the bridge's opening in January 1981.

Half a mile east of the bridge the Severn Wharf and Warehouse (now open to visitors) stand at the entrance to Coalbrookdale, which runs out of the gorge to the north. Another half-mile up it lies the Museum and Furnace Site, embraced by the curving railway viaduct of 1864. The Old Furnace, where Darby's work began in 1709, is at the centre of it, directly below the Upper Pool, where water was stored for turning the big wheels to work the bellows.

The Museum will eventually be in the Great Warehouse, the tall brick building with the gaily-painted clock tower, its windows set in iron frames made on the spot. The present temporary exhibition summarises the history of the site and the growth of the Company. The first room is dominated by an excellent portrait of William Reynolds, a partner in the late 18th century, whom we shall meet again. Do not miss the delicate pencil drawings of the Dale and the gorge made by Joseph Farington in 1789. The second and larger room displays the Company's products, from its early railway equipment to modern domestic appliances, parts for which are still cast by the Company's successor in Coalbrookdale. The chief interest here lies in the decorative ironwork that was one of the Company's specialities: firegrates, umbrella stands, garden furniture, firescreens, lamps, inkstands, as well as a whole range of ornaments, figurines of animals – tortoise, lion, camel, stag – and knights in armour. It offers an instructive anthology of the taste of the Victorian middle classes.

The Coalport China Works Museum lies two miles east of the bridge. Coalport was a waterway junction, where boats from the Shropshire Canal were brought down to the Severn by means of the Hay Inclined Plane (to be mentioned shortly). From this port coal was distributed widely. Other industrial activities were pursued here too. There were rope and timber yards, and a linseed mill. But the place is famous for its china works, established through the enterprise of William Reynolds not long before 1800. Coalport china continued to be made here until 1926, when the business was transferred to Stoke-on-Trent. Some of its buildings have been most skilfully converted into a museum. The techniques of the craft are described with care (the commentary is much more informative here than in the Coalbrookdale Museum), and examples of the firm's products are displayed in the cone-shaped Glaze Kiln, which has been excellently adapted for the purpose. Here is the story of Victorian commercial art, as developed in Coalbrookdale, in another medium.

Finally, Blists Hill Museum, a mile away up above. It extends over 42 acres, and it is being developed to display comprehensively the industrial history of the whole district. Some of its chief exhibits are in their original position; others have been brought here from the neighbourhood. Close to the entrance stands a noble pair of double beam engines, *David* and *Sampson*, built in Glasgow for the Lilleshall Company, six miles away at Priorslee, in 1851. Their task was to blow air into blast furnaces, cutting out the earlier operation that had used bellows. Behind the engines are the furnaces themselves, which are gradually being reconstructed.

A group of structures is being assembled to recreate a small industrial town of the late-Victorian age. There is a printing shop and a pottery here, adjoining the Red Clay Mine, whose shaft reached a maximum depth of 600 ft, to yield coal, ironstone, and clay for making bricks. Beside it runs the Shropshire Canal, to its terminus at the top of the Hay Inclined Plane, by which boats were lowered and raised to and from Coalport, partly by steam power and partly by the force of gravity. It was working by 1793 and continued in use for a century.

Close to the entrance is a tollhouse from the Holyhead

Road, whose reconstruction was one of the achievements of Thomas Telford. A section of road is laid in front of it according to his principles. He was the most refined of all road engineers, and this is an appropriate tribute to him, here in Shropshire, which the Holyhead Road crossed and where so much of his work was done.

These are a very few of the things to be seen in this large group of sites and buildings. The Trust that manages them was established in 1968. Its work has been impressive. There is much more of it to come, its speed and scale depending largely on the funds that can be provided. It is a demonstration of ideas and techniques in the study of recent history, of industrial archaeology and the ways of presenting its findings, that belongs especially to our own time. The whole gorge has much to offer: a series of remarkable buildings and their equipment, many small exhibits of great interest, all set in a striking landscape. It is still a rather remote place. But then remoteness is part of its special attraction; and once you are there, whatever your effort has been, you are likely to think that effort justified.

Coggeshall: Paycocke's Essex 5B3

Coggeshall is an ancient little town, whose history is different from what its appearance suggests today. In the Middle Ages this part of Essex reared sheep. Much of their wool was exported, but from the 14th century onwards it was made into cloth on a large scale. Coggeshall became a cloth-manufacturing town, and remained so prosperously throughout the 15th and 16th centuries. Paycocke's is a handsome witness to that prosperity: a late-medieval town house, not large but of high quality, well restored and cared for.

John Paycocke, who died in 1505 owning the house, described himself in his will as a butcher; no doubt he was a grazier too, with large flocks of sheep. The timbers of the house show the initials TP and MP, referring to his son Thomas (who died in 1518) and to Margaret, Thomas's wife.

The structure is timber-framed throughout. It is by no means a unity. Two wings project to the back, into the garden, which are very much older; and on either side of "Paycocke's" proper there are other buildings that are structurally part of it, under the same system of roofs: to the east a cottage, to the west what is now the Fleece Inn (formerly known as Drapers: the house in which the last male Paycocke died in 1580). The central part of this complex is the most distinguished. At one time it was divided into three tenements, and this accounts for some of the uneven spacing of the ground-floor doors and windows. At the east end there is a cartway, with good 16th-century timber gates – probably brought from elsewhere. The horizontal beam below the upper storey, which overhangs slightly, is handsomely carved, with numerous references to the Paycocke family. The five upper windows are all timber-framed oriels, uniform in height but

(Janet & Colin Bord)

differing slightly in width. The brick infilling dates from the restoration of the house in 1905.

Here is something subtler than the run-of-the-mill "black and white" that is usually chosen to represent the timber building of the late Middle Ages. Like most timber buildings it has needed drastic restoration to preserve it, but that has been conservatively managed and the house retains its original character clearly. It is a work of architecture, something more than a mere piece of building. Its present colour too is delightful: the timber pale silvery-grey, the brick a soft dull red.

The front door opens directly into the hall, the ceiling beams of which are carved with trails of foliage. The patterns are not wholly repetitive. The central east–west beam is perhaps the best of them all. The walls of the dining room are covered mainly with 16th-century linenfold panelling; but there are three small 14th-century Gothic panels behind the door, delightfully patterned, reminders of an earlier mode. These two rooms show the richest carving in the house. The principal bedrooms upstairs have ceiling beams excellently moulded but not decorated; elsewhere the timbers are left plain.

Walk down the pretty garden, long and narrow, behind the house. Looking back, you see the whole group of buildings, with their rear projections (so different from the trim *façade* they present to the street) and the irregular scatter of roofs, in rich red tile. It is a thoroughly English composition.

Coggeshall lay off the main highway to London, on the Roman Stane Street that ran from Colchester to St Albans. In the Victorian age the railway kept at a distance – there was no station nearer than Kelvedon, over two miles away – and that delivered it from much ugly development. Misfortune has assailed it in the 20th century, however. Its spacious 15th-century church was largely destroyed by a German bomb in September 1940, and has had to be rebuilt. Stane Street now carries very heavy traffic along the narrow main thoroughfare of the town. How can its many timber buildings stand up to this ceaseless pounding? One cannot truthfully describe Coggeshall as beautiful, or even as picturesque. In one respect indeed it is hideous. Electricity wires have been allowed to dominate several of its streets; the total wirescape here is almost like what one encounters in the United States. It is a place with a very distinct history, a character of its own: no longer an industrial town, as it was in the later Middle Ages, but still a place of trade and, with its extensive seed-growing business, the centre of the economic life of the rich corn lands that surround it.

Conisbrough South Yorkshire 2C4

Conisbrough is a small town not far from Doncaster, on the way to Sheffield. It has had two quite separate phases of importance: as a dependency of its castle in the Middle Ages and of its coal mines in the past 100 years. Its site, on two hills rising steeply above the valley of the River Don, is naturally defensible. On the more westerly of the hills stands the church (St Peter), in which there is still Saxon masonry; and it was probably this hill that the Saxons fortified, with earthworks. William the Conqueror bestowed Conisbrough on one of his chief supporters, William de Warenne, who seems to have begun to develop a fortification on the eastern hill, the origin of the present castle. In the 12th century the property came by marriage to Hamelin Plantagenet, half-brother of Henry II; and the keep of the Castle, the signal distinction of Conisbrough, was erected by him soon after 1180. It exemplifies the circular plan, carried out with exceptional thoroughness and elegance.

The keep stands at the north-eastern edge of the bailey: an enormous cylinder clasped in six buttresses running up the full height of the tower (nearly 80 ft) and above it to provide platforms from which a watch could be kept on assailants. These buttresses are solid, except that on the third floor the south-eastern one accommodates the chapel. The walls of the keep are immensely thick throughout – 15 ft on the first floor. It is possible that the stonework was made so massive in order to allow each storey of the castle to

Conisbrough Castle: the Keep (Bowling & Beauchamp)

be vaulted inside; but the floors have now all gone – apart from the domed roof of the lowest, at ground level. The entrance was, as usual, on the first floor.

The keep of Conisbrough is an unforgettable sight on account of its masonry: faced to the very top in finely-dressed magnesian limestone. (Great quarries of that stone, still worked, are only a mile away to the north-east.) It is a distinguished design, both as architecture and as military engineering, and superbly executed. Moreover it has lately been cleaned, with the greatest care, so that the stone shines almost as when it was new.

Climb to the top of the keep and you can see, in summary, much of the history of England: the castle directly beneath, the town at its gates, and the church (Saxon in its origins, but clad outside in English Perpendicular Gothic); the valley of the Don, canalised in the 18th century; the railway striding across it on a tall viaduct, and the big Cadeby Colliery, still active; seven miles away to the north-east, the tower of Doncaster parish church, one of the grandest works of the Victorian Sir Gilbert Scott; and on the hills in the opposite direction good ploughland, much as it was before industrial development began.

Cotehele Cornwall 3B4

Cotehele is a house of the late Middle Ages. It was given its present form chiefly by Sir Richard Edgcumbe and his son Sir Piers between about 1485 and 1520. Sir Richard was a Lancastrian, who escaped death at the hands of a Yorkist enemy by an artful trick, passed on into the service of Henry VII, and died at Morlaix, fighting for the Duchess of Brittany against Charles VIII of France. It was the principal house of the Edgcumbe family, with one brief interlude, until the later part of the 17th century, when they moved to another estate, Mount Edgcumbe opposite Plymouth. Cotehele then served sometimes as a dower house for the widowed Countesses of Mount Edgcumbe; the east wing was built for one of them in 1862. The sixth Earl of Mount Edgcumbe persuaded the Treasury to accept the house in lieu of death duties and to hand it over to the National Trust: an important negotiation, the first of its kind, which set a precedent frequently invoked since then, resulting in the preservation of many great houses that would otherwise have been sold and probably pulled down.

Sir Richard Edgcumbe and his son took an already existing house and altered it to make the present one. Some fragments of the older building appear on the left of the Hall. They are distinguishable by small single-light windows and by the use of a rough shaly stone, contrasting with the dressed granite,

Cotehele: the Hall Court (A. F. Kersting)

much smoother and more refined, used from Sir Richard's time onwards. The Hall Court is one of the most complete pieces of late-medieval English building, to be compared with some of the Oxford Colleges.

You enter, abruptly, the Hall itself; a more perfect survival of its time than any College hall, completely unaltered. Sir Piers erected it, and it was finished by 1520. It is still wholly medieval in character, untouched by the Tudor age or the Renaissance; lofty, with a fine arch-braced roof and furnished, save in one respect, in the traditional manner. There are no pictures, only pieces of armour, weapons, and hunting trophies. Originally the walls would have been hung with some kind of textiles, of silk or wool, making them dark and rich, where now they are white. If that seems a deficiency here, it is compensated for in the rest of the house, where nearly every room is hung with tapestry. Though none of it is as old as the house itself, the impression it produces could not be bettered. The tapestries are mostly of the 17th century, Brussels and Mortlake. They have been cut about and the series separated (the noble figures in the Brussels set depicting the foundation of Rome, for example, appear in several different rooms). This is the way most such hangings were used: not as works of art but as wall-coverings, for warmth as much as for decoration. Here and there they even hang across an archway, in substitution for a door.

The furniture is entirely in keeping with the house, though little of it is of the same age. The most important 16th-century piece is the remarkable bed-head now placed in the Staircase Lobby, with its inscription in Welsh, recording that it was made by Harry ap Griffith. This must have been brought by Katherine, widow of Sir Griffith ap Rhys, who married into the family in 1532. Notice the Welsh elements in the decoration, especially the musicians playing the Welsh harp and crewth. Angular and clumsy as it is, this is a precious piece of the 16th century.

The chapel, replacing an earlier one licensed in 1411, is Sir Richard Edgcumbe's work, though a good deal restored in the Victorian age. The screen is of his time, more or less intact, and so are the two figures in the south window, of St Catherine and St Anne. The triptych on the altar is Flemish, of the late 16th century. The altar has a silk frontal, but this is too fragile now to be displayed in the light. The clock, in a recess at the back of the chapel, is believed to be the oldest in England that stands unaltered in its original position. It formerly operated a bell, in the little bell-cote above, which struck the hours.

The house stands near the top of the steep western bank of the Tamar, one of the loveliest of English rivers, every yard of it from its source near the north coast through winding gorges down to its termination in Plymouth Sound. There are falling gardens below the east front, and then thick woods right down to the water's edge.

Other things are to be seen here too: the little chapel built by Sir Richard Edgcumbe in thankfulness for his escape from death (though not much of it is now of his time); Cotehele Mill with some of its equipment; the Quarry; and upstream the railway viaduct at Calstock, opened to traffic in 1908 – one of the few elegant structures ever made out of concrete blocks. This is a place to spend a long time in, and it may be added that a simple restaurant of unusual merit is to be found in the big 15th-century barn close to the front entrance of the house.

Coughton Court Warwickshire 4E1

The great majority of Englishmen accepted the religious changes imposed by successive governments in the 16th and 17th centuries. Under the Tudors there was great division, however, and opposition to the Elizabethan Church settlement. There were always some who refused to accept it on any terms, incurring the disabilities, the penalties, even at times the persecution, that attached to the old religion. Persecution ceased at the end of the 17th century, but political disabilities continued to be imposed until 1829 on those who did not conform to the Anglican Church.

Throughout those years some families continued obstinately Catholic; a few have stayed so until the present day. One of the most remarkable of them is the Throckmortons of Coughton. One must say "of Coughton", for not all Throckmortons remained Catholic. Another branch of the family, at Haseley (10 miles away), was just as obviously Protestant. There was division on these matters, in this family as in so many others elsewhere.

Coughton Court is, before all things, a Catholic house. That gives it a peculiar character of its own. It lies on the west side of the broad valley of the River Arrow, standing back from the Redditch–Alcester road across a wide meadow, its Gatehouse glowing in the sunlight. Beside it are two

Coughton Court: the Gatehouse and west front (A. F. Kersting)

churches: the medieval parish church, close to the house, and a little further away the graceful Catholic church by J. A. Hansom, of 1857.

The Throckmortons acquired the estate in 1409. A little over 100 years later, in the reign of Henry VIII, Sir George began to reconstruct the house. He kept to the traditional courtyard form. The Gatehouse he built is one of the best works of its time to be seen in England; a gatehouse domesticated by its multitude of windows, with the two-storeyed oriel in the centre. The wings beside it are less satisfactory. They were refashioned in 1780, and again some 50 years later, and the stone was covered in cement. This rendering, however, is now being taken off, effecting a great improvement to the whole west front. At the back of the house the north and south wings of the Tudor building face each other across the courtyard; they are tall, mainly in brick and timber with some strong Elizabethan carving on the barge-boards of the windows on the south side. The east range, which formerly closed in the courtyard, has gone; it was pulled down by an anti-Catholic mob from Alcester in 1688. So the house looks out across a great expanse of green to the little river, and the rising parkland beyond it.

That moment of violence in 1688 was not unique in the history of Coughton. In the Civil War Sir Robert Throckmorton was, as we should expect, loyal to the King. His house was occupied by a Parliamentarian force, and in January 1644 was bombarded by the Royalists' guns, set on fire, and seriously damaged. Before that there had been echoes of violence here, at a distance but not less poignant. In November 1605 a party of ladies sat in the Drawing Room over the Gatehouse. They were the wives of conspirators in the Gunpowder Plot, waiting for news of its outcome. When they heard it had failed, they moved off to another Catholic house in Staffordshire. Twenty years earlier, young Francis Throckmorton (not a son of the house, but first cousin of its owner) had been the central figure in a plot in favour of Mary Queen of Scots against Elizabeth; he was racked three times in the Tower, and afterwards hanged. This dark history of violence and conspiracy, transmuted later into a quiet, tenacious rejection of the established religious order, overhangs Coughton everywhere.

The ground floor of the Gatehouse was enclosed early in the 19th century to make an entrance hall; it has a pretty fan vault. The two rooms above it on the first and second floors are full of light, from the big oriel windows facing east and west and the little additional windows placed in the corner turrets. The Drawing Room, on the first floor, is dominated by a sumptuous French portrait of Sir Robert Throckmorton painted by Largillière in 1729, in a fine rococo frame. Complex and superbly rich, it makes all English portraiture of its age insipid by comparison – though England's time came in the second half of the century with Reynolds and Gainsborough, who achieved a richness and expression of their own. Opposite this picture stands a case of missals and books of hours of the 15th century, illuminated and exquisitely written. Above is the Tower Room, which was formerly used as a chapel, reached by a narrow staircase in one of the turrets. In another turret there is a second staircase, used in emergency by priests and leading down to a concealed space in which a bed and a portable leather altar were discovered in 1870. Documents are shown in the Tower Room, from the very rich store of the family's archives. Stairs then lead out on to the roof, whence the whole broad valley of the Arrow can be surveyed.

The interior of the Dining Room, as we see it, is of about 1630, with a chimney-piece in a sober combination of marbles and excellent panelling all round the walls. The room displays very well the refinement of Caroline taste, by comparison with the overblown exuberance of the Jacobean age before.

A short flight of steps leads out of the Dining Room, up to the Tapestry Drawing Room and Bedroom. From the foot of the steps, to the left, a tiny room can be reached, another concealed "hole". It contains a good panel of Nottingham alabaster of the 15th century, depicting the Nativity: a "superstitious image" hidden away, no doubt, when that was necessary after the Reformation, but jealously guarded and kept.

The next room, the Tribune, contains the most precious historical relics in the house: the white chemise worn by Mary Queen of Scots at her execution and a splendid purple velvet cope, embroidered in gold – it is said by Queen Katherine of Aragon. There is also a small case of things with Jacobite associations. A portrait hangs here of Sir Nicholas Throckmorton, ambassador to France under Elizabeth. His daughter was a lady-in-waiting to the Queen, whom she enraged by secretly marrying Sir Walter Ralegh; a story fascinatingly told, with the aid of a diary kept at the time, by A. L. Rowse in his *Ralegh and the Throckmortons*.

The Saloon, below the Tribune, was once used as a chapel and given its present form in 1910, incorporating the big staircase, removed from Harvington Hall in Worcestershire. Here pictures and other memorials reflect the history of the family in the 19th and 20th centuries. A case of documents stands in the low-roofed passage-way under the staircase. They are a miscellany, admirably contrived to indicate the range of the family's connections and associations. Not all of them have Catholic references. Here is a letter from John Wesley; a manuscript volume of Cowper's poems, written in his delightful hand; and an account of Byron's death in a letter from his valet to his father, a Venetian gondolier.

The guidebook to the house carries at its centre a broad genealogical table of the Throckmortons from 1409 to the present day. It also includes a list of 80 portraits of members of the family and their relatives. Such matter is often of interest only to specialists. Not so here. These pages reveal the nexus of kinship that bound the old Catholic families of England together. The names of those they married form almost a roll of the history of Catholic recusancy, in Warwickshire and elsewhere: Sheldon, Tresham, Catesby, Petre, Stonor, Plowden, Stapleton, Acton, Stourton. In war, here is one killed at the battle of Pavia in 1525, two more in the World Wars of our own time; in peace, an abbess and a nun in Paris convents in the 18th century, a lady-in-waiting to the Empress Elizabeth of Austria. Nowhere perhaps can one listen better to the special inflections, national and international, of historic English Catholicism.

Coughton Court, with about 150 acres of land adjoining it, was made over to the National Trust by Sir Robert Throckmorton, the present baronet, in 1945. By an unusual arrangement he retained the contents of the house. So all that the visitor sees now, of furniture, pictures, and relics (except that Largillière portrait alone), still belongs to him, and is shown by his kind leave. In view of the special character of these possessions, one rejoices. Even a non-Catholic must wish this wise arrangement to continue.

Dorchester and Maiden Castle Dorset 4D4

Though not distinguished, in history or architecture, Dorchester has some endearing merits. It has been less affected than any other English county town by modern development. There are no tall concrete buildings here; no road system has torn any part of it asunder. It remains quietly busy, an administrative centre and a market town with some small industries and a population of 14,000. It is sensibly content with that.

No town of its kind figures more happily in English literature. For Thomas Hardy was born and died immediately outside it. He set one whole novel here, *The Mayor of Casterbridge*, and made it the scene of many stories and poems. He died 50 years ago; but if he revisited Dorchester now he would find much of what he knew and wrote about still recognisable, and some of it quite unchanged.

The town has one special charm, in the tree-shaded walks that it enjoys, laid out along the line of the walls, like similar towns in France. Those walls were not medieval in origin, but Roman. For Dorchester was the Romans' Durnovaria, sharing with Ilchester the chief place in their administration of this part of England. It was a centre of communications and a market. Among the amenities it enjoyed was an aqueduct, bringing in water from the north, over a distance of 10 miles. A series of tesselated pavements – one of them to be seen almost complete in the excellent Museum – tells us something of the town they lived in. Their walls have all disappeared, except for a fragment in the West Walk. But these avenues of trees, planted in the 18th century, commemorate for us the Roman founders of Dorchester.

High East Street and High West Street, which are continuous, carry A35 through the town, and in the second of them there are many pleasant buildings of the 16th and 17th centuries. At the centre, where they are joined by Cornhill, stands St Peter's, the civic church of the town. Close by are two coaching inns, the Antelope and the King's Head, both with Georgian bow-windowed fronts, and down South Street (Cornhill's continuation) on the left is Napper's Mite, a tiny 17th-century almshouse now converted sensitively into a set of shops and a restaurant.

If you carry on down that street and follow the Weymouth road at the next crossing, you will climb a hill and notice

(Frank Rodgers)

Dorchester: High West Street, with St Peter's church

a big grassy bank on the left near the top. Scramble up it, and you stand on the top of a green amphitheatre. This is Maumbury Rings, a henge monument of the late Stone or early Bronze Age: a high enclosure, that is, built to contain a ceremonial circle of stones or timber trunks. The type is peculiar to Britain. The hollow here is about half an acre in extent, with an entrance on the north-eastern side. When the Romans established their Durnovaria and desired an amphitheatre for public spectacles, they took this existing work of their predecessors and adapted it by levelling the floor, covering it with gravel, heightening the surrounding banks and furnishing them with seats cut in the chalk. In the Civil War it found another unexpected use, being adapted as a fort by the Parliamentarian forces defending Dorchester. A gun platform was then erected on the south-western side, which became an advanced outpost in the defences of the town and was linked to them by a flat-bottomed trench designed to form a covered way. It was not put to the test, however, in any assault. In 1705 Maumbury Rings was brought into use once more, for the burning of Mary Channing, convicted of witchcraft. Thereafter it relapsed into silence, broken in the 1840s by the picks and shovels of navvies, building railways one on each side of it. Had it not been for a local antiquary, Charles Warne, it would have been damaged, or destroyed entirely. As it is, it is tightly hemmed in but still tenaciously intact.

The Weymouth road (A354) runs south-westwards out of the town in a dead straight line. It was the Roman road to Radipole (part of Weymouth today), which served as the port for Durnovaria. To the right another earthwork, far bigger than the one just described, soon comes into view, making a serrated skyline of the green chalk hills: Maiden Castle.

This is for many people the most exciting of all English prehistoric earthworks. Several things help to give it that pre-eminence. First, its enormous size. Its defences enclose an area of 47 acres – though there are others still larger: Cissbury in Sussex covers 60. Secondly, its complex nature: the long series of successive occupations of the site, and the elaborate defensive works that resulted. Thirdly, its history, beginning in the Stone Age and stretching down to the end of the Roman dominion. Finally, and most strongly of all, Maiden Castle thrills the eye. The earthworks form a series of vast sculptures in the grass-covered chalk. That is revealed in air-photographs; but it cannot be appreciated fully except on foot. One's first experience of climbing these ramparts and walking on them remains with one for life.

The earthwork embraces two knolls and the slight depression between them. The site was first used, so far as we know, in the Stone Age, perhaps about 3000 B.C., when the eastern knoll was occupied. For how long, there is no telling; but it is clear that this part of the site was used again in the Iron Age, in the 4th century B.C. Then, perhaps 100 years later, occupation extended to the other knoll. Finally,

Maiden Castle (Janet & Colin Bord)

in a series of operations prolonged over about 100 years from 150 B.C., the multiple defences were completed: three high ramparts all round, with a fourth on the southern side, and two very deep ditches.

There were two entrances to the great enclosure, on the east and west sides. That on the east was protected by a long outer fortification, with rounded ends – what in modern military engineering is called a hornwork. The interior has revealed several things of special note. The first of them, and perhaps the most remarkable, is the long barrow – gigantically long, a third of a mile. Buried deep inside it was the body of a man aged between 25 and 35, whose head and limbs had been hacked from his trunk after death; three separate efforts had been made to extract the brain from his skull. It seems clear that this is a case of ritual human sacrifice.

When the Romans began their main invasion of the country,

the Britons defended Maiden Castle. It was carried by storm in A.D. 44 or 45 by troops commanded by the future Emperor Vespasian. The bodies of the slain were buried roughly in a pit; one of them with the iron head of a Roman dart still stuck into his spine.

After that bloody episode, Maiden Castle continued to be occupied for a time, until its people moved away, many of them drawn no doubt eventually by the Roman town as it developed in the valley below. But late in the 4th century, during a revival of pagan religion, a temple was erected in the eastern part of the fort. It cannot have been used for long before the Romans in their turn departed, and the building was left to decay.

The whole of this tract of chalk downland, covered thickly with prehistoric earthworks (118 round barrows have been counted in the single parish of Winterborne St Martin, in which Maiden Castle is situated), now ceased to be inhabited, though much of it here and there came to be ploughed or turned to pasture. A barn went up inside the Castle, near the eastern entrance, in the 16th century; a square pond was dug in the 19th. Maiden Castle was safe from any wanton destruction. Its exceptional interest was recognised and proclaimed by antiquaries, from Aubrey and Stukeley onwards. It was scientifically investigated by Cunnington in the 1880s and by Sir Mortimer Wheeler 50 years later. Much more, no doubt, remains to be discovered in those parts of the earthwork that have not yet been excavated. But enough is known, and we can see enough for ourselves, to allow it to be claimed for Maiden Castle that it is, in construction and in history alike, one of the most remarkable monuments of the ancient world in northern Europe.

Dover Kent 5C4

Dover Castle must surely be reckoned the pre-eminent fortress of England. It has not the august history of Windsor or the Tower of London; there are others, like *Warkworth*, that might be reckoned finer works of architecture. But it remains a fortress, only just indeed out of commission, for the last units of the army did not relinquish their occupation of it until 1958.

It stands on a natural site of great strength: on the eastern and higher of two bluffs that flank a deep valley, immediately above a little bay affording some shelter from south-westerly winds and close to the narrowest point of the English Channel. An Iron-Age camp was established on this hill, and that was re-used in the 12th century as the base of the outer wall of the Castle. Although we do not know much about the settlement the Romans built at Dover, the value they attached to its harbour is attested by the two lighthouses they erected above it, one on each side of the valley, to guide their ships. The one on the west has now almost entirely disappeared, but the eastern one still stands to a height of more than 40 ft (with 19 ft of medieval work added) in the Castle enclosure, cheek by jowl with the church of St Mary-in-Castro. That church dates from the late Saxon age, about A.D. 1000. It is a fine Romanesque building, surprisingly large and elaborate for its date and handsomely enriched in the 12th century. But it was allowed to fall partly into ruin, as you can see from old photographs at the back of the building today. Gilbert Scott put it to rights quite acceptably, and then – how hard the busy Victorians found it to leave well alone! – Butterfield was allowed to befoul its walls with mosaic decoration not merely hideous but blatantly vulgar. So the poor church is now a thing of interest but not of beauty.

The first castle here, in the full sense of the term, was built in the 20 years or so following 1168. That produced the Keep and the walls of the Inner Bailey – a most unusually elaborate complex, perhaps the first of its kind in western Europe. In the 13th century the outer defences were completed, with their 14 surviving gates and towers. This castle, as a work of national defence always in the hands of the Crown, never of a subject, was far too important to be allowed to decay, like most other English castles, in the 16th and 17th centuries. It remained fully in use, and in the 18th century it began to house a greater military population than ever before, in the barracks that were built within it. Its defences extended underground, and during the Napoleonic Wars both hills became in effect subterranean fortresses, honeycombed with tunnels and gun emplacements. The main developments of the later 19th century were maritime: the construction of the Admiralty Pier, and of a harbour of refuge. Early in the 20th century Dover harbour was capable of containing the whole of the British battle fleet. In the German wars Dover's importance continued still: at its highest in the evacuation from Dunkirk and the Battle of Britain in 1940.

In colour Dover Castle is rather sombre, for it is built of a brownish ragstone, rendered darker by the white chalk and the green grass from which it rises. But a good deal of the lower part of the walls of the Keep is, or was, faced with limestone ashlar from Caen, which is also used at the corners, providing just the vertical emphasis that the building needs.

Dover Castle: the keep and (right) Constable's gate (A. F. Kersting)

The public entrance is through the Constable's Tower, a complex three-lobed structure, rising impressively sheer out of the moat on the south side. Within, you are at once aware of the modern history of the Castle, from the 18th- and 19th-century houses and storerooms that stand inside the walls. All the rooms of the Keep, as usual, are on the upper floors, well above the ground. At a turn in the stairway, by what is now the ticket office, you are suddenly confronted with the Lower Chapel: a very small room, no more, but decorated with richly-carved stonework. You ascend into the two principal rooms, the Great Hall and Great Chamber, which lie side by side. Their appearance was marred in 1800 when the brick vaults were inserted, to provide support for heavy guns mounted above. On this floor are also the Well Chamber – the well goes far down into the natural chalk below the Keep, and two lead pipes are still to be seen, providing a more sophisticated water supply than was usual in the 12th century – and the Upper Chapel, similar in size and structure to its fellow (which is directly below it), except that it is vaulted in stone. Climb up again on to the roof, from which you can take in the whole layout of the Castle, the town, and the harbour.

Though one must think of Dover first in terms of defence by land and sea, the town has always been a considerable commercial port, once noted for its fisheries (whence "Dover soles"), always a point of departure for France. It is not a distinguished place in its own right, but it has a few things besides the Castle that are worth seeing. The Town Hall, originally the Maison Dieu, a medieval hospital, has a range of fine 14th-century windows (filled however with deplorable glass). On the floor below is the town's Museum: a crowded Victorian collection, well kept and recently improved by new lighting. Close by is the tiny chapel of St Edmund, consecrated in 1253 and now repaired with affection and care. The impressive 12th-century refectory of St Martin's Priory forms part of Dover College. The sea front, facing on to the harbour, has two fine things to show: the long handsome range of Waterloo Crescent by Philip Hardwick (1834–8), and – a

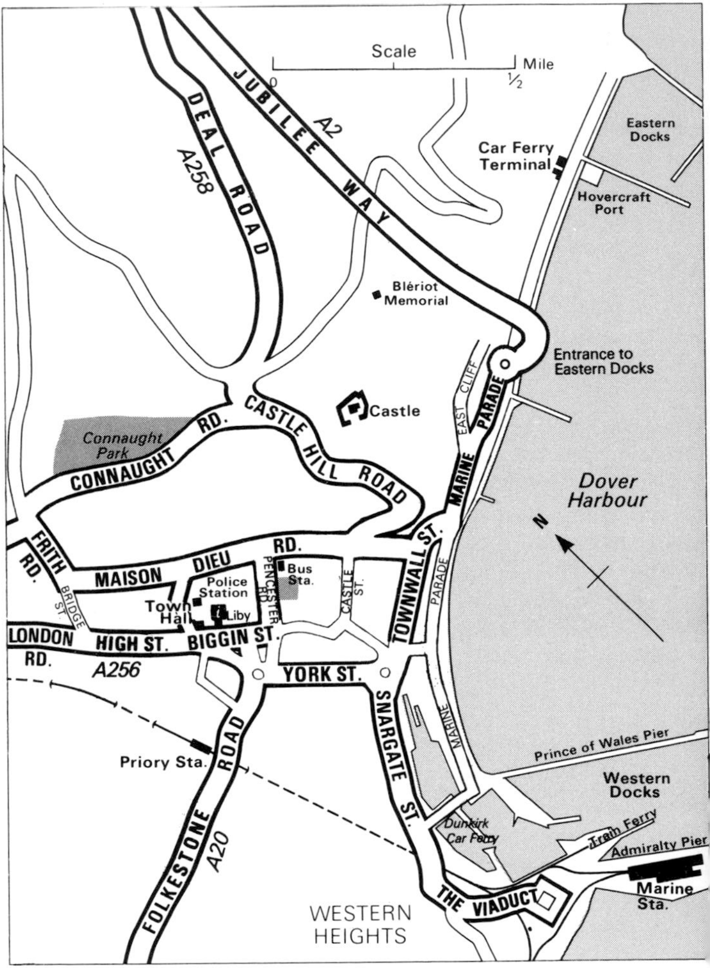

great rarity – an hotel of the 1950s that is a delight to look at. This is the Dover Stage, by Louis Erdi (1956–7), and it shows how good building in concrete can be if it is handled with skill. (For its opposite – of which we have far too much – look at the great slab of the Holiday Inn

The Dover Stage (Architects' Journal)

just across the street at the back.) The name of the Dover Stage was happily chosen, to commemorate the long history of the port as a packet station, just when the car ferries were beginning to revive its road traffic to and from the Continent on a wholly new scale. Since then this business, together with that brought by the hovercraft, has immensely increased Dover's importance. Nearly eight million people now pass through it in a year.

Perhaps I may add that this is by far the finest way to arrive in England, by sea across the English Channel. Where is there, to any country in Europe, an entrance more striking than Dover?

Durham Durham 1C2

Whatever a traveller sees or does not see in England, he must not fail to see Durham.

No one will forget the massing of the cathedral and castle together; and the cathedral itself is one of the great medieval buildings of Europe. They stand on a precipitous hill, rising from a loop in the River Wear, which almost surrounds them. In its site Durham is like Shrewsbury, like Toledo, Besançon, and Berne. It is a town that should be explored on foot. The narrow streets impose numerous parking restrictions; some are closed to cars altogether. The distances involved are not great, and walking offers many rewards. The Durham City Trust publishes some useful leaflets, describing walks. *A Short Tour of Durham*, by B. Colgrave and C. W. Gibby, is based on a single itinerary throughout. Another, much shorter, is sketched at the close of this account.

The city as we know it takes its origin from a particular moment in time, when in 995 the body of St Cuthbert was brought to rest here on its long journey from *Holy Island*. Its guardian Bishop Aldhun and his clergy built a cathedral, consecrated in 999. There was also some kind of fortification, twice besieged by the Scots within the next half-century.

Medieval Durham had a triple importance. The shrine of St Cuthbert made it the most venerated place of pilgrimage in the north of England; the cathedral was the spiritual and administrative centre of a huge diocese; and it was a vitally important fortress in the long warfare between

England and Scotland. Royal powers of government were exercised by the bishops, including a large measure of responsibility for the defence of northern England against the Scots. They amassed great wealth, and the see became one of the richest in England.

Let us begin by looking at the cathedral, with its precinct, and the castle, moving out then into the little city surrounding them.

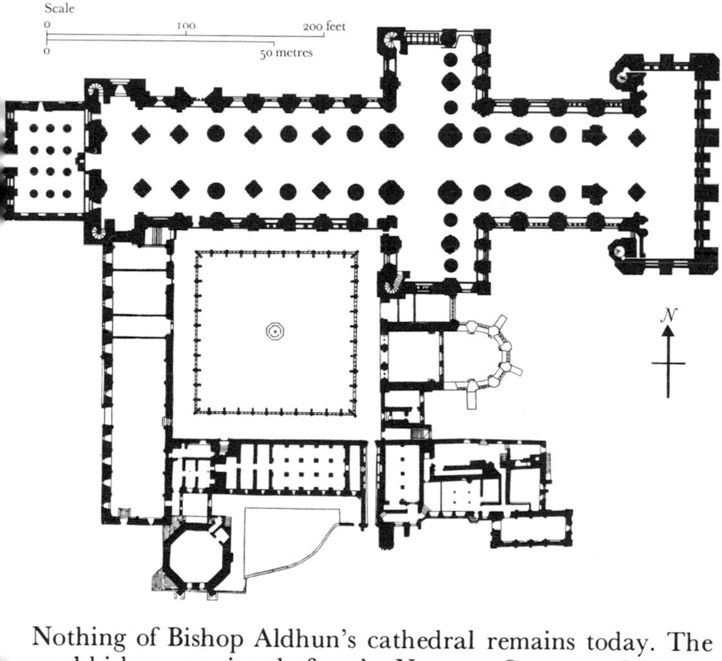

Nothing of Bishop Aldhun's cathedral remains today. The second bishop appointed after the Norman Conquest, William of St Calais, invited Benedictine monks to Durham, and a monastic cathedral of the type peculiar to England (as at *Ely*) resulted. Under him the present cathedral was planned and begun, and most of the building was completed in 40 years (1093–1133). The only substantial additions made to it since are the Galilee at the west end, with the towers that flank it (about 1175–1226); the eastern arm, the Chapel of the Nine Altars (about 1242–80); and the central tower, built in two stages (distinguishable by their differing stone) about 1465–90. The monastery was dissolved in 1539, and its buildings partly destroyed. The cathedral suffered much from Puritan iconoclasm then and in the next century, especially in 1650, when a large number of Scottish prisoners were shut up in it after the battle of Dunbar. The republican government in England treated them inhumanly, denying them fuel to provide them with any warmth. Naturally they tore up the ancient woodwork and burnt it. Much damage had to be repaired after 1660, and largely through the efforts of Bishop John Cosin the cathedral was refurnished. The fabric was restored, not always judiciously, in the 18th century, and again by Sir Gilbert Scott in the 19th.

The cathedral is built of local carboniferous sandstone. It is at first sight sombre, especially outside on a grey day, but it often lights up to a honey colour; inside, under some conditions of light, it glows.

The nave is high, majestic throughout but never ponderous. The eight bays are divided into four pairs, the central pier of each being ornamented with a simple pattern, heavily incised – a diagonal network, zigzags, fluting. The scheme is repeated in the transepts and the chancel, though not so completely.

The Dean and Chapter have resisted the current craze for nave altars, and for that every lover of the building must thank them. The crossing remains unobstructed, and so do the transepts to left and right; the lofty vault of the tower is open above.

Of Scott's marble pulpit and screen Archdeacon Strank says truly that "they might not look so bad anywher else". The chancel, beyond, is richly furnished. The stall (1665) were erected by Bishop Cosin. The bishop's throne

Durham Cathedral: interior from the west (A. F. Kersting

on the right, is a rather florid piece of medieval ostentation due to Bishop Hatfield (d. 1381), who is himself commemorated in effigy beneath it. At the east end, behind the high altar, the pinnacled Neville Screen (1372–80) forms a reredos. It is now a piece of delicate openwork, deprived of all the statues that formerly filled its niches. Though their loss is regrettable, it is a mercy that no Victorian dean thought fit to replace them with statuary of his own time.

On a platform behind the Neville Screen the shrine of St Cuthbert was placed. It was destroyed in 1540, but by a surprising decision of Henry VIII himself the saint's uncorrupted body was preserved. Reburied under a plain slab, it is still there now.

Beyond lies the Chapel of the Nine Altars, which forms a vast eastern transept – and from the outside what is perhaps the finest east front of any English cathedral except *Wells*. It is a magnificent extension in high Gothic to the Romanesque building. The floor was made lower than that of the rest of the church, so giving the arches and the vault above that sense of soaring height so often lacking in the great English churches of the 13th century. The colour was varied, in the way that was then fashionable, by dark columns of marbled stone, from Frosterley, 20 miles west of Durham. The finest element in the whole composition is the north window, best seen from close underneath it at the east wall. Here the double structure is apparent, and the strong, graceful mouldings of the arches, two of them intersecting at the top.

At the opposite end of the cathedral is the Galilee (for that term, see *Ely*): a strange building, broader than it is long, extending westwards to the very edge of the cliff above the river. When compared with the main nave of the cathedral, it strikingly illustrates the range of Romanesque design. The earlier grandeur has gone entirely, giving place to a slender lightness, even a touch of fantasy imparted by the saw-tooth decoration of the arches. It is faintly reminiscent of Moorish Spain. The eastern wall of the Galilee provided for three altars. Above the left-hand one are parts of three paintings of the 11th century: a rare survival in England. In front of the right-hand altar is the tomb of the Venerable Bede (d. 735) – his bones having been stolen by a Durham monk from the monastery at Jarrow.

The cathedral contains no other monuments of outstanding interest. But notice two more magnificent legacies from Bishop Cosin: the towering font-cover and the organ-screen, now disused as such and standing at the back of the south aisle of the nave. Near it is the entrance to the cloisters and (immediately to the right) the staircase leading up to the Monks' Dormitory.

This enormous room, nearly 200 ft long and 40 ft wide, covered by a massive timber roof, was built in 1398–1404. It is now a library, and also a museum, with an important collection of Anglo-Saxon stone crosses and gravestones, two fine embroidered copes, and a changing display of documents from the very rich archives of the cathedral.

Its finest possessions are now assembled in a new Treasury (1978: architect Ian Curry) in the undercroft below. The relics of St Cuthbert and the objects associated with them are the greatest treasure of all. St Cuthbert's coffin, made of oak with figures and symbols incised in it, is the one borne by his followers through their wanderings from *Holy Island*. His pectoral cross, of garnets set in gold, is here, and a portable altar that was probably his too, encased in a silver covering made a little later. There are also some vestments – girdle, stole, and maniple – dating from early in the 10th century, perhaps given by King Athelstan to St Cuthbert's community at Chester-le-Street in 934. They are English work of exceptional beauty; judged as fine as anything of the same age in Italy or France, perhaps finer.

Many of the cathedral's other possessions are also shown here: service books, two of them given to the monastery by Bishops St Calais and Pudsey; the head of a 12th-century crozier; silver-gilt plate – gorgeous pieces from Cosin, chaster ones of the 18th century; two more embroidered copes. Riches have here been compressed into a little room, with much ingenuity of arrangement and display.

A doorway leads out of the south-east corner of the cloisters into College Green: a delightful enclosure lined with good houses, presenting a Georgian appearance now, though some are older than the 18th century. A gateway leads out into the South Bailey, a street we shall be traversing later from another direction.

For the moment, let us go back through the cathedral and out the other side, on to Palace Green. (The north door bears a splendid bronze sanctuary knocker, which is at present removed for restoration.) At this point a new element in the history of Durham has to be taken into account. In 1831–2 the Bishop and the Dean and Chapter were persuaded to establish a University here, by the sacrifice of some of their possessions and revenues: a sacrifice that might perhaps have been forced on them (they were exceptionally rich), yet was made voluntarily and with benevolence. The Castle passed into the hands of the University, and the buildings that face on to Palace Green, later, one by one. The Green itself is under the University's control.* Some of the buildings now contain lecture rooms. Most of the western range forms part of the University Library. At the north-east corner stands a tall 17th-century brick house with a handsome porch. From beside it there is a good view of the Keep of the Castle, into which we can now move.

A small part of the present building dates back to abou[t] 1080. There is work in it of every century since. Th[e] Keep, the highest part and in the distance the most impressive is virtually the work of Anthony Salvin, for it was a dilapi dated shell when he undertook its reconstruction in 1840 to provide accommodation for the newly-founded University

* Would that the University would bring itself to forbid the parkin[g] of cars at least for one brief period in the week! Their presence dreadfull[y] disfigures the amplest of all views of the cathedral.

The gateway, with its richly-carved Romanesque main arch, set in an 18th-century framework, gives admission to the courtyard, round which all the chief buildings of the castle, except the Keep, are ranged. Bishop Cosin's hand is in evidence here again, in the porch and in the powerful buttresses beside it. On the left inside are the Buttery and Kitchen, a remodelling by Bishop Fox in the late 15th century; on the right, the Great Hall, a 14th-century work (with a fine timber roof of that date) much Victorianised – and agreeably in the case of the big window, with Kempe's glass of 1882.

The Black Staircase is one of the most remarkable of Cosin's undertakings, dating from 1662 (compare *Astley Hall*). The balustrades are lusciously decorated with foliage. The staircase was designed to stand clear, without pillars; but support soon proved necessary, and the present plain columns were inserted. On the first floor Bishop Tunstall created a Gallery in the 16th century. Pudsey's Doorway (the former entrance to his hall, now destroyed) is in the centre of it: one of the most splendid pieces of late Romanesque in the country. At the end of the Gallery notice the fine terracotta bust of George II by Rysbrack.

Tunstall's Chapel comes next, lengthened by Bishops Cosin and Crewe late in the 17th century. The Chapel contains some interesting woodwork: the early Tudor stalls were brought from the palace at Bishop's Auckland, and the screen is Cosin's. The organ is part of one made for the cathedral in 1683.

On the floor above is the Norman Gallery, built by Bishop Pudsey and showing in its window-frames the brilliant effect to be produced by zigzag decoration, exemplified also in the Galilee of the cathedral.

Finally, a plunge below into the basement, to the Norman Chapel, part of the first castle building, dating from about 1080. It is a small rectangle with six lofty circular piers and a groined vault, dark, mysterious, deeply impressive. This is the oldest room in the Castle, and in Durham.

There is still much more to see in the little city. One

or two things may be mentioned here, lying close by; and then a walk will be proposed taking in another most notable element in the place, hardly yet hinted at.

The ancient commercial centre of the city was the Market Place, with the good Victorian church of St Nicholas lying

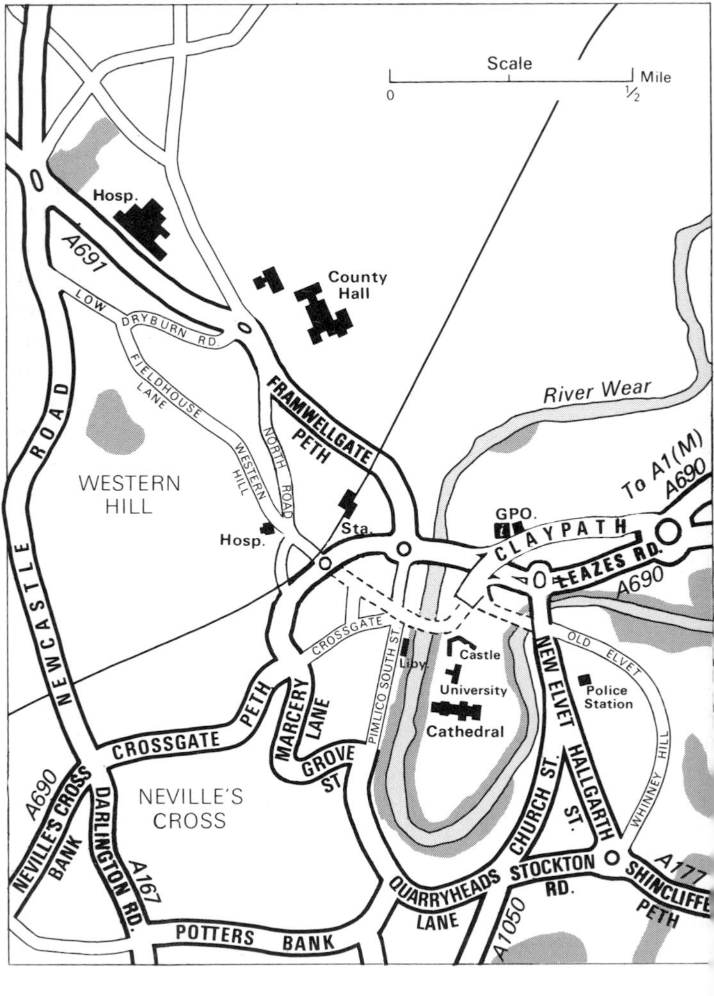

along its northern side. The streets swirl away from it steeply down to two medieval bridges: Framwellgate Bridge on the west and Elvet Bridge on the east, both medieval structures sympathetically widened, and both now carrying pedestrians only. Durham used to be a notorious traffic nightmare. Resolute and careful replanning has now shown what can be done, even on such an intractable site, to alleviate this evil.

Across the river to the east Old Elvet is a handsome street, leading to an agreeable green, with the low Assize Courts on the right. The street is disgraced by a building of 1895, fiery, arrogant, and coarse-grained. The sin of erecting it is not to be ascribed to its present occupant, the University. It is the former Shire Hall. This is the only ugly building of any large scale or pretensions in Durham.

Now for the walk. At the foot of the steep hill leading up from Framwellgate Bridge, on the right, is a narrow passage, Moatside Lane. It affords a better idea than can be got anywhere else, at close quarters, of the Castle as a fortified building, the Keep rising on the almost sheer rock. The Lane was used by pilgrims arriving from the west to visit St Cuthbert's shrine. It leads into Sadler Street, which is continuous with two others, North and South Bailey. They form the spinal cord of the peninsula. Though there are individual buildings of special interest in them (the Georgian double shopfront at No. 44 Sadler Street, for example; No. 3 South Bailey) it is the streetscape as a whole that is remarkable. South Bailey curves gently, cobbled for most of its length, with the tiny church of St Mary the Less delicately set in an opening in it. (The building is of 1846, with old materials re-used, and contains a fine 13th-century figure of Christ on the north wall of the chancel.) The end of South Bailey brings a great surprise: the Water Gate of 1778 and then the Prebends' Bridge across the river. The bridge is itself a splendid piece of masonry (George Nicholson, 1777), and it is the introduction to a fresh and exquisite pleasure: the River Banks.

Durham cathedral from the Wear (A. F. Kersting)

Both the steep sides of the Wear are planted with woods. There are no buildings visible whatever except two very small ones at the water's edge: the Old Fulling Mill, and opposite it the Old Corn Mill (regrettably washed the colour of tinned salmon). In and out of the trees and along by the river there are walks. They are walks only: wheeled traffic is entirely kept away. Here one can stroll or sit by the hour. The west front of the cathedral, with the Galilee, soars up out of the trees. Then, two-thirds of the way round the loop, the new Kingsgate foot-bridge has been built, as firmly of the 20th century as the Prebends' Bridge is of the 18th, or the other two of the Middle

Ages. It is a slender concrete structure (Ove Arup, 1963). Climb up to it, walk across, and you receive the full impact of the cathedral's broad east front. So back on to the peninsula, up to the North Bailey and on to Palace Green.

This is certainly one of the best town walks in England. And where, outside England, will one find a landscape of woods and water so closely integrated with a town itself?

Ely Cambridgeshire 5B2

Ely is a very small town, of about 10,000 people: with *Wells*, the smallest ancient cathedral city in England. Except for Cambridge, 17 miles away, it is far from any large centre of population. It stands isolated on a low hill on the edge of the Fens. Why should there be a cathedral here at all?

A monastery was established on this hill by Etheldreda, formerly Queen of Northumbria, in 673. It was a dry place above the Fens, which were then quite undrained. Etheldreda's monastery was a double house, for men and women. She ruled the whole institution. The Danes ravaged the monastery in 870, but it was reconstructed 100 years later as a house of Benedictine monks. In 1081 Simeon, a relative of William the Conqueror, was appointed abbot. He put in hand a reconstruction of the church. In 1106 relics of the foundress, now recognised as a saint, were placed in a shrine in the new building, which became a place of pilgrimage. Three years later Ely was made the seat of a bishop. The church became the cathedral of his diocese, but the monastery also continued until 1539, when it was dissolved by Henry VIII. Under Henry VIII also St Etheldreda's shrine was destroyed, and pilgrimage ceased. Since 1539 the church has been a cathedral, and nothing else.

If you arrive at Ely by train, or by road from Newmarket (off the A11), go up Station Road and turn right into Broad Street. Then walk left through an iron gateway 200 yards further on. That will bring an immediate surprise. The cathedral appears in its entire length, across an open meadow.

Ely cathedral from the south (Eric G. Meadows)

It might almost be in open country, like *Beverley Minster* – like no other great church in England, and very few anywhere else.

The elevation is almost unique, a single tall tower at the west end and a centrally-placed octagonal lantern. The cathedral is built mostly of limestone from Barnack, beyond Peterborough, brought round by water. Its roofs are covered in silver-grey lead.

The church was erected in four distinct stages. The transepts, the nave, and the tall western tower belong to the 12th and 13th centuries. The chancel was reconstructed from 1234 onwards. In 1322 the central tower fell in, necessitating an immediate reconstruction. The result was the Octagon, erected in 1328–42. The Lady Chapel (on the far side of the cathedral) was built in 1321–53. About 1400 the west tower was heightened by its top stage, a second octagon; and there all major building stopped.

The footpath up the meadow arrives at a burly medieval

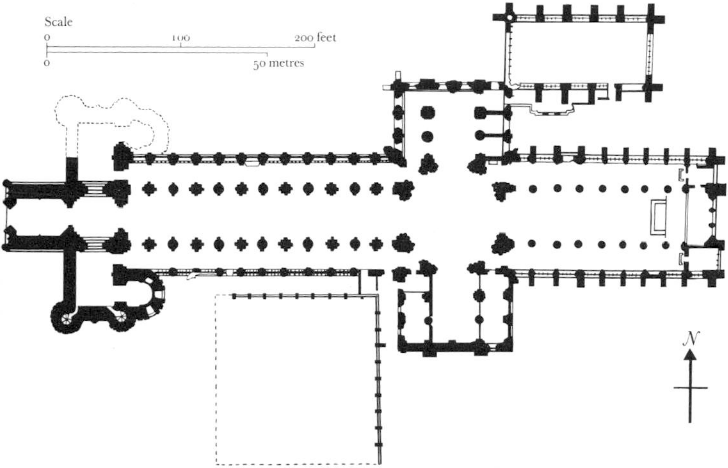

gateway, the Ely Porta. You then turn right into a street called The Gallery. On its right-hand (south) side all the buildings are medieval, belonging to the monastery and now part of the King's School. The street leads to Palace Green, a grassy forecourt in front of the cathedral.

In every English cathedral the west front is a weak element. At Ely the weakness is due not to an architect's failure, as it is at *Salisbury* and Winchester, but to the disappearance of the northern (left-hand) wing, which collapsed in the 15th century and was never rebuilt. Had it been there, this would have been a fine composition. It is still, in its mutilated form, powerfully impressive.

The west tower, standing singly, is found commonly in parish churches, but in no other English cathedral. The entrance at its foot is through a very big Galilee porch (so named because the celebrant, heading a procession, entered it first, as Christ led his disciples into Galilee after the Resurrection). This was added about 1250.

Inside the door the nave stretches away, immensely long, narrow and therefore apparently high, surmounted by a flat wooden ceiling painted in the 19th century. Immediately to the right is the surviving arm of the west front, now forming a baptistery, its walls richly patterned with 12th-century arcading. The nave is lighted by very large windows, both in the south aisle (those opposite are a reconstruction of the 15th century) and on the first floor, in the spacious gallery. There is no figure carving; everything is entirely plain.

As one walks from the nave up to the central Octagon, the whole space broadens out, lighted by windows diagonally placed (a device rare in medieval building). The tower that collapsed was of stone. The Octagon was built largely of timber. If that lessened the weight placed on the piers beneath, the construction was made more difficult by the decision – vital to the effect – that the whole space was to be enlarged; the nave, the transepts, and the choir were all shortened for this purpose. When the lantern was added, about 1335, it was of timber too, its weight supported largely on a frame behind the vault. The colouring and the glass are of the 19th century; but much lower down, on the diagonal walls, there are eight carvings of the life of St Etheldreda, which are a delightful part of the original decoration.

The Octagon is one of the greatest strokes of genius in English architecture. Who designed it? A monk of Ely, writing later in the 14th century, said that the idea came from the Sacrist, Alan of Walsingham, and there is no good reason for rejecting that statement. But how far did the "idea" extend? Whose advice was sought, in a work so complex and unprecedented? All we can say with near-certainty is that the master-carpenter in charge of the timber work was William Hurley, the most distinguished man of the time in that business.

The choir beyond is full of elaborate stone-carving. The three western bays were reconstructed as part of the scheme for the Octagon and covered with a lierne vault (see p. 188). They now contain the very rich wooden stalls that originally stood under the Octagon. These are among the finest sets in England, though unhappily their canopies now bear feeble figures added at the instance of Sir Gilbert Scott. The six remaining bays are vaulted more plainly. They were built under Bishop Northwold between 1234 and 1252, with a free use of Purbeck marble to provide a contrast with the limestone.

The Lady Chapel is unusually placed, beside and not beyond the chancel, and reached now through the north transept. It is a very broad rectangle, decorated with sumptuous carving round its walls and covered with the most elaborate vault in the building. Plain glass makes everything clear: the fascinating decoration, which as Sir Nikolaus Pevsner says "gives the vivid impression of a movement swinging and rocking forward and upward"; and also the abominable vandalism that has wrecked the figures and obliterated their meaning. In the Puritan eastern counties, Ely cathedral was a target for destruction of this kind, at the Reformation and again in the 17th century. Hence the paucity of ancient glass throughout the building. Barbarism has mauled here a complex work of art.

Although nothing important was added inside the cathedral after the Lady Chapel was completed, two small chantry chapels were built at the east end. The earlier is Bishop Alcock's (north side), begun in 1488. The decoration of its canopied front is extraordinarily rich, even over-ripe, the knobbly shapes assorting strangely with the fan vault behind them. Bishop West's chantry, opposite, is later, built in 1525–33, and plainer. It has kept its original fine iron gates.

The cathedral contains some notable monuments. The outstanding medieval ones are in the north choir aisle. Bishop Northwold's stands abreast of the high altar. The effigy was splendid, though it is decayed and has suffered from vandalism. Further west is Bishop Kilkenny's (d. 1257), more perfect now, a very pure piece of sculpture. At the back of the aisle is Bishop Nigel's (d. 1169), in black Tournai marble, depicting his soul held in a napkin by an angel with magnificent wings.

Two other monuments, very different from these, are near the entrance to the remaining fragment of the cloisters, reached by a door in the south nave aisle. One is a tombstone mounted in the wall with an epitaph entitled "The Spiritual Railway"

(1845). The other, beyond an outer door, is to Humphry Smith (d. 1743) with a pleasant portrait bust and an admirable inscription composed by a London architect for whom he worked.

Near the west end of the south aisle is the Prior's Door (kept bolted in winter, but opened on request). Its exterior presents splendid carving of the 12th century, especially the two angels, looking back over their shoulders at the seated figure of Christ in the middle.

To the south of the cathedral, within the King's School, is Prior Crauden's chapel, reached by a spiral stairway. It dates from the same time as the Octagon. The stone vault has gone, replaced with a plain wooden one, and it is dominated by five Victorian figures in the east window, big and extremely coarse; they seem to occupy the whole minute space. However, the floor is really notable: one of the most perfectly preserved medieval tiled floors in the country. The tiles are laid as a mosaic, and lovely in patina and colour.

On the opposite side of the cathedral, bordering the High Street, is a range of 15th-century monastic buildings, including the Almonry and the Sacristy, with the Steeple Gate leading into the precinct. They demonstrate clearly the relationship between a large monastery and its town. The precinct is enclosed tightly. One side of the street is for trade alone; the other belongs to the Church, fortified against external interference.

At the east end of the High Street the Market Place opens out, quite small, with a good Georgian building, Archer House, at the diagonally opposite corner, roofed in the nice variegated tiles of Cambridgeshire, buff, yellow, and red. The High Street is continued by Fore Hill, dropping downwards and framing a prospect of the Fens, far away into the distance.

The little city is pleasant, without any secular buildings of distinction. It has one agreeable thing to show. Palace Green – so named from the red-brick Bishop's Palace (now a school) begun by Bishop Alcock and remodelled in the 17th century – is a triangular space, opening out into another beyond. St Mary's, the parish church, stands here: built about 1200, with a good doorway and elegant arcades inside. Nothing could be simpler, more unconsidered, than these two communicating greens. They make a very happy piece of informal English townscape.

One's final thought of Ely is likely to be of the cathedral seen from a distance, perhaps from far away across the Fens. Its hill rises up less than 70 ft. But that lift is enough. It dominates the countryside for miles in every direction.

Esthwaite Cumbria 1A3

A little has been said about the Lake District already (p. 19). Two lakes are described here. *Ullswater* is large and famous. Esthwaite Water is small, and though it is beloved by naturalists it is not in general well known. But it is deeply endearing from its own qualities and associations, all brought together within a very small compass.

The lake and its vale form a miniature: the water barely two miles long, and at its broadest half a mile across. The hills that rise from it are not high, running up to only 700–800 ft. But the presence of the mountains is here nevertheless. The Langdale Pikes stand out in the background to the north, the Old Man of Coniston, much closer, to the west.

Esthwaite can be approached easily from any direction. A good way is to come across the ferry over Windermere from Bowness, through the village of Sawrey, along the eastern shore of the lake to Hawkshead, then back down the opposite side, either to Sawrey again to complete the circuit or on by the road through the woods to the south. The important thing is to go right round the lake, for its aspects are all different.

If you take this way, there is at the beginning – unless you are prepared for it – a surprise. The village of Sawrey comprises two hamlets, Far and Near. Hill Top Cottage in Near Sawrey was bought by Beatrix Potter in 1905, chiefly from the earnings from the first six of her tales for children.

When she died, well-to-do largely owing to the success of her writing, she left it to the National Trust, together with 4,000 acres of land, in Troutbeck below the Kirkstone Pass and in this neighbourhood.

She was a most remarkable woman: intensely lonely for more than half her life, confiding in a journal kept in cypher. She was brought to the Lake District on holidays and came to feel for it with passion. It fills her little books: the village shop at Sawrey in *Ginger and Pickles*, the flowers in the cottage gardens, her own farmyard – they are all there, every detail observed. Sawrey has thus made its way, to be read of in half a dozen languages and in millions of copies of her books across the world.

Esthwaite Water from the north-east (Roy Nash)

The lake lies immediately below. To many people, especially those coming from across the Atlantic and from hotter and drier countries, the pre-eminent beauty of England is its colour, the green it displays all the year round. Anyone who wishes to see that green at its most intense should come here. The whole landscape is green, in every tint from lime and emerald to the quietest sage. There are patches of bracken, and the water is fringed with reeds that are buff or pale pink according to the light; but they and the water itself are hardly more than foils to the green.

That is one thing striking about Esthwaite. Another is that its banks are totally uninvaded by any development. This is not accidental. It is due to the protection of the whole vale by its landowners, the Sandys family of Graythwaite Hall. They have shown the same jealous and salutary care for it as, in the far south-west, the Hamlyn-Williams have shown for *Clovelly*.

At the head of the lake, and back from it, is the tiny town of Hawkshead: a town not a village, with a little square, a court house at the north end (now a museum), a grammar school, and a church worth visiting, where judicious repair has brought up the 17th- and 18th-century paintings on its walls. It contains a monument to the parents of Archbishop Sandys of York. He came from Hawkshead and founded its grammar school in 1575. The little building lies just below. Among its pupils was Wordsworth, who was here from 1778 to 1787. The memories of his schooldays are the stuff of the first Book of *The Prelude*, the brilliant climax of it the boys' skating on Esthwaite at night.

The Hawkshead end of the lake, Esthwaite North Fen, has been carefully studied over the past 60 years and is now a national nature reserve. The Fen is advancing at an appreciable rate into the lake. Esthwaite Water is very shallow, and its vegetation particularly rich and varied. The western shore is more carefully planted than the other, with a little classical house, Esthwaite Lodge, in its own small park, and Esthwaite Hall further down. Still the same green prevails everywhere, but on the heights opposite the trees are broken into by a large tract of bracken. These heights are easily accessible by a road and path from Sawrey. They form a saddle between Esthwaite and Windermere. On one side is Windermere, big, busy with boats, lined on the far bank with houses – and on the other the tiny Esthwaite, still quiet and completely retired.

Farnham Surrey 5A4

There are two towns of Farnham: the old one lying along the north bank of the River Wey, the new one to the south of it. Rather unusually in England, the two have been kept separate, to the advantage of both. The new town is a pleasant place, brick-built in the English idioms of the past 30 years. The old town is one of the most completely harmonious in England.

The place enjoys a combination of advantages: its site, in a narrow but ample valley, rich land famous for its hops; the Castle, built and held by the powerful bishops of Winchester, on the valley's steep northern flank; delicately-toned brick, readily available for building in the 18th century; the jealous care exercised over development in the past 60 years. The result is something remarkable indeed when one considers that London is less than 40 miles away, with electric trains to and fro every half-hour.

The plan of the old town is simple. The Borough, the central link in the chain of streets, is narrow, noisy, and short. The two most interesting streets open out of it, at right angles to each other, close to the arcaded Town Hall. This is a building of 1930, designed by Harold Falkner, the architect chiefly responsible for the town's preservation. It replaced a fearsome Victorian Gothic affair, harshly out of sympathy with all its surroundings. This represented a notable achievement in promoting the harmony of the townscape, made possible by the leadership of a jeweller and citizen, Charles Borelli.

Castle Street, wide and curving, is entirely satisfactory from bottom to top: the houses predominantly of red brick, just

Farnham: Castle Street (A. F. Kersting)

sufficiently variegated with white or grey stucco, the Georgian character agreeably broken once by the sharp pointed gables of the little Windsor Almshouses, half-way up on the right. There is a contrast between the two sides of the street. The left-hand (west) side consists of quite small houses, single or occasionally in pairs, uninterruptedly delightful. Opposite, there is more variety, higher up some pleasing self-consequence. At the top of the curve, buildings disappear. The trees close in to form a tunnel; and a long flight of shallow steps gives access to the Castle.

Directly you are through the gate-house another scene, totally different, opens out in front: a smooth, level lawn, part of a walled garden, dominated by the brick tower built by Bishop Waynflete about 1470. This is a noble work, at once massive and refined: one of the masterpieces of brick building in England. Behind it lies the main body of the Castle. It was really a large country house, for the use of the bishops on their constant journeys between Winchester and London, built first by Henry de Blois in the 12th century and substantially refashioned by George Morley late in the 17th. The upper windows, and the lawn in front, survey the whole town and its valley.*

Descending Castle Street (admirably terminated by the early-Victorian building of the National Westminster Bank) and turning right, you come into West Street. Though busy with traffic, it reveals its character straight away through its slightly sinuous course; and as soon as you look above the level of the shop-fronts the real interest of its houses becomes apparent. Some of that interest extends into the shops themselves. No. 20, for example, has a heavily-decorated plaster ceiling of the late 17th century. Further on, shop-fronts grow fewer. Two grand brick houses appear on the left: Willmer House of 1718, now the town's admirable Museum, and Sandford House (1757) next door. But, except at the Castle, grandeur is alien to Farnham. Fine though these two houses are, one may well prefer No. 90, on the opposite side of the street. The most enjoyable thing of all, throughout Farnham, is harmonious diversity: the irregular line of red and yellow roof tiles, for example, on Nos. 70–73 and 80–88. Walking slowly along the street, one becomes aware that it occupies a shelf in the valley. Here and there, looking up a side turning to the north, hedges and cornfields are to be seen, only a few hundred yards away; and Downing Street, again on a falling curve, leads south to the church and the river.

The church (St Andrew) was very harshly restored in 1855, though a valiant effort has recently been made to repair that fatal damage. It is not a mean building, however: big throughout, with a huge four-square tower, set in a spacious churchyard, bounded by a wall of trim and ancient brick. Here is the grave of the town's most famous son William Cobbett, who derived many of his best qualities

* The Castle (now an educational institution) is open to visitors every Wednesday afternoon; the best time to visit Farnham, for most of the shops close early on that day, and the traffic is reduced in proportion.

from his ancestry and nurture in Surrey. His birthplace, once the Jolly Farmers inn but now renamed after him, stands by the river. If he came back and looked at Farnham now he would find much to growl at – he was the world's most accomplished grumbler. But a fair-minded visitor today must think chiefly of the town's good fortune, in the vigilant zeal of those who have loved and cherished it.

Fingest and Turville Buckinghamshire 4F2

A broad belt of chalk lies across south-eastern England, almost continuously from Dorset to Norfolk. The Thames cuts through it, and the hills for some 25 miles to the north-east of this gap are known as the Chilterns, stretching as far as the neighbourhood of Tring. Geologically they are no more than the central section of the chalk belt, but the landscape of the Chilterns is quite different from that of the bare hills adjoining them to the north, in Bedfordshire and Cambridgeshire, and the Berkshire Downs on the south (see *Uffington and Ashdown*). The Chilterns are not bare at all but heavily wooded, above all with beech trees, and in that lies their special distinction.

The southern end of this country, in Oxfordshire, is characterised by commons and heaths, by small clearings in the woods. Then further north in Buckinghamshire the hills and valleys become steeper and more frequent. Within this large tract of country there is not one substantial town – though Hemel Hempstead, High Wycombe, and Aylesbury are not far away, and it is only 30 or 40 miles to London.

There are two ways of approaching the Chilterns, and you can choose which you prefer or find easiest. To see them at their most dramatic you need to come at them from the plain to the north and west, from Oxford say or from Aylesbury. Then they appear as a ridge of chalk hills, filling the skyline, and you climb up them quite steeply. If you approach them from the London side, you will see them in another shape. From the south and east the hills rise almost imperceptibly until you find yourself in a tangle of little by-roads running through woods and down into valleys. There is no drama here, but a gradual slow entry into seclusion. Let us take one journey of this second sort as a sample. It starts from Marlow and ends up at Henley – two pretty riverside towns, both worth visiting in their own right.

North-westwards out of Marlow you take A482, a pleasant but uneventful road, for four and a half miles to Bolter End and then turn off to the west, dropping down to Fingest. The old village is tiny; two rows of brick and timber houses in an L-shape, embracing a churchyard screened by tall trees. Behind lies the church (St Bartholomew), whose tower is massive in relation to the rest of the building, with pairs of round-headed openings at the top and surmounted by a double gable. The lowest stage of the tower may originally have comprised the whole nave of a small church. The pairs of lights at the top are the only sophisticated thing here. The bishops of Lincoln had a manor-house at Fingest; perhaps this adornment owed something to them. The gables are of brick and timber, an incongruous addition to the flint and rubble tower yet one that now entirely accords with it. Behind, there is a steep green slope, crowned by woods. If you go on to the west towards them, in less than a mile you reach Turville.

This is a slightly larger village, also shapely in a quite un-selfconscious way. Its centre is a small three-sided green, with the pub at one corner, low red-brick cottages on two sides and on the third the church. The church (St Mary) turns away, again at an acute angle. The tower is again broad, but this time low; the uplift comes from the tall trees behind it. No landscape architect could have created anything so satisfying. In its own way the centre of Turville is a perfect village composition – except that it was never deliberately composed. Everything is well kept, without any tiresome fussiness; but how fragile it all is can be seen from the unpleasant row of council houses just across the road from the church. It is mercifully tucked away from the view of anyone standing beside the pub; but another such row, and the whole thing could be ruined.

Fingest church (A. F. Kersting)

Turville: the Green (B.T.A.)

High above, the hill to the north is crowned by a white-painted windmill, lacking its sails and used now as a house. It makes a splendid eye-catcher, seen for miles around.

From Turville the road leads on to the north-west through woodlands to Christmas Common, then to Watlington Hill on the north face of the Chilterns with the whole plain of Oxfordshire lying below. You can come back another way, no less delightful, by Turville Heath, and then southwards down the Hambleden Valley to Hambleden itself, a beautiful brick-built village, and so to Henley.

Some people think the Chilterns tame, and their scale is certainly small. Yet they have their surprises. The road from Turville to Ibstone climbs up, on curves and through a tunnel of trees, at 1 in 6; there is room on it for one car only, with no passing-place. And no one who has seen the Chiltern beeches in October will ever forget the sight.

Gibside Tyne and Wear 1C2

Here is the ruin of a great estate, which yet possesses three of its finest elements in perfection. It came into the possession of the Bowes family through marriage in 1713. They were already rich coalowners. This addition much augmented their wealth and their political power in County Durham. Sir George Bowes, who succeeded in 1722 at the age of 21, was distinguished as a man of business – one of the "Grand Allies", who largely dominated the development of the Durham coalfield – and as a man of taste. He took the Jacobean house he inherited and added to it a wing, not in the Georgian mode but in the style of the original, together with a series of other detached buildings, stables, a Gothic banqueting house, and an orangery. Meanwhile he was redesigning the whole surrounding landscape in the steep valley of the Derwent. About 1747 he laid out a broad avenue above the house, planting it with Turkey oaks, and 10 years later he terminated its north-eastern vista with a colossal statue of British Liberty, placed on a pillar 140 ft high. At the opposite end of the avenue he decided to erect a mausoleum, but he died in 1760 before it was built. His successor began it. It was carried through to completion, not as a mausoleum but as a church, in 1812. The design was due to James Paine; but he died in 1789, and the last stage of the work may have been undertaken by David Stephenson of Newcastle.

In form it follows closely the general plan of Palladio's Villa Rotonda. It is a square building with a portico, crowned

Gibside church (Country Life)

by a low dome. When you enter you find that each corner is also a miniature domed building. Perfectly plain Georgian sash windows flood the whole interior with clear light. The altar is centrally placed, and behind it rises what must be one of the supreme examples of the three-decker pulpit, with clerk's desk and reading desk below. This belongs to the last phase of the work and is very like what Stephenson put into his splendid church of All Saints, Newcastle, though more lofty and perhaps even finer. There are four square pews for the Bowes family and their dependents, one in each corner of the building; with two others, semicircular, for what general congregation there might be. The unusual timber chosen for all this work is cherrywood. Except for the blue of the altar-cloth and carpets, no strong colour appears here at all.

When you come out, walk slowly down the length of the noble avenue, running along a ledge in the thickly-wooded valley towards the monument. This brings you past the wreck of the orangery and the house – the trees growing up inside its walls. The contrast between the ruins of all this wealth and elegance and the perfection of what remains intact is poignant.

Gloucester Gloucestershire 4D2

Among the chief medieval English churches as we have them today, Gloucester cathedral is one of the great innovators. It may claim a rarer distinction than that. The earliest works in a new style can seldom be reckoned among the best. Gloucester is an outstanding exception to that rule. In the 14th century it produced what had been seen never before on so large a scale, and this first effort came close to perfection.

Gloucester was not a cathedral in the Middle Ages but a Benedictine abbey; the see of Gloucester was created only in 1541, after the abbey had been dissolved. The cathedral was reconstructed from a smaller church over a period of about 30 years from 1089. To that time belongs more than might appear of the present building. The nave, the crypt under the chancel, the ground-plan and part of the lower structure of the chancel itself, all date from these years, round about 1100. Already here there is innovation: for the Romanesque arcades in the nave seem to be the earliest in a series confined to the Severn basin – found also at Tewkesbury and Pershore – in which very plain, massive cylindrical piers are used, rising to a great height, carrying arches that are markedly narrow. The proportions are entirely different here from those of the big Romanesque churches going up elsewhere in the same years, at *Ely* and *Norwich* and *Durham*. This nave was given an elegant Gothic vault

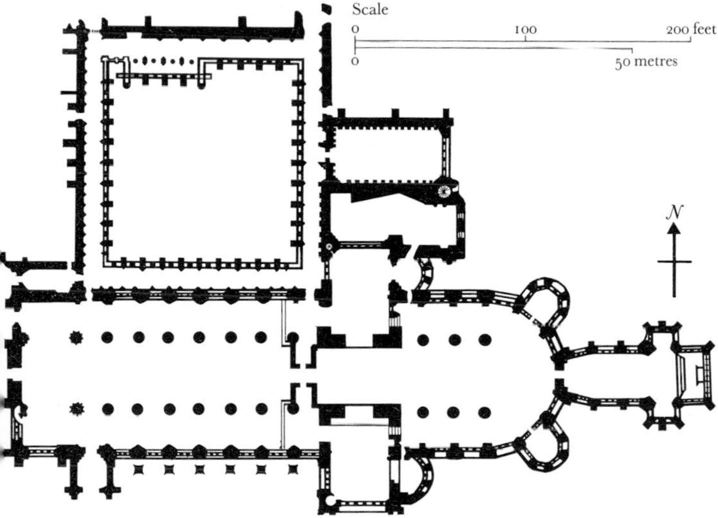

in the mid 13th century; the south aisle was rebuilt about 1320, its windows elaborately decorated with the ball-flower ornament then in fashion. From the middle of the nave one can see the whole development of stone vaulting, the successive modes from the 12th century to the 14th: from the Norman in the north aisle to the Early English high vault and the richer one over the south aisle. Beyond the organ there appears something richer still.

Such then was the church in 1327. In that year Edward II

was murdered at *Berkeley*, 16 miles away. Abbot Thoky of Gloucester took a bold political gamble in agreeing to accept the corpse for burial. The gamble succeeded. Very quickly the dead king came to be venerated as a saint. His son Edward III soon came to favour the cult, and with the money that poured in from its devotees the Abbot was able to begin a reconstruction of the eastern part of the church. The work started with the south transept, rebuilt into its present form in 1331–7. The design came from London, from the Chapter House of St Paul's and St Stephen's Chapel, Westminster – buildings both destroyed by fire, in 1666 and 1834. The London innovation consisted in running the mullions of the windows vertically to the top of the frame. But at Gloucester a variant emerged in the use of horizontal transoms, producing, except at the upper edge where the Gothic curve persisted, a series of rectangular panels. The 19th-century architectural historians called the style "Perpendicular", on account of its vertical emphasis. "Rectilinear", the alternative term devised then, is really more accurate.

The rebuilding of the south transept was followed immediately by that of the choir, which began about 1337 and was completed within about 20 years. Here, on the largest scale, the new ideas came into their own. The earlier Norman work was not wholly destroyed; it survives in the ambulatory behind the high altar. Rather, the new work of the 14th century formed a skin covering it, together with a great vertical extension, which takes the vault to a height of 92 ft. The vault is an early one of the lierne pattern: the liernes being minor ribs (multiplied here very numerously) not connected with a central boss or with one of the main springers at the sides. It was a design that came to find great favour in England and was developed further, for example at Canterbury and *Norwich*. The east wall of this choir at Gloucester is virtually one huge window, the largest with stone tracery in England. It retains most of its original glass, much of it commemorating the distinguished dead who had fallen at Crecy and elsewhere in the early campaigns of the Hundred Years War. The window does not present a uniformly flat surface: it is slightly canted at the sides. The very big windows of the same sort that follow this prototype at Gloucester but lack the slightly bowed effect – the west windows at Winchester and York, for example – are dull, tame by comparison.

The work so boldly and gloriously begun in the choir was extended over the next 150 years throughout the church. The north transept was reconstructed in the 1370s. Then, about 50 years later, an attempt was made to bring the nave into line. The west front was rebuilt, the south porch, and two bays of the nave itself. There the work finished. That rejoices some people and makes others sad. For my own part I am sorry. I should dearly have liked to see one cathedral clad entirely in late English Gothic. It would have been unique, and here at Gloucester splendid.

Although this part of the nave was not completed, the urge to rebuild was not spent. The central tower, as we see it, dates from the 1450s. At the crossing below, a pair of delicately thin double-curved arches were inserted at the openings into the transepts, perhaps to provide some additional support. It is a brilliant device, with that touch of the fantastic which appears so often at Gloucester. Finally, at the very end of the 15th century the Lady Chapel was added behind the high altar to a beautiful plan, again with canting at the west end; the building is almost detached, to avoid masking the east window.

There the work of reconstruction at last stopped. The origin, the mainspring of it all, had been the Abbot's decision to accept the King's body for burial; and the royal tomb is therefore, in a sense, the focus of the whole church. It stands high in the choir, a little north of the altar. The canopy is superb, its decoration with ogee arches and pinnacles elaborate, yet strictly disciplined. Beneath it is the alabaster effigy of the King, lying on a chest of Purbeck marble. It is to be taken not as a portrait but as a representation of ideal kingship. Politics and religion made this tomb a place of pilgrimage in the 14th century; as a work of art it is equally one for us today.

There is still one more thing of the highest class to be seen here, not inside the church but in the monastic quarters that adjoined it to the north. The cloisters were rebuilt in the third quarter of the 14th century. The fan vaulting with which they are covered is the earliest now to be seen anywhere: the earliest and, once again, unsurpassed. The inner walls are solid, not open to the green enclosure as they usually are elsewhere. On the south side they are shaped to provide little carrels for the monks' studies. But this does not make these four walks into gloomy tunnels. The sun comes in through little windows to illuminate the roof and form a diaper on the richly-patterned walls. Here too the decoration is lavish, but it is kept under the firmest control.

It must be said with regret that the city of Gloucester is unworthy of its cathedral. I first visited it 40 years ago and was disappointed to find it a rather sordid place, totally without inspiration. On subsequent visits I thought it got

Opposite: the cloisters, Gloucester cathedral (A. F. Kersting)

Below: Gloucester cathedral from the east (A. F. Kersting)

worse. Now, some valiant efforts having been made here and there, it is somewhat better. But it remains unattractive, without any building or streetscape of real distinction. It seems characteristic of Gloucester that a sizeable part of the cathedral close should have been allowed to become a car

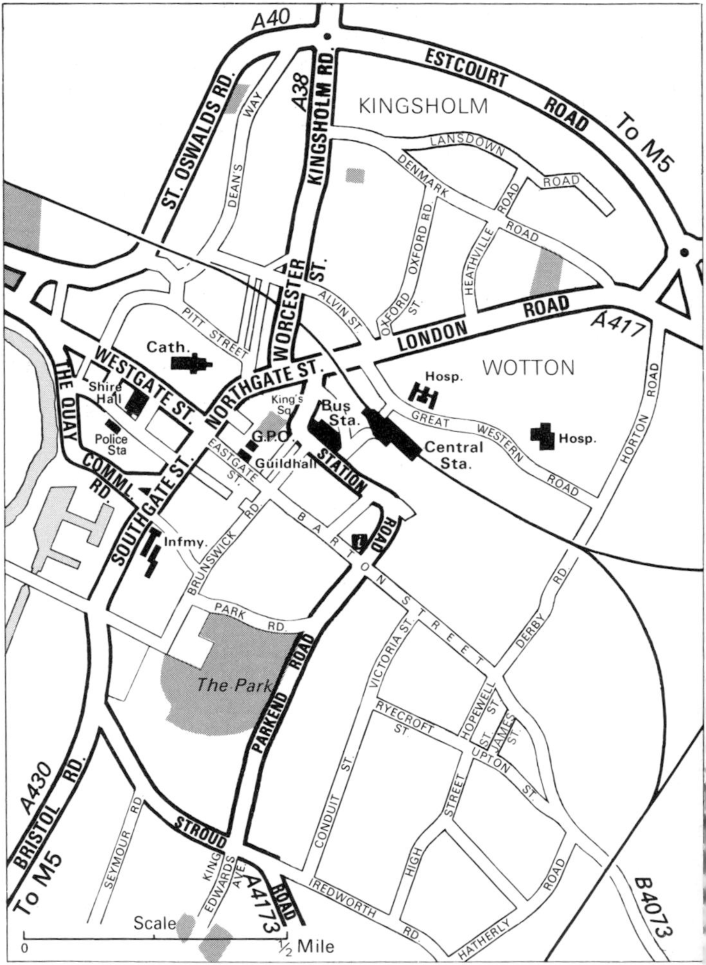

park. Much of the eastern part of the old city is now a big shopping centre. Though a praiseworthy attempt has been made to give it some coherence in King's Square, the result is too small and crowded. And yet – how dare one grumble? Walk out of King's Square by St Aldate Street. Turning your back on the supermarkets, lift up your eyes, and there is that tower with its graceful crown and the filigreed parapet of the chancel below. From a distance too, in any direction, it presides with serene assurance over the city and the water meadows of the Severn. As Henry James's Italian prince cried, in *The Golden Bowl*: "Gloucester, Gloucester, Gloucester. Look at it over there!"

Golden Cap Dorset 4D4

No county in England has a finer coast-line than Dorset: not even Devon, with its curving sweeps (see *Hartland and Clovelly*), nor Cornwall, whose estuaries are unrivalled (see *Trelissick*). Dorset shows extraordinary variety, from the long inlets of Poole Harbour round the Isle of Purbeck to Lulworth and Weymouth Bay, protected by Portland Bill. The Bill is unlike any other English promontory in its bold outline and the thrust it makes into the sea, and the Chesil Beach that follows, though certainly not picturesque, is unique. Then comes Lyme Bay, which Dorset shares with Devon. The highest point on the Dorset side is Golden Cap, reaching 617 ft.

Golden Cap stands midway between the two little towns of Lyme Regis and Bridport. It is only a mile from the village of Chideock, as the crow flies; but earthbound man has a toilsome hill to climb, up the noisy A35 road, until a track diverges from it near the top to the left. It is passable for cars a little way, and then they have to be put into a small park provided for them. From here onwards you must move on foot, through a wood (a piece of economic planting, of beech and fir) and then up over grass and stones to the Cap.

There the whole of the bay is spread out before you: west to Lyme not far off, east (if the weather is clear) to

Golden Cap from the east, looking across Lyme Bay (A. F. Kersting)

the Chesil Beach and Portland Bill. The cliffs vary endlessly in height and colour and shape. Inland to the north rises Hardown Hill, with a group of barrows on it, one of them containing a Saxon burial; beyond that the green slopes of Marchwood Vale, watered by the little River Char. Immediately below, to the west, is the tiny settlement of St Gabriel's, with a church of which only a few stones remain. This is one of the classic points on the English coast.

It lies far away from any large towns, and its configuration is not favourable to building. Yet like all pieces of natural landscape it is extremely vulnerable. One has only to look at the little clutch of caravans below to the east at Seatown and to think what would have happened if that place had been allowed to grow into a settlement justifying its name and then to consider the possibilities of improving the road to St Gabriel's and yanking caravans along it there too. That these things have not happened is due to the public spirit of some landowners, and in recent years to the determined action of the National Trust.

Golden Cap itself was protected in 1936, by covenants entered into by its owner, Lt-Col. Weld. Then, 25 years later, nearly 300 acres of land at Stonebarrow Hill, to the west, were given to the Trust. The Trust's imaginative project for protecting the natural coastline, Enterprise Neptune, has achieved a notable success here, with 13 tracts of land, nearly 1,700 acres, given or bought, mainly from Neptune funds, in 1966–72. The 27 acres of Golden Cap itself are not included. It is now proposed to purchase them as a memorial to Lord Antrim, the Trust's wise and revered Chairman from 1965 to 1977. No better memorial to him, and the work to which he devoted himself, could be imagined.

Having climbed Golden Cap and surveyed the scene from its summit, the whole of the Trust's estate below is there for walking: six miles continuously along the coast, 15 miles of paths altogether. This is country for a most enjoyable holiday, with two small towns at hand to enrich the mixture. Lyme Regis is steep, with its tiny harbour protected by the Cobb, from which Louisa Musgrove had her fall in *Persuasion*; little echoes of the spirit of Jane Austen can be heard there still. Bridport is calmly urbane, with a centre, nice Georgian houses and one or two very good shop-fronts, as well as a view of the green countryside at the end of each of its chief streets, north, east, and west. It was Thomas Hardy's Port Bredy, at the western end of the country he made his own. His spirit too is present, faintly here perhaps, more and more powerfully as one moves eastwards to his capital, *Dorchester*.

Great Amwell Hertfordshire 5B3

An agreeable excursion on a hot afternoon from London. If you are driving, you make for Ware – once an engaging small town, now martyrised by the motor-car. It is really better to take an electric train from Liverpool Street to St Margaret's, whence it is a walk of a mile along the trim

(Thames Water)

New River, tall trees on the far side and below you a bank covered in Queen Anne's lace.

The New River was an enterprise undertaken by Sir Hugh Myddelton in 1606–13, to supply London, chiefly from springs in and around Amwell, with fresh water. It was a great work, 36 miles long, and the beginning of an improvement in one of the city's prime amenities. Though Myddelton himself died poor, the New River Company, which he founded, continued in prosperity until it passed into the hands of the Metropolitan Water Board in 1902.

Among the engineers of the New River in the 18th century was Robert Mylne; a member of an interesting Scottish dynasty, architects and engineers through 12 generations. He designed the first Blackfriars Bridge, completed in 1769. He served the New River Company from 1767 to 1800, when he retired to live at Amwell. There he erected a family mausoleum, still standing east of the church (St John the Baptist: interesting, but totally ruined by Victorian "restoration"). Immediately below the church, on a tiny island in a curve of the river, Mylne put up at the same time a monument to Myddelton, an urn on a plain pedestal in Portland stone. It stands close to the water on a lawn always kept close-shaven, beneath a yew tree flanked by weeping willows. The dead-white monument shines through their foliage. It is a cool, peaceful place. Here is the English 18th century at its simplest, in classical perfection.

Great Chalfield Wiltshire 4D3

Great Chalfield lies about four miles north-west of Bradford-on-Avon – a steep stone-built town with a notable Saxon church and many good houses, large, small, and tiny. You turn off the Trowbridge road to the right. Almost at once you start to descend a steady slope, a tongue of land between Box and the vale of Corsham on the left and, on the right, the rich pastures of Trowbridge, with the chalk downs above Westbury in the distance. You skirt a field, of enormous size for England, and there beyond is the house, screened by trees.

It was given its present form by Thomas Tropnell, who acquired the estate, as a result of persistent litigation, in 1467. There was an earlier building here, moated and walled, which he pulled down. The house reflects with precision both the new security and the continuing unease of life in his time. It first appears across the.moat, the central building in a group of three, with the church on the left and the long west wing (an addition of the 16th century) on the right. The entrance is through two gateways in a corner of the courtyard. In essence the structure comprises a hall block in the middle, running east and west (that is left and right, as you look at it from across the moat), with gabled projections and a wing at each end at right angles to it, the upper floors lighted by large oriel windows. But the symmetry is varied, by the placing of the entrance porch, by the hall chimney-stack, and in the oriels' decoration: the left-hand one delicately crested, the other plainer, both supported on fluted brackets, with different windows underneath them. The roof lines, running at different heights and in different directions, are picked out by a series of sculptured figures of griffins and knights. There is nothing restless here, however. It is all bound together by the beauty of the limestone, which is used everywhere: buff, fawn, yellow – it can

Great Chalfield: the north front (A. F. Kersting)

be all those colours according to the light, and shot with gold too.

On this side the house is perfect and complete, almost exactly as it was finished for Tropnell about 1480. On the other side, the south, it is different. There some of his buildings have gone; their foundations can be seen, and one wing has been entirely rebuilt. For in the 19th century the house fell on bad times. The eastern wing became ruinous, though happily its south wall, with the oriel, stood; the great hall was cut up into four rooms for a tenant farmer, two up and two down. Just before this happened, in 1837, a pupil of Pugin's made a very careful set of measured drawings of the whole building; and from them Sir Harold Brakspear was able to undertake a thorough restoration in 1905–12.

His work was admirably done, with great care and restraint. But he necessarily had to make some changes, in the interests of modern convenience, and it must be said that the inside of the house does not quite equal the first view of it from across the moat.

The hall has a panelled ceiling, some of the timbers painted with Tropnell's device and motto; but the bosses were unhappily defaced in the makeshift reconstruction for the farmer. The three grotesque masks, with eye-holes for observation from above, are a rarity. At the east end there are two projecting windows, charmingly vaulted. Tropnell was at the front of the fashion of his time in providing himself with a separate dining-room, at the west end of the hall. The room was panelled and the ceiling plastered in the 16th century. This covered up a portrait painted on the wall in one corner, which was revealed again at Brakspear's restoration. It is a remarkable piece, a crude but powerful representation of a man of Tropnell's time, probably – though not certainly – himself.

The two large upper rooms are given distinction by their bay windows, in the oriels. The one above the dining room has its original timbered roof, open to the gable; the other, in the wing that was ruined, is a careful copy.

The church (All Saints) is older than the house; there

are some fragments of Norman masonry to be seen by the pulpit. But it too was given its present character by Tropnell, with the pretty bell turret and spire, answering to the decoration of his house, and with his chantry chapel, behind a stone screen carrying his armorial bearings, on the south side. There have been pleasant additions since his time too: the 17th- and 18th-century furniture, especially the pulpit and reading desks, and the vestry, dated 1775 in noble Georgian characters.

In the end, this is one man's place, and Tropnell lives in it for us still: a cautious, patient business man, infinitely long-headed, far shrewder than the Percies and Hungerfords he displaced here and elsewhere. His wariness is to be seen again and again: in those watchful masks, in the slit in the dining room to allow visitors to be espied, and the small wicket within the big front door. "A perilous covetous man" one of his enemies called him; but that is the small change of a law-suit. In the end he won, and died at a very great age. In the 15th century that was no small feat. He has the last laugh at all his opponents. He left his fortune undiminished, and here is his achievement extant 500 years afterwards.

Hadrian's Wall see **Housesteads**

Hartland and Clovelly Devon 3B4

These are two adjacent parishes in North Devon. Between them they offer a remarkable diversity of interest and pleasure. They can be visited very well in any order, separately or together. The route suggested here moves roughly from west to east. It can be reversed or varied, with one restriction, to be indicated at the point where it arises.

Hartland lies just off the main road from Barnstaple to Bude (A39). Hartland Point is a familiar object in English geographical textbooks: the place at which the coast along the widening mouth of the Bristol Channel turns sharply southward, to face on to the Atlantic and confront America. It is a very wild coast indeed, with no harbour worth the name now for 40 miles down to Padstow: savage, high, and steep, the grave of innumerable ships driven on to it in the furious gales of winter. It can hardly be more inhospitable anywhere than at Hartland Quay – which is a quay no longer now, the little harbour having been destroyed by the sea at the end of the last century. The shore here comprises nothing but a series of ribs of rock, razor-sharp, with a few larger promontories of the same kind. The cliffs are by no means at their highest at Hartland – further south, between Crackington Haven and Boscastle, they rise more than twice as high, to nearly 700 ft; but they are more terrifying nowhere. Hartland Point itself, to the north, is tamer: the slopes more rounded, the cliffs already of the red colour associated particularly with Devon. The lighthouse, built in 1874 (part of it can be visited), nestles snugly into them. If this is a turning-point on the English coast, it is not a dramatic one.

The parish of Hartland, with its 17,000 acres, is one of the largest in the south of England. It has two centres, besides a number of scattered hamlets: Stoke, the "church-town", and Hartland itself. The church is one of the noblest in Devon, with a superb tower 128 ft high, visible for miles inland and from far out to sea. Its proportions are faultless, and the sharp geometry of the buttresses clasping the corners is admirable. The whole interior is characteristic of Devon: the massive, boldly-carved Norman font; the timber-framed ceilings throughout; above all the 15th-century wooden screen, the longest in the county (which is celebrated for them), and one of the richest. The carving and colouring are appreciated best from the chancel, looking back at them. Just below the altar to the left there is a 15th-century table tomb made of the dark-grey stone called catacleuse, quarried in Cornwall. Another pair of memorials brings one abruptly into the modern world. In the north aisle there are wall tablets commemorating two figures famous in literary history. One is John Lane of the Bodley Head, publisher of *The Yellow Book* of the 1890s, who was born at West Putford

(C. Wheeler)

and went to school here; the other Sir Allen Lane, founder of Penguin Books, which in the past 40 years has been a powerful influence in the education of our time. These two are commemorated again on a seat outside the south porch, the lettering most elegantly cut in slate.

Close by the entrance to the churchyard is the Church House, a small stone building of a kind necessary in places like this, where the people came together from the distant parts of a large parish: the medieval equivalent of a community centre.

In the long valley running up from the sea north of the church an Augustinian abbey was founded about 1169. Only a few fragments of it remain now, incorporated into a mansion in the Gothic style built in 1779. It can be seen in the distance from the road from Stoke to Hartland.

Hartland itself is unremarkable. Its former town hall was demolished in 1839, the materials being used to construct a plain little church, serving as a chapel-of-ease to the parish church two miles away. The road then goes on eastwards for about four miles, to reach the turning to the left for Clovelly.

★

Clovelly is celebrated as one of the most picturesque villages in England, its single street climbing up by steps 300 ft from the harbour. Dickens was there in 1860 and described it admirably in "A Message from the Sea". "No two houses in the village were alike", he remarked, "in chimney, size, shape, door, window, gable, roof-tree, anything". It is all just the same, totally unchanged. Donkeys still ply up and down, as they did in Dickens's time. If the service of a Land-Rover is available for the less energetic it travels on a by-road, out of sight. Cars are firmly halted, and parked at the top of the hill.

To all this Clovelly owes its fame; what superior persons might call its notoriety. It is unique and preposterous. It is also irresistible, to anyone who will go and look at it without prejudice – though not, if possible, in July or August, when the pressure on the tiny place is overwhelming. It

(Eric G. Meadows)

is no arty village out of Disneyland. It is in fact, when looked at closely, a natural and sensible settlement, taking its form from the exceptional configuration of the country. A convenient little harbour was constructed here, with a stone quay of 1587; the only one on the west side of Bideford Bay. It formerly drove a good trade in herrings, and its fishermen lived on the hill above. Now the herrings have gone, and the fishermen too. Visitors have taken their place; their needs are catered for all up and down the street. Clovelly is among the most striking examples in the country of a "preserved" settlement: preserved not dead and mummified or with silly olde-worlde devices, but living and going its own way.

It is all due to one family: the Hamlyns, later Hamlyn-Williams. They acquired the manor from the Carys in 1724, rebuilt their house (which stands away from the village on the top of the hill, near the church), and cherished the estate in two special ways. They planted trees on a large scale and laid out walks and drives in both directions along the coast. And when the fame of the village spread, to bring visitors by hundreds and then by thousands, they imposed the firmest possible control on it and its surroundings, in order to prevent any undesirable development. So there has been no new building – though much unobtrusive reconstruction, candidly indicated by the dates some of the houses carry. There are no overhead wires here: that hateful curse of our time, in town and country, is entirely absent. The visitors come – and why not? They are provided for in a quiet and orderly way, without fussiness. The control and management are as deft as could be.

But for many people the village will not be the thing to remember longest about Clovelly. It will be the drives and the planting. Sir James Hamlyn-Williams (who died in 1829) and his wife Diana were chiefly responsible for them. In particular they laid out the Hobby Drive, which stretches nearly four miles eastwards through woods above the cliffs. It is open to walkers through a gate near the top of the village street. It is also open for cars, on payment of a toll, but they must enter it from the other end, by the Hobby Lodge on the Bideford road. One way or the other, it is an experience on no account to be missed. Here is the picturesque moulding of the natural landscape in the great English tradition, descending from *Stourhead* and the terraces at *Rievaulx*. Yet it is different from them: for it respects the natural wildness of these magnificent hills falling to the sea. Sir James and his wife clothed them with trees. They cut the drive, making serpentine bends into little valleys, with views east and north and west in succession. For the rest they let Nature speak for herself. They knew exactly what they were about. The natural scene is superb: cliffs rising up 600 ft, the whole vast curving sweep of Bideford Bay, 12 miles across, in front, and the granite hump of Lundy Island 10 miles away to the north. The cliffs are pink to purple, with green fields above, and over in the distance the five miles of yellow sands at the mouth of the Taw. It is one of the finest stretches of the English coastline, seen from here to perfection in the self-effacing framework the Hamlyn-Williams made.

Hatfield Hertfordshire 5A3
Hatfield is a place of politics. Nowhere else in England, except at Westminster and Windsor, can one feel so well the long continuities of power.

The manor belonged to the monastery of *Ely* and was assigned to the bishopric when that was established in 1109. The most powerful man who ever occupied that see, Cardinal Morton, built himself a palace here in the 1480s. He was then one of the chief ministers of Henry VII. At the Dissolution 40 years later, it passed to the Crown, Henry VIII making the house a residence for his children. His young son Edward VI heard the news of his accession here. Elizabeth was kept a half-prisoner at Hatfield during the reign of her sister Mary. Here she learnt in turn that she had become Queen, and in the Great Hall of the Palace she held the first council of her reign, in 1558. At her side was William Cecil, whom she at once made Secretary of State, presently Lord Burghley and Lord Treasurer. She trusted him without interruption until his death 40 years later; and by then his son Robert was already Secretary of State, trusted by the Queen almost equally.

James I, who succeeded Elizabeth, did not care for Hatfield. He took a fancy to another house in Hertfordshire, Theobalds, built not long before by Burghley, and in 1607 he persuaded Robert Cecil (now Earl of Salisbury) to accept Hatfield in exchange. Salisbury inherited from his father a passion for building. He started at once on a new house at Hatfield, pulling down three-quarters of the former Palace and using many of its bricks again in the fabric of his own. He died shortly before it was completed in 1612.

Thereafter for a long time Hatfield took a rest from high politics. The first Earl of Salisbury's successors were either quiet men or foolish, and none of them played any important part in public life until late in the 18th century. Then the seventh Earl (and first Marquess) of Salisbury was Lord Chamberlain to George III. His grandson the third Marquess was three times Prime Minister under Queen Victoria: one of the greatest of her servants, as his ancestor

Lord Burghley had been to Elizabeth. The fourth and fifth Marquesses were both Ministers of the Crown, influential in many fields of public life. The tradition of the family is of a highly independent conservatism. In the 1930s both the fourth Marquess and his son stood on the right wing of the Tory party over many issues, yet entirely rejected their leaders' policy of appeasement with Hitler's Germany. In religion the Cecils have been, almost without exception, strong Anglicans.

This long political history is written all over Hatfield itself. If only a quarter of Morton's palace remains, that quarter contains the Great Hall, much as it was when it was built and when Elizabeth was there. After the completion of the new house, it survived as stables; today it is a restaurant. The timber roof is among the finest of its kind. The building is a splendid example of late-medieval brickwork: 230 ft long – one has to think of it as one side of a courtyard only, matched by three other ranges stretching back up the hill, to get the full sense of the scale on which Morton built.

Hatfield House is perhaps, with Bramshill in Hampshire, the most complete of the great Jacobean houses now in existence; and Bramshill is not open to the public. Holland House in London was destroyed by bombing. Audley End in Essex – by far the biggest of them all; one of the largest houses ever built in England – survives, but only in part, and much modified since. At Hatfield there has been no substantial change. Alterations made in the 18th century were themselves altered back in the 19th.

The north front is powerfully plain in outline: four-square, even box-like. The Hall is eminently Jacobean in its character, with two immense carved wooden screens facing each other, and galleries above. Fine portraits hang here: one of Elizabeth – Nicholas Hilliard's famous Ermine Portrait, with the little creature climbing up the Queen's left arm; one of Mary Queen of Scots, whose chief antagonist in the end was Burghley. The rest are of Burghley himself, his second wife (an austere bluestocking), and his son, the

Hatfield House: the south front (Eric G. Meadows)

builder of the house. Round the corner is the Rainbow Portrait of Elizabeth, painted probably by Isaac Oliver, full of the elaborate symbolism that she and her age liked.

The staircase is one of the most gorgeous pieces of its time. The carving throughout, here and in the Hall, is outstanding in its technical skill. In King James's Drawing Room, above, the King presides in person, a statue over the fireplace. To the right hang two portraits: a smooth Romney of the first Marquess and a much more interesting Reynolds of his wife. Under her direction this room was redecorated and refurnished. Although some of her elegant furniture remains here still, most of her work was undone in her son's time, when Jacobean taste came into fashion again under Queen Victoria. The contents of the house reflect each successive age, naturally and freely (down to two portraits, for example, by Augustus John); but the character everywhere is Jacobean still, as if the spirit of the house forbade any marked alteration.

The ceilings were redecorated in the 19th century: that of the Long Gallery entirely in gold. This room is sumptuous. It is one of the longest of all such galleries and has a special feature, uncommon and delightful: a subsidiary gallery leading off it to the north, with windows looking down into the Hall. The Gallery's many treasures include an exquisite posset set, in crystal decorated in gold and enamel, given by the Spanish ambassador to Philip II and Mary on their betrothal in 1554; and Queen Elizabeth's stockings, gloves, and garden hat. The portraits are numerous, and one or two quite unexpected. What are we to make of the presence here of Ravaillac, who murdered Henry IV of France?

Hatfield House: the Long Gallery (A. F. Kersting)

The Library, right at the west end of the house, is a notable one. The Cecils have been a bookish family, in the last 100 years markedly intellectual; and this is a library designed not for ostentation but for use. The books themselves make that clear, and the Victorian iron-framed gallery, giving easy access to the upper shelves. Some documents are displayed too. No private family in England can have richer archives than those at Hatfield. Many of Burghley's state papers are here, as well as those of his son. The third Marquess, Queen Victoria's Prime Minister, transacted much of his public business from the house, and his papers survive at Hatfield in meticulous order. Anyone who has ever consulted them, here or in the national archives, will remember the annotations, in red ink in his clear flowing hand, his crisp and caustic comments.

His touch is to be felt strongly in the Chapel below. He was a devout high Anglican, and he began embellishing the Chapel directly he succeeded his father in 1868. Here the union of the Jacobean and the Victorian is complete. The glass was bought for the house in 1611: Flemish in character and partly in design, but made in Southwark. Almost all the furnishings – notably the white marble altar and its yellow reredos – are of the 1870s.

The interests of this great man were various. He was primarily a statesman; but also a theologian, and an experimental scientist. Hatfield was the first great house to have an internal telephone system, installed in 1877, and the first to be lighted by electricity, four years later. The Marquess's system was erratic at first, and the family were accustomed to throwing cushions up to the ceiling of the Long Gallery, to extinguish the flashes and sparks from its wires. In his portraits he is powerfully impressive. But he was never in any degree pompous. He had an impish sense of humour, and his deep piety was combined with a scepticism about human behaviour that made him also a profound realist.

Coming out of the house, turn into the West Garden and move along under the great trees. You will then see the whole south front, a composition far more varied than its fellow on the north. Here is nothing box-like. The two wings advance boldly. They are capped with lead cupolas, and sets of big chimneys rise behind. The central part is crowned with a tall clock tower. This and the arcade below (now unfortunately filled in) may be an early work of Inigo Jones, who was at Hatfield in 1609 and received £10 for drawings. This front shows a strong contrast in colour: between the white Caen limestone and the red brick of the wings, and between the reds themselves, which vary from the palest pink to a darkened vermilion and plum.

Three buildings are visible from here, ranged together in a sequence: the tower of St Etheldreda's church (which contains the noble monument of the first Earl), the old episcopal palace, and then the present house above it. The town is out of sight below, and that adds its own element to the others: one charming Georgian street and some interesting recent buildings, part of an expansion that has been in progress since the 1930s. Hatfield has always been a busy place of traffic. The Park is enclosed by a long wall and gates; but it is open liberally to the public, 10 hours a day. This is no princely palace, secluded and aloof. It has been an intimate part of the unfolding history of England.

Haworth Parsonage West Yorkshire 2B4

Visiting Haworth is a strange experience. How could it not be, associated so closely with the Brontës, one of the strangest families of genius that we know of? There are two Haworths: the larger and newer, down in the valley with the railway (lately defunct, and now resuscitated successfully by enthusiasts for the steam locomotive) and some small industry; the old township, high up on its steep hill, with the church at the top and the Parsonage close beside it. Everything goes black: the natural colour taken on with age, and even without much smoke, by the Yorkshire millstone grit.

(Yorkshire Post)

The church the Brontës knew has gone, except for its tower. But the Parsonage is much as it was when they lived there: a simple Georgian house of 1779. It was bought and given to the Brontë Society by a rich man, Sir James Roberts, born in Haworth, in 1928; and it received a notable addition not long afterwards when Mrs Henry Houston Bonnell of Philadelphia gave it the collection of Brontëana assembled by her husband – a characteristic gesture of American generosity.

No house in England is more impregnated with genius than this one. There are others, little changed, in which masterpieces were written: Shandy Hall at Coxwold, Coleridge's cottage at Nether Stowey and Jane Austen's at Chawton, Lamb House at *Rye*. But these compose parts of literary lives. Here the whole working life, not of one but of three writers, is concentrated: for all the novels of the Brontë sisters were written in these small rooms. Here they lived their sad, often grim short lives; and here their lives ended in the dining room is the sofa on which Emily Brontë suddenly died. There is something terrifying about the way in which this house reveals the lives of its inhabitants. But what could be more characteristic of them than that?

The Rev. Patrick Brontë (born Brunty), an Irishman with a Cornish wife, came here in 1820. Haworth was not a good living, but about as much as he could hope for. He brought with him six children. His wife was ailing, and within 18 months she was dead of cancer. Thereupon her austere sister, Aunt Branwell, came to live in the Parsonage to bring up the young family. Two of the girls died in 1825, aged 10 and 11, from illness contracted at the dreadful Cowan Bridge school, for which Charlotte – who also went there, with Emily – conceived a life-long detestation. As the surviving girls grew up, they became governesses and school-teachers. There was very little joy in their lives: they were poor, their father was morose and exacting, their brother Branwell – they came to recognise it – a wastrel. The resource they all turned to was writing: writing that arose from their children's games of make-believe, the fantasies they had created of the countries of Angria and Gondal. Out of all this came their poems, Emily's pre-eminent among them; and their seven novels, all written in as many years. Within a space of eight months, in 1848–9, Branwell, Emily, and Anne died, leaving Charlotte the one survivor of the whole large family of children. She battled on, living here at Haworth in her father's company, travelling modestly as her work became known. At last, after much opposition from her father, she married his curate, Mr Nicholls. Nine months later she died. The men survived: old Mr Brontë to the age of 85, Mr Nicholls – it is curious to think of – until 1906.

The house is a simple one, everything small, plain, and spare. The dining room opens off the narrow hall to the left, and on the opposite side the parlour, Mr Brontë's study in which he spent most of his time, shut away from his family. Behind these is a tiny store room, which Charlotte turned into a study for her husband, and the kitchen. Upstairs is the little bedroom occupied by the faithful family servant

Tabby (Tabitha Aykroyd), and the bedrooms of the Brontës themselves. They changed their use as time went on. The right-hand one, above the dining room, was Aunt Branwell's. When Charlotte married it became hers, and she died there. The central small room was the nursery ("the children's study", as it was called by the servants: the figures those children scratched on the walls are still on them), and then it was occupied by Emily. The other principal bedroom was Mr Brontë's, with Branwell's little room beside it. At the back of the house, reached by another staircase, is the room fitted up to house the Bonnell collection, with some of its treasures displayed.

That is all – all except the Haworth Moor and the wild country stretching out beyond it, the country of *Wuthering Heights*. There has been a good deal of quarrying here, and one of the quarries is a municipal refuse dump; the unbroken expanse of moorland has been interrupted with small reservoirs. The stream of visitors is unending, and it has induced some twaddle – a mile or two down the valley there is a Brontë Zoo. But these are small things, soon forgotten under the spell cast by these women. Their house is now admirably displayed, a witness of the devotion they have called forth. It is not a mere museum. It is more than a centre for the study of their works. The Parsonage is a part of the books they wrote, an inspiration to anyone who reads them.

Heveningham Hall Suffolk 5C2

On the map of England, Suffolk looks close to London. That proximity can be felt at Ipswich, and at several other points on the county's southern and eastern borders. But over most of it London seems quite forgotten. No motorways traverse the county, and only two other roads of importance: A45 from Felixstowe to Newmarket and on into the Midlands and A12, running parallel with the coast from London to Lowestoft and Yarmouth. To the west of A12 there is a large tract of very quiet country. Its only towns, and those small ones, are Framlingham and Halesworth. It used to be called the Woodlands, or High Suffolk: a plateau about 150 ft above sea-level, cut into by tiny rivers, crossed by narrow, crooked roads; a landscape, a whole countryside, little changed for 100 years past. Heveningham Hall lies here, approached from the south by a long drive through a wood, bordered thickly by primroses in spring. The house stands on the side of a hill, facing northwards into the shallow valley of the River Blyth.

The Heveningham estate was purchased by Sir Joshua Vanneck in 1752. The Vannecks had come from the Netherlands to England at the beginning of that century and grown rich as merchants in London. Sir Joshua was content to occupy the Queen Anne house he found here, but immediately he was dead, in 1777, his son Sir Gerard determined to reconstruct and greatly enlarge it, to make of it an imposing Palladian mansion. He turned to Sir Robert Taylor as his architect. Taylor was surveyor to the Bank of England and had an extensive practice among City men in London. His work was carried through quickly, and by 1780 the Queen Anne house had been wholly disguised behind a massive Corinthian front, with wings – each in itself longer than the original house – added on either side of it. There then occurred a breach between architect and patron, and nearly all the internal work was designed by James Wyatt, a much younger man, still in his thirties, with ideas very different from Taylor's. No reason for this change is recorded. Perhaps Sir Gerard Vanneck felt that his new house was already a little old-fashioned and that he wanted something lighter, more colourful, varied, and gay, than Taylor offered him. Certainly Taylor's design for the Entrance Hall (it is shown in a room upstairs) appears ponderous and angular beside Wyatt's, which we see today. Sir Gerard Vanneck called in Capability Brown to refashion the park around the house. Something will be said of that later.

The Vanneck family continued to own Heveningham until 1970, when they sold the house, with some of its furniture and a large part of the estate, to the Government.

The visitors' entrance to the house is by a small door

on the west side. The interesting Print Room comes first – an untouched example of a short-lived fashion – and then the Morning Room. This is decorated more plainly than the rest of the chief rooms and may be the sole part of the interior that was designed by Taylor. The contrast with the Entrance Hall, which follows, is most striking.

This is a room of extreme distinction. If a trifle low in colour now – it needs to be seen in sunlight – it is outstanding in design and decoration. It has been compared with Adam's Hall at *Syon*. That is misleading. Both are entrance halls, but there the resemblance between them ends. Wyatt's is a rectangle treated symmetrically, its prevailing colour green, accented with the yellow scagliola columns and pilasters and the rich mahogany doors. A high segmental vault crowns it – so high that it is almost semi-circular. Both Adam and Wyatt ordinarily made their curved ceilings shallow. Here the greater roundness changes the proportions decisively, making the whole room lofty and enlarging all its scale. The brackets supporting it show the influence of the fan-vault, a device that particularly pleased Wyatt and other Gothic revivalists of the 18th century – inserted here into an architectural scheme that is otherwise wholly classical in its origins.

The Hall is the first of a sequence of seven rooms: Dining Room, Library, Drawing Room, Saloon, and Etruscan Room, ending with the Staircase Hall. Taken together, they show Wyatt's powers in interior design at their highest. There is endless variety here in shape, line, and colour, realised largely owing to the delicate talents of the painter Biagio Rebecca. The Dining Room is much brighter than the rest at present because it was severely damaged by fire in 1949 and was then repainted, with meticulous adherence to the original colour-scheme. Much of the furniture, though not all of it, belongs to the house, and some pieces (most of the small chairs, for example) were designed by Wyatt. Notice in the Library the Sheraton elbow chairs and the splendid movable steps, folding up to make a table. The little Etruscan Room again reflects a fashion of the time. Adam had given Osterley an Etruscan Dining Room a few years before. That

Heveningham: the Entrance Hall (A. F. Kersting)

was a much larger and more elaborate work; this one has the charm of intimacy.

The floor above is curious. Here one can see the difficulties that arose from fitting the new house into the existing one, and from the changes that Wyatt introduced into Taylor's plan. There are no state bedrooms, as we should expect, on the first floor of the central block. The windows in the *façade* are blank, with the vault of the Entrance Hall rising behind them. The rooms now to be visited are a storey higher. The Yellow Bedroom contains some very fine furniture: a Hepplewhite four-poster bed in walnut; stools, mirrors, and a commode by Wyatt. In the Dressing Room next to it, and the room beyond, are some of his drawings for other pieces of furniture that were not made for the house, as well as an important series of Brown's plans for landscaping the park.

The terraced garden behind the house is a pleasant Victorian creation. The kitchen gardens above are striking from their noble red-brick walls, especially the long serpentine one, of a design sometimes called "crinkle-crankle", favoured pre-eminently in Suffolk for the growing of fruit trees. Beyond the walls, at the top of the little ridge, is a green open space, shaded by magnificent cedars of Lebanon and graced by Wyatt's lovely white orangery, with a semi-circular portico. It is built largely of wood, and not at present in sound condition. Will it soon be treated with the care it deserves?

The park at Heveningham is delightful. It is possible to see with some precision what was done here in the 18th century. At the foot of the staircase hang two pictures of the house and park as they were when Sir Joshua Vanneck acquired them in 1752. They show a pleasant, well-timbered scene, big trees rising haphazardly on the slope from the house down to the river. Brown's designs for remodelling the landscape were not all carried out. But his plans show what he intended in detail. We have contemporary pictures displaying what was in fact done, and finally the scene as it is today, 200 years later.

All the big trees in front of the house were swept away.

Smooth turf now stretches down, unbroken by any planting, into the valley. The Blyth runs in its natural course still, augmented by another little stream flowing into it from the north-east, and a lake has been formed here. (Brown wanted a chain of lakes, but he was permitted to make only one.) Beside the house and behind it there is liberal planting, though much of it is of a later time. Not many of the trees we see now were there when the grounds were thus laid out, apart from the big cedars that cap the ridge; but there are new young trees, and the succession is being revived. It is all relatively simple. The Vannecks had not the same passion for planting as the Hoares had, one after another, at *Stourhead*. They went for something quite different: a landscape entirely green, in which brilliant exotics, like rhododendrons or maples, would have been wholly out of place.

The planner of it all, Lancelot Brown, was a delightful character – see the brilliantly humorous portrait of him by Nathaniel Dance in the National Portrait Gallery. He is one of the few important men of the past who is invariably referred to by a nickname. He is always called Capability Brown, from his own habit of speaking to his clients of the "capabilities" of the landscape they presented to him for his treatment. He had a wonderful eye, and he was both imaginative and shrewd. With that combination of talents he redesigned many parks like this one. He made a great contribution to an art that was recognised as peculiarly English.

Moving away from the house to the west, you can go down into the valley and turn right along the Halesworth road at the bottom. That brings you to the north side of the lake, from which you look back up the green slopes to the house, clasped in its gardens and trees behind.

Hoar Cross: church of the Holy Angels Staffordshire 2C6

The Hoar Cross estate, in Needwood Forest, was a possession of the Meynell family. Col. H. F. Meynell-Ingram died young in 1871, and his widow determined to erect a church in his memory. As architects she chose the firm of Bodley & Garner. G. F. Bodley was then making his reputation: a perfectionist if ever there was one, with the supreme good fortune here of a patron with almost unlimited wealth, who placed her full confidence in him to the end. The building was begun in 1872 and brought into full use four years later. Its decoration proceeded throughout Bodley's life and was not completed until just after his death in 1907.

It stands by the side of a road, in a clearing in the trees, which screen it from the house of the family, Hoar Cross Hall. It is built of red sandstone from Alton, near by, and from Runcorn in Cheshire. The massing of the parts is splendid, drawn together by the central tower, which differs totally from the prevailing patterns of its time: firmly rectilinear throughout, rejecting pinnacles and every thought of a spire. It prefigures the Anglican cathedral in Liverpool, on whose design Bodley had a strong influence. Historically, the church is a notable landmark in the evolution of the last phase of Gothic architecture in England.

Inside, the building presents a harmony of systems, com-

(N.M.R.)

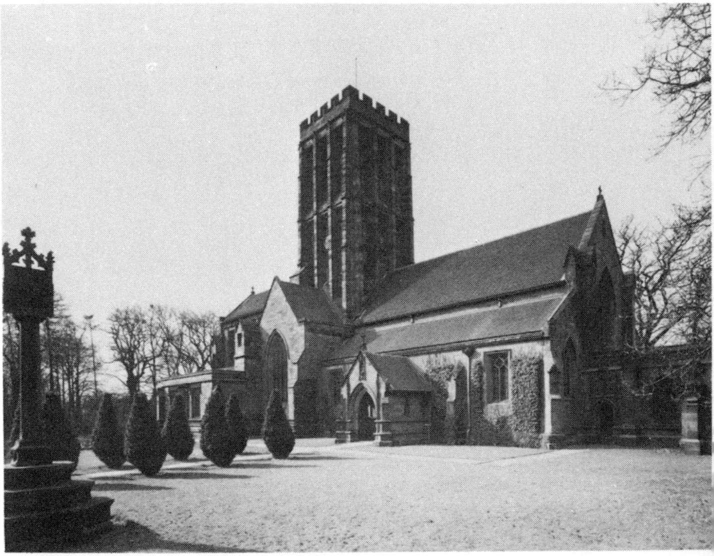

pletely realised, from the black-and-white paving of the floor to the stone vaulting of the roof. The proportions are soaring, but never exaggerated or spindly. The chancel is enclosed with a set of delicate iron screens, the organ sunk into its south wall, concealed in a richly-decorated case. On the south side are the sumptuous tombs of the foundress and her husband.

The building is beautifully kept, and it contains not a single ugly object: none of the clutter that is to be found in the ordinary parish church. It reveals the power of money in the 19th century no less surely than the Beauchamp Chapel at Warwick in the 15th. In both we see lavish expenditure in the service of the most refined English taste of its time; directed here – more evidently than at Warwick – by an absorbed devotion of the spirit. It is one of the most perfectly beautiful monuments of the Mid-Victorian age.

Holy Island Northumberland 1C1

Holy Island is a place of peculiar sanctity, consecrated by the Northumbrian monastery of Lindisfarne and its achievement. "Island" is something of a misnomer: for it can now be reached by road during many hours of each day. That has become in our own time a danger. A place that was chosen because it was secluded, inaccessible, has lost a great deal of that character. Its fame has exposed it to invasion, so that in the summer it can look like a fairground.

The see and monastery of Lindisfarne were founded in 634 by Oswald, King of Northumbria, to be ruled by Aidan, a monk from Iona. Aidan was a missionary, whose task was to preach Christianity over the whole of Oswald's kingdom – that is, throughout the country now called Northumberland and south-eastern Scotland. The site was excellent for this purpose: easily accessible from the mainland yet sufficiently withdrawn to be protected against hostile raids from that quarter, and only a few miles from the King's capital at Bamburgh. Aidan travelled ceaselessly until his death in 651.

The monastery he set up at Lindisfarne was of a Celtic

pattern, ruled by an abbot but also affording quarters to the bishop when he chose to reside there during an interval in his journeyings.

The sixth bishop of Lindisfarne was Cuthbert, a Lowland Scot, who arrived there first as prior in 664. He became bishop in 685 but lived only two years longer, dying on Farne Island in 687. His body was brought back to the monastery and buried there. Cuthbert had been much admired and beloved in life, and his resting-place became a centre of pilgrimage. In 698 his body was exhumed and, together with some personal relics and the portable altar he had carried with him on his travels, placed in an oak coffin by the altar of the church. In 793 the monastery was attacked and plundered, in one of the earliest Scandinavian raids on the east coast. Exposed though it was, however, the community held on for another 80 years. Then, when the danger became too great and continuous, it was decided to abandon Lindisfarne. The whole community of St Cuthbert left the place, bearing his body and the other relics, settling for more than 100 years at Chester-le-Street and then at length at *Durham*. But their tribulations were not over. In 1069 the community of Durham fled before William the Conqueror's savage attack, retreating to Lindisfarne once more. They stayed there less than a year, going back to Durham in 1070. Throughout this journey of evacuation they had borne with them St Cuthbert's body and relics, as the most sacred of their treasures. Now at last those things could rest, in the magnificent cathedral that grew up around them at Durham; and there in part, they remain.

With Jarrow and Monkwearmouth, Lindisfarne was now re-established as a cell of Durham, a small priory. Soon afterwards the Old English name by which it had always been known began to give place, in ordinary usage, to "Holy Island". The church became the ecclesiastical capital of a unit called Islandshire (later North Durham), reaching as far up the coast as Tweedmouth, opposite *Berwick*. It remained administratively part of the County Palatine of Durham, and separate from Northumberland, until 1845.

The priory never recovered any of its predecessor's importance, and it was dissolved in 1537. The church then quickly fell into disrepair, and in 1613 Lord Walden, who had secured the property in right of his wife, stripped the lead from the roofs of all the buildings. Thereafter they were ruinous, decaying gradually into the condition in which we see them now. The parish church, which had always stood outside the monastic enclosure, continued in use, to serve the small population of the island.

Holy Island itself is almost flat except at its south-eastern corner, where Beblowe Crag rears up dramatically to a conical peak immediately east of the small harbour. Strangely, this natural point of defence seems never to have been occupied until 1542 when, as a consequence of war between the English and the Scots, two bulwarks were planned here, to be constructed largely out of stone taken from the disused monastery. By 1550 there was a fort surmounting the Crag. It saw no action in that Anglo-Scottish strife, but it was used during the English Civil War, and it was seized for a day by two Jacobites, in a harum-scarum episode that might have come from *Redgauntlet*, in 1715. A tiny garrison continued to be stationed in the fort for another 100 years and more. In 1865 the Island was occupied by about 500 people, mainly farmers and fishermen, together with some workers at a lime-kiln, then recently opened. The population is not more than 200 today.

No fragment survives above ground of the Northumbrian monastery, which was built of wood. All that is to be seen here from that time are some carvings in the little Museum – "pillowstones", which were laid flat on graves, and upright headstones. One of these is notable, showing on one side the sun and moon, with worshippers adoring the Cross, and on the other a group of seven warriors brandishing battleaxes.

The buildings themselves belong to the later priory. The church is a splendid work, erected at the same time as Durham cathedral, with which it shows some plain affinities, for example in the piers of the nave. Its scale is, however, very much smaller: the length of the whole church is 142 ft, compared with the 460 ft of Durham as it is today. You get the best sense of what the building was originally like by standing on the south side of the nave, where only the stumps of the piers now survive, and looking back: to the west wall, a grandly-composed screen, and to the north arcade opposite. At the same time, if you have seen Durham, another difference will strike you forcibly. The building here is of a sandstone reddish in colour (quarried at Cheswick on the mainland) as against the yellow-brown sandstone used in the cathedral. This is no miniature version of Durham. For all the remoteness of its situation – by the flat sea-shore, ungraced by trees – it is warm, even intimate, where the greater building is formidably austere.

As originally erected, the chancel was smaller than it is now, with a round apse. About 1140 it was enlarged and made rectangular, in the English way. The monastic buildings on the south side of the church date mainly from the 13th and 14th centuries. They are of a different grey stone, which comes from Scremerston, towards Berwick. It is unusual in this country to find religious buildings fortified; but here in this exposed place, swept by the intermittent warfare between England and Scotland, it was necessary. Hence the battlements on the west wall of the outer court, and the cross-shaped slits for bowmen cut in the top storey of the west front of the church.

Except for one short interlude, however, and a single day of melodrama, Holy Island remained undisturbed. At the beginning of the 20th century something surprising happened. Edward Hudson, who had founded the admirable magazine *Country Life*, purchased the fort from the Crown and called in Edwin Lutyens to convert it into a house for him. Work began at once, and it was carried through quickly. Although Hudson loved it and entertained much distinguished company here, that life fell to pieces in 1914 and he sold it soon after the war was over. It then passed through one other owner to Sir Edward de Stein, a merchant banker, who gave it in 1944 to the National Trust. It is now to be seen very much as Lutyens left it.

(A. F. Kersting)
Holy Island, looking to Beblowe Crag, surmounted by Lindisfarne Castle

Standing on its bare basalt rock above the sea, approached by a stone ramp, under a portcullis and up a staircase, Lindisfarne Castle resembles one other English house alone: St Michael's Mount in Cornwall. But the Mount is historic and grand. This is not. What Lutyens aimed at was to make a modest manageable dwelling, to satisfy the standards of comfort of the 20th century, within the fabric of a crumbling Tudor fort. He succeeded, furnishing Hudson with four living rooms, a kitchen, and nine bedrooms, originally served by one bathroom and subsequently by a second. He allowed stone to predominate everywhere inside the house, as if one were living in the rock itself: notably in the low vaults of the Dining Room and Ship Room on the ground floor. Most of the furniture is of dark oak, some of it designed by Lutyens himself, the rest antique, English and Dutch. Perhaps the most charming room is the Long Gallery, with a flat timber ceiling. Above it, you step out on to the Upper Battery, which commands, as it did when the fort was in commission, a long sweeping view up and down the Northumberland coast.

What a story there is here, from Aidan and Cuthbert down to the publisher and his architect, the merchant banker, the visiting crowds today! The original monastery has gone, its fabric vanished without trace; and yet in the end it outshines everything else, its memory preserved in part at Durham, in the relics of St Cuthbert and the *Liber Vitae*, and above all in the Lindisfarne Gospels, one of the greatest possessions of the British Library.

The Gospels were written by Eadfrith, who was bishop of Lindisfarne from 698 to 721; and the book was bound by his successor. It is distinguished especially by its decoration, extraordinarily elaborate yet always closely controlled. Though strongly Celtic in character it does not derive from Irish models, like the Book of Kells, which belong to a later time. Rather, it is to be seen as an English work, fusing perfectly the Celtic and the English spirits, achieved here in the peaceful, well-governed kingdom of Northumbria. The peace and good government did not last, but the book survived their destruction. It is one of the supreme works of what are sometimes called the Dark Ages.

Houghton Norfolk 5B1

Sir Robert Walpole was one of the strongest, the most intelligent and effective politicians who have ever ruled England. He was in power for more than 20 years, from 1721 to 1742, and during that time he built this house for himself in Norfolk. The Walpoles were deeply rooted at Houghton. Sir Robert began to consider rebuilding the Jacobean house he inherited in 1721, and Colen Campbell prepared a plan for the purpose. This was in essence the basis of the house we see now, though the final responsibility for it rested with another architect, Thomas Ripley. The work began in 1722 and was largely completed in nine years, but the finishing touches were not put to it until 1735.

The only building stone available anywhere near was the yellow-brown car stone quarried near Snettisham. That was used for the huge stables, which stand to the south of the house. It is a rough material, however, and could not meet the standards that the architect and his patron required. To achieve that they had either to use brick (as had been done at Raynham in the previous century, and was to be done again at Holkham a little later) or to import stone, at enormous expense, from elsewhere. Happily this last decision was taken, and the choice fell on a jurassic sandstone from Aislaby in Yorkshire, shipped from Whitby to Kings Lynn and thence conveyed overland. It is a superb stone, immensely durable, as fine today as it was when it was new, and showing a whole range of colours from dark brown to yellow and grey. It is simply a facing; the core of the house is of brick.

Campbell's original design comprised a square block with a square turret at each corner, influenced by Wilton, near *Salisbury*. That was retained, but the whole character was altered by Walpole's decision that the turrets should be crowned by cupolas. Ripley added them, accordingly, and the result is exactly right, giving the house an element of curvature that redeems what might otherwise have been too foursquare. Externally, save in one respect – to be mentioned later – the house stands just as it was built.

The interior was largely planned by William Kent, and executed under his supervision. Two of the state rooms only have been much altered since his time. Those rooms all lie on the first floor, the *piano nobile*, reached by a staircase contained within one of the corner turrets. It is of mahogany, like all the doors – a wood just then becoming fashionable. It is lighted from the cupola above, and the well of the staircase is occupied by a copy of a Roman statue of a gladiator, raised up on four Tuscan columns to stand level with the first floor.

The rooms that follow vary greatly in size. The first to be seen, the Common Parlour, is intimate, and then next door to it is the most architecturally splendid of the series, the Stone Hall, a perfect 40 ft cube, descending directly from

Houghton: the Stone Hall (English Life Publications Ltd)

Inigo Jones's hall in the Queen's House at Greenwich. The furniture is all Kent's, the chairs covered in their original green velvet. The reliefs over the doors are by Rysbrack, and so is the great chimney-piece, which also bears Rysbrack's wonderfully living head of Walpole himself: powerful, tough, calm, and humorous, it is a more convincing representation of the great man than his painted portraits.

The state bedrooms are hardly less notable, hung with Brussels tapestries. In the Green Velvet Bedchamber the bed itself is for many people the most memorable single object in the house. The dominant *motif* is the scallop shell, huge at the back of the bed and picked up repeatedly in the trimmings; and again the original green velvet, made for the house, is here. In line, colour, and texture it is a masterpiece.

The two rooms that have been somewhat altered are, first, the Cabinet Room, where the green velvet hangings were replaced by Chinese wallpaper in the 1790s, and other Chinese furniture, two exquisite mirrors and two cupboards, was brought in during the present century; and the White Drawing Room, now hung with Spitalfields silk, a gift from the Prince Regent, and furnished predominantly in the white and gold of the late 18th century.

With such changes, these rooms are not as Walpole and Kent left them; even so, they remain perhaps the finest set of interiors of their generation in the whole of England. On the other hand it must be said that what has been introduced is also of very high quality, and the variation it provides may well enhance the delight of the house. But there have been two changes, one inside and one out of doors, that are grievous.

In nearly all great families – in most others too, if the records were known – there has been at least one notable black sheep: a fool, a spendthrift, or a blackguard, whose misdoings have impaired the inheritance he left behind him (see *Stourhead*). Here it was the third Earl of Orford, Sir Robert Walpole's grandson, eccentric and incompetent, who to meet his financial difficulties sold the great man's collection of pictures to the Empress Catherine II of Russia. So that what was once at Houghton is now in the Hermitage at Leningrad.

The house was originally approached, on both its main fronts, by large and noble external staircases, giving access direct to the first floor. The same Lord Orford had them removed, to save the cost of repairing them. A new one was erected on the west front in 1973 to the original design, the masons' work most commendably executed. It is a generous attempt to put right a grave wrong; but unfortunately it does not wholly succeed, since the new staircase is in a different Aislaby stone from the original. It is to be feared that it will always stand out too prominently as an addition.

There can be no other regrets here whatever; nothing but admiration, and gratitude for the care with which everything has been cherished. It is a tribute to eight generations of owners, to the piety they have felt towards the memory of the statesman who built the house. Few houses anywhere can be more strongly impressed with the personality of their original owner. Sir Robert Walpole's is everywhere: intensely masculine, so strong that it never needs to domineer, disciplined by the education of his age and the fine taste that came partly from himself and partly from the artists who worked for him.

One enlargement of the splendours of Houghton wa planned to Walpole's orders, though never seen by him. Th house was part of its landscape, and that was remodelled under him, by Charles Bridgeman. The work was in progres in 1731, when planting had started and the plans were show to a visitor. The hindrance was the lack of full-grown timber on this light heathy soil, but that, the visitor commented could be repaired in 200 years' time. He was right. Th avenues and the spacious rides between them have no attained their maturity; ample and undulating, they stretc out from the house on every side.

A final word. One should contrive either to approach th house or to leave it by the road from the south, comin up from Castle Rising by a noble avenue to the tiny villag of Houghton, another deliberate creation, begun in 1729. Trim and whitewashed, spick and span, it attends at the park gates in the perfect dignity of its age.

Housesteads Northumberland 1B2
Hadrian's Wall is the grandest Roman monument in Britain; it ranks indeed among the great works of the whole Roman Empire. Many antiquities are important without being impressive. This one is both. It has always amazed those who looked at it, with any eyes to see. Bede mentions it, writing about the year 730. It has been examined and discussed ever since the 16th century, and in our own time more thoroughly investigated than ever before. It is a complex work, with a discontinuous history. A very large literature has accumulated about it, analysing the examinations that have been made, comparing this fortification with others that are similar elsewhere in the Roman Empire. So anyone can go to the Wall now well prepared; but the going is essential. It is beyond the power of any writer or any photographer, however skilful, to convey the full impression made by this extraordinary work. You must see it for yourself.

We speak of Hadrian's Wall, as if it were a single structure, all built at once. But "the Wall" is only a phrase to denote a very elaborate work of defence, of the delimitation of a frontier, built and then rebuilt over a long period of time. The main elements in the plan were four, not all of them present throughout the Wall's length.

The work began with the laying-down of a road from Corbridge to Carlisle by Agricola, about A.D. 80. This road is known by its English name the Stanegate, and much of it is still in use. Along the road a series of forts were erected, of which Corbridge is the best known and Chesterholm (close to Housesteads) is now being carefully examined. After a rebellion in Britain in 118 the Emperor Hadrian visited the province and ordered the building of the Wall, protected by a ditch parallel with it on the north side except where the wall ran along naturally defensible cliff. The troops were soon moved up from the Stanegate forts to new ones on the Wall itself. Finally, at the same time or soon after, another equally great work was undertaken, parallel with the Wall to the south: the Vallum, a very broad ditch flanked by earthworks. The Romans had to meet attacks from north and south. The Vallum defended the Wall, which could now be reached from the south only through gateways, placed opposite each fort. It completed the isolation of a military zone.

So there were the four elements: Ditch, Wall, Vallum, and Stanegate.

The use made of this set of defences changed according to military and political needs. Most of the work was completed by 128. About 10 years later the Wall was evacuated in favour of a new one built in Scotland from the Forth to the Clyde. The relative importance of these two works fluctuated for a time, but the Scottish wall was abandoned, perhaps as early as 163, and Hadrian's Wall permanently re-commissioned. It was destroyed, or at any rate gravely damaged, in at least four major attacks subsequently, and abandoned at last with the gradual decay of Roman imperial rule in Britain at the close of the 4th century.

The whole work was some 80 miles long, from Wallsend-on-Tyne to Bowness-on-Solway. The eastern part has been almost entirely submerged in the urban development of Newcastle and its neighbourhood. The western section, where the Wall was built of earth, not of stone, has almost entirely disappeared. So the visitor does best to make for the central part, some 30 miles in length, between Corbridge (which lies south of the Wall itself) and Birdoswald.

The best possible introduction to the Wall is afforded by the Museum of Antiquities in the University of Newcastle. This has a notable collection, especially of Roman inscribed and sculptured stones, and offers a re-creation of the building and defence of the Wall itself. The re-creation has been imaginative. Here, for instance, is the interior of a temple of Mithras; and a legionary soldier in his armour. There are models of types of building associated with the Wall. And, to bring everything together, there is one of the Wall and the associated defences throughout their length, which makes them an intelligible whole.

If you have a car, the principal points on the central section can be visited in about three days, with one more for Newcastle and another for Carlisle. Both of those are interesting towns in their own right, and Carlisle has another important collection of Roman antiquities in its Tullie House Museum. The whole length of the Wall can be walked – that is usually reckoned to take about a fortnight. Here, on the pattern of this book, one site alone, Housesteads, has been selected for brief discussion, and as a base from which other important points on the Wall can be reached.*

Housesteads was the Roman fort Vercovicium. That means "hilly place", and it lies on the Wall's hilliest section. It was sited so as to watch the steep valley of the Knag Burn, immediately to the east.

The fort is a rectangle 610 ft × 367 ft. It stretches southwards, down hill, from the Wall itself, which is pierced by the fort's north gate. The fort itself is enclosed by a wall, with a gateway on each face. Another gate was added in the 4th century down by the Knag Burn itself, for controlling commercial and civilian traffic across the frontier.

A street runs directly between the south and north gates, with the commander's residence and the headquarters building on its left (west) side and the granaries above. Behind the headquarters building is the hospital (now under investigation: the only Roman one so far examined in Britain). On the opposite side of the street, in the north-eastern sector of the fort, are the barracks. At the south-eastern

* It is not, however, a place for the visitor to stay in. There is no accommodation in Housesteads itself, and little in the neighbourhood. The nearest village (with a bus and railway service) is Bardon Mill; the nearest towns Hexham and Haltwhistle. Consult the Tourist Information centres in those towns about accommodation.

corner is the latrine block, where the arrangements of Roman sanitation are shown better than anywhere else in the country.

Here are some of the fort's chief elements, as they are now known from excavation. More is to be learnt about it from the small Museum on the site. Though none of the buildings is at all complete, the walls show not only their external outlines but sometimes, as in the case of the commander's house, the disposition of the rooms. The masonry is wonderful, squared and dressed, as sophisticated as it is in many town buildings. In its present form, it is all of the 4th century.

The fort did not stand on its own. Outside it there grew up a considerable village, a civilian settlement, which has not yet been fully investigated. The Vallum to the south has disappeared here; there is a good stretch of it to be seen four miles to the east, by Carrawburgh.

The Wall itself was fortified by "milecastles", placed at intervals of a Roman mile (1,620 yards) along it. In

Hadrian's Wall, west of Housesteads (B.T.A.)

between each pair were two turrets serving as watch and signal towers. One of the milecastles (no. 37) is at Housesteads, reached by a walk along the Wall itself quarter of a mile to the west. This was constructed by the Second Legion, and the superbly massive stonework of its north gateway may be dated to the time of Hadrian.

The conception and achievement of the Wall can be appreciated here in their full grandeur. It strides away to the east up to Sewingshields Crags, and to the west up Cuddy's Crag towards Hotbank. Northwards, across Broomlee Lough, you gaze over a seemingly illimitable distance into the hostile territory that the Wall was designed to face. In the opposite direction you are looking towards the valley of the South Tyne (parallel with the Wall) and then beyond over Alston Moor to the Pennines, where Cross Fell rises to nearly 3,000 ft. Only a few isolated buildings are visible over the whole of this sweeping prospect. All that is to be seen in motion here will often be the sheep. It is empty country, wild and grand. And yet, not empty: for if the Wall is anywhere in sight it compels one to think of the men who conceived and built and defended it.

Ile Abbots: church of St Mary Somerset 3C4

Wherever one travels in England, the church steeples – towers and spires – delight one in the landscape, varied endlessly in shape and colour and scale. Sometimes one of them seems to stand on guard, near the entrance to a county: as Church Langton does, where Leicestershire rises up from the valley of the Welland. A lofty spire can preside, in one's thoughts, over a whole journey: like Hanslope in Buckinghamshire, the finest thing to be seen anywhere on the railway between London and Liverpool.

The best series of towers is in Somerset. And with good reason. All the conditions for building them were favourable: great wealth in the Middle Ages, from farming and from the clothing industries; building stone of very high quality, various and abundant; a cathedral near the centre of the county, *Wells*, whose masons influenced the whole of the country around them. The beautiful tower at Ilminster, for instance, is manifestly modelled in design and proportion on the central tower of the cathedral: though its decoration is different, and it is built of another stone.

Stone lies at the heart of the matter, and in that Somerset is uniquely endowed. It has four outstanding varieties; not all of the same quality, but affording between them an extraordinary range of colour and texture.

At the very top, among the best building stones in the whole of England, is the oolitic limestone of the eastern part of the county, wrought to its highest perfection at Wells; and the Ham Hill stone of the upper lias – golden, honey-coloured, sometimes almost orange or tawny – seen for example in the houses at *Brympton d'Evercy* and *Montacute* or in the tower just mentioned at Ilminster. Then, widespread through the southern part of the county, the blue lias, very much inferior though sometimes agreeable from its curious colour. And finally, to the west round Taunton and in the Quantocks, red sandstone, delicately pale in colour, though like most sandstones not suitable for carving of any refinement.

Given these materials, with good communications by water to transport them and with plenty of money to spend, the builders of the Somerset church towers were fortunate, beyond any other builders in English history who used local materials only, drawn from so small a space. Their handiwork, created in a century and a half, between about 1380 and 1530, has survived abundantly. Most of the church towers survive without alteration. The stone is so good that it has not often perished, so as to require rebuilding or drastic refacing; and when they have had to be rebuilt, the splendour of the originals has demanded reconstruction and no more, loving and exact. The outstanding example is the glorious tower of St Mary's at Taunton, rebuilt with reverent humility in 1862 by Benjamin Ferrey and Gilbert Scott.

Some of the finest of these towers, like that one, are the showpieces of towns, where there was a concentration of wealth

(N.M.R.)

to pay for them. The church of Ile Abbots exemplifies, and not in its tower alone, the village church of Somerset in perfection.

To begin with the tower. Its west front, the first thing one sees on approaching, is an entirely satisfactory composition. The Somerset builders were beset by a great temptation. With all this money, with wonderful materials to their hand, in a spirit of rivalry as one town and village after another rebuilt its tower after the new fashion, their work sometimes became showy and over-ornate, decoration obliterating structure. From that criticism this tower is entirely free. The disposition of the windows (no merely decorative element; they were there to provide light and, in the upper stage, openings for the sound of the bells) is admirable: two single windows below, of diminishing size, offset by a pair above, the pinnacles and parapet exactly right in placing and scale. Notice how the uppermost pair of side pinnacles is set diagonally: one of the small devices that help to give movement to the whole design. All this is of yellow Ham Hill stone. But it is conceived as a front, no more. The rest of the tower, and the whole body of the church beyond, are built of blue lias, though the more elegant stone is also used here for dressings and for such elaborate work as the fan vault of the porch. On its own the blue lias is seldom attractive. Here, in combination with its finer counterpart, it is refreshing. Had the church been reconstructed entirely in Ham Hill stone, might it perhaps have seemed monotonous, too rich?

The rest of the exterior is relatively simple, apart from the north aisle, an elaborate piece of the 15th century. As soon as you go inside, different things begin to strike you. The body of the church is much older than the tower. The chancel – it appears at once from the lancets of the east window – is of the late 13th century. It has four excellent windows in the side walls, with plate tracery; the eastern pair still have the original grisaille glass in their upper lights. At the south-east corner is an elaborately framed piscina, and beside it a set of priests' seats, shaped like no others anywhere. The north aisle, rich outside, is rich inside too, with a panelled timber roof. Its generous windows are now filled with plain glass. The whole church is blessedly unencumbered with anything ugly, or incongruous. There is a clear light everywhere, accentuated by whitewash and coloured only by the green of the trees outside.

The most distinguished parish churches of all in England are those that were once monastic or collegiate, like Selby and Sherborne and *Beverley*, or the principal churches of big medieval towns – St Mary Redcliff at *Bristol*, *Boston*, Hull;

together with some in places that were once towns and have become, as we think today, villages, like *Patrington*. But the great majority of medieval parish churches were built to serve villages, and they do so still. Though it would not be sensible to put them in any order of merit, this much may be said: that none exemplifies the village church more happily, blending refinement with plainness to make a satisfying whole, than Ile Abbots.

Ironbridge see **Coalbrookdale**

Kedleston Derbyshire 2C5

The manor of Kedleston has been in the possession of one family, the Curzons, for at least 700 years: an exceptionally long tenure, still maintained, of one estate. They have played their full part in the social and political life of Derbyshire, as M.P.s and magistrates. They acquired a baronetcy in 1641. Sir Nathaniel Curzon was raised to the peerage in 1761 as Lord Scarsdale. And late in the 19th century they produced one man of outstanding eminence: George Nathaniel, first and only Marquess Curzon of Kedleston, Viceroy of India, Foreign Secretary, and in 1923 almost Prime Minister.

The Hall here was built by the first Lord Scarsdale, entirely replacing an earlier one. Matthew Brettingham put forward the general plan of a central block with four wings linked to it by colonnades. James Paine then took over and erected the north front. He was succeeded by Robert Adam, who designed the centre of the house, as we now see it, and the south front in 1765. The Latin inscription on this front gives the date, with the courteous addition that Lord Scarsdale intended the house *amicis et sibi*, for his friends and himself.

There are two approaches: one from the west from Kirk Langley and the village of Kedleston (removed to its present site in order to allow the park of the new Hall to be laid out in satisfactory amplitude), the other from the east, from Derby. The second is to be preferred, traversing a long stretch of the park with some splendid old oaks, crossing the noble bridge designed by Adam, with a delightful boat-house close by, and affording a broad view of the calm, majestic north front of the Hall. The whole central section is built of buff-coloured sandstone. The upper parts of the wings are of brick, covered in a dark cinnamon rendering.

Directly you open the front door you are inside the Marble Hall, one of the grandest things of its kind in the country. It is a rectangle, its roof supported on 20 richly-fluted Corinthian columns, of red alabaster from Nottinghamshire. Everything here is sumptuous, yet under the firmest discipline, from the inlaid floor (of Italian marble combined with Derby-

Kedleston: the Marble Hall (A. F. Kersting)

shire Hopton Wood stone) to the fireplaces and their furniture, and the exquisite plasterwork of the ceiling.

The hall had been intended by Paine to lead to a big formal staircase. Adam changed the plan, moving the staircase to the west side of the house and putting here instead of it a circular saloon under a low dome. This is as formal as the hall itself, but different in shape and proportion – it is smaller and half as high again – as well as in colour, very low in tone with accents provided by the pilasters of blue scagliola.

The state rooms are grouped around this central core. Notice, among many other delights, the Venetian window and the doorcases in the State Drawing Room, in alabaster; Adam's noble furniture in the same room; the severely rectangular staircase. Every piece of equipment in the Dining Room is memorable. The jasper wine-cooler and the curved tables fit perfectly into the apse that Adam designed to hold them. There is surely no finer Georgian dining room to be seen anywhere.

Having enjoyed the inside, go round the house to see the gardens to the west of it, and the south front. This front displays the ideas of "movement" that possessed Adam on his return from Italy and Dalmatia in 1762. Adam owed much to Roman example; but this front departs from it very strikingly, in the shallow ellipse of the external staircase. The whole composition is alas incomplete. There were to have been two more wings here (in accordance with Brettingham's original plan), and in them these swirling curves might have reappeared.

Adjoining the house on the west is the church (All Saints), a small cruciform building notable for its monuments. Two stone heads sunk into the floor of the chancel, which date from about 1275, may commemorate Richard Curzon and his wife. They are without inscriptions, but it is highly probable that they represent the lord of the manor and his lady. If we accept this, then the sequence of Curzon monuments here stretches over nearly 700 years: something unique in England as the memorial of a single family. In the south transept there is a fine alabaster monument to Sir John Curzon, who died about 1450, and his wife; a poor one to the first baronet, erected 20 years before his death; and one opposite it to Sir Nathaniel Curzon, father of the first Lord Scarsdale, designed by Adam and executed by Rysbrack. The north aisle of the nave, designed by G. F. Bodley in 1906, was built to contain the monument to Lord Curzon's first wife; the white effigies are by Sir Bertram Mackennal. The iron grille is a fine one, of a kind lovingly developed by Bodley in his later years.

As one goes away, looking back once more at the house and the church and their setting, and reflects on the exceptional continuity of this family's tenure, one understands why one of their mottoes should be "Let Curzon hold what Curzon held".

Kempley: church of St Mary Gloucestershire 4D2

A very small church, reached by narrow and winding lanes. It is built entirely of limestone, the roof included, and comprises a Norman chancel with a 13th-century nave and tower. On the south side one large 14th-century window has been inserted, and a timber porch of the same date built on. The interior seems equally plain and simple until one's eyes grow accustomed to the subdued light and one begins to take in the paintings in the nave and, much more remarkable, the painted vault of the chancel.

No English church is decorated inside today exactly as it was in the Middle Ages. Every surface was then usually ornamented, with painting or sculpture. Much of this was destroyed by the vandals of the Reformation and the Civil War; most of what still remained perished through neglect in the 18th century or mistaken restoration in the 19th. It is quite impossible to recover now the full character of the decoration of medieval buildings in England; in this respect they are entirely different from what they were designed to be, and were when they were erected. Where sculpture and glass are concerned, the loss is an irreparable disaster; the

(N.M.R.)

efforts of the Victorians at imitation, painstaking and hardly ever successful, demonstrate that everywhere. But the painting is another matter. Enough original fragments remain to enable us to see that much of it was crude, some of it indeed perfunctory – ornamentation commissioned, so to speak, by the yard. Worse, it is clear that it was often garish: zigzags and rectilinear patterns in harsh reds and yellows. Still, if one wishes to appreciate medieval architecture one must take account of this important element in it.

There is no surviving decoration in England to be compared with what is to be found here and there in France (as at St Savin-sur-Gartempe), still less with the best in Italy. All we have, for the most part, are little fragments, usually of very poor quality, or, when good, faded beyond the power to give us pleasure; together with a very few more elaborate and extensive schemes that come nearer to being intact. Here at Kempley is the best in any English parish church.

These paintings were whitewashed over after the Reformation and rediscovered only in 1872. The whitewash was then taken off and they were covered with a shellac varnish to preserve them. Under this, over the years, they faded, until in 1955 Mrs Eve Baker removed the varnish, to reveal that they were still in good condition. The paintings had been executed on wet plaster (this was the Italian, though not the English practice), and that had helped to preserve them.

The whole scheme of the paintings in the chancel is clear: the seated Christ in the centre, surrounded by the sun, moon, and stars, and the symbols of the Evangelists; the Virgin Mary and St Peter; standing angels, one at each corner; below them the twelve Apostles, six on each side, and some detached figures, a pilgrim and a bishop. The colours are red, yellow, and white, and (much more faded) green. The faces have mostly been obliterated – presumably by the religious yahoos – and one figure in the north-east corner has entirely gone because a wall tablet was placed over it. The tall Christ and the great angels are most majestic, and so likewise are the conversing Apostles. There is much delightful detail, such as the towered buildings over the north and south windows and the perspective in chequered patterns painted on their splays. Apart from the mutilations, nothing interferes with one's admiration and enjoyment except perhaps the sickly little east window – effusively cheerful, and quite inappropriate – by C. E. Kempe. Electric lights are provided low down in the chancel. The paintings should be looked at with their aid, and then again without it.

The fine Norman chancel arch is also painted delicately In the nave the decoration is of the 14th century, and very much less clear, though a Wheel of Life can be seen on the north side and a Last Judgment is discernible high up on the east wall.

The only entrance to the tower is from inside the church an arrangement adopted to make it defensible if necessary

– as it might well have been in this secluded place, not far from the Welsh border, in the time of Edward I.

Apart from the former vicarage and a large farmhouse of the 17th century, there are no buildings at all in this little valley. The village is up on the hill, with a new church of its own – an interesting Arts and Crafts building by Randall Wells, of 1903. The old church has therefore now been declared redundant. One is bound to speculate about its future. Mrs Baker's admirable work was accompanied by an equally admirable engineer's job of underpinning the chancel with a concrete U-bolt to prevent subsidence. So all that the skill of our age can do to preserve this wonderful chancel has been done. But what, in the long run, can be the fate of a building like this, disused, so remote and so vulnerable?

Kirkleatham Cleveland 1C3

An extremely strange place, at once melancholy and inspiriting.

The village stands quite on its own, in the plain between the Cleveland Hills and the sea. Redcar, a residential town and seaside resort, is two miles to the north; to the west are the works of Imperial Chemical Industries at Wilton, the advanced outposts of Teesside, peering down insistently. Kirkleatham belongs to another world, made by the Turner family in the 17th and 18th centuries.

The estate was bought by John Turner in 1623. His younger son William made a fortune in London, was knighted, and served as Lord Mayor in 1668 and 1669. Sir William endowed Kirkleatham munificently with a Hospital providing for 20 elderly men and women and 20 orphans, founded in 1676. When he died in 1692 he bequeathed £5,000 to establish a Free School. His nephew Cholmley Turner carried on his work, opening the school in 1709 and largely reconstructing the Hospital. He also began to rebuild the family house, Kirkleatham Hall, and the parish church; but he did not complete the work, turning aside to erect a mausoleum to the memory of his only son, Marwood Turner, who died on the Grand Tour of Europe in 1739, aged 22. The rebuilding of the church and the Hall was completed in the next generation.

The last of the Turners died in 1810. The estate then came into the hands of others, Vansittarts and Newcomens. The charities were maintained, on the basis of the original foundations. But presently the place decayed. The Hall was demolished in 1955. Since then a good deal has been done to renovate and improve the village, notably by the construction of a by-pass, to take away the choking traffic.

Now that the Hall has gone, Kirkleatham does not make a readily intelligible whole. To the visitor it is a loose group of units. The church of St Cuthbert is tucked away down a side road. The tower is of 1731, the rest rebuilt to the plans of John Carr of York and a local man, Robert Corney. The masonry is very good. Unfortunately the original fittings have been altered or replaced. The monuments include a fine 17th-century brass to John Turner's father-in-law, Robert Coulthirst. There are two Turner monuments in the chancel, but the most important are in the mausoleum, which adjoins the church on the north side.

This is a curious building by James Gibbs, erected in 1740. It is an octagon crowned by a pyramid, a very oddly assorted neighbour to the four-square chancel, when seen from outside. Within everything is plain, not as Gibbs left it but as it was refashioned in 1839. In the middle stands Sir William Turner's monument, moved out from the chancel. The young Marwood Turner is here with books about him, in a fine monument by Scheemakers; his grieving father, by Cheere; and Sir Charles, who brought the line to an end in 1810. There are all the chief characters in the story.

A little way to the south is the Old Hall, which is a puzzle. It was the Free School erected by Cholmley Turner but what was the disposition of its parts? The building is big – really three houses in one; and nobody knows how it was intended to be used. The school was moved to Coatham in 1864.

The Hospital is another very large building. The Turner

always thought on the generous scale characteristic of Yorkshire. Few charitable institutions of the sort can match it. (A southern rival would be the Somerset Hospital at Froxfield, near Marlborough in Wiltshire.) The building is on three sides of a courtyard, entered through splendid iron gates ascribed to Warren of Cambridge. Two fine statues, of an old man and woman (perhaps by Scheemakers), face inwards, and in the centre is another, of Justice (by Cheere?). The orphans' schools of the original foundation are in the two buildings in front, which flank the chapel.

The chapel was begun in Sir William Turner's lifetime, the interior finished in 1724, the exterior (including the tower) in 1742. No architect can be named with certainty, but it may well be by Gibbs. The plan is a Greek cross within a square. The whole building is painted white inside, and it combines strength with opulence. The strength comes from the plan and from the dark woodwork, including the capacious galleries above. The opulence is in the fluted Ionic columns, the delicate ironwork of the altar rails, the east window (glowing painted glass of the early 18th century), and two pieces

(The Trustees, Sir William Turner's Hospital)

of furnishing, imported yet both entirely at home. The superb pair of chairs by the altar are by William Kent, identical with some of those at *Houghton*; and the gorgeous baroque chandelier, made of limewood gilded, came from the Duke of Chandos's house Canons, outside London.

In view of what has happened to the City churches in London and to almost every other parish church of Wren's time elsewhere, this chapel is now one of the most completely untouched works of its kind anywhere in England. It comes very close to perfection.

The strangeness to be felt everywhere at Kirkleatham is also present here. At the back of the north aisle there is an inconspicuous glass case. From inside it Sir William Turner looks straight at you. This is his death-mask, dressed in his own wig: not ghastly at all, except in its pallor, but the face of a calm and sensible man, about to speak. Death-mask though it is, it keeps him uncannily in life.

The decay of Kirkleatham is still visible. However lovingly it is cared for, it can never retrieve what has been lost, become once again a complete whole. But the love and the care are evident, privately in the church and the Hospital (both faultlessly kept) and throughout the village no less than on the part of the local authority. The village was made an early Conservation Area, in 1970. If that gives it a paper protection only (dreadful things have been done in Conservation Areas here and there), it represents, on the part of the planning authority, a firm statement of intent. Ceaseless vigilance is still needed, for Kirkleatham is very fragile, vulnerable to strong pressures that are evident and close. But a good effort is being made. Here is something to be grateful for, and to salute.

Knightshayes Court Devon 3C4

The Victorian age is generally held now in great respect. "Victoriana", in many forms, are popular with collectors; the literature concerned with the age grows fast; the Victorian Society works hard to protect its monuments when they are threatened with damage or destruction. Yet the appreciation of it remains limited. The student of Victorian architecture has thousands of churches at his disposal – half a dozen are discussed in this book. But very few Victorian houses are open to the public, and of those few some are scarcely worth visiting. *Standen* was the first to be acquired by the National Trust as a building in itself, not primarily for its contents or its gardens. But that – it has been truly said – is an anti-Victorian house, in which current conventions were not followed but flouted. Knightshayes is different: a house of the high Mid-Victorian age, built in 1869–73, displaying strongly the ideas and principles of its time.

It lies three miles north of Tiverton and was built for John Heathcoat-Amory, head of the large lace-making business there, a Liberal politician as well as an industrialist, made a baronet in 1874. His architect was William Burges, then engaged in reconstructing Cardiff Castle for the Marquess of Bute. Burges was fastidious, and worked slowly. The fabric took four years to complete, and then its internal decoration was barely begun. His client apparently lost patience, discharged Burges and engaged J. G. Crace, a successful commercial practitioner, to finish the work instead. Not much of the original decoration remains within the house today. The

(A. F. Kersting)

complicated story of its displacement and restoration is recounted in the notes given to visitors.

The exterior states the ideas of its architect powerfully. The house stands up well, facing south over its park down the Exe valley. It is built of local sandstone, red and purple, with golden dressings from Ham Hill in Somerset (see *Ile Abbots*). Two wings thrust themselves forward, ending in three-storeyed bays. The chimney-stacks are big but not dominant. Long water-spouts shoot out from the eaves, boldly grotesque. The carving of animals everywhere, outside the house and in, is forceful. There is nothing over-assertive or pugnacious about the building, as there was in some of its immediate predecessors and contemporaries, like Teulon's Elvetham or Waterhouse's Eaton Hall. Its surroundings have been altered and softened since. Burges designed the house to rise not from lawns but from stepped terraces flanked by big stone drums.

There has been much more change inside. The Hall originally had a screens passage, in the medieval tradition, linking the entrance door with the one opposite, and a gallery above. That passage has gone. The staircase is a notable piece of craftsmanship in teak, worth looking at from underneath. The Dining Room, Morning Room, Library, and Drawing Room make a fine series, *en suite* facing south. The animal carvings that Burges designed are seen at their best in the Dining Room and the Billiard Room (now in use as a restaurant). But most of the specifically Victorian character of the decoration has gone. The Drawing Room is now distinctly 18th-century in its feeling, with its glass chandeliers and lovely apple-green Worcester porcelain.

The house is ennobled by some distinguished paintings, including a small self-portrait by Rembrandt, a fragment of a Raphael cartoon, a Claude, and a Turner. They were acquired by the late Sir John Heathcoat-Amory, to whom Knightshayes owes much. He and his wife remade the gardens, enlarging and beautifully diversifying them. The Garden in the Wood on the east side of the house is an outstanding achievement: a delectable flower garden set within the wood itself. This part of the work, completed in 1972, was commemorated by the erection of the simple Cedar House, looking on to the open Glade and containing some of the carved oak bosses designed by Burges.

So although Knightshayes is a monument of the Mid-Victorian age, it has like most country houses been freshly handled by succeeding generations. The process continues happily still, in the hands of the National Trust.

Lanercost Priory Cumbria 1B2

A good way to come to Lanercost is by turning off the Carlisle–Newcastle road about two miles east of Brampton and walking or driving down through the park of Naworth Castle. The Castle was a stronghold of the Dacres and later the Howards (restored with restraint by Salvin), and the road skirts round it, then descending under fine beech trees to the River Irthing. At the foot of the hill there is an agreeable inn, and a medieval bridge of note: high, humpbacked, its two arches divided by a big triangular cutwater. Lanercost Priory lies quarter of a mile to the east.

It was founded for Augustinian canons about 1165. A little of the first church remains, but most of the present fabric dates from the 13th century. Here, as everywhere else near the Border, one has to think of the long warfare between the English and the Scots. The Priory was repeatedly battered in Scottish raids between 1296 and 1346. Edward I stayed here three times in the Guest House, which is now part of the vicarage, immediately west of the church. On the last occasion he arrived in September 1306 and was taken so ill that he remained here all through that winter until March 1307. He never left Cumberland again, dying at Burgh-by-Sands on the Solway two months later.

The church is approached now through a fragment of its ancient gateway, across a broad green. It displays an admirable west front, in the pure style of the earlier 13th century, with a beautiful figure of St Mary Magdalen, undamaged, standing in a niche in the gable. The nave remains

(A. F. Kersting)

in use as the parish church, its eastern wall and window built up about 1740. Three windows in the aisle are filled with glass by the firm of William Morris.

The eastern parts of the church are now unroofed, but not ruinous. There are 16th-century tombs of the Dacres here, the heraldry splendidly executed on that of Sir Thomas Dacre (d. 1525) on the south side of the chancel. Of the domestic buildings of the Priory the undercroft of the refectory, the cellarium, survives. Adjoining it is the Prior's House, which the Dacres incorporated into a house for themselves after they had acquired the Priory at the Dissolution.

The special charm of Lanercost, as of so much in this part of Cumbria, arises from the delicate rose-pink sandstone of which it is chiefly built (in the chancel, however, there are two tones, of pink and buff). It is also fortunate in its site, in the green valley of the Irthing. Nothing could be more peaceful now. But along the northern slopes of that valley, only a mile away, runs the Roman Wall: another reminder of the dangerous proximity of Scotland.

Launcells: church of St Swithin Cornwall 3B4

Like most other things in Cornwall, the churches have a strongly-marked character of their own. They are small, and built low to withstand the winds. Nearly all of them are of one storey only, and the few that rise higher are all in the south, away from the gales sweeping in from the Atlantic. One major building stone predominates, granite, and that is too hard for any but the simplest carving. Where delicate decoration appears, it is either in monuments, in local slate or alien marble, or in the woodwork of roofs and screens and seating. So the great qualities of these churches are simplicity and a massive strength. But the strength is not rude; it is given shapeliness, even grace, by the towers, relatively slender for their height and made to look higher still by the groups of pinnacles that crown them.

Though some of these churches stand on hill tops and are seen from afar, like St Breward and St Dennis and Goran, the great majority are sheltered down in the valleys. No scene is more characteristic of Cornwall than one of these small valleys thickly clad in trees, with a church tower springing out of them.

All this is exemplified at Launcells. As elsewhere in England, so in Cornwall, the Victorian restorers were active: the county produced one of the busiest and least sensitive of them all, J. P. St Aubyn. But none of them ever came to Launcells. When repairs were needed, they were undertaken tenderly and carefully in the 1930s, and again about 10 years ago. There have been only two losses: the screen and the medieval glass. But the second of those is a loss with compensations. Even in this sequestered place the church could hardly have retained its original glass; in nine cases out of 10, the Victorians would have filled the clear windows strongly. As it is, the building is full of plain daylight, accentuated by the white-washed walls.

Though the present church had a Norman predecessor (its font remains), it is now entirely of the 15th century. The two arcades are closely similar in design, but in different materials. The northern one is of the usual granite, the southern (a little earlier) of polyphant, a blue-grey stone quarried 15 miles away to the south near Launceston and seldom used except here for anything larger than a font or the tracery of a window.

The nave is furnished with a complete set of medieval pews, comprising not merely bench-ends but some of the seating too. The bench-ends, 60 and more of them, are fascinating. The carving is not refined, but each panel conveys its allusion directly and with a terseness almost telegraphic. There is not one human figure, yet they range over the

(Janet & Colin Bord)

whole story of the Passion: the 30 pieces of silver, pincers and ladder and spear, coffin and spice-box. They refer to some of Christ's followers: the cross of St Andrew (to whom the church was originally dedicated) with three tears, the incredulity of St Thomas, Mary's heart pierced with a sword.

In the chancel there is another survival from the Middle Ages. Almost the whole sanctuary is paved with 15th-century embossed tiles, made in Barnstaple, green, yellow, and red, showing griffins, lions, pelicans, fleurs-de-lis, and roses.

The rest of the chancel furniture is remarkable in a different way. It is Georgian Gothic. The reredos is of white marble, in a black wooden frame, carrying the Ten Commandments; the altar rails very prettily carved; the pulpit of the same age. This church was well cared for in the 18th century. The nave was then given a plain plaster ceiling (those in the aisles are original, showing their medieval carved timbers), and handsome box-pews were brought into the north aisle, though happily they did not displace their predecessors in the nave. On the north wall is a magnificent representation of the arms of King Charles II, one of a group to be seen in the neighbourhood by Michael Chuke of Kilkhampton.

Altogether this church has been fortunate. It is admirably looked after now, and it richly deserves all the care and affection that have been devoted to it in successive generations.

Leeds West Yorkshire 2C4

Leeds is a great commercial city: that is its character, as compared with its rivals Bradford (where, to a larger extent, woollen goods were actually made) and Sheffield, the town of steel. It wears, more than they, the air of a metropolis. In Leeds – as in *Liverpool*, most abundantly – there is a palpable civic pride. Its warehouses and mills, the monuments of its rise to greatness, are disappearing very rapidly, in favour of the faceless concrete of our own time. But it still includes, at its centre or in its suburbs, at least five buildings of great note: one medieval, two of the 17th and 18th centuries, and two Victorian.

LEEDS

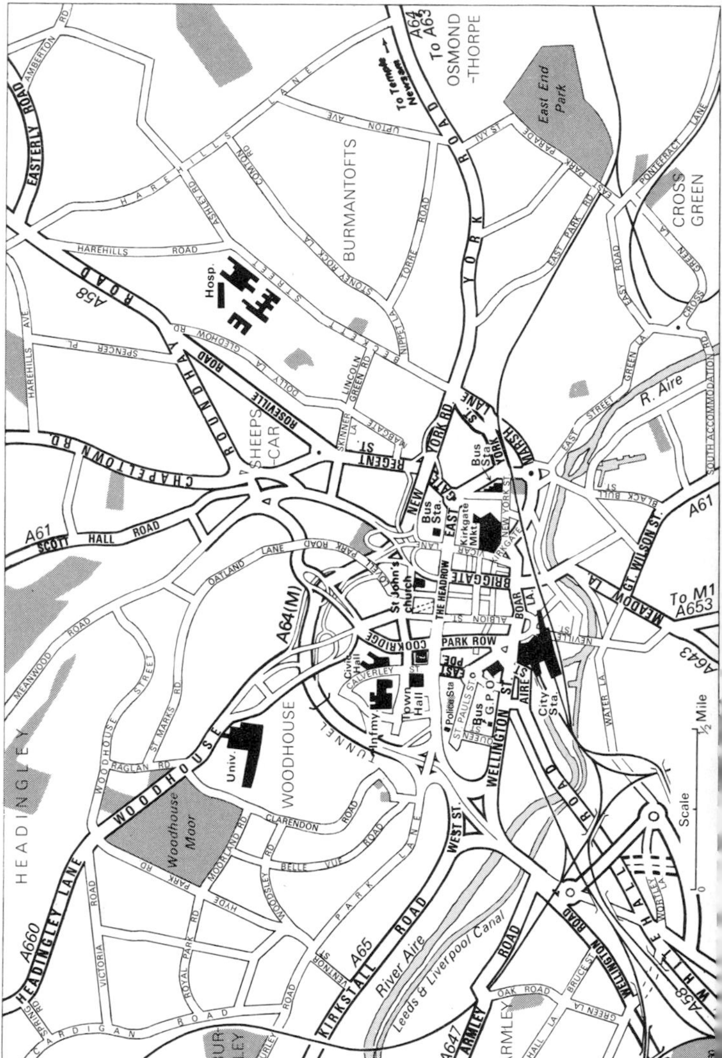
HEADINGLEY
WOODHOUSE
BURMANTOFTS
OSMOND -THORPE
CROSS GREEN
SHEEPS -CAR
ARMLEY
BUR- LEY
East End Park
Woodhouse Moor
Univ.
Hosp.
Town Hall
Civic Hall
Infmy
St John's church
Kirkgate Mkt.
Bus Sta.
City Sta.
G.P.O.
Police Sta
R. Aire
River Aire
Leeds & Liverpool Canal
To Temple Newsam
To A63
A64
To M1 A653
A643
A61
A660
A65
A647
A58
A64(M)
YORK ROAD
EASTERLY ROAD
HAREHILLS LANE
HAREHILLS ROAD
ROUNDHAY ROAD
CHAPELTOWN RD.
SCOTT HALL ROAD
ROSEVILLE ROAD
REGENT ST.
NEW YORK RD.
THE HEADROW
BRIGGATE
PARK ROW
BOAR LA.
WELLINGTON ST.
WEST ST.
KIRKSTALL ROAD
WOODHOUSE LANE
HEADINGLEY LANE
MEADOW LA
GT. WILSON ST.
MARSH LANE
EAST ST.
ARMLEY ROAD
WELLINGTON ROAD
WHITEHALL ROAD
CARDIGAN ROAD
CLARENDON ROAD
MEANWOOD ROAD
Scale
½ Mile

Let us begin with the Victorian pair, both at the centre, both planned within a space of 10 years and by the same architect: Cuthbert Brodrick, a Yorkshireman (see also *Scarborough*).

The first is the Town Hall, which dates from 1853–8.

(Leeds City Council)

A large number of such buildings went up throughout England during the Victorian age. For many people – I am one – this is the king of them all. It rises nobly from a great flight of steps to a Corinthian portico; and above that soars a tower, crowned by a domed spire with concave sides, attaining a height of 225 ft. The outline is unique, and recognisable in any distant view of Leeds – upbraiding, as the dome of St Paul's does in London, the mass of dull building that now closes it in. The *façade* is the most splendid part of the Town Hall, but the whole exterior is worth looking at; walk up the hill behind, to see it from above. Inside there is a high elliptical entrance vestibule and then, beyond that, an ornate concert hall, with a celebrated organ (lately rebuilt). The interior is imposing, but the decoration is restless and it does not achieve the same perfection as the *façade*. That embodies, no single building better, the conviction, the pride in achievement, of Early Victorian England.

Brodrick's Corn Exchange (1861–3) is a very different work. It is of two storeys, oval in shape, and not ornate in the least: strictly functional, in fact. The big hall inside is lighted by a partly-glazed dome. As its furnishing indicates, it is still in use as a Corn Exchange. It rides with complete assurance above its crowded and rather squalid surroundings.

The third building, still in the centre of the city, is a church: St John's, built at the expense of a Leeds cloth merchant, John Harrison, in 1634. It was strictly traditionalist when erected: still in the late-Gothic manner, though to an untraditional plan comprising two naves of equal size. The woodwork, however, is not Gothic but Jacobean in its character, and it fills every part of the building. Not many churches of this date survive, with their furnishing intact; none at all that expresses, so completely as this one, the pious intentions of a middle-class founder, in sympathy with Laud's desire for seemliness of worship without accepting his theology.

And so back into another world of piety, quite untouched by anything commercial. Improbably, Leeds contains the most complete example of a medieval Cistercian church in Britain; and one of the earliest, founded about 1152. This is Kirkstall Abbey, well within the whole urban complex, less than four miles from the City Square. Its situation is characteristic of such monasteries: low in a valley, close to running water and – when it was built – remote from towns. The church survives unaltered, though roofless except at the east end. The chancel affords a very early English example of pointed rib-vaulting. The only addition that was made was a central tower (something actually forbidden in the original statutes of the Order), and that was heightened early in the 16th century, just before the Dissolution, which swept the monks away. Only one wall of this upper storey survives, but it provides, with the empty tracery of the windows, a romantically beautiful silhouette – rendered beautifully in a watercolour by Girtin nearly 200 years ago.

This one fragment of the 16th century is all that shows elaborate patterns of decoration. Everywhere else things are either plain or carved in severe geometrical forms. The church delights one by its simple, undisturbed purity, enhanced by the millstone grit of which it is built, now blackened by smoke and time. The same is true of the monastic buildings, notably the vaulted chapter house. It all stands in a public park, close to a main road. But it is not just a curious ruin. It is still to be seen as a fine work of architecture.

Finally, move across the city, into yet another world: to Temple Newsam, the great house of the Ingram family, which passed to the Corporation of Leeds in 1922. It is strikingly placed on a ridge, three miles east of the centre. High-rise buildings peer over its western horizon. Southward of it is the valley of the Aire, this part of it now wholly industrialised. To the east there were formerly fine woods, cut by a cleft designed to lead the eye into them, looking from the house; but the south part of this woodland is now raw from open-cast coal working, the trees felled. One cannot therefore fail to be aware of the presence of industry, hemming in the house and its park on every side. The estate, when it was bought by the city, comprised over 900 acres. It has been put to various uses, including a golf-course; the stables provide a restaurant, a café, and a room for exhibitions; below, in a dell to the north-east of the house, there is a garden.

One needs plenty of time for seeing the house. Outside, it seems at first sight to be a Jacobean building, something in the tradition of *Hatfield*, though coarser in its rough northern brick. Its history is in fact more complex than appears, and more interesting. The estate was once a possession of the Templars. In the late Middle Ages it belonged to the Darcy family, until the last of them forfeited it, with his life, for rebellion. It then passed to an Earl of Lennox, whose son Lord Darnley (the future husband of Mary Queen of Scots) was born here in 1545. Much plotting against the government went on at Temple Newsam during Elizabeth's reign. The estate was again confiscated, and then granted by James I to his cousin the Duke of Lennox; but he was a spendthrift and sold it to a wealthy financier and politician, Sir Arthur Ingram, in 1622. With the Ingrams and their descendants it remained for exactly 300 years.

The building reflects a good deal of this story. The oldest part of it is the centre of the west wing, which is Tudor, with diapered brickwork, and was probably erected by the last Lord Darcy. This Tudor house was built round a court. Sir Arthur Ingram reconstructed it entirely soon after he bought it, demolishing the east wing, which he replaced with a stone screen and a gatehouse, and heightening the whole, to give it approximately its present bulk and shape. The house was much altered inside in the 18th century, the south wing rebuilt in 1796. Ingram's inscription in letters of stone around the roof was then replaced, in handsome gilded iron. A century later, an effort was made to restore the Jacobean character of the house. This was the responsibility of Mrs Meynell-Ingram, the builder of the church of *Hoar Cross*, and here too she employed her favourite architect, G. F. Bodley. So the house displays with precision the cycle of taste as it has revolved over more than 300 years.

The most remarkable of all these alterations is to be seen in the Saloon. Like every other house of its date, Sir Arthur Ingram's had a Long Gallery. To the 18th century these immense apartments, low-ceiled and tunnel-like, were uncongenial. Robert Adam devoted exquisite ingenuity to remodelling the one at *Syon*. Here at Temple Newsam a simpler solution was adopted. The Gallery was drastically shortened by making separate rooms out of it at each end, and broadened by taking in a corridor on the south side. Since it was already

Temple Newsam; the Saloon (N.M.R.)

tall in comparison with many of its kind, this gave it, to the eye of the time, something much nearer the correct proportion. The result is a superb room, filled with furniture made for it in 1735, a harmony of red and gold.

It is easy, all the same, to see why Mrs Meynell-Ingram felt that, inside, the original character of the house had quite gone – the character that the whole exterior still bore. The staircase (designed for her by C. E. Kempe, the glass-painter) is the chief monument of the changes she made.

The house contains fine pictures and some splendid furniture, all described in each room with care and accuracy. Here is a personal selection of five pieces. Two of them are pictures: the grave, direct Portrait of a Man by Pourbus and the elaborate Reynolds of Lady Hertford (mother of the Marquess of Steyne in *Vanity Fair*); Roubiliac's bust of Pope; the brass chandelier now in the Great Hall, made for Cheltenham church in 1738; and – one among a score of first-rate pieces of furniture – the *bureau-plat* by Bernard van Risenburgh, one of the great craftsmen of Paris under Louis XV.

The pride of Leeds, and the pride of Yorkshire, of which it is the outstanding commercial city, have given it a touch of grandeur, seldom found in the English provinces though much more often in France – as at Lyon or Bordeaux – and in the United States of America.

Lincoln Lincolnshire 2D5

The position of Lincoln is lordly; one's first sight of the cathedral, lying along its escarpment, a thing to remember through life. First and last, it is always the cathedral one thinks of at Lincoln. But the town was there long before a stone of the cathedral was laid. For Lincoln was one of the leading cities in Roman Britain.

It was placed on the southern edge of a limestone plateau, where the ground falls steeply to the River Witham. The site was already occupied in the Iron Age, before the Romans arrived. They built a fortress there, in which the Ninth Legion was stationed, and then at the end of the 1st century A.D. it was turned into a *colonia*, a settlement for veteran soldiers who had got their discharge. Hence the name "Lincoln": a contraction of *Lindum colonia*, where the first element is a Celtic word for a lake (the modern Welsh *llyn*), a reference to the widening of the river, still to be seen in Brayford Pool. No town bears a name that personifies its history better. The two syllables unite Celtic and Roman speech, and at the same time reflect the dual nature of the town – the settlement on the hill, and the extension of it towards the river below.

We know nothing of what happened in Lincoln when the Roman government was withdrawn in the 5th century. The place was important again, as we learn from Bede, about the year 630. It became a centre of Danish power for a time in the 9th century; at the Norman Conquest it was one of the largest towns in the country. A castle was then founded on the west side of the Roman town and the seat of the bishop of Lindsey was removed from *Stow* to Lincoln in 1072. The cathedral and the castle rose, close together, on the hill. New walls were built to protect them both (as the cathedral grew bigger in the 13th century, the Roman east wall was swept away in its favour). This enclosed town on the top of the hill became known as the Bail; its main street is still today called Bailgate. The lower town was also walled in the Middle Ages, as it had been under the Romans, the southern wall running along the line of the river. There seem to have been altogether 46 parish churches within the walled area, or close to it; only four of these survive.

It was essentially a town of a single street: the Bailgate, continued southwards by what is rightly known as the Steep Hill, then the Strait, and then the High Street. The street crosses the river at the High Bridge. Brayford Pool opens out to the west, the port of Lincoln. But Lincoln is 40 miles from the sea, and *Boston* came to displace it for this purpose in the 14th century, much as *Bristol* displaced *Gloucester*. When that change became marked, Lincoln's commercial prosperity began to decline. It remained an important centre of administration, and the cathedral city of the largest diocese in England. But those were things that chiefly concerned the Bail, the town Above Hill, in the common local phrase. The one Below Hill was a poor relation.

No new development occurred in Lincoln until the 19th century. When that century began it had become a backwater, with a population of only 7,000, rather shabby and poor - except in the Bail, occupied by the churchmen and lawyers. It lay off the chief lines of communication, the Great North

LINCOLN

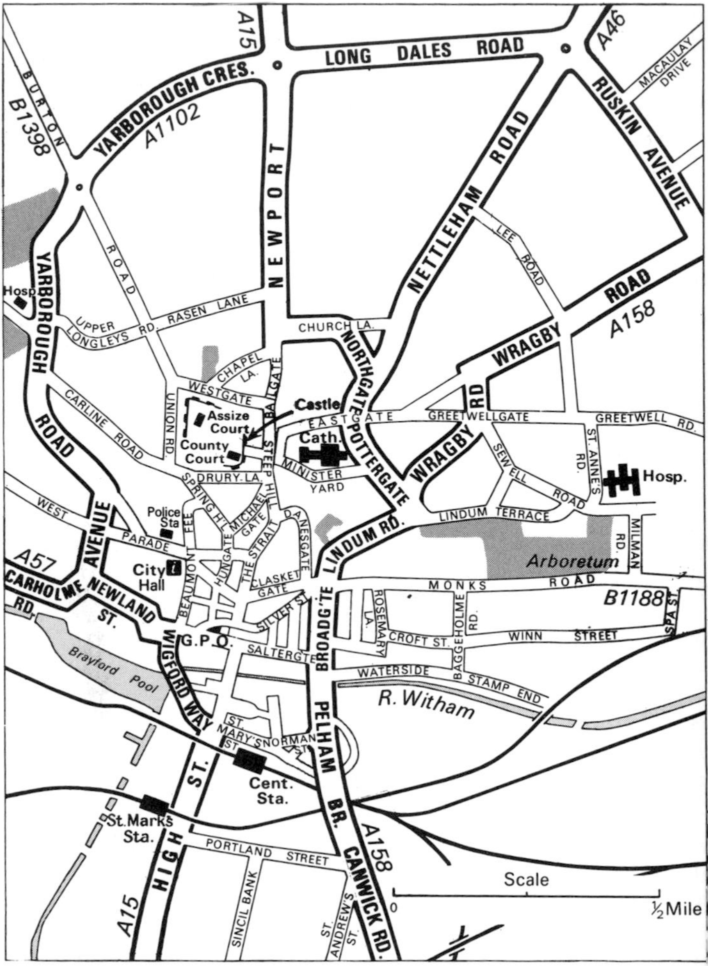

Road of the coaches and then the main railways. But it seized the advantage that the railways offered and developed a new commercial importance as a centre of manufacturing industry, especially of agricultural machinery. By 1900 its population was about 50,000; today it is half as big again

In that process the balance of power between the city Above Hill and Below Hill changed.

The cathedral is a most essentially English building – even though all the chief influences that went to its making were Continental. So much is clear outside at the west front. The central part of that is Romanesque, the one substantial portion of the first cathedral of Lincoln that survives, erected under a bishop from Normandy and enriched about 1150 with a portal owing much to St Denis in France and a sculptured frieze derived from Modena in Italy. But, from about 1190 onwards, the whole of the rest of the original church was rebuilt and this front, already large, was made much larger still both in height and in width. It became a vast screen, and it ceased to express accurately the building that lay behind it. Something similar happened at *Wells*. Inside, one is in a building that could not be anything but English. Its proportions are quite different from those of the great churches in France. Here is breadth, dignity, sure repose, but none of the ecstatic leaping upwards that thrills one at Reims and Amiens.

The earliest part of the present church, except for the west front, is the pair of eastern transepts and the choir – that is, the choir used as such today; they were built at the very end of the 12th century. Next come the nave, the main transepts, and the chapter house; then, lastly, the Angel Choir, which extended the church eastwards in 1255–80. So the whole building we see, behind the west front, was completed in about 90 years. Only one major addition remained: the towers. There was already a central tower, the lowest stage of which is still visible. In 1305–11 it was heightened to its present form: tall, bold, and graceful, one of the loveliest in England. Presently, in the 15th century, the two western towers were similarly raised, to match up to it.

Of the architects responsible for all this work we know one by name, the most original and curious of them: Geoffrey de Noyers, who was brought in as "constructor" in 1192. He left his marks powerfully on the eastern transepts and

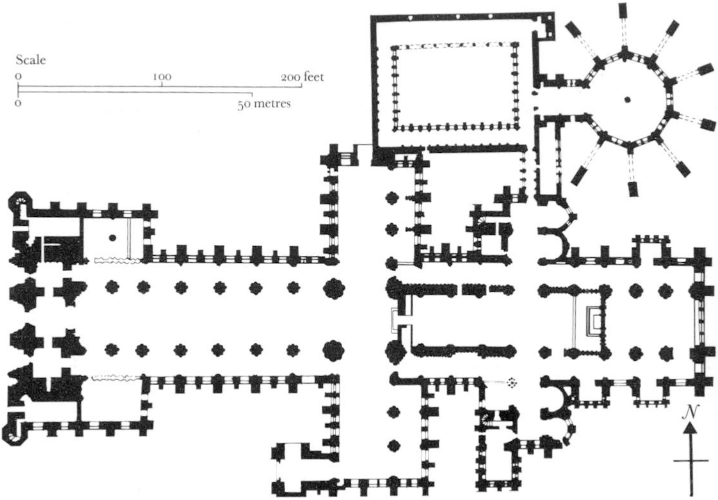

the choir: in the beautiful double arcading on the walls, in the mixture of round columns and octagonal piers, and of broad and narrow pointed arches in one arcade. He used the grey Purbeck stone then becoming fashionable in England (see *Salisbury*), in combination with the local Lincolnshire limestone, though much less lavishly than his successor in the nave. He had his mannerisms and faults, and his geometry seems to have been weak. The vault of the choir is a fascinating design, the earliest we know in which a rib runs straight along the ridge. But the arrangement of the ribs that curve up to meet the central one is lop-sided. This engaging irregularity occurs again and again at Lincoln, not only in the work of Geoffrey; look at the miscalculation in the vaulting of the north transept, and the frequent uneven number and size of arches in a series.

The Angel Choir is a very different matter. Here there are no such irregularities. The work is totally accomplished It was designed as a great enlargement of the existing choir to accommodate the shrine of St Hugh of Lincoln, the bishop who had been largely responsible for the rebuilding of the church in the 12th century and had been canonised in 1220. It was an enlargement in breadth, giving spacious aisles and a square east end in place of a series of rounded chapels on the plan still to be seen at *Norwich*. But the height remained exactly the same, preserving and enhancing the external harmony of the building as a whole. The Angel Choir is very richly decorated – by contrast with the old choir and nave – with clusters of leaves, with 28 carvings of angels and of Christ and the Virgin high up between the arches, and a magnificent series of bosses in the roof. It is lighted by an enormous east window, filled now with 19th-century glass. That is not bad of its kind. But there is some superb glass at Lincoln, of a quite different order of merit: above all in the rose window of the north transept, "the Dean's Eye", a sparkling jewelled composition of the 13th century, and in the "Bishop's Eye" opposite in the south transept, whose flowing tracery contains a great many fragments, irregularly set.

There are notable things to look for in every part of the church. Best of all perhaps the details of the carving and sculpture: in the arches at the entrance to the choir aisles (one of them is delicately illuminated), for instance; in the great south-east porch, much restored outside but containing three wonderful sequences in the vault inside, almost untouched; the female statue standing immediately to the east of this porch, impertinently hemmed in by the parapet of a 15th-century chapel. Nor are all the good things at Lincoln medieval. There is a splendid brass chandelier in the choir, given in 1698; the pulpit in the nave is a noble piece that came from the English church at Rotterdam; and the Honeywood Library, above the cloisters, was added to the design of Sir Christopher Wren in 1674. This is a handsome great room, built above a Tuscan arcade, opening out of the surviving part of the medieval library: a notable building, in which some of the cathedral's treasures are shown.

Another group of those treasures is to be seen inside the cathedral itself. On the Continent most cathedrals have a treasury: a museum of relics and plate, often remarkable.

That custom has been little followed in England. Lincoln was the first English cathedral to have one made for it – in 1959–60. The work was ingeniously contrived by Louis Osman, inserted into a very small space in the north-east transept. Some beautiful plate is shown here, from the cathedral and from churches in the diocese; and two documents. One is the foundation charter of the cathedral of 1072. The other is Lincoln's copy of Magna Carta, one of the four originals that survive.

There is no close at Lincoln, in the proper sense of the word, as there is around most English cathedrals. The Minster Yard, which surrounds it on all sides but the north, is not an enclosed space except at the south-west corner, where it is screened by the 14th-century Exchequer Gate. On the east side the traffic roars and grinds on the hill, shaking the foundations of the notable houses that line it.

To the west of the cathedral, through the Exchequer Gate, is an open space, a cross-roads. The Judges' Lodging on Castle Hill is a calm yellow-brick building of about 1810. The Castle has a 14th-century gatehouse, enclosing the original Norman core. What chiefly remains of the Castle itself is the circuit of its walls and their medieval towers. The main building inside the spacious enclosure is now the former gaol (1787), which accommodates courts and the Lincolnshire Record Office. The chapel, which can be seen, is grimly devised to keep the prisoners separate from one another. At the far end of Bailgate – a street of modest shops appropriate to a country town – stands the Newport Arch, the Roman north gate. Only the inner face survives, the rest having been demolished to form another gateway in the Middle Ages. It looks unimpressive now because it has lost 8 ft in height through the gradual raising of the road level. Part of the Roman ditch and wall are visible from East Bight, which starts here and leads round to the Eastgate Hotel, in front of which the foundations of a tower of the Roman east gate are now exposed. From this point there is a splendid view of the whole length of the cathedral.

The best way to leave – or approach – the upper town

is on foot, by the Steep Hill or the Greestone Stairs, further east. In the Steep Hill there are at least two Norman buildings, both traditionally associated with the Jews, who were a flourishing community in Lincoln in the 12th century. Nos. 25 and 26 incorporate a fragment of the Roman south gate.

The continuation of Steep Hill southward is The Strait. Beyond that is the High Street, spanned by the Stonebow, a medieval gateway used as the Town Hall. The Council Chamber is immediately above the arch. The city's regalia include two notable medieval swords. Just beyond, the High Street crosses the river by the High Bridge, which carries tall timbered houses on its west side and can be seen by turning in through a passage beneath one of them to the right.

All this section of the High Street is now pedestrianised. Three of the four surviving medieval churches stand on it: St Benedict, crouching behind an unsympathetic war memorial on the right; then St Mary le Wigford, which has a beautiful 13th-century chancel; and further on St Peter at Gowts. These last two have tall thin towers, built just before the Norman Conquest.

(Frank Rodgers)

They survey an amiable bedlam of shoppers, not to mention two of the most inconvenient level crossings in the country. The reward of the visitor is to look back from here, up the street, to the cathedral on the hill; and then to walk westwards by the river to Brayford Pool and look up again from there. Nothing could be better than this enormous building, long, relatively low, but soaring upwards through its towers. It can be seen, in clear weather, 30 miles away, up the Vale of Trent, or from across Lincolnshire to the south, a distant magical vision.

Little Moreton see **Astbury**

Liverpool Merseyside 2A5
Liverpool has a quality to be found, in the same abundance, nowhere else in England: the quality of grandeur. There are of course English buildings and streets here and there that can truly be called grand – what could be grander than St Paul's cathedral? But St Paul's sits in isolated magnificence; there is nothing else like it, in scale or character, in London. What else can one bring into comparison? *Durham* indeed, perhaps the gorges of *Bristol* and Newcastle, and one or two of the great Norman castles, *Dover*, Rochester, or *Richmond*. But the list cannot be a long one. The quality appears abroad, though less commonly than one might think: at Lyon and Amiens and Laon, at Antwerp and Würzburg, in Rome and repeatedly in Spain.

Liverpool has it through and through: in its site on the broad Mersey (more than half a mile wide, an estuary) and the terraces rising above it; in its great dock buildings, in the amplitude of its streets, its two enormous cathedrals; in its monuments of civic pride.

The older approaches to Liverpool proclaimed it all to the stranger at the outset. The Atlantic liners moored close to the Pier Head. If that is a thing of the past, the descent into Lime Street station by railway is still awesome. Much of the original tunnel was opened out in the 1860s, to produce cyclopean cuttings up to 80 ft deep, their sides hewn vertically in the solid rock. In some conditions of light, this can be a series of scenes from Piranesi.

But grandeur may have little to do with beauty; and there are many aspects of Liverpool that are ugly and heart-breaking. Poverty abounds there, much of it springing from the mass Irish immigration in the 19th century. Large tracts of the city are seedy and decaying. Liverpool was famous for violent crime long before that became a fashionable pursuit in most great towns in England. As for its amenities and historic buildings, it has no very good record in preserving and caring for them.

I first went to Liverpool in 1930. It made at once a powerful impression on me, far beyond my schoolboy's understanding. Since then I have been there again and again, and the impression has only grown stronger. Like London and Edinburgh and Glasgow, like Oxford and Cambridge in a different sense, but like no other British town at all, this is a European, a world city. By comparison with it, Birmingham and Manchester seem merely large.

The grandeur and the horror confront each other everywhere. Some people hate Liverpool, its squalor and brutality and brashness. But if you have never seen it you must go there and take it in, without illusions. The experience is unforgettable, for the eye and the heart.

★

Although it was chartered as a town in 1207, Liverpool did not become a place of any consequence until the middle of the 18th century. It then rose fast, in successful rivalry with Bristol, through the Atlantic trades, in sugar, tobacco, and slaves. In 1801, with 82,000 people, it was the largest provincial town in England. A hundred years later the Liverpool Steamship Owners' Association possessed nearly a quarter of the steamship tonnage of the whole world. In the 20th century everything has changed, with the decline of British shipping. The Mersey is unrecognisably different from what it was before the war, still more from what it was in the

LIVERPOOL

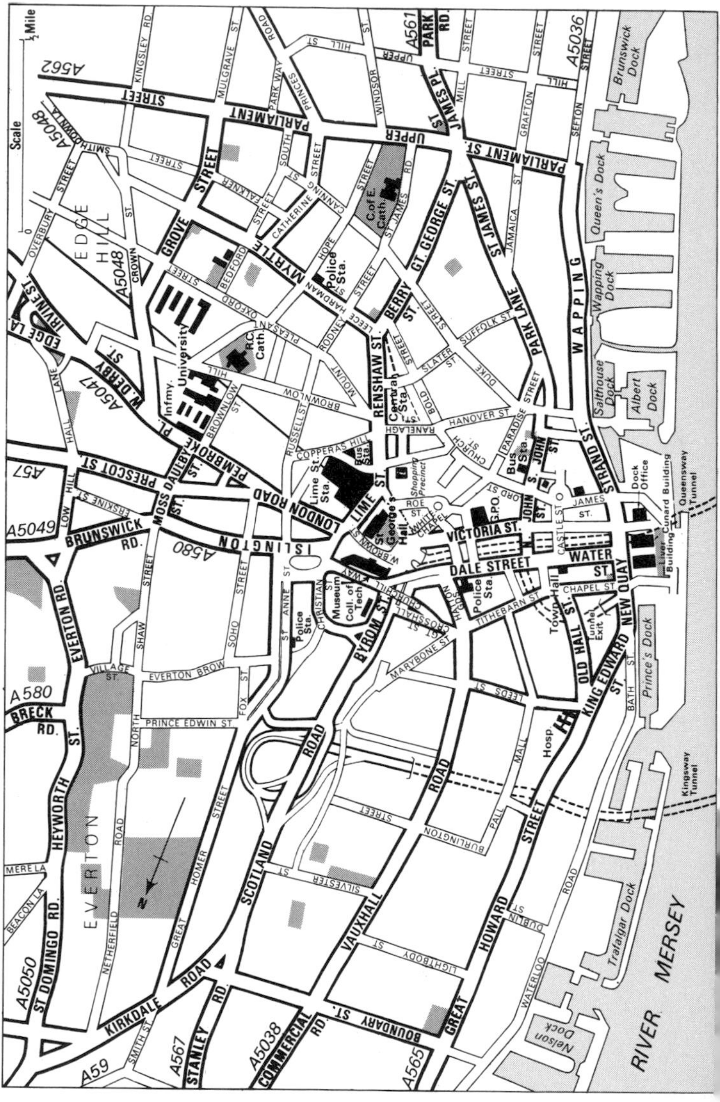
Scale
½ Mile
0
EDGE HILL
EVERTON
RIVER MERSEY
Brunswick Dock
Queen's Dock
Wapping Dock
Salthouse Dock
Albert Dock
Prince's Dock
Trafalgar Dock
Nelson Dock
Dock Office
Cunard Building
Liver Building
Queensway Tunnel
Kingsway Tunnel
Tunnel Exit
Town Hall
Police Sta.
Bus Sta.
Lime St. Sta.
Central Sta.
St. George's Hall
Museum
Coll. of Tech.
University
Infmy.
R.C. Cath.
C. of E. Cath.
G.P.O.
Shopping Precinct
Hosp.
PARLIAMENT STREET
UPPER PARLIAMENT ST.
WAPPING
STRAND ST.
NEW QUAY
KING EDWARD ST.
GREAT HOWARD STREET
VAUXHALL ROAD
SCOTLAND ROAD
GREAT HOMER STREET
KIRKDALE ROAD
STANLEY RD.
COMMERCIAL RD.
BOUNDARY ST.
ST DOMINGO RD.
HEYWORTH ST.
EVERTON RD.
BRECK RD.
BRUNSWICK RD.
LONDON ROAD
ISLINGTON
PRESCOT ST
PEMBROKE PL.
W. DERBY ST.
GROVE STREET
MYRTLE ST.
BERRY ST.
RENSHAW ST.
LIME ST.
GT. GEORGE ST.
ST JAMES ST.
PARK LANE
DALE STREET
VICTORIA ST.
WATER ST.
OLD HALL ST.
BYROM ST.
MOSS ST.
DAULBY ST.
A562
A5048
A5047
A57
A5049
A580
A5050
A59
A567
A5038
A565
A5036
A561

Victorian age. The city was heavily bombed. Since 1945 it has had to adapt itself to a new way of life. The task has been a hard one, pursued with varying success.

In terms of buildings and streets, it can almost be said that Liverpool is a town of the 19th and 20th centuries. No trace remains of its castle, which stood beneath Derby Square and was first examined archaeologically in 1976. It had six 18th-century churches; four have gone. Very few houses of that date survive, and no squares. On the other hand the city has two 18th-century buildings of special note, the Town Hall and Bluecoat Chambers; and its range of buildings between 1800 and 1914 is perhaps larger than any other English provincial city can show. It has also one major building erected since the second World War, and a number of minor ones that are eminently enjoyable.

The account given here starts at the Pier Head. It follows a course roughly sickle-shaped, northward to St George's Hall, then east up Brownlow Hill to the two cathedrals; finally descending back again to the river. It is designed for walking and ignores the one-way traffic system. The docks stretch for 10 miles up and down the east bank of the Mersey. They include some of the most notable of all the city's buildings, the warehouses and offices designed by Jesse Hartley and Philip Hardwick – especially the Albert Dock of 1839–45. This monumental structure, of brick resting on cast-iron drums 12½ ft round, is now disused, and its future is tragically uncertain.

The Pier Head is the focal point of the whole district, the meeting-place of buses and the ferries across the Mersey. Three big buildings overlook it, completed in 1907–16 for the Royal Liver Friendly Society, the Cunard Steamship Company, and the Mersey Docks & Harbour Board. The tallest of the three is the Royal Liver Building; but the Cunard Building in the middle is the distinguished one, a work of real breeding, erected at a time when that quality was growing scarce.

Inland from the Pier Head the streets mount a series of terraces. Water Street contains a Victorian building of note:

Oriel Chambers of 1864, whose narrow *façade* (returned round the corner) consists largely of glass, set in projecting windows – the oriels that give the building its name. It is an astonishing forerunner of much that we are familiar with in the 1970s, which is nicely reflected indeed in the very next building up the street. Here we are looking at a work of originality, far ahead of its time, which is also a thing of distinction and charm. Its architect, Peter Ellis junior, is very obscure. This work was fiercely attacked when it was new; he tried again not far away, at 16 Cook Street, in 1866 (go up the steps and out to the back to see his spiral staircase clad in iron and glass) and then he totally disappears, as if he had given up in despair.

At the top of Water Street stands the Town Hall, which was designed by John Wood the elder of Bath, and erected in 1749–54. James Wyatt enlarged it in 1789–92, and then it was burnt out in a fire in 1795. It was reconstructed over the next 30 years by John Foster the elder, a Liverpool architect, with Wyatt's advice. Wood's work survives at the back, on the east side; the other three sides, as we now see them, are Wyatt's, and the high dome was added in 1802. The City Council still meets in the building, which is otherwise used chiefly for civic hospitality. The interior is not shown except by special permission, though it is now open to the public for a fortnight in August. The set of six rooms opening out of one another on the first floor is the finest that any English municipality can boast. They comprise three reception rooms, two ballrooms, and a dining room, and they are distinguished alike by their decoration, in the richest manner of Wyatt's time, and their splendid Regency furniture, chiefly of rosewood with brass inlay, made in Liverpool about 1823. The portraits include Lawrence's lively and quizzical one of Canning.

The Town Hall faces Castle Street, which is handsomely broad. On its left-hand side is the Liverpool branch of the Bank of England, a distinguished work of C. R. Cockerell (1846–8) with a most satisfying narrow *façade* looking straight down Brunswick Street to the river. Cockerell and his son

Liverpool: St George's Hall from Lime Street (A. F. Kersting)

also designed the Liverpool & London & Globe Insurance building in Dale Street, just north of the Town Hall; and opposite that is the Queen Insurance Building (1837–9), with an exuberant front and a peaceful courtyard behind.

Now move north up Dale Street. The ground dips and then rises again, to bring a full view of St George's Hall lying athwart the next hill. This is the supreme civic building in England, designed by H. L. Elmes in 1839–41 and completed after his death (at the age of 33) by C. R. Cockerell and Sir Robert Rawlinson in 1856. In one huge pile it provides a great hall, a small concert room, and law courts. It is a superb monument of the Greek Revival. Again access to the interior is not very easy, but the trouble is worth taking. The Great Hall is magnificent; the Concert Room, decorated entirely by Cockerell, is among the most delightful public rooms in the country. The building is not only an architectural masterpiece; it is also technologically important for its system of heating and ventilation, and for some points in its construction too.

Its setting however is unworthy. It stands opposite the former hotel of Lime Street railway station, a dignified building but not within two classes of it. To the west and south it surveys a mean commercial muddle. Only to the north is there something better. There, in William Brown Street, the city placed in a row its chief cultural buildings, the Walker Art Gallery, the Central Library, and the main Museum. No other English town did anything comparable to proclaim the importance of the arts. These buildings make good satellites to St George's Hall, with the Wellington column shooting up between them; but the whole site cries out to be made a great civic square.

From St George's Hall go south past the station along the left-hand pavement of Lime Street, where the charming tower of St Luke's church (John Foster, father and son, 1802–31) comes into view, backed by the massive one of the Anglican cathedral. Turn left up Brownlow Hill. It is now a street with no qualities at all but breadth. At the top of the rise on the left is the Victoria Building of the University, designed by Alfred Waterhouse (a native of Liverpool) and completed in 1892. Behind and around it are the buildings of the University, which are numerous and diverse – so diverse indeed as to call forth Sir Nikolaus Pevsner's witty and accurate remark that "the whole is not a whole but a zoo, with species after species represented". Yet it should be said that the University of Liverpool possesses some good buildings, where many British universities, growing fast since the war, can show few or none.

First things first. The approach to the Catholic cathedral, which lies opposite, is by a flight of steps from Mount Pleasant. The history of this building is curious. The site was acquired in 1928, and Lutyens planned a cathedral for it that was to be the largest, after St Peter's, in the world. The vast crypt was constructed in 1933–40, and there the work stopped. A competition was held in 1959 for completing the cathedral on a smaller scale, won by Frederick Gibberd. His building was erected with astonishing speed, in little more than four and a half years, and consecrated in May 1967.

Liverpool: Catholic cathedral from the south-west (A. F. Kersting)

The cathedral is circular and provides seating for 2,000 people round a central altar, with a series of 13 chapels radiating out from the circumference. It is something like a vast tent inside, lighted entirely with coloured glass, by John Piper and Patrick Reyntiens, predominantly blue, but also violet, grey-green, and red, with yellow and white in the Lady Chapel alone. Above the altar hangs an immense corona in tubular steel. The altar itself stands on a beautiful pavement of polished marble, and it bears a moving crucifix by Elizabeth Frink.

There are some elements in the exterior that it is difficult to like or admire: the shapes of the clustering chapels, and particularly the great wedge reared up over the main entrance, with its sculpture of violence. Above it all, however, rides the circular central tower with its delicate crown: a superb composition, making poetry out of metal and concrete.

Mount Pleasant curves round here. Walk down it a few yards to look at what is now the Irish Centre (on the right-hand side, just below the cathedral). It was built as the Wellington Rooms (architect Edmond Aikin, 1815), and its charming *façade* is another piece of the Greek Revival. Now move along Hope Street, which provides an axis between the two cathedrals. It includes two notable buildings: the Philharmonic Dining Rooms, completed in 1900, with their bronze gates, a sumptuous riot of *art nouveau*; and the Philharmonic Hall (1939), showing the strong influence of Dutch brick architecture. The main streets leading off Hope Street up and down the hill – Hardman Street, Falkner St, Canning St – show the full scale of Liverpool's urban planning in the opening years of the 19th century; and out of the last of these opens Percy Street, different from the rest in being built of stone, instead of the plum-coloured brick that appears almost everywhere else in Georgian Liverpool.

The Anglican cathedral, which you have now reached, was built like its neighbour in the 20th century and also as the result of a competition; but those are almost the sole points of resemblance between them. It is a Gothic building of red sandstone (quarried at Woolton and Rainhill, only a few miles away), dignified, massive, immensely solid. Its construction has been in progress for over 70 years, and the work is still not quite finished. It was interrupted by two World Wars, in the second of which the building suffered some damage. From 1904 to 1960 it was supervised by its original architect, Giles Gilbert Scott, who won the competition at the age of 22, and he introduced considerable changes into the design as the building progressed. Its plan comprises a nave and choir of equal length, with a central space, underneath the majestic tower, that is somewhat longer and broader incorporating shallow transepts with porches between them. The vast scale of the building is its essence. It is noble, well proportioned, immensely grand; yet, for many people, it is too large. One can feel a sense of fatigue even at mounting the steps of the great porch to go in; and when one is inside the littleness of the human beings – even if it is acceptable symbolically – is oppressive. The colour of the interior is monotonous, and the figure sculpture, like most modern representational work, totally unsatisfying.

The cathedral rears up above St James's Cemetery, overgrown and intensely romantic, with a distant prospect, down to the river, across it, and away to the Welsh hills beyond. Here in Liverpool, in an age of no faith, are two cathedrals each asserting a faith of its own.

To walk along Rodney Street now brings you back to plain Georgian prose. The first house here seems to have been begun in 1783. No. 62 is notable: Gladstone was born in it in 1809, and it was subsequently lived in by Edward Cardwell, the reformer of the Victorian army. Here and there, in this and the neighbouring streets, there is excellent ironwork on the first-floor balconies.

Rodney Street leads back into Mount Pleasant. Go down it and cross into Ranelagh Street, which will bring you into Church Street, now given up to pedestrians and full of large shops. What sort of town can this be, one asks, when Marks & Spencer's is housed in a Victorian palace all of stone? Immediately behind Woolworth's is the most delightful building in the whole city: Bluecoat Chambers. This was the former Bluecoat School, erected in 1717: a brick building enclosing three sides of a paved courtyard, the fourth comprising a screen of trees and elegant iron railings. It was disused as a school in 1906 and might have been pulled down had it not been for the devoted efforts of some Liverpool citizens and the first Lord Leverhulme. He saw it as a centre for the arts (well before such things had become a commonplace), and at length, long after his death, that was realised, as a result of many tough struggles. So today this beautiful building provides a gallery for exhibiting pictures, meeting rooms, and offices for cultural societies. It has been an excellent enterprise.

Two very agreeable small pieces of the modern world now lie close at hand: the extension to the Playhouse in Williamson Square (Hall, O'Donohue & Wilson, 1968), with a glass drum delightfully managed in placing and scale; and on the corner of Lord Street and St John Street the Mariners Restaurant (Christopher Riley, 1954), a clean and enticing interior of circular shapes, revealed through window walls. Across Derby Square James Street leads on downhill. Turn aside at the bottom into the Piazza, where there is a fascinating waterwork (Richard Huws, 1966), which you may be lucky enough to see playing. The Piazza commemorates the old "Goree Piazzas", Goree being a West African base of the slave trade, to which Liverpool owed much of its prosperity in the Georgian age. The big office building on the Piazza today is called Wilberforce House: a symbolic act of reparation, commemorating the man who did most to put the slave trade down.

In front now is the Pier Head. No one should leave Liverpool without crossing the river by one of the historic ferries – historic indeed; for one of those of a former generation, *Daffodil*, played an heroic part at Zeebrugge in 1918. They go in two directions, south to Birkenhead, north to Wallasey. The Birkenhead one has more to offer: a good general view of the Albert Dock buildings, and then from the opposite shore the whole panorama from the Pier Head up to the cathedrals. It is from across the river that one best appreciates the poetry of the Catholic cathedral's crown, an ethereal element in what is otherwise a townscape of solid shapes, massive and powerful.

LONDON

The treatment of London here presents special difficulties. It is not only the largest city, by far, in England; it is also, in many of the things with which this book is concerned, very much the richest. St Paul's cathedral is one of the great buildings of Europe; Westminster Abbey and the Tower embody the nation's history as no other buildings can; and what Romantic group of the 19th century surpasses the Houses of Parliament? Though the aristocratic town houses that used to be among London's prime distinctions have been ruthlessly destroyed in the past century, there are still a few that remain; and within Greater London there are at least half a dozen major country houses. The London parks present a special and delightful kind of landscape. As for the streets of the city – and what has, historically, been the chief of them, the river – they are full of interest, of surprise and delight, often to be discovered under the very shadow of a featureless "development" of our own time. Nobody could claim that London is the most beautiful capital city in Europe; but anyone with a sense of history, a student of human life from Roman times to our own, may well feel there is no other town to touch it.

So, how is one to select from all this abundance? My decision has been this. From within Greater London I have included two houses, one small and one large; a group of three of the churches in the City – a sadly diminished band, yet still one of its chief possessions; one other church, very different; and two secular buildings of the 19th and 20th centuries. For the townscape I have chosen one of the parks, and the group of buildings at Greenwich by the river.

There is the sample I offer. But let me reiterate what I have said in another connection (p. 22) in discussing the way to look at towns in general. You can get excellent impressions of London from the top of a bus – the No. 11, from Chelsea to the City, offers one of the classic rides of its kind to be had anywhere. But having got some such general views, it is much better to walk in and out of the streets, the still-numerous byways and lanes.

Church of St Andrew Undershaft City 6
No building holds more richly and intimately than this one the character of the old City of London. Apart from mild Victorian restoration, it is in its fabric and memorials almost entirely a work of the 16th and 17th centuries.*

Its tower is older, built in the 15th century, though heightened by one storey in 1883. The body of the church was rebuilt immediately before the Reformation, in 1520–32.

The church is virtually a rectangle, with a chancel projecting very slightly at the east end. It comprises nave and aisles, divided by arcades of six bays. The flat timber ceilings are the original, the one in the nave looking newer than the others since it was cleaned and restored in 1950 after war damage.

The west window is a late-17th-century composition showing figures of five sovereigns from Edward VI to William III. Beneath, against the west wall, is the elegant font, completed by Nicholas Stone in 1634. The organ was made by Renatus Harris in 1696, and it is in its original case. The iron altar rails are by Jean Tijou, a French craftsman whose work is superbly seen at St Paul's cathedral, but only very rarely in the parish churches.

The monuments mirror the life of the City. Look at the brass of Nicholas Leveson to begin with, at the east end of the north aisle. He was a mercer, and Merchant of the Staple of Calais, and he died in 1532, the very year in which the present church was completed. His wife bore him 18 children and lived on until 1560, when presumably this monument was made. It is entirely medieval in its character, with Latin tags emerging in prayer from the mouths of husband and wife, "whose souls Jesu pardon".

* The church has lately been converted into an under-30s lunch-room and exhibition centre.

St Andrew Undershaft: John Stow's monument (N.M.R.)

Immediately adjacent is the monument of John Stow, the historian of London. He died in 1605, in poverty we are told: yet his widow was able to commission this handsome memorial to him, in alabaster, from Nicholas Johnson. It shows a scholarly balding man writing at his desk, with books around him; the quill pen in his hand, by a graceful custom, is annually renewed by the Lord Mayor. At the top are two pithy Latin sentences: "either do what is worth writing about or write what is worth reading".

Further west in the same aisle are Sir Hugh Hammersley and his wife, a fine pair of kneeling effigies. He died in 1636 and was, as the inscription tells us, Governor of the Levant Company and a member of all the chief companies trading overseas, from Virginia to Russia and India. Sir Christopher Clitherow (Lord Mayor in 1635) is another figure from the same world, but more important, M.P. for London in 1628 and a power in the delicate game of politics and finance played between Charles I and the City in the succeeding years. As a moderate King's man he was perhaps fortunate to die just before the Civil War began, in 1641.

Forty years earlier he had been one of the foundation members of the East India Company; and that great institution figures here again and again. The old East India House was in Leadenhall Street – it stood on the diagonally opposite corner – and St Andrew's was its parish church. From another age, on the same wall, is a tablet commemorating William Ramsay, Secretary of the Company, who served it for 50 years. He was no more than 64 when he died in 1813. The Company was in many ways a good employer; it paid for this memorial, as a tribute to his work.

One must think of the Company here, of its huge commercial business, the foundation of British power in India; and of some of its other servants too – not only men like Ramsay, who gave it the whole of their lives, but also those who worked honestly for it in office hours (short, and not always very exacting) and then led another life when they went home: Charles Lamb, for example, Peacock the novelist, and John Stuart Mill. Lamb wryly remarked: "My printed works were my recreations – my true works may be found on the shelves in Leadenhall Street, filling some hundred folios". Outside, in St Andrew's graveyard, lies Peter Motteux, who published one of the chief English translations of *Don Quixote*, in 1712.

One last remembrance, of the early 16th century when the present church was built. It was dedicated to St Andrew the Apostle; but it had long been known as "Undershaft" with reference to the maypole that was set up in the street outside on May morning, taller than the tower of the church. It was the scene of "Evil May Day" in 1517, a riot directed against foreigners, which led to 14 executions. The maypole was then laid up, unused, against the wall of the church until again it became a centre of disorder in 1549, when a fanatical Protestant preacher, alleging that the maypole was an idol, stirred up some of those who lived near it – "after they had well dined", as Stow says – to take it down, saw it in pieces, and burn it.

Church of St Mary Abchurch City 6

Perhaps, taking everything into account, the most satisfying interior of a Wren parish church now left in London. Abchurch Lane, at the east end of Cannon Street, brings you into a tiny square, the church forming its northern side. There is no better place to eat your mid-day sandwiches in the course of visiting a series of these churches, all around you.

The building (erected in 1681–6) is of brick, with a tower at the north-west corner bearing a shapely lead spire. Hemmed in closely by tall offices, it looks small, though carrying itself with the most assured self-confidence. In fact, as with a number of these churches, the impression it makes inside is not of smallness but of grandeur. The church is a perfect square on plan, and the whole internal space is covered by a dome rising immediately from the walls, not supported on any columns nor buttressed outside. Here Wren demonstrates his genius for attaining a mathematical and aesthetic perfection.

The north wall is solid; the church is lighted chiefly from

the south. All the glass – blessedly, here – is plain. The colours inside are few and entirely harmonious: off-white on the walls, buffs and greys on the monuments; the darkest oak for most of the woodwork; touches of gold here and there, applied with restraint; a crimson carpet before the altar.

The woodwork is truly magnificent. It is dominated by the reredos, made in 1686. This and the font-cover at All Hallows by the Tower are the only two pieces by Grinling Gibbons in any City church, other than St Paul's. It is enriched with superb garlands of flowers and fruit, falling down to the altar from a great height. The pulpit beside it dates from the previous year and was made by W. Gray. It is a splendid piece, excellently proportioned in all its parts,

(N.M.R.)

with a very big hexagonal tester, lavishly carved. The dome of the church was painted in low colours by William Snow in 1708. The organ, at the back, is a modern one, in a case of 1717 brought here from All Hallows, Bread Street, one of the churches demolished in the Victorian age. The gallery in which it stands used to be occupied by the boys of Merchant Taylors' School, which stood near by until 1875.

There are fine monuments: that to Sir Patience Ward (d. 1696), for example, placed just rightly to the south of the altar; and the one to Matthew Perchard in the north-west corner, its marbles delightfully variegated.

The church suffered severely in the war. In the autumn of 1940 the dome was badly damaged and the great reredos blown into 2,000 pieces. It has all been repaired beyond criticism (under W. Godfrey Allen), to yield us now a vision of the genius of Wren, faultless and complete.

Greenwich 6

There are several ways of getting to Greenwich. The steamer from Westminster Bridge or the Tower is attractive, but it has one drawback: a facetious commentary is often brayed forth through a bad public-address system. The London river steamer is a rough affair compared with the *bateau-mouche* in Paris. In this matter they order things better in France. It is preferable to return that way to London, when the commentator usually keeps silent.

The 53 bus offers a good approach, from Piccadilly Circus or Charing Cross. After about 40 minutes through south-east London, noisy and drab, the road climbs steeply up to a wide green plateau. This is Blackheath, with the wooded Shooter's Hill in the distance and some handsome houses near by. If you are minded to explore, have a look at the far corner of the Heath to the right: at the Paragon, a noble colonnaded crescent built in the 1790s, and Morden College close to it, in a warm red brick of 1695.

But our business is with Greenwich. Retrace the road you have come by and go through the wall into Greenwich Park.

The trees here are venerable, especially some fine Spanish chestnuts. At the end of the avenue ahead is one of the great views of London. Below lies Greenwich: the Royal Naval College with its domed towers; the white Queen's House, flanked by colonnades; hard left, the tall masts of *Cutty Sark*; beyond that the river curving away towards London, with the dome of St Paul's rebuking the anonymous slabs around it. The statue by which you are standing commemorates Wolfe, who went to school at Greenwich and is buried in the parish church. It was given by the people of Canada and unveiled in 1919 – with what magnanimity! – by the Marquis de Montcalm, descendant of the French commander he defeated at Quebec in 1759. Immediately beside you is the old Royal Observatory of 1675, the octagonal building in plum-coloured brick. Through the Meridian Building close to it the Prime Meridian of Greenwich passes, by which modern time is measured.

A house was built at Greenwich by Humphrey Duke of Gloucester in the 15th century, which grew into a palace, one of the chief royal residences of the Tudors. Henry VIII and Elizabeth were both born in it and lived here a great deal. James I bestowed it on his Queen, Anne of Denmark, and she began the erection of the Queen's House, much smaller than the palace, in 1616. It was completed for Henrietta Maria about 1638. The old palace was pulled down under Charles II and a new one begun, but not finished. Then William and Mary abandoned Greenwich altogether for Hampton Court and started to build a Naval Hospital here, under Wren's direction, instead. This was completed slowly and eventually accommodated nearly 3,000 pensioners. It was closed in 1869. Four years later the buildings became the Royal Naval College, as they are still.

The College occupies the site of the palace, along the river. To appreciate the superb disposition of the buildings one has to look at them from the opposite bank: easily managed by walking through the tunnel (quarter of a mile long; lifts) to the Island Gardens, which face the College directly. Here is the precise view that Canaletto put into

(A. F. Kersting)

Greenwich: Royal Naval College and Queen's House

his famous picture, painted about 1755 (now in the National Maritime Museum). The focal point of the design was the existing Queen's House. The buildings run, a symmetrical pair capped by domes, down to the river and then open out into two great ranges. The right-hand one incorporates King Charles's Building, designed by John Webb in 1669. Most of the rest of what is visible here is by Wren, though Hawksmoor and Vanbrugh played their part in it too. The whole was not completed until 1750; extensions and embellishments continued down to 1814.

The College is not open to the public, but its two chief rooms are accessible on most weekday afternoons: the Painted Hall and the Chapel. The Painted Hall (built in 1696–1704 and painted in 1708–27) is a misleading name. It is really three rooms, its special magnificence arising from the conjunction of them, and their disposition. The first, smallest, and highest is the Vestibule. A broad flight of stairs then ascends to the Lower Hall, the largest division. A tall arch at the end, and a second staircase, lead into the Upper Hall, sufficiently screened from the Lower to give the sense that it is another room. The majesty of the whole sequence is unsurpassed in England.

The decoration matches it. Ceilings and wall-paintings of the time abound in English country houses. A few are good (see *Sudbury*, and Kimbolton Castle in Cambridgeshire); most are extremely dull. The painting here by Sir James Thornhill is not. It is a very complete scheme, realised with great freedom and power, presenting the triumphs of Britain in the wars against Louis XIV's France and glorifying the sovereigns who successively presided over them (and over the building of the Hospital), William and Mary, Queen Anne, and George I.

The character of the Chapel is entirely different. It too is approached up a broad staircase; but there the resemblance ends. It was burnt out in a fire in 1779 and redecorated to a quite new scheme by James ("Athenian") Stuart and William Newton. The colours are the palest blue, grey-green, and white, accented powerfully by the yellow scagliola columns. The furnishings are of the highest quality, the limewood pulpit with its curved mahogany stairs, the font and the altar rails. The huge painting at the east end, representing St Paul and the Viper, is by Benjamin West.

The Queen's House (across the main road), designed by Inigo Jones, was the first Palladian building to be erected in England: a work of great historical importance and (what may not be the same thing) of great beauty. Cool, elegant, quietly rectangular, it was a striking work of "modern" architecture when it was new. The plan was curious. It was not one house but two, lying parallel with each other on either side of the old Dover road, which then ran at the foot of the hill, the two parts being linked by a bridge. The house was enlarged in 1662, which involved the making of two additional bridges. When the road was eventually diverted, to run along its present course, the house became secluded, standing then quite on its own. The colonnades linking it to new buildings were added from 1807 onwards.

The Hall of the house (originally the entrance from the river) is a complete 40 ft cube, with a wonderfully-patterned black-and-white pavement by Nicholas Stone, best seen from the gallery above. The upper floors are reached by a spiral staircase in the south-east corner of the room: one of the most beautiful in England, from its design and from the ironwork of the balustrade, representing fleurs-de-lis (the French royal emblem, in compliment to Henrietta Maria), though looking like tulips. The rooms are partially furnished in the style of the 1630s. They contain the older paintings of the National Maritime Museum, within which the Queen's House is now incorporated.

This is one of the best museums in the country. It was opened in 1937, inheriting older collections from the Government, of models and plans of ships, paintings and relics of many kinds, and it has been continuously enriched since from private donations and public funds. Its galleries have lately been enlarged to a remarkable extent. Neptune's Hall, built round a complete steam tug, with the Barge House leading off it, and the New Galleries in the west wing, have all been opened within the past seven years.

The Museum enjoys a special combination of advantages. It has a splendid site and forms part of a group of distinguished buildings. Its collections are extremely diverse, including some fine pictures. The technologies it demonstrates are fascinating, sometimes crossing the boundaries between science and art. The presentation of them is crisp, informative, and often visually delightful. Its treasures cannot be catalogued or described here. All that can be done is to offer a few examples of them.

The Nelson relics are among the most remarkable relating to an Englishman anywhere – and properly, for he is one of the supreme figures of English history. They show that combination of intimacy and public flair that Nelson had himself; they also display him as a popular hero, of a peculiarly compelling power. This collection is in the New Galleries, not far from another relating to Cook, showing Cook's qualities as a seaman and something of the vision of a new world opened up by his exploration. The paintings of the South Pacific by William Hodges, who accompanied him, were a revelation in the 1780s. They can take one's breath away still.

The Navigation Room, one of the most important parts of the whole Museum, displays the developing knowledge of the oceans, and a succession of the instruments enabling them to be crossed. Outstanding among them is the series of marine chronometers produced by John Harrison in 1735–59, imaginatively displayed and described with meticulous care.

Finally, a word about portraits. What a gallery of characters is here, of English, Welsh, Scottish, and Irish faces! Take a few in the immediate neighbourhood of Nelson: Sir Thomas Graves, his second-in-command at Copenhagen, firm, plodding, without fire; Hardy, who commanded the *Victory* at Trafalgar – the bluff, genial seaman; two of the very young men, finely rendered, Peter Rainier and Sir Peter Parker. One can follow this line through the centuries here. It is endlessly rewarding.

There is much else to see in Greenwich besides. Five minutes' walk away *Cutty Sark* lies in dry dock, famous as a clipper in the wool trade from Australia in 1883–95. She has been well restored, and fitted up to show the life and working of an ocean-going ship in the final days of sail. Close to her is another historic ship, the tiny *Gypsy Moth IV* in which Sir Francis Chichester sailed round the world alone in 1966. One moves at Greenwich from the 15th century to the 20th, and over all the centuries between.

Hampstead: Fenton House 6

To a larger extent than most of the world's biggest cities, London is a city of villages. The Greater London we know today has engulfed more than 100 communities, each of which has a recognisable, sometimes a very long, history of its own. Many of these villages have lost nearly all their old identity in the process – though they may retain more of it than is commonly supposed. Some, on the other hand, still keep their village character, clearly and obstinately; and of these one of the chief is Hampstead.

It ancient history is not remarkable. It begins to become

interesting only towards the end of the 17th century, when with the steady growth of London it emerged as a place of suburban residence for city men. High and open, it was the very antithesis of the close-packed, stinking London that burnt so readily in the Great Fire – and grew up again, in some ways scarcely changed, when that disaster was repaired. If one kept a coach, it was an easy journey out there; with the use of one's legs, no great walk. At the same time the village's popularity increased through the discovery of chalybeate springs, which turned it into a little spa.

A few houses built at that time survive, and this one especially, which seems to date from 1693. Nothing is known of the architect or his client. The house belonged to a family named Gee for a large part of the 18th century and was acquired in 1793 by a merchant in the Baltic trade, Mr Fenton, from whom it got its present name. Lady Binney bought it in 1936, filled it with her collection of porcelain, and left it on her death to the National Trust. The Trust has placed in it the collection of early keyboard instruments given to it by Major Benton-Fletcher.

The contents of the house, as we see them now, are no less important than the house itself. Lady Binney's collection is of high quality, in German and English porcelain of the 18th century. It is displayed very well in two big cases set in alcoves in the Porcelain Room on the ground floor, and in the Drawing Room above. One might single out any number of things for special mention: the Nymphenburg Scaramouche – along with many other characters from Italian comedy; the cherry-pickers and a whole group of people at various occupations from Meissen. In the Drawing Room are more Meissen pieces, including a superb pair of parrots mounted in ormolu, and a teapot with a mask and hat for its cover. The English collection includes figures from Bristol, Plymouth, and Chelsea downstairs, and in the Drawing Room some delectable Worcester.

There is Chinese porcelain here too. The best pieces are in the Oriental Room on the ground floor (accommodated

Fenton House: the south front (B.T.A.)

in an 18th-century cabinet of Chinese style); and upstairs the Blue Porcelain Room is wholly filled with porcelain made in China roughly at the time of the building of the house.

The musical instruments are distributed through most of the rooms. The majority of them are on the top floor, but there is a notable harpsichord in the Dining Room, a Shudi-Broadwood with two keyboards dating from 1770; to be compared with a Kirckman instrument of the same sort, upstairs in the Drawing Room, made in 1777. Much earlier instruments are to be seen elsewhere in the house: English virginals of 1664, Italian harpsichords of the 16th and 17th centuries. The sequence is rounded off by a grand piano, still shaped like a harpsichord, made by Broadwood in 1805.

As you move round, looking at all these things and many

more (including much delightful furniture), you become aware of the highly individual character of the house, its compelling charm. It has one peculiarity, most endearing. In many of the rooms there is a little closet opening out of one corner, just big enough to hold a small writing-table or an armchair: a delightful arrangement in itself and for the sense of enlargement that it gives to the room. There are no big rooms here, nothing grand; but also – it is a secret of such houses as this – nothing mean.

All around Fenton House things have changed greatly in the space of nearly three centuries since it was built. Trees have grown up, houses have multiplied, Fenton House itself is now hemmed in. But the process has been friendly here, not uncomfortable, because the house has managed to keep a substantial garden. One might even say three gardens: the grave formal green one in the front, facing Hampstead down the hill, and two, parallel with each other but different, at the back. The one chiefly visible from the house is a walled-in open space, with a large lawn, the other at a lower level includes a tiny orchard.

When it was built, high on its ridge, Fenton House enjoyed that view over London which has made Hampstead famous. Most of that has now gone, blocked out by later building; but subtle glimpses of it are to be had between trees, from the closets on the first floor, and in the opposite direction, out to the south-west, from the top landing.

Leaving the house, walk down hill to the right, and do not fail to look back at it through its splendid wrought-iron gates at the south end of the front garden. Hampstead then lies all around you to be explored: Church Row (one of London's best 18th-century streets), the Victorian amplitude of Rosslyn Hill; northwards the Heath, and with it a notable great house, Ken Wood.

Harefield: church of St Mary Hillingdon 6

The church stands on a frontier between suburbs and open country. A hundred yards away is a narrow and roaring main road, lined with semi-detached houses; beyond, the gravel pits and waterworks of the Coln valley. To the north of the church lies the old village, with tiny brick almshouses founded by the Countess of Derby (she will appear again in a moment) early in the 17th century, their big chimney-stacks set diagonally and dominating the hill. Everywhere else, farm land and trees.

The church is a modest building outside, with its tower at the north-west corner, nicely battlemented in brick. The south aisle is faced with flint, chequered with stone. The building is full of furniture and monuments; in no disorder, however, but carefully disposed. Nearly all the furniture is good: simple early-19th-century pews, a complicated pulpit-cum-reading-desk. Round the altar (raised up aloft, for the church is built into a hill) the woodwork is of the 17th century, and opulent. It was presented to the church in 1840 and is said to have come from Flanders. Two carved angels support the Tables of the Law, painted in black ink on glass. The walls are white throughout. There is a plain 18th-century ceiling in the nave; the chancel vault is delightfully ribbed (Henry Keene, 1768). Clear glass almost everywhere, except in the upper lights of the windows and their borders, which are filled with cheerful Victorian glass in strong colours; a few roundels of older glass in the north chapel.

There are over 40 wall monuments, ranging in time from a brass of 1440 to a plain tablet of 1936. Indeed, if you want an introduction to English monumental sculpture, not at its highest (for that you go to Westminster Abbey) but consistently enjoyable and instructive, you could hardly do better than spend an afternoon in the church and churchyard of Harefield.

Two families preponderate: the Newdigates, who acquired the manor of Harefield perhaps about 1440 and held it, with one interruption, until 1925; and the Ashbys, who owned that of Breakspears from much the same date to the early 19th century.

Among the Newdigate monuments there are two by Grinling Gibbons in the north-east corner of the chancel: fine

(A. F. Kersting)

Harefield: the Countess of Derby's monument; right, Lady Newdigate's

artist as he was, they show that he worked less well in stone than in wood. On the opposite wall are three white marble urns commemorating members of the family who died between 1765 and 1800, set beautifully in alcoves, painted black. They were erected by Sir Roger Newdigate, celebrated as the founder of a prize at Oxford. The south aisle contains seven more of their monuments. Four, of the 17th century, are well set, diagonally against the corners of the aisle. The monuments in this church were arranged in the 18th and 19th centuries, with unerring taste, to make a studied picture. Nothing has been done since to change the composition.

Among the Ashby monuments one is of distinction: that to William Ashby (d. 1760), high up in the north wall of the nave. It comprises a bust, again set in a black alcove, with a deliciously decorated inscription below. The bust is attributed to Sir Robert Taylor.

The most spectacular of these monuments is in the south-east corner of the chancel. It is to Alice, Countess Dowager of Derby (d. 1637); a bizarre performance, said to be by Maximilian Colt of Arras. There she is lying as if in a four-poster bed, in her peeress's robes and coronet, with her children below, guarded by heraldic eagles of theatrical ferocity. This Countess held the manor of Harefield during a brief interval in the Newdigates' possession of it. It was for her that Milton wrote his masque of *Arcades*, first performed at Harefield in 1635.

Outside the church there is still more to see and think about. Three simple monuments are built into its wall, commemorating faithful domestic servants. One of these, close to the north door, was erected by William Ashby to his gamekeeper Robert Mossendew. A relief shows him out with his dog. Below, the inscription is a charming piece of genuine simple poetry. The churchyard contains many plain wooden "bedhead" memorials, up to the end of the 19th century. Facing the wall of the church, and worth looking for, are three headstones to members of the Trumper family from 1782 to 1803, most admirably lettered. And then to the north a regular range of little white stones indicates a military cemetery: here are over 100 Australians, most of them casualties from Gallipoli, who died in hospital at Harefield Park in 1915–19. We have moved a long way from the world of the Newdigates and Ashbys, enclosed, assured, and secure.

The Monument and the church of St Magnus the Martyr City 6

The Great Fire of London broke out in Pudding Lane* in the small hours of 2 September 1666. It raged four days and destroyed nearly all the city's public buildings, St Paul's Cathedral, 87 churches, and 13,000 houses. Fire was a terrible incident to which all towns were liable when most buildings were of timber. It consumed Northampton in 1675, and Warwick in 1694. But this, which ravaged the capital, is pre-eminent. It remains *the* Great Fire of English history.

Rebuilding began quickly, but to plans that were not at all consistently carried through. It was five years before the first stage of the work was at an end, with the inauguration of the reconstructed Guildhall for the Lord Mayor's Feast in November 1671; five more were required to complete all the secular buildings; many of the churches were not finished until the opening years of the 18th century.

So great a disaster called for some conspicuous public commemoration. The form it took was appropriate to the event: a single Doric column supporting an open platform and then, above, a gilded urn with flames rising out of it, emblem of the Fire itself. The column was made big enough to accommodate an internal staircase, by which citizens and visitors could ascend to survey the city and the river valley – and so, at the time, to observe the work of reconstruction as it went on. The Monument rises from a massive pedestal, bearing on its western side a relief (by C. G. Cibber) depicting the Fire and the rebuilding, to which King Charles II offers

* Pudding Lane runs down from the west end of Eastcheap to Lower Thames Street.

(A. F. Kersting

his support. On its other faces it carries long inscriptions in Latin and English, cut in gilded Roman letters.

The design may have been Wren's, though on the evidence we have Robert Hooke has as good a claim to it. Work on the Monument began in 1671 and took at least four years, or longer if we accept the date of completion on the pedestal, which is 1677. The inscription is (pardonably) a little ebullient, and at some points it is not accurate. It explains how the Monument came to be sited where it was, telling us that it was 202 ft high, and 202 ft away from the baker's shop in which the Fire began. Today the site appears low, lacking in prominence. But the Monument was, when erected, a very conspicuous object from the river (crowded then with passenger traffic), and it stood close to the head of London Bridge. For the old bridge stood a little east of the present one. Fish Street Hill provided its main northern approach, and the Monument was placed close to the cross-roads where that street intersected Thames Street, the highway running close to the river along the north bank. The Monument was tall enough, too, to be seen from all over the city, above the rim of the valley in which it stood, readily identifiable by the golden flames surmounting it. The 19th and 20th centuries, having what they considered bigger business to think of and caring little about a fire 200 or 300 years ago, allowed the Monument to become choked with the big erections that surround, and from some points of view obliterate, it now.

The Monument stands on the site of St Margaret's church, which was destroyed in the Fire and not rebuilt. Below it, however, and adjoining the Bridge, was another important church, St Magnus the Martyr, which contained the tombs of many rich citizens and was among the earliest to be re-erected to Wren's design. The work was in progress at exactly the same time as the Monument, in 1671–6, except for the steeple, which was added in 1705.

All the traffic off London Bridge surged by immediately outside the church, across Thames Street and up the steep Fish Street Hill. Some 90 years later the aisles were shortened at the west end so that the bottom stage of the tower became a porch, a thoroughfare for foot passengers. Then in 1831 the new London Bridge was opened, and the passage was disused. In 1921, alas, Atlantic House was erected, immediately alongside, towering over it with thick insensibility. St Magnus is now therefore generally seen from the viaduct at the north end of London Bridge, crouching beneath its overbearing neighbour. When Wren designed its lovely octagonal steeple, capped by a dome and a concave spire, it

(A. F. Kersting)

was to serve as an upstanding landmark, a foil to the Monument just above.

The church is rectangular, with nave and aisles, the arcades a little different now from what they were at first. The woodwork is splendid: the gallery at the west end, with its two fine twisted staircases, the pulpit, and the reredos behind the altar, carrying paintings of Moses and Aaron. The original pews have gone, and that is regrettable since the low seating that has replaced them exposes the bases of the pillars, which the pews were designed to fit exactly. Still, the right dark tone has been preserved in the woodwork everywhere.

Among the monuments notice the one in the south aisle to Miles Stringer, a spice merchant who displayed "the most pleasing and unaffected urbanity of manners"; and against the east wall of that aisle the two tablets to Miles Coverdale. There is ripe irony here. Coverdale was a strong Protestant, translated the Bible into English, was Bishop of Exeter in 1551–3 and then, under Elizabeth, rector of this church, until he refused to conform to Anglican requirements and resigned. In the 20th century St Magnus became a stronghold – almost the only one in the City – of Anglo-Catholicism: representing all that Coverdale would have detested most. It retains that character still.

The Museum of London City 6

The Museum of London figures in this book on two accounts. Its collections are very remarkable. As a museum devoted to the history of a single city it is unexcelled anywhere, and probably unequalled. And its building is remarkable too. The other buildings chosen to represent Greater London here are of all centuries from the 15th to the 19th. Here is one to keep them company from the 20th.

London formerly had two principal museums to display its history, arising from the ancient division between the City proper and the rest of the great town. The Guildhall Museum was established by the City Corporation in 1826; the first to be set up in England by any municipal body. In 1912 it was joined by the London Museum, occupying apartments in Kensington Palace. The two were widely different. The older museum was largely concerned with archaeology. It was unobtrusive, not seen by many visitors. The London Museum owed much to an illustrious predecessor, the Carnavalet in Paris. It was housed more agreeably than its colleague in the City, its interests were wider: it assembled, for instance, notable collections of costume and of material relating to the women's suffrage movement. And it drew more attention to itself, in particular by the publication of catalogues that were models of their kind.

The two museums were managed separately. Both were shut down in the second World War; the Guildhall Museum was not reopened until 1955. By that time it was obvious that the maintenance of two museums devoted to the history of London was not justifiable. It was uneconomic, confusing to visitors, and involved a serious overlapping of functions, particularly in fieldwork. Yet any proposal to make a single museum for London as a whole had formidable obstacles to overcome. Where should a new museum be placed, in the City or outside it? What would it cost to build, fit out and run, and who was to pay? How was it to be governed and managed? These were delicate questions. Parliament decided at last in 1965 that a new Museum of London was to be established, combining the two older ones, under a Board of Governors representing the City, the Greater London Council, and the Government. A specially designed building was to be erected for it, on a site within the City. Another 11 years passed before this plan was realised, with the opening of the new Museum by the Queen on 2 December 1976.

This political history is very characteristic of London itself which for the last 900 years has been not one city but two (London and Westminster), as well as an agglomeration of communities, each in some ways different from its neighbours. It has never been easy to create any institution to serve London as a single whole. The new Museum was constituted on the bold assumption that that could be done.

Its site is excellent – perhaps not far from ideal: at the

junction of Aldersgate Street with London Wall, five minutes' walk from three Underground stations, St Paul's, Barbican, and Moorgate. The entrance is from a high walk that threads its way between tall buildings, above the traffic. The Museum itself forms part of a tall building, but its quarters are on the lower floors; the tower block is let as offices.

Powell & Moya, the architects, had great difficulties to contend with in their planning. The site has one special awkwardness: the presence of Ironmongers' Hall, one of the halls of the ancient City Companies (though not itself an old building, erected only in 1924). This was not to be removed. It lies uncomfortably close to the new building, at an acute angle to it. To the north, also, a stretch of the medieval wall of the city was standing, with two of its turrets. Clearly there must be no encroachment on that. Rather, the new Museum must try to form some relationship with it.

Within these constraints and others (not least those arising from inflation and mounting costs) the architects had to work. And like the best architects – like Wren, a king among them, in his City churches – they turned constraint into opportunity: to make a museum building that is notably compact, flexible, and convenient to visitors. The display is on two levels only, linked by a lift and a ramp. It is arranged chronologically. The point of division arises at the year of the Great Fire, 1666. The upper floor, by which one enters, treats the history of London from its origins down to that catastrophe; the lower continues it to the present day.

The arrangement is free and open throughout, with few structural walls. The building surrounds an internal courtyard, visible everywhere through glass, and by an excellent device the visitor can move along the left-hand side of it, by-passing what he may not want to see in order to reach quickly what interests him most. A gentle ramp slopes down to the floor below, enclosed in a tall glass-lined tunnel framed with steel ribs. The descent is delightful, an architectural experience to be remembered. The story is then taken up again with the reconstruction of the city after its most spectacular disaster.

(The Museum of London)

The lower floor includes a series of shop-fronts facing on to the suggestion of a street, and a dozen Victorian commercial units, well selected: a tailor's, a bookseller's, a barber's; two offices; part of a pub. A brief glance at the hectic years of Queen Victoria's two Jubilees and the glittering reign of Edward VII – and we plunge into the two World Wars.

(The Museum of London)

The Museum of London: part of the Roman gallery

The second is evoked chiefly in terms of the air-raids that destroyed almost every building on the site of the Museum, and around it.

Well over 7,000 objects are exhibited in the Museum. They are described with exceptional care, on labels containing about a quarter of a million words all told. It is perhaps invidious to pick out any single groups or objects for special mention. Yet it must be done, to give an indication of the range of interest of this great collection, and to offer a sample of what is to be found here, as an invitation to discovery. Here is a selection: a handful of different objects, and only that.

The origins of human settlement in and around London are well illustrated, with pottery and tools from the Thames Valley. When Heathrow airport was being constructed in 1944, a remarkable wooden temple was discovered, with a farm, dating from about 600 B.C. Some of the finds from that site are here: layers of culture on top of one another indeed!

Roman London is splendidly presented; many people will find this the most striking part of the whole Museum. The sculptures from the Temple of Mithras discovered in Walbrook stand out. They reflect the wealth of the city. That wealth arose from trade; and trade is – very rightly – the unifying theme of the Museum as a whole. So here are workshops, a carpenter's bench, a fascinating cutler's stall, and a selection from the goods imported from the Continent.

Similarly in the medieval section, there is an excellent display relating to the leatherworking trades, from shoes to *cuir bouilli*. The pilgrims' badges are delightful. Some of them relate to the cult of St Thomas Becket, which sprang up quickly after his murder at Canterbury in 1170. He was a Londoner through and through – he often signed himself "Thomas of London": the city's own saint. Close by, another small display, imaginatively conceived, relates to the religious life of London immediately before the Reformation, when the worship of saints – above all of St Thomas, the priestly opponent of monarchy – was forbidden.

Tudor and Stuart London provides a rich mixture, well symbolised by the Cheapside Hoard, the stock of a jeweller's shop at the beginning of the 17th century. We are shown a little of the Civil War, in which London played a decisive part. Oliver Cromwell's death-mask is an exceedingly powerful reminder of it.

The old London Museum constructed a diorama of the Fire. Here it is again, with a clearly-spoken commentary, an endless attraction to more visitors than the small space allotted to it can hold. The reconstruction of London afterwards, the wealth that went into it and the still-increasing wealth of its citizens, are convincingly portrayed, with a glance at Pepys and another at Wren – don't miss the iron garden gate from his house in Love Lane. In the 18th century the emphasis is placed again very heavily on trade, on the crafts of London (like the making of Chelsea and Bow porcelain) and on its misery, vice, and crime. A prison cell and the gates of the old Newgate gaol are incorporated into the display.

By the beginning of the 19th century London had become the largest city in the world and in many respects (notably economic) its metropolis. Its buildings and streets never quite reflected that. Such achievements as Haussmann's boulevards in Paris lay outside the scope of its thinking. Yet it had fine new buildings, widely admired, and some as the Museum reminds us have gone already: the Crystal Palace, destroyed by fire in 1935, the Euston Arch and the Coal Exchange by philistinism in 1961–2. The domestic and commercial life of Victorian London are well reflected in the shops and offices that have been lifted and brought in – though where is a working-class kitchen, or a bourgeois drawing-room?

The changes of the 20th century are unfolding themselves before us still, and with relentless speed. It is extraordinary to be confronted with the gates and car of a lift from Selfridge's store, put in there just 50 years ago: gilded, ambitiously ornate, they belong to an era as decisively past as the Iron-Age temple at Heathrow.

The most spectacular object in the Museum is surely the Lord Mayor's coach, resplendent in scarlet and gold: built by Joseph Berry in six months of the year 1757. Its display is admirably contrived. It looks handsomer than ever now, its gorgeous colouring set off by the austerity that surrounds it: concrete well dressed, clear glass, York stone, a shallow black-lined trough of water below, to keep the atmosphere moist and prevent cracking in the paint. The baroque world and the 20th century confront one another here sharply. No clash results, however, only a final harmony.

There is one thing more to be seen at the Museum, which should not be missed: the views down to the City wall and along it to the two bastions. One of these is to be had from a window in the Roman gallery; the other from a corner of the building, by the medieval antiquities. The Museum plans to undertake excavation here, which may well reveal more about the Roman and medieval defences of London.

All these things can be seen by anyone who steps into the Museum. But a great deal more lies behind the public display: workshops and laboratories, for the servicing of the Museum and the conservation of its possessions on the spot; an energetic educational service, taking the Museum's work out into the schools and bringing them into it; a library and a large print room where students can examine a splendid collection of pictures of London of all kinds. Here is a major new force for learning and teaching, in the heart of the City. Its establishment, in the face of so many difficulties, and its physical realisation in this excellent building, represent one of the best achievements of England in the 1970s.

St James's Park Westminster 6

The open spaces of London are one of its special amenities. They are of different kinds. To begin with, the Royal Parks, part of the estates of the Crown: this one and the Green Park that adjoins it, Hyde Park, Kensington Gardens, Regent's Park, and Richmond Park 10 miles out. Then the squares, at first associated with the aristocracy and generally laid out as part of a plan of systematic development: St James's Square, for example, by the Earl of St Albans about 1680. Presently, squares came to occupy the sites of great houses that had been demolished: Berkeley Square is one, created about 1740 in the grounds of Berkeley House. The Dukes of Bedford laid out a series of these squares north-west of the centre of London; the largest of them, bearing their family name, Russell Square, in 1801. Then thirdly the Commons, the property of the commoners, which could be sold off only with their consent. These form the chief pleasure of south London. Clapham, Wandsworth, and Wimbledon Commons lie close together, with Richmond Park just beyond. And finally there are Hampstead Heath, Blackheath, and Epping Forest, whose acquisition by the municipality of London is a valiant epic of the Mid-Victorian age.

Even in those parts of the city where there are few or none of these things, tiny open spaces abound. Some of them adjoin Wren's churches (one is at *St Mary Abchurch*). On a hot day Charterhouse Square, close to Smithfield Market, is a delicious cool place, shaded by magnificent planes. Those trees have adapted themselves better than any others to the conditions of life in the city, which owes them an inexpressible debt. They achieve perhaps the height of their splendour in Berkeley Square, compensating at least in part for the destruction of nearly all its fine houses. There they have been growing grander every year since 1790.

St James's Park is the oldest of the Royal Parks, and the smallest. It was a low-lying swamp until Henry VIII had it drained, to form a pleasant addition to St James's Palace; stocked with deer, it had a pond at its western end. It soon became a place of public resort. Charles II took to it immediately on his return from exile and set about refashioning it with all the energy he devoted to the things that amused him. The pond was enlarged into a rectangular shape in 1660, and an ice-house built; a variety of birds was introduced, which the King enjoyed feeding. He walked here constantly, attended by his dogs, conversing affably, though always with caution – Halifax observed that "he would slide from an asking face, and could guess very well". In December 1662 skating began here, a pastime that Pepys had never seen before.

So the Park came to minister to everybody's pleasures, to be used for wrestling matches and buck-hunting and assignations of all kinds, including duels. The Hanoverian sovereigns – one cannot altogether blame them – disliked the way in which the Park, although their property, had passed into public use. Queen Caroline asked Walpole what it would cost to shut it up and turn it into a private garden. "Only three crowns" was his dry answer. As usual, he was right. The Park had become a highly prized possession of London. Immediately outside its limits, streets had grown up with gardens leading down to it. Milton lived in one, in Petty France on the south side, by Birdcage Walk. About 1704 Queen Square was erected here, much associated with the great South Sea Company. Today it is known as Queen

Anne's Gate, and it includes the most perfect set of houses of that time left anywhere in the city, with elaborate canopies over their front doors.

In 1814 the Park provided the setting for elaborate festivities in honour of the allied sovereigns who had gathered in London to celebrate Napoleon's abdication and retreat to Elba. The Prince Regent's architect John Nash built a Chinese bridge with a pagoda in the centre and two pavilions at each end. It was flimsily constructed, but the pagoda had an even shorter life than had been intended, for it caught fire and tumbled into the lake. Then, when the Prince Regent had become George IV, he determined to make some permanent changes in the Park. Again Nash was responsible. He erected

St James's Park: looking eastwards to the Horse Guards

(A. F. Kersting)

Carlton House Terrace, a noble piece of architectural scenery on the Mall to the north, and replanned the landscape of the Park itself, giving the lake an irregular outline, in the shape of a mutton-bone as we see it today. He also improved Buckingham House at the north-west end of the Park, pleasing the King so much that he decided to move there. It thus became Buckingham Palace; its main front was changed into something much more grandiose by Sir Aston Webb early in the 20th century. This was part of a plan for turning the Mall into a processional way entered from Trafalgar Square by the Admiralty Arch. The work was carried through in 1901–13. It made the Mall the English equivalent of the Champs Elysées in Paris, yet something very different: on flat, not rising ground, much smaller, far less grand.

As you stand on the bridge in the middle of the lake (the second successor to the gimcrack affair of 1814) you look one way to Buckingham Palace, the other to the Foreign Office. On the north side is the Mall, on the south the lofty trees that screen the Park from the traffic of Birdcage Walk. Or go to the eastern gate. You are close to Duck Island, full of exotic birds, the descendants of Charles II's, and you look over the Horse Guards Parade to Kent's elegant composition of towers, with the Admiralty building (Imperial Renaissance) on the left and the plain backs of the official residences of Downing Street, the seats of power, on the right. One memory prevails here, perhaps above all, from the English Revolution: of Charles I, on the icy morning of 30 January 1649, walking across from St James's Palace to his execution at Whitehall, pausing on the way to point out a tree planted by his elder brother Henry. Had that brother lived, there might have been a different revolution, or none.

St Pancras Station Camden 6

This was the metropolitan terminus of the Midland Railway Company, a rich provincial corporation that had its headquarters at Derby and thrust its way up to London rather

(Geoffrey Drury)

St Pancras Station: the train-shed. Photograph taken in 1967, the girders on the roof recently repainted

later than most of its rivals. To achieve that end it had to undertake an extension 50 miles long from Bedford. Work began on the line in 1864. It was opened for goods (which meant above all coal) traffic in September 1867. The passenger station was brought into use on 1 October 1868.

The building comprises two elements, closely related but not quite fused together: the station – that is, the train-shed, with the platforms, booking-hall, and other rooms required by passengers – and the hotel, in front, facing the Euston Road. The train-shed, designed by W. H. Barlow, is both technically and visually a masterpiece. It comprises a single vast hall, overarched by a glass-and-iron roof 240 ft wide, its immense weight carried not on any internal columns nor by walls shored up with huge buttresses but by being tied in underneath the platforms. This solution allowed several things to be achieved at once. The absence of internal supports left the planning of the interior entirely flexible – and in fact two new platforms, the present Nos. 3 and 4, were added some 20 years after the station was opened. The construction of the roof enabled the shed to be excellently lighted from the top. The vaults underneath were designed to accommodate beer traffic from Burton-on-Trent. Apart from those two additional platforms, the station remains, in essence, unaltered. A very large goods station was added on the west side in 1883–7. It is shabby now and quite disused; but its curtain wall is a splendid piece, the quality of the bricks matched, in smoothness and precision, by the delicacy with which they are laid.

The hotel did not receive its first guests until 1873, and it then took three more years to finish. It was designed by Gilbert Scott and was very much larger than had been originally intended. Scott's ambition – which had been frustrated in some ways, for all his enormous practice and great success – leapt at the opportunity; the Midland Railway's directors responded to his enthusiasm. When they saw Scott's drawings, they recognised that they had here the chance to proclaim that their provincial company had successfully arrived in London. They took it, even though in the end it cost them half a million pounds, as much again as the rest of the station.

The building ceased to be an hotel 40 years ago and now accommodates offices. Its exterior is almost exactly as Scott left it: a tremendous cliff of Gothic red brick, rising up from a plinth of steps and crowned by a tower, a spire, and numberless pinnacles. It makes everything in its neighbourhood look featureless and inert by comparison – except King's Cross station, which preserves a dignified composure. The outline of St Pancras is still to be seen memorably as it emerges again and again over the roof-tops between gaps in the streets and buildings to the south.

The station distils the very essence of Mid-Victorian power: for it is the most magnificent commercial building of the age, reflecting more completely than any other its economic achievement, its triumphant technology, its assurance and pride, suffused by romance.

Syon Park Isleworth 6

There was a nunnery at Syon in the 15th century. After its dissolution in 1539 its property was secured by the Duke of Somerset, Protector of the young Edward VI, and he built a house here. It surrounded a courtyard (perhaps laid out on the lines of the nuns' cloister) and is the shell of the house we see today. The estate came into the hands of the Percy family, Earls and later Dukes of Northumberland, in 1557. It has been with them ever since.

Syon is the only one of the riverside palaces of the nobility near London to remain in private ownership. The approach to it is frankly disagreeable. It lies on the western fringe of Brentford, a dingy Thames-side town. Even when you are inside Syon Park a miscellany of buildings appears, and you wonder how far the commercial spirit has overspilled from the London Road outside. Your first sight of the house too, whether you get it from the river or from its entrance, is disconcerting. It is a large square pile, battlemented and with little turrets at the corners but otherwise perfectly plain. Pausing before you open the front door, you may well fear that your tedious journey has been wasted.

But the moment you open that door, enchantment begins. You are in the Great Hall, at the beginning of a sequence of rooms at once so sumptuous, so refined, and so varied that they can scarcely be matched anywhere else in England.

Robert Adam worked on the house from 1762 to 1769. His task was to remodel the 16th-century building; to remodel, not to demolish and start again. The outside of the house had already been given its mildly medieval character; Adam's attention was given exclusively to the inside.

His difficulties are to be seen at the outset in the Great

Syon House: the Ante-Room (A. F. Kersting)

Hall, where the levels are awkward but the problem is solved by the use of two little flights of steps and, at the eastern end, a screen of Doric columns. With its antique sculptures, including a copy of "The Dying Gaul" made in Rome in 1773, it provides a calm and noble introduction to the rest of the house.

For some people the greatest delight of all comes next, in the Ante-Room, an astonishing harmony of the richest colours. Harmony is the final result: for no one colour – neither gold nor red nor the greyish-green of the scagliola columns – prevails.

The Dining Room follows, the first room furnished by Adam, terminated at both ends by the screened-off apses that he particularly liked. The colours here are white and gold, set off by those of the Red Drawing Room, which opens out of it: red predominantly, from the crimson silk hangings of the walls, but tempered by the endless varieties of the ceiling. This comprises a series of medallions, octagonal and diamond-shaped, divided by gilded bands, each of the medallions painted differently by G. B. Cipriani. Adam designed the carpet for the room, which has the maker's name Thomas Moore and the date 1769 woven into it at one end. The white marble chimney-piece is enriched with ormolu work by Matthew Boulton of Birmingham.

And so through the next pair of doors – every detail of them is magnificent throughout Adam's part of the house – to the Long Gallery. It is long indeed, a tunnel of a room in its proportions, for its height and width are no more than 14 ft and it is 136 ft in length. It was inherited from the older house and Adam was not at liberty to cut it up as Lord Irwin had done for example at Temple Newsam about 1740 (see under *Leeds*). He gave the ceiling cross lines which induce a sense of breadth, and he broke up the long inside wall with three doors and two fireplaces, as well as a range of books, for this was the library of the house. In use, as a drawing room intended particularly for the ladies its confined proportions may have been turned to good account: for the chairs could group themselves closely round the fires, to give the warmth that must often have been much needed, since the windows of the room face east, out on to the damp cold meadows of the Thames. Over it all Adam threw an indescribable texture of colours, sage green and buff and pink primarily, laced everywhere with gold. Two centuries have done the rest: the patina now is exquisite.

Here the sequence of Adam's work stops, abruptly. He never touched the north side of the house. He was not able to fill in the courtyard, as he intended, with a circular saloon, or to construct two oval rooms and a double staircase between it and the east front. The circuit of the house on the ground floor is completed through one small room and two passage ways, hung with portraits and other small pictures. Through the second of these you descend once more into the dazzling white splendour of the Great Hall.

Adam created one other thing at Syon: the screen on the London Road, with its gateway surmounted by the lion of Northumberland. It is at present in a lamentably dilapidated condition – much at risk too, as the eternal traffic pounds by. It is an outstanding piece. Should it perhaps be removed, for safety, inside the grounds?

The Park is flat, and not large: half a mile from the London Road to the river, less than a mile the other way. Capability Brown did wonders with it in 1767–73, sweeping away the old formal gardens, creating two lakes and allowing the house to stand in a setting of grass, trees, and water. Fresh improvements followed, notably through the building of the Great Conservatory, a most elegant structure of glass and iron, one of the precursors of the Crystal Palace, in 1820–7. Syon has a long and distinguished history as a centre of horticulture. William Turner, chaplain and physician to Protector Somerset while he owned Syon, wrote his *Names of Herbs* in the house, published in 1548. He also made here what claims to be the first botanical garden in England. A hundred years later the tenth Earl of Northumberland imported a series of exotic plants and again made the gardens famous. In our own time, in 1965, the present Duke established here a gardening centre, which provides a delightful complement to the pleasures afforded by the house. The Great Conservatory is in splendid order and contains not only exotic plants and shrubs but a fine collection of moths, clinging to the leaves of bougainvillea and plumbago, and an aviary; a rock garden and a notable rose garden are here too. But it is the trees that make the park at Syon memorable: swamp cypresses, catalpas, great cedars, rare oaks.

A whole delightful day can be spent within the walls of Syon Park. It is a pleasant walk of a mile (westwards of the house) to the river, to the old village of Isleworth with its church, bombed and now reconstructed, and the London Apprentice, a hospitable pub. If you want to add something else the choice is varied, from what lies close at hand. Two miles away to the north-west is another Adam house, Osterley, very different from Syon but in quality fully comparable. Eastwards a bus through Brentford will bring you in 10 minutes to Kew Bridge. There, if you have a mind for such things, is a Pumping Station now open as a museum. Its huge engines are put into steam at the week-ends; the sight and the sound of them is majestic. Across the bridge is the pretty Kew Green and then Kew Gardens, delightfully laid out and rewarding at every season of the year; the parent of many botanic gardens throughout the world.

Lytes Cary Somerset 4D4

A complete small manor-house of the late Middle Ages. It lies in the flat plain of Somerset, close to the Fosse Way (the road the Romans built to run diagonally across the country from Devon to Lincoln). The earliest part of the building is the 14th-century chapel. An older house appears to have been entirely replaced between about 1450 and 1550: first the hall, which is chiefly of the 15th century, then the adjoining rooms, one of which bears the date 1533, and those above. The greater part of the work was due to John Cary, who succeeded in 1523 and died in 1568.

Two things distinguish it particularly. One is the lavish provision of oriel windows – elaborate projecting bays, set in a stone frame: beautiful both in enlarging rooms and giving them a cross-light as well as in decorating the exterior. The arch of the oriel in the Great Hall has the panelled decoration that is an especially delightful regional element, appearing in the arcades and the tower-arches of many of the Somerset and Dorset churches. The other notable thing is the number of small rooms adjacent to the hall, and in particular the one known as The Oriel, so designed and placed as to allow it to be screened off to form a tiny private room on its own: a clear stage in the evolution of the later dining room, separate from the hall.

Lytes Cary exemplifies the pursuit of privacy everywhere. It has no large room anywhere; it never acquired a long gallery, of the kind that was soon to be demanded even in houses of quite modest size (see *Little Moreton*). There is nothing ostentatious here. Everything is comfortable and homely, yet dignified and never rustic. The only piece of clumsiness is due – surprisingly – to the Georgian age. The Carys fell on hard times then and sold the property. The north part of the house (to the right of the entrance) was pulled down about 1800 and replaced by a much taller new building, which sits uneasily in relation to the rest. Throughout the Victorian age the place was sadly neglected, until it was rescued by Sir Walter Jenner, who acquired it in 1907, added to it discreetly on the far (the west) side, brought the whole back into repair, and bequeathed it to the National Trust in 1948.

The house is well furnished throughout, largely with pieces collected by Sir Walter Jenner. Most of them date from about 1680 to 1730, but they include two later pieces of particular interest: the curious semicircular drinking table in the Little Parlour and the elegant 18th-century bed in the smallest bedroom, with its arched and hooded top. The bed in the Great Chamber comes from Burton Pynsent, not far to the west, a house that was given to the Elder Pitt, and it may have been used by him. The chapel has simple 17th-century furnishings and some very curious glass of about 1830.

(A. F. Kersting

The Carys who built the house and lived here were plai country gentlemen. Only one of them achieved any specia distinction: Henry, son of John the chief builder, who comple mented his father's work in stone by laying out a garde that became famous. He translated a Flemish work on horticul ture and dedicated it to Queen Elizabeth on its publicatio in 1578, "from my poor house at Lytes Cary".

Nothing of Henry Cary's garden remains now; but if h revisited the place he would find it all recognisable, muc of it unchanged – including the landscape. There is nothin in sight or sound to destroy its harmony: the harmony i shows of green grass, yew-hedged alleys, the plain grey wal of the house enlivened with the oriels, all in the rich golden stone from Ham Hill.

Maiden Castle see **Dorchester**

Maidenhead Berkshire 4F3

The town of Maidenhead has experienced ups and downs of fortune, arising chiefly from changes in transport. It grew up as a settlement on a main road from London to the west, beyond the crossing of the Thames. Though it became, in consequence, a place of inns, it did not grow into a town of any importance for general trade. With the growth of coach travel in the 18th century it flourished, and the bridge was rebuilt, to allow it to carry the increased traffic, in 1772–7. Then came the Great Western Railway, opened to this point from London in 1838–9 and on to Bristol in 1841; and the town's business shrivelled away. The railway did not even think it necessary to provide Maidenhead with a station. What it called "Maidenhead" was at Taplow, on the opposite side of the river, one and a half miles from the town centre. The present station was opened only in 1871. Victorian Maidenhead became a quietly sedate little place. A pleasant residential quarter grew up on Boyne Hill, west of the town – dominated by Street's All Saints church (1854–7), which with its parsonage and school buildings still forms a striking group; and towards the end of the 19th century it began to draw profit from pleasure traffic on the river. Its revival came with the motor car. Revival, and presently a fearful problem: so that today, in spite of a by-pass road, the town is apt to be a maelstrom.

These changes have left two signal monuments behind them. The 18th-century road bridge is a work of an elegance outstanding even in that age; and the railway bridge is one of the English masterpieces of bridge-building in any shape. They are within quarter of a mile of each other and can be seen together.

The road bridge is the work of Sir Robert Taylor, an architect who began life as a mason and sculptor. It is, like nearly all pre-railway bridges, slightly bowed; resting on seven heavily-rusticated arches. The limestone of which it is built – white with a creamy tinge – has lately been cleaned to excellent effect. It is a beautifully refined work throughout. Notice for instance the sweeping curve of the walls at the approaches; and the little blind circles let into the parapet of the bridge itself. Harassed by the ever-growing pressure of traffic, the local authorities must have been much tempted to demolish it and build a new one. It stands to their credit that they have succeeded in keeping it unaltered.

The railway bridge of 1838 presents a strong contrast. Its top is horizontal, not bowed; it is built of red brick; and it leaps across the river on two arches, each 128 ft wide. The whole viaduct is completed by four narrow arches at each end, almost concealed by trees and buildings. The great pair in the centre are rightly famous. They are the widest brick arches in the world. I. K. Brunel, who designed them, was the boldest railway engineer of his time. His plan for the bridge was ridiculed. He was told it would sag, it would inevitably collapse directly the centerings were removed. He went on unperturbed. The eastern arch gave a little trouble, for which the contractor accepted the blame. It was put right, and the bridge has defied the critics ever since.

Unlike the road bridge it has been altered. It was widened to take four standard-gauge tracks (in place of the two broad-gauge, for which it was designed) in 1893. The work was carried out with great care, to preserve entirely the lines of the original, building out on each side of it. Standing underneath on the towing-path, you can see how the enlargement was made; the new work is actually 2 ft wider in span than the old. There is a change in the brickwork, from Brunel's English bond to the stretcher bond of 1893.

The two bridges can be seen together from River Road, Taplow, which follows the eastern bank. Pass under the railway bridge and about 100 yards beyond, and then look back. There Taylor's elegant white bridge is framed within

Maidenhead: the two bridges (A. F. Kersting)

Brunel's monumental brick creation: the 19th century at its most powerful, overlaying – one might say, superseding – what had gone before.

There is more, much more, to see in the neighbourhood. Northwards, beyond the road bridge, lies one of the finest lengths of the Thames, with the magnificent gardens of Cliveden falling down to it. The whole stretch past Marlow to Henley is one of the classic pieces of river scenery in England, enhanced by accomplished planting and backed by the natural woods of the Chilterns (see *Fingest and Turville*).

Mildenhall Suffolk 5B2

The ancient churches of Suffolk are extremely numerous: there are at least 500 that can be reckoned to be of medieval foundation. The great majority of them are, as we see them now, Perpendicular buildings of the 15th century. They are distinguished for their woodwork: their seating, with elaborately carved bench-ends, their painted screens, special fittings like font-covers, and above all their magnificent timber roofs. Fine roofs are to be found elsewhere: across the border in Essex, in Norfolk (see *Sall*), in the West Country (see St Cuthbert's, *Wells*). But no other county can show so many, of such high quality, as Suffolk. It seems invidious to choose any one example. Let us take Mildenhall, not only for its roof but also because it is a noble building, well set.

The church (St Mary) stands right at the middle of its little town in a grassy churchyard, open to the High Street though screened by trees. The building is large in all its parts, with a very tall tower, constructed of the local flint and rubble but with liberal dressings of expensive limestone.

The eastern part of the church is much older than the western. The chapel on the north side of the chancel is of the early 13th century, of stone throughout and carrying a very chaste and simple vault. The chancel arch is a little later, splendidly proportioned like the chancel itself, whose windows are worth special study. Those on the north and south sides are agreeably varied, whilst the east window (later still; probably put in after 1300) is a fascinating composition: a double arch with quatrefoils between the two frames and a pointed oval as the central feature. There is something like it at Ely, but the design was never repeated anywhere else.

The rest of the building is more like what one expects in Suffolk: Perpendicular on a grand and lavish scale, with tall arcades and unusually broad aisles. The roofs are exceptionally elaborate and accomplished. The one in the nave is dominated by angels with outspread wings, and the transverse brackets have delicate tracery. The carpenters' work is even finer in the aisles, especially the northern one. There the carved figures are not winged, but there are Biblical scenes in the spandrels of the brackets and delightful small figures of animals in the cornice above the windows. At least nine figures can be counted for each bay. Nor does that exhaust the riches of these aisles. Both have big porches towards the west end; again the one on the north side is out-

(A. F. Kersting)

standing. It is vaulted and it carries a Lady Chapel above, reached by a staircase in the west wall (notice the carving of the Annunciation at the entrance). The tower has a gallery, open, like the Lady Chapel, into the church; underneath it there is a beautiful fan vault.

The church is sadly marred by its Victorian glass, in which a gruesome pink is conspicuous; a few fragments of the mediæval glass are to be seen in the east window of the north chancel chapel. The monuments are undistinguished, but one inscription is worth recording: to the memory of Lt-Gen. R. Armiger (d. 1770), "in whom were happily united the politeness of the courtier, the integrity of the gentleman, and the bravery of the soldier, cemented with universal benevolence".

There is nothing else in Mildenhall to rival the church. But it keeps a pleasant country-town centre, with a six-sided wooden market cross and to the north of that a row of small shops and houses roofed in the pretty tiles, mottled in red and yellow, that are peculiar to this part of England.

Try, if you can, to take the road from Mildenhall to Newmarket. It runs over great sweeps of chalk, covered with grass and edged with beech trees. No wonder it should be the country supremely favoured for English horse-racing since the 17th century.

Molland: church of St Mary Devon 3C4

Molland may take some finding. It is easily reached from A361, the main road from Taunton to Barnstaple. But the smaller by-roads in this part of the country are capriciously signposted, or not signposted at all, and it is not difficult to get lost in them. Still, there are ample compensations in the country itself, with its steep valleys and bare hills, and Exmoor always a broad presence to the north. It is perhaps best to come in spring. There are not many trees here, but the deep hedge banks are full of primroses and the small wild daffodils.

The village is unremarkable. It clusters below the simple

15th-century church, with its plain and handsome tower. The exterior gives no idea of what is to be found when the door is opened. If the fabric is entirely medieval, its contents are nearly all of the 18th century. The nave and aisle are filled with tall oak pews, reaching high up the piers of the original arcade. In the aisle is a big three-decker pulpit, complete with its sounding-board surmounted by a trumpeting angel. At the entrance to the chancel there must formerly have been a carved rood-screen (no doubt a simpler version of the one at *Hartland*); the reredos behind the altar is probably composed of some of its panels, re-used. A very plain Georgian screen stands there now with an arch giving access to the chancel. Above it are the Ten Commandments and the royal arms, painted on boards in 1808. At the east end there are monuments to Courtenays (that great Devon family held one of the manors here) and to David Berry, a vicar who was ejected during the Civil War.

The church is admirably kept, the fabric well maintained. There is nothing at all dilapidated about it. Yet it is what is often called "unrestored". The Victorians in general, finding such a church, tried to put it back into its medieval condition, casting out the box pews and over-large pulpits,

(A. F. Kersting)

erecting new screens of the medieval type, to incorporate any fragments of the original that might remain. Here is a church where that was never done. This interior remains a very perfect piece of the Georgian world: not elegant but homely, rural, even a little rustic. One can only rejoice that it has been left unchanged, to be cherished and respected in our own time.

Montacute see **Brympton d'Evercy**

Mottisfont see **The Test Valley**

Newark Nottinghamshire 2D5

Newark is a town of great interest. Its importance derives from its position on the Trent. In the Middle Ages it stood on the main stream of the river, which has now been diverted a little way from it, to improve navigation. It was then a depot for the trade in wool, from the sheep of the good grazing lands in Nottinghamshire and Lincolnshire, much of it exported down the river to the Continent. The bishops of Lincoln had a castle here, of which a noble fragment remains. It survived, not indeed in good repair but strong enough to serve a military purpose in the Civil War of the 17th century, when Newark was one of the bases of the King's power and underwent several attacks. In the Victorian age the town became notable for its brewing; the low chimneys of maltings formed an important element in the skyline until recently. It is a place of light industries today.

Through all these changes two things have been constant. Very close to the bridge here over the river, the Fosse Way met the Great North Road (A1); the multiplicity of big inns reminds us of the coaching age still. Although the A1 has now been re-routed, to pass at a short distance from the town, a stream of traffic continues to battle through. The town's centre is still the Market Place. Newark has not tidied away its market into some hygienic and featureless hall. Here it is, out in the open, the natural centre of the town's life.

In a visual sense, the best approach to Newark is from the west. As you arrive at the bridge, a striking group of buildings confronts you. On the right is the castle, seen from this point at its most impressive: its west wall, nearly intact, rises up sheer from the river. In the centre is the spire of the church: very tall and richly decorated, presiding still over the whole town and its neighbourhood. Below it, in the foreground, as symmetrically placed as if it had been in a composed picture, is a Queen Anne house – marred unfortunately by a projecting shop front. And on the left is a remarkable building of the late 19th century: what was originally the Ossington Coffee Palace, a temperance hostelry (1882). The architect was Ernest George, and it is a ripe piece of the 17th-century revival. Big, and dominant on its commanding site, it was certainly calculated to impress this brewing town with the power of the doctrines of temperance. But it has now passed into other hands. Today it accommodates public offices.

The gatehouse of the castle, on the north side, is a grand ruin of the late 12th century. The brave front facing the

Newark: the Castle (A. F. Kersting)

river is now a *façade*, no more. But notice the elegant oriel window, inserted about 1475, when defence was giving way to comfort.

Kirkgate (away to the left, on the opposite side of the road) contains one or two half-timbered buildings, but is to be remembered chiefly for its approach to the church, running up to the steeple at a diagonal. Go on past it and turn into the Market Place on the right. The buildings here are a miscellany, reflecting the history of the town. The huge church lies parallel with it, to the north. Below the church stands the Moot Hall, an early-18th-century building carefully refashioned to form commercial premises by Currys Ltd in 1965–6. Further east there is a building of the same date with a distinguished door-case, notable (as a tablet recalls) because it was the place where the first youthful poems of Byron were printed, in 1806–7. At the south-east corner is the White Hart, the most important domestic building, in an archaeological sense, in the town: a 14th-century timber structure, painted externally in red and green, heavily decorated with small figures. It is now empty and in a bad state of repair.

The south side of the Market Place shows a long arcade, a covered walk of the kind first popularised in England by the piazzas of Covent Garden. This is in front of what were formerly the two principal coaching inns, the Clinton Arms and the Saracen's Head. A little to the west of them is the fine half-timbered Governor's House – the house, that is, occupied by the Governor of the town, under the King, during the Civil War in 1642–6. And then, in the middle of the west side of the Market Place, comes the Town Hall, completed in 1773 to the designs of John Carr of York. Newark is in general a town of brick, orange-red, rough in texture; and this extends even to the roofing, which is of pantiles. The church and the castle are built of limestone from Ancaster in Lincolnshire. The Town Hall is of white Mansfield stone, dressed smooth throughout. There is a fine assembly room inside. Calm, precise, assured, it is an aristocrat surrounded by burgesses.

One more set of burgess buildings, leading north out of the Market Place: Wilson Street. Down to the 1950s this was intact on both sides: a complete pair of 18th-century terraces facing each other, plain and cheap but showing the unfailing dignity of their time. Now most of one side has gone, and the other, having fallen into grave disrepair, is being renovated. The "Wilson" refers to a Georgian vicar, one of the less pleasing of his kind, who erected these houses as a speculation.

The demolition on the right-hand side of the street allows you to walk straight into the churchyard: a very large one, admirably tidied up and laid out as a garden in 1950. The whole north side of the church (St Mary Magdalen) can be seen from here. Its grandeur appears if you go to the north-east wall of the churchyard and look back at the whole composition, building up to the steeple. The east front is intriguing, the broad aisles seeming to pinch in the tall chancel: yet, though odd, the total effect is fine.

The splendour of the interior, when you enter by the west door, bursts on you at once. It has a strong unity of its own. But it is not a single composition. The piers of the crossing belong to the 13th century, and so does the tower. The spire was raised shortly before 1300, and the south aisle was given its present form immediately afterwards. The rest of the church, replacing the earlier structure, dates from about 1460–1510. The transepts came last, their walls glazed to the utmost limit of safety.

Like the churches of *Boston* and St Mary Redcliff at *Bristol*, the church as we see it today is a splendid monument of the piety, the wealth and taste of the commercial middle class in the late Middle Ages. The whole of this great interior soars upward. Yet its proportions seem exactly right; the vertical is counteracted by the horizontal of the painted timber roofs and the transepts that open out to left and right. This balance between vertical and horizontal is shown again in the noble screen at the entrance to the chancel, made by craftsmen of York in 1508. The chancel itself is flanked by two chantry chapels. To build and maintain the one on the north side, Thomas Mering bequeathed "all my clipped wool and all my flock of sheep". The very large brass of Alan Fleming (d. 1361) reveals again the wealth and pride of these townsmen. The east window of the south aisle is filled with medieval glass, formerly a jumble but now skilfully reassembled. The eight panels in the centre date from about 1300 (look at Adam and Eve, expelled from Paradise and then delving and spinning), the remainder from the late 15th century.

It is much to the credit of Newark that, though not a large or rich place, it has carried through a loving and at most points successful renovation of the church – which very badly needed it – in the past 15 years. The town shows a continuing pride in itself. Even its minor Victorian buildings have been cleaned up and freshened, like the Corn Exchange of 1847 in Castlegate. British Rail have similarly cleaned the stations – the smaller of which, the Castle station of the old Midland Railway, is a handsome structure, in the Italian manner, of 1848.

Norwich Norfolk 5C2

Norwich was one of the chief provincial cities of medieval England, with *Bristol* and York. It was exceptionally extensive. When its walls were constructed in 1297–1334 they enclosed almost a square mile, an area as big as that of the City of London. By that time it had become the unquestioned capital of East Anglia. The seat of the bishop was removed from Thetford to Norwich in 1094; it was a river port, the commercial centre of a large hinterland, and from the 14th century to the 19th a major textile manufacturing town. Most of those things are evident today. It is still a cathedral city and regional capital. If its cloth manufacture has departed, it has other industries on a considerable scale, the making of footwear, printing, brewing light engineering. The city proper has a population of about 120,000 now; the whole built-up area, Greater Norwich perhaps 180,000.

Norwich was substantially bombed: over 2,000 houses in the city were damaged beyond repair. In the 30 years since, it has had that damage to overcome, together with many other insistent problems, notably the unrelenting demands of motor traffic. Norwich shows a marked civic pride. The tradition goes back a long way. In 1932 it commissioned a new City Hall much bolder and more remarkable than any other of its time in the country. In the 1950s and early 1960s, before "conservation" had been much heard of elsewhere, it set itself to protect and encourage the refurbishing of some of its notable streets and buildings. The treatment of the delightful Elm Hill, with the aid of the Civic Trust, was a landmark in urban improvement.

Norwich is not an easy place to describe systematically. It lacks a main street, to form a spinal cord. Its centre is the Castle, high on its mound, and the valley below it to the west with the Market Place and the City Hall beyond. The cathedral, within its ample precinct, lies a few minutes' walk away. But there are over 30 medieval parish churches in Norwich and many buildings of other kinds not less notable. Some of these things are hidden obscurely. Still, it is never long before one catches sight of the massive four-square castle or the bulky steeple of St Peter Mancroft church by the Market Place or the cathedral's bold spire; and those things provide one's bearings.

Norwich is a place of hills: gentle hills within the old city itself, steeper ones outside. It lies in a shallow amphitheatre in the valley of the meandering River Wensum, which is joined there by two others, the Tas and the Yare. Most of the medieval town lay on the west bank of the Wensum, set well back from it on account of flooding. But to the north it crossed the river; and more than a third of the ancient churches are to be found in this quarter.

The account given here starts at the Castle, goes on to the Market Place and the close-packed old city, and ends with the cathedral and its precinct.

The first castle was erected to the orders of William

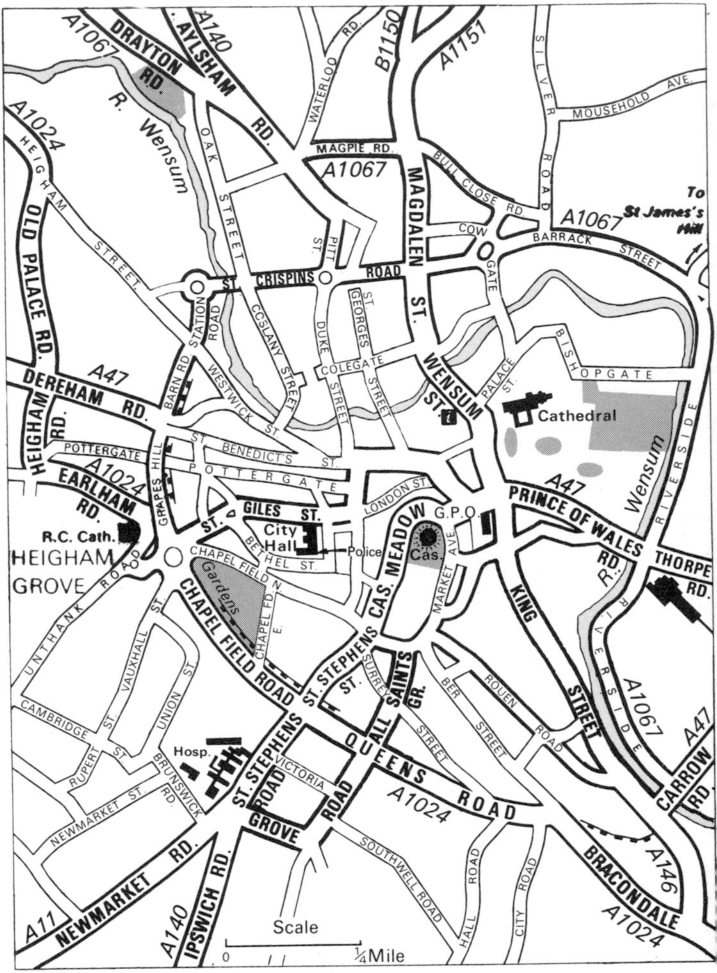

the Conqueror on a natural hill, heightened for the purpose, with a ditch dug round it. The buildings were probably all of timber. The present square stone keep dates from about 1160. It was refaced in 1834–9, which makes it look hard and new. However, the remarkable decoration of the exterior, in a series of arcades, reproduces the original faithfully. It was a powerful symbol of the Norman Conquest. At *Lincoln* and *Durham* the castles, erected at the same time, were matched by cathedrals close by, so that Church and State appeared together. Here at Norwich the castle stood high up, alone.

When the castle was no longer needed as a fortress it became a prison and continued so until 1887. Then it was converted into a museum, opened as such in 1894. It has since been much extended, with a series of galleries attached to the Keep, to a roughly octagonal plan of much ingenuity: an excellent job completed in 1969 (David Percival, City Architect).

This is one of the best museums in England. The Keep is appropriately given over to the medieval collections. The natural history of Norwich and Norfolk is displayed in six galleries in the new building; archaeology in another two. Most of the remainder is given to Lowestoft porcelain and to the Museum's outstanding possession, the watercolours and paintings of the Norwich School. Crome and Cotman each has a gallery to himself, with the lesser men – Stark and Vincent and Thirtle and many others – well represented. A happy day can be spent in this building, the pleasure increased by the refreshment facilities. This is one of the few museums in England that offer their visitors a good welcome of that kind.

Descend from the castle and cross the street that skirts the foot of the mound, to the narrow Davey Place leading out of it on the opposite side. This leads into the Market Place. Here is a scene unchanged in its essentials for 200 years and more. True, the houses and shops on the opposite side were removed to make way for the new City Hall, and every space is now filled, in tightly-disciplined rows of market stalls. When Cotman drew it in 1807 it was less tidy, and there was an empty space at the north end. But those are all the differences. The coloured awnings are gay, the houses at the south end (the tallest of them now a pub, the Sir Garnet Wolseley) are just as they were. So is one of the two public buildings that flank the Market Place: the Guildhall, with its elaborate 15th-century front, chequered in flint and stone. The other, lying along the top, is the City Hall (C. H. James and S. R. Pierce, completed 1938). Its models were Swedish, but it is well naturalised here: dignified yet not pompous, agreeable in colour and scale, it presides admirably over the old Market Place.

One more public building may be mentioned in conjunction with it: the Assembly House, in Theatre Street close by. This was erected in 1754 (the architect either Thomas Ivory or James Burrough), subsequently served for many years as a girls' school, and returned to something like its original purpose in 1950. The Music and Banqueting Rooms open out of an octagonal hall and are in constant use. Norwich deserves great credit for what it has done here, generously aided by H. J. Sexton, shoe manufacturer, who bought the building, restored it, and gave it to the city.

Facing down to the Market Place is the big church of St Peter Mancroft: a "market-church" of a kind rare in England (though see *Boston*) but common on the Continent (as at Haarlem, Dôle, and Frankfurt). It exemplifies most of the original qualities found in the churches of Norfolk, on the largest scale. It was built in 1430-55. The tower, much decorated outside, stands on open arches, to allow the free movement of processions. Inside the church is almost a rectangle, with three shallow projections, a pair of transepts and a chancel of one bay only; the south transept is now occupied by an organ, enclosed in excellent woodwork of about 1707. There is a fine original hammerbeam roof. The east window is filled largely with 15th-century glass, much rearranged.

This is the civic church, an extremely opulent work. There were nearly 60 parish churches in Norwich in the Middle Ages. More than half of them remain today, in spite of the loss of five by bombing. This is the largest number to be found in any English city: York has 19

Bristol 12. Though some retain older towers, the great majority of them date from the 15th century. Nearly all are of flint and rubble; most are rectangular in plan, without transepts; many have good timber roofs. They display a great range of interesting monuments. There are no Georgian churches, though some have fine Georgian fittings, and no Victorian ones of any importance either. That is true of the Church of England. The Roman Catholics and the Protestant Dissenters have, as we shall see, important post-medieval buildings of their own.

Churches will not be described individually here. There is an excellent guide to them: *The Old Churches of Norwich* by Noel Spencer and Arnold Kent. Many of them are kept locked. It is no longer possible to stroll from one to the next (sometimes only 100 yards away) comparing, contrasting, and enjoying the differences. The vandalism and theft of our day have forbidden that. Since it often takes time and trouble to get the keys of these churches, the casual visitor can hope to see only a small number of them in a short time.

Let us begin by considering two lying close together, with notable features to be seen from the outside. St Mary Coslany has a round Anglo-Saxon tower, attached to a conventional 15th-century building. These towers, and their Norman successors, are a local speciality: nearly four-fifths of those surviving in England are in Norfolk and Suffolk. Of the three in Norwich, this is the most striking, with its triangular-headed bell-openings. Close by, St Michael Coslany offers on its south side, facing the street, a display of East Anglian flintwork at its finest. Rough flint is not often attractive. But here – with the flints split and smoothed, and then ornamented with patterns cut in stone, to form "flushwork" – it can be splendid. The enormous windows are set in a frame, their tracery reflected in the patterning of the walls. The flushwork of the chancel is entirely of the 1880s, and scarcely inferior in its craftsmanship.

In architectural terms one of the most striking of these churches is St Giles, building up to a very tall and shapely

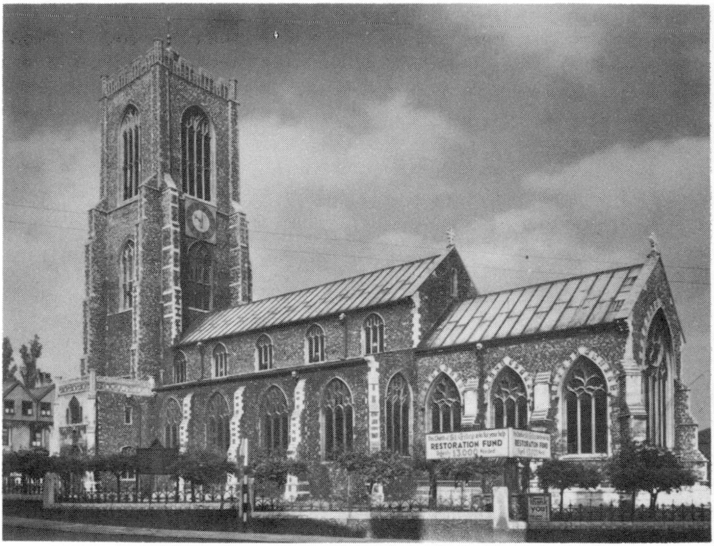

Norwich: St Giles's church (A. F. Kersting)

tower. (Its churchyard is enclosed in a splendid hedge of wistaria, at its best usually early in June.) St Stephen's has a very fine interior, the boldly-moulded arcades surmounted by a rich clerestory and a good hammerbeam roof. This is very late work, dating from about 1510 to 1550. Medieval fittings of note include the sanctuary knocker and lectern at St Gregory's and the delightful brass chandelier at St John Timberhill. There are good 18th-century pulpits at St George Colegate and St George Tombland. None of these churches escaped earnest Victorian restoration. Numerous drawings in the Castle Museum, and some at St Peter Hungate (now a museum itself) show what they looked like before that. Very few town churches anywhere were left alone: a rare and precious exception is Holy Trinity Goodramgate, York.

As for monuments, St Giles has good 15th-century brasses,

besides a pair of nice Georgian wall-tablets to members of the Churchman family, whose elegant house stands opposite. There is a fine Renaissance table-tomb, at present in poor condition, at St George Colegate, and at St Peter Parmentergate a characteristic Jacobean monument to Richard Berney (1623). The inscriptions are endlessly worth perusing. In St George Colegate there is Mary Calvert, who died in 1749 aged 66, having borne 13 children, 12 of whom died as infants. These memorials (often most beautifully lettered: see for instance Robert Harvey's in St Clement's, of 1816) offer a running commentary on life and death for 500 years and more.

The Catholic cathedral (St John Baptist) was built at the expense of the Duke of Norfolk in 1882-1910. The architect was George Gilbert Scott, and after his death in 1897 his brother John Oldrid. It is sumptuous (built of stone throughout, with a complete set of stone vaults) yet austere. The style is 13th-century Gothic – well chosen, as the one great style missing in the medieval buildings of Norwich. The glass, by John Powell and his son Dunstan, is worthy of the building. This is the finest modern Catholic cathedral in England, except the very different one at *Liverpool*.

Norwich also possesses the most complete surviving medieval friars' church in England: the church of the Dominicans, now in public use as Blackfriars Hall (the chancel) and St Andrew's Hall (the nave). It was built in 1440–70. Its amplitude is not easily appreciated because of its division into two. The nave was a great preaching-house, 140 ft long and 60 ft wide.

Nonconformist chapels were also preaching-houses. The two best lie together in Colegate. The Old Meeting House of 1693 (Congregational) has a plain brick front, enlivened with pilasters and decorative capitals. Inside, much of its furnishing has remained unchanged since it was built. The Octagon Chapel (Unitarian) was designed by Thomas Ivory and completed in 1756. The pulpit and organ were enlarged in 1887–9, but otherwise it keeps its original elegance:

as Wesley found it in 1789, "furnished in the highest taste and as clean as any gentleman's saloon".

Like almost every Nonconformist chapel in the whole of England, these two are kept tightly locked.

And so, at the end, to the cathedral. It lies low, at the level of the river; but its spire is visible everywhere. It is a very big Romanesque building, like its neighbours

Norwich cathedral from the south-east (B.T.A.)

Peterborough and *Ely*: greatly changed and enriched by the stone vaults that gradually replaced the original flat timber ceilings between 1450 and 1520. Norwich cathedral unites two quite different styles, Romanesque and late Gothic, and welds them into a harmony of its own.

Two things particularly distinguish the exterior: the apsidal east end and the spire. The rounded apse, imported from Normandy, did not suit the English, who preferred the ends of their churches square. This one was never reconstructed. The Lady Chapel is modern; it replaces a 13th-century one destroyed under Elizabeth. The excellent flying buttresses were added to take the weight of the stone vault placed over the choir about 1480. The steeple is Romanesque up to the series of bell-openings; Perpendicular above, reconstructed after the previous spire had been struck by lightning in 1463.

The building is smaller than Ely, and the difference is accentuated by the crowding at Norwich with chairs. Architecturally, the nave at Norwich is the richer, with splendid aisles and elaborate decoration on some of the

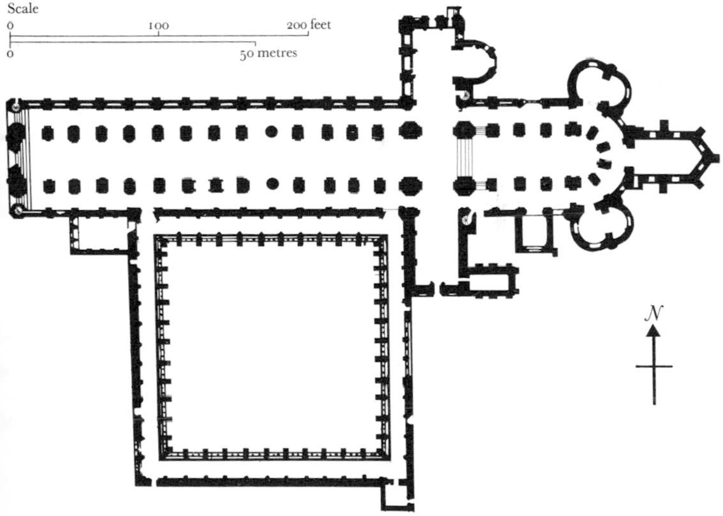

piers. The vaults are fascinating everywhere. There are over 800 carved bosses altogether, and many are of great individual interest; movable horizontal mirrors in the nave make it easier to study them. All have been recoloured in recent years, with great care. The east end of the chancel is superb: one of the great achievements of English medieval architecture. The ambulatory, round the back of the high altar, is an impressive curved tunnel. Chapels open out of it: St Luke's, on the south side, notable for the fine late-14th-century painting on its altar, of the East Anglian school. On the north side of the choir a bridge spans the aisle to the former Reliquary Chapel, which has been made into a Treasury for displaying some of the plate of the cathedral and diocese; admirably designed by Stefan Buzas and completed in 1973. It was the gift of the Goldsmiths' Company in London.

Some of the minor monuments in the cathedral are worth looking for. Notice Osbert Parsley's, on the north side of the nave, a tribute to an Elizabethan musician from his colleagues; and in the chancel the Georgian Bishop Horne's. His *Commentary on the Psalms*, we are told, "will continue to be a companion to the closet till the devotion of earth shall end in the hallelujas of Heaven".

The cloisters (built about 1295–1430) are again notable for the carved bosses on their vaults. Those in the south walk mostly portray scenes from the life of Christ, with one bay devoted to the Virgin and one to St Thomas Becket. The Prior's Door, at the north-east corner, giving access to the cathedral, has seven figures under rich canopies, arranged around the head of the arch. It is an outstanding piece of the early 14th century.

The close at Norwich is not laid out with ample green lawns, as at *Salisbury* or *Wells*. It falls into two divisions, lying at right angles. The larger part, the Upper Close, has two approaches from the city, St Ethelbert's Gate and the Erpingham Gate. The walls are still there, though masked by later houses, mainly Georgian. Houses of that sort continue delightfully in the Lower Close. This leads to the Water

Gate, whence there used to be a ferry across the river.

That convenience has now gone. Instead, one can return to the north side of the cathedral, pass through the Bishop's Gate, and walk to the Great Hospital, with the parish church of St Helen attached to it. The Hospital was founded in 1249 and at the Reformation passed to the city, which used it for the treatment of the sick poor. The road leads on to Bishop Bridge, the only surviving medieval bridge in Norwich. Across the river to the right is the brick Cow Tower (under construction in 1378), part of the fortifications of the city. The walls extended in a great arc, leaving only the river bank unfortified. They had 23 towers. The best surviving stretch is at the south end, by Carrow Bridge and up Carrow Hill. St James's Hill (off Gurney Road, above the Cow Tower) affords a view of the city from above, including the towers of more than half the parish churches. This is on the edge of Mousehold Heath, the main approach from the north. One of the numerous breweries of Norwich stood here, and the Nelson Barracks; Jarrolds' printing works are in this quarter still. These are all ingredients in the history of this remarkable city, rich in its inheritance from the past and bustling still today.

Patrington: church of St Patrick Humberside 2E4

The approach to Patrington is curious. You will almost certainly come to it from Hull, eastwards through the small town of Hedon (once much more considerable, and still distinguished by a noble church), and over the plain of Holderness, so dead flat that Keyingham, less than 30 ft above sea-level, seems to stand on an Alp. Glimpses of the spire of Patrington appear in the distance, but you do not see the whole church until you are almost beneath it, in the village itself: a village now, but the shade of a tiny town, the central focus of commerce – it once had two markets a week – in this tip of the old East Riding of Yorkshire, running down to Spurn Head.

If you were drawing up a list of the finest churches in

Patrington church from the south-east (A. F. Kersting)

England, you would have to consider Patrington as a candidate. Its exterior makes a superb composition, particularly from the south-east. It is cruciform, with steep-pitched lead roofs and surmounted by a marvellous spire, springing from an octagonal arcade. This spire, added in the 15th century, is the latest element in the whole fabric. The main body of the church dates from about 1280 to 1340. It is distinguished by the quality of its stonework, exemplifying the Decorated style at its apogee, like *Beverley*, not far away.

The building has an unusual plan, with double aisles provided for the nave and both transepts (a very uncommon feature indeed in a parish church), but none at all for the chancel. This, like everything else here, is nicely calculated, to make the narrowed chancel the climax, the focal point of the rest of the church. The mouldings are rich, and the capitals have beautiful carvings of foliage. All that is deficient – and the lack is much to be regretted – is stone vaulting. One has only to look at the vaults generously furnished to the aisles of the nave about 1900 to see how splendid an addition they would have been to the main body of the building. One small medieval vault was, however, erected: over the shallow apse of the little Lady Chapel in the south transept.

The church has no furniture of special interest – it would look much better if most of the furniture were removed. The building is grotesquely over-pewed. But at least it is not marred by ugly and powerful glass.

One returns to the outside, to walk round it with the deepest satisfaction. From Church Lane on the south side, take in the patterns of light shining through the glass and its tracery in the chancel, and look once more before you leave at the whole structure as it builds up from the east. There is here a classical, an ultimate justness of proportion.

Penshaw Monument Tyne and Wear 1C2

As you approach Newcastle from the south by the A1 you descry a puzzling object on the horizon to the right. (It is visible also from the train.) Getting nearer, you see that it looks like a temple. Turn off the road (at Chester-le-Street), drive up to it, and you find that indeed that is what it is: a Greek temple crowning a rocky hill, very large, and roofless. There is not the simplest notice to inform you what it is, or how it came to be there.

It is in fact a monument to a politician, John Lambton, first Earl of Durham. The rock on which it stands was part of his estate; but it is not a piece of vainglory on his part, nor a demonstration of family pride. It was erected by a local public subscription as a memorial to him in 1844, that is four years after his death.

Lord Durham was one of the ablest politicians of his time: a strong left-winger, nicknamed "Radical Jack". He was one of those who framed the first Reform Bill, under his father-in-law Earl Grey; he played a considerable part in the diplomacy that created the independent state of Belgium, and was twice ambassador to Russia. He was vain, and an awkward colleague (his temper sharpened all his life by spinal disease). Melbourne, who succeeded Grey as Whig Prime Minister, disliked him and saw a chance to get rid of him, perhaps even to break him as a politician, by sending him as Governor-General to Canada in 1838, charged to report on the causes of the rebellion that had taken place there in the previous year. The mission was a thankless one. In his absence Durham was attacked by his enemies. Melbourne made no attempt to defend him. Durham threw up his commission and returned to England after spending only seven months in Canada. But that was long enough to enable him to complete his report on the way home, in collaboration with his first-rate assistants Charles Buller and Edward Gibbon Wakefield. Published in 1839, the Report is one of the classics of English political literature, brilliantly written, incisive in its analysis of the causes of the Canadian troubles, and constructive in the remedies it proposed for them. It laid the foundations of the "responsible government for colonies" that became a peculiar feature of British colonial policy, leading to the creation of the Dominions as sovereign states within the Commonwealth, side by side with the United Kingdom. Durham saw none of this himself. He died in 1840 (aged no more than 48), exhausted, isolated, and in apparent defeat, less than a year after his report was published.

The Northumbrian Liberals had just signalised their pride in Earl Grey by the erection of his statue, on a lofty column, which still presides over central Newcastle. Durham's admirers, spurred on no doubt by the treatment to which he had been subjected, determined to do no less for him. This monument is the result.

It stands up majestically on its rock above the valley of the Wear, five miles inland from the sea. It used to be ringed round quite closely with collieries, but today most of them have gone. The monument has been a target for modern vandalism. Its plinth is daubed with illiterate scrawls, and the National Trust (which now owns it) has felt obliged to fence it in with wire and to deface some of its columns

(A. F. Kersting)

with minatory white notice-boards. But it rides calmly above all such insults. The strange form conceived by its sponsors is exactly right. It was never roofed. If it had been, that would have rendered it useful, a public building like the Town Hall of Birmingham, its contemporary. This was intended to be nothing but a monument. It stands up in solitude, as if it were at Paestum or Segesta, symbolising a long continuity, from the political speculation of the ancient Greeks to the liberal-minded imperialism of the 19th century, reaching out across the Atlantic to the New World.

Plaxtol: Old Soar Manor Kent 5B4

It is not easy to visualise the life of a medieval house. Most of those that remain either are in ruins or have been greatly changed, adapted by subsequent generations to their own habits and conveniences of living. No medieval house survives in this country quite unaltered and complete (though see *Burton Agnes*). Here however in Old Soar is a substantial fragment of one, which is fortunately intact and has escaped alteration of any kind.

The house lies in deep lanes west of Maidstone, on the slope of a hill. It was built, of Kentish ragstone, about 1290. It was never big, and the fragment that remains now is very modest, comprising three rooms on the first floor, with vaulted store-rooms and passages below them. The largest of the three is the solar, the private living-room; it is flanked by the chapel on one side and the garderobe (lavatory) on the other.

The hall, which was the heart of a medieval house, has now gone, submerged in the later house adjoining. But it is easy to see the surviving rooms in use. The owner and his wife would withdraw from the noise and turmoil of the hall up the narrow spiral staircase still used today into the quiet of the solar: a delightful room, brick-paved, with a raftered ceiling, a good-sized window to the west, and part of its original fireplace. It is bare now, the shell of a room only; but it would have been sparsely furnished when it

(A. F. Kersting)

Plaxtol: Old Soar Manor, the medieval house on the right

was new, with a table, perhaps a chair or two and a few benches, the walls hung with some kind of woven fabric, probably nothing as elaborate as a silk tapestry. The garderobe is large, but now totally bare; even the shoots have gone. The chapel, however, on the other side retains one of its fittings: a piscina, a drain for washing the communion vessels, placed in the thickness of the wall close to where the altar stood, under a pretty carved stone canopy.

So, with the hall below and its outbuildings, Old Soar remained, growing totally out of date and perhaps used only for storage and the purposes of a farm. In the 1740s its owner decided to build himself a new house. But he displaced the old one only in part. He pulled down the hall and erected his house on the site of it; yet he left a sizeable piece of the medieval house untouched. One wonders why. Perhaps it was from piety towards his predecessors; or perhaps he found the medieval building useful for the purposes of his farm. Anyway, he left it. What he put up is a plain house, in the agreeable manner natural to its time, and built of the warm red brick that is one of the delights of south-eastern England. The contrast between the two parts of the building as we now see it is piquant: the charming red house and its venerable predecessor, in pale yellow stone. Here, on a tiny scale, two civilisations touch.

Portchester Hampshire 4E4

Portchester Castle has an exceptionally long continuity of occupation. It stands on a promontory at the head of Portsmouth Harbour, eminently defensible from the water. A fort was built here by the Romans late in the 3rd century A.D., becoming one of the series developed as a defence against Teutonic pirates and generally known as the forts of the Saxon Shore. It seems to have been abandoned after serving for more than 30 years, to have been recommissioned about 340 and then abandoned again, in favour of Bitterne near Southampton, about 369. Thereafter, so far as we know, the Romans used it no more. But what is so rare about Portchester is that the Roman walls of the fort remained intact. They are intact to this day. Portchester is the only Roman fort in northern Europe whose walls still stand complete, to their full height.

In the 6th century it was occupied by Saxon invaders – descendants of the very people it had been built to repel. It may perhaps have been an early centre of Christianity. But no considerable town grew up here, as it did around some of the other Saxon Shore forts, like *Dover*.

Under Henry I and his successors Portchester became one of the main bastions of the defence of the south coast. The present keep was built, and the King founded an Augustinian priory inside the ample enclosure of the walls in 1133. It did not remain there long, before being removed to Southwick; but the church continued in parochial use.

Portchester was a constant place of embarkation and arrival

for the crossing to and from France. Though its position was in many ways admirable, it had drawbacks corresponding to its merits. If it was sheltered and well defended by the water, it could be a trap. Ships could easily be hemmed in at the narrow southern neck of Portsmouth Harbour; inland, Portchester lay uncomfortably close to the high chalk downs that dominated it. Edward I did nothing to strengthen it, as he did Dover; the king who showed it most affection, building a palace within its walls, was the unwarlike Richard II. He was deposed before he could occupy it himself. It was at Portchester that Henry V, assembling his forces for the campaign that ended at Agincourt, learnt of the Earl of Cambridge's plot to kill him – an event transferred to Southampton in Shakespeare's play. In the 15th and 16th centuries the castle gradually decayed, though it was repaired under Elizabeth and James I by Sir Thomas Cornwallis. Out of commission for good as a fortress, it was frequently used to house prisoners of war down to the early 19th century. There was an idea, thrown up during the Crimean War, that it might be made into a permanent military hospital, but that was rejected in favour of Netley. So the castle remained untenanted but intact, until it came to be repaired, and its history investigated by prolonged excavation by the archaeologists of our own time.

Unless you arrive by water you approach the castle up the main street of the old village of Portchester: a delightful haven of quiet after you have battled out to it through the ugly suburban sprawl of Portsmouth. It comprises a gently winding street, lined with agreeable small houses, leading to a tiny green shaded by an oak tree. Here two lanes diverge, one to the sea and the other to the castle. You enter by the Land Gate and find yourself inside the Roman enclosure, nine acres in extent, which became the Outer Bailey of the Norman fortress. The walls are of flint and rubble, bonded by courses of red tile and stone. They had originally 20 turrets, of which 14 still remain. The medieval castle occupies the north-west corner of the enclosure, defended internally by a moat, and by walls enclosing an Inner Bailey. The

(H. Tempest, Cardiff, Ltd)

Portchester Castle and church, enclosed within the circuit of the Roman walls

tall Keep is built into the right angle of the walls, overhanging them slightly. It may be dated about 1125, with a top storey added some 50 years later. From that top the whole fortress is spread out below you, together with all Portsmouth Harbour (still lined at the far end with warships), its narrow opening, the Solent, and the Isle of Wight beyond.

Richard II's extensive work, of 1396–9, lies along the west and south sides of the Inner Bailey. The ruins of it are substantial. The ground floor provided lodgings for the Household; the principal rooms, the Great Hall, the Great Chamber, the rather small bedroom for the King, are above. On the eastern side of the Inner Bailey are the remains of a building erected by Cornwallis about 1600.

The 12th-century church (St Mary) stands in the diagonally opposite corner of the great rectangular Roman enclosure. It has unfortunately lost its south transept and all but one bay of the chancel; but for the rest it is a complete Norman building, unmarred by bad restoration. It has an admirable west front, a nave of satisfying dignity, and a splendidly sculptured font. Sir Thomas Cornwallis has an alabaster monument on the east wall, by Nicholas Stone; the bust (originally painted) in a circular frame, shows the convincing quality of a portrait. Spare a thought for James Lind, who is commemorated by a simple memorial tablet on the north wall. He is described on it merely as having served for 35 years as physician at the naval hospital at Haslar. But he made a great contribution to the welfare of the world, through his discovery of lemon juice as a preventive of scurvy on long sea voyages. He published it in 1768, and the practice he advocated was adopted by Cook, with complete success, on his great Pacific expedition of 1772–5.

So Portchester keeps its place, from Roman to modern times, in the vital relationship between England and the sea.

Richmond and Swaledale North Yorkshire 1C3

The site of Richmond is arresting. Turner seized the drama of its Castle, rising up sheer from the north bank of the Swale, when he drew it (with marked exaggeration), probably in 1816. It is indeed a splendid fortress. In plan it is roughly triangular, the apex, towards the town, containing the Keep, which was defended by the Barbican, now destroyed. The work of building it began soon after the Norman Conquest, and most of the present walls, other than those to the south facing the river, are of that time, together with the towers on the eastern side and Scolland's Hall at the south-east corner. The Keep was built in the second half of the 12th century, together with the southern wall. Some time in the 14th century a Great Chamber and Chapel were erected immediately north of Scolland's Hall, but of them very little remains. A survey of 1538 depicts the Castle as ruinous, and it was never subsequently repaired.

The Keep is the most impressive part of it all now, a rectangular building 100 ft high, massively thick. The ground floor of it was the original gatehouse of the Castle. That was superseded by another, which has now gone, when the Keep was built. (The arrangement seems odd, but the same thing was done at Ludlow.) There are two storeys to the building, each containing a large room and several small ones, and then a staircase leads up to the battlemented roof. Scolland's Hall, though less exciting to look at, is an important building of the 11th century: one of the earliest castle halls to be found in the country, if not quite the earliest. It is on two storeys, the hall standing above cellars, and it must have served as the sole principal apartment until the Great Chamber was constructed north of it in the 14th century.

The Castle never proved to be of any military importance. But it was the administrative capital of the Honour of Richmond, a group of estates that passed several times into the hands of the Dukes of Brittany, and finally to the English crown when Henry Tudor, Earl of Richmond, became King in 1485.

There are other English castles as strikingly situated as this one – Corfe, *Scarborough*, *Warkworth* for example. What gives Richmond its special character is the intimacy of the physical relationship between castle and town, and the plan of the town itself. Its centre is a sickle-shaped market place on the side of a steep hill, swirling down from the entrance to the Castle: a very broad crescent, embracing the tower of Holy Trinity church. The Market Place is paved with dark stone and lined with houses mainly of 18th-century brick, with the principal inn, the King's Head, as its centrepiece. At the top stands the Market Cross, an obelisk erected in 1771 and sited at exactly the most effective point.

The parish church (St Mary), which lies oddly outside the medieval walls, was largely rebuilt in 1859–60. Below it is the pretty Gothic building of the station (now disused as such) and the handsome bridge put up by the railway company in a style that seemed proper to mark the approach to an historic town.

Richmond has one other building of note besides its Castle: the Theatre, which dates from 1778. It is one of the oldest in England still in regular use, to be compared with the larger one at *Bristol.* It kept going, prosperously at first and then with waning success, for over 50 years from its opening. Then it fell into disuse and became a corn merchant's store and a furniture repository. It was rescued from this condition in 1960–3, repaired and restored with skill. Since then it has taken a valued place in the life of its neighbourhood, offering a range of delightful entertainment – Shakespeare, Vanbrugh, Turgenev, Bernard Shaw; the Torteliers and Mattiwilda Dobbs.

The auditorium is very small and intimate, holding just over 250 people, the seating rather more comfortable now than it was in the 18th century but otherwise very little changed. When not in use, the Theatre is shown to visitors by admirable guides; and it is described in a booklet that is, in all respects, a model of its kind.

Make your way back now into the Market Place. Take Finkle Street on your right, and then Bargate. This is another good street, chiefly of 18th-century houses, running down to the river. At the foot on the right The Green opens out, a pretty space like the centre of a village. Above it is the Culloden Tower, erected in 1746 to commemorate the Jacobites' defeat in the previous year. Cross the bridge, look up, and there is Turner's view of the Castle.

The Castle was placed here for one reason: it is at the point where the valley of the Swale broadens out into the Plain of York. Each of these north-eastern Dales has a corresponding castle – Bishop Auckland, Barnard Castle, Middleham, Skipton – guarding the approaches from the hills to the wealthy and fertile plain. If Richmond Castle saw no military action, it was a mighty warning nevertheless.

The river itself invites one to pursue its course upwards, and Swaledale, though less well known than Wensleydale or Wharfedale, has a strong character of its own. It was never invaded by a railway, like its neighbours to the north and south; the one road that follows it is narrow and grows progressively steeper. Of all these valleys this one is the most secluded.

Richmond Castle from the south-west (D.o.E)

Upper Swaledale, between Muker and Keld

(Spectrum Colour Library)

Lead was formerly mined in the hills above. The industry declined in the 1850s, and the population fell. A faint industrial flavour persists nevertheless, not at all disagreeably. More than one of the Swaledale villages has a Literary Institute of its own: that in Muker dates from the late 1860s. The signs of the Victorian desire for self-improvement are to be found even in places as remote as these.

Reeth stands at the meeting-point of two valleys. Arkengarthdale, formed by the Arkle Beck, comes down here to join Swaledale. Muker is at the end, with the hamlet of Thwaite beyond. The little road then forks. The more important branch climbs north-westwards to Kirkby Stephen; the other rises higher, much more steeply, to the Buttertubs Pass and then drops down into Wensleydale. Another fine road, shorter and not so steep, rises up from Crackpot (there is a hamlet called Booze not far off: what names these places have!), half-way between Reeth and Muker, and runs south over Askrigg Common. This is fine walking country, whether you keep to the Dale or climb up on to the moor above; and if you want wilder country still you can find it to the west on Mallerstang Edge or southwards in Langstrothdale Chase.

Rievaulx North Yorkshire 1C3

Rievaulx (pronounced *Ree-vo*) is famous for its abbey; and rightly, for no more beautiful ruin is to be found in England. It also offers something else, less well known: no ruin indeed, but a matured achievement, perfect and intact.

The abbey was the earliest Cistercian house in the north of England, founded in 1131. Others of the same Order sprang from it, notably Melrose in Scotland. It soon flourished exceedingly. In the time of its most celebrated abbot Ailred, who ruled it from 1147 to 1165, there was a community of 140 monks here, with 500 lay brothers. About 1230 the house was rich enough to begin a complete reconstruction of the abbey church, which produced the choir we see now. But this work seems to have overstretched the resources available. Thereafter the abbey declined in numbers and wealth. At the Dissolution in 1538 the community had dwindled to 22, and its income was only about a fifth of that of Fountains, the largest of its Order in England.

When the abbey was first built the River Rye ran on the eastern side of the valley, and the buildings had therefore to be disposed on a relatively narrow site between it and the steeply-sloping hill. For this reason the church was laid out, unusually, to run north and south. The course of the river was altered in the 12th and 13th centuries, so that it now runs entirely on the western side of Ryedale. This was much to the benefit of the abbey, giving it room to extend, as well as good meadow and pasture land of its own.

The 12th-century founders used a dark-brown stone in their building. Plain and simple like everything else undertaken by the original Cistercians, it must have looked solemn, perhaps a little heavy. The 13th-century reconstruction was undertaken in a much lighter sandstone, quarried lower down the valley on the opposite side, and its style was not plain but as rich as anything to be found in the cathedrals that were being built or rebuilt at the time, like *Salisbury*. The choir of Rievaulx lacks its vault, and only a fragment of the aisles is still standing. Otherwise it is complete.

The monastic buildings all lie below the church, towards the river. The main lines of their disposition can be seen: the cloister, with the apsidal chapter house opening out of it, parallel with the choir of the church; the refectory or frater, facing on to it behind an arcade of three windows on the first floor; then, lower down, the novices' rooms and the infirmary. The gatehouse by which the monastery was approached lay up the hill, close to the little parish church, which was the *capella extra portas*, the chapel outside the gates.

After the Dissolution the monastic property passed into the hands of the Manners family, Earls of Rutland, and from them to George Villiers, second Duke of Buckingham. When his extravagant life ended in 1687, the estate was bought by Sir Charles Duncombe, a London goldsmith. His nephew

Thomas built Duncombe Park for himself in 1711–13, on the same side of Ryedale but high above, not in the valley. He then laid out a terrace to the south of the house: a free and natural landscape of grass and trees, in contrast to his formal gardens. His son, another Thomas, went on in the 1750s to add a second terrace further up the valley, immediately above the ruined abbey. He perhaps intended to bridge the gully between them; but if so, that idea was never carried out.

The two terraces are similar in that both are broad green rides framed in trees, with a temple at each end. The earlier temples, in Duncombe Park, are round. One is Tuscan and includes a circular room; the other, Ionic, is entirely open. The second pair, on the Rievaulx terrace, both contain rooms. The northernmost, again Ionic, is an exquisite dining room. Inside, with 16 places for diners round a table and a kitchen below, one thinks of hospitality. But the point of bringing

Rievaulx: the abbey church from the terrace. An old photograph, taken when the trees had lately been cut back

(Aberdeen University Library)

guests here, for Mr Duncombe, was to display his terrace and the view of the ruined abbey church. That view is revealed with the utmost subtlety at several points along the broad walk by clefts made through the trees. The edge of the terrace is serpentine, and the views, looking down, constantly change. Each is different, a freshly-composed picture.

Going back to the abbey and looking up with all this in mind, one sees the Ionic temple. Here is a union of three civilisations, all entirely different and yet blended into one: the classical world above, the medieval Christian world below, and both harmonised by a third, the landscape art of 18th-century England.

Rycote Oxfordshire 4E2

There are two things to take one to Rycote: the memories arising from a house, now gone; and a church, which still survives.

The estate was bought by Sir John Williams in 1542, a wary and successful politician. He reconstructed the modest house he found there on a much larger scale. When he died in 1559, as Lord Williams of Thame, he left no son. His heir was his daughter Marjorie, married to Sir Henry Norris.

Norris had shared with Sir Henry Bedingfield the duty of keeping the young Princess Elizabeth at Woodstock while her sister Mary was Queen. He had been a milder and more congenial warder than Bedingfield, and she became attached to him and his wife, whom she affectionately named her "black crow". She had visited Rycote once in Williams's time, in 1554. Then, after she became Queen, she returned four times, to stay with the Norrises. She was here in 1566, accompanied by Leicester, on her way from a week's state visit to Oxford. Norris served as ambassador to France, and became Lord Norris of Rycote. He had six sons, who all served the Queen valiantly in Ireland and France and the Low Countries, and all died comparatively young. Elizabeth came for the last time in 1592, returning from her second visit to Oxford. The mood now was different. She was close on 60, burdened with all her experience, her achievement, the dangers she had passed through; her host 10 years older. He received her with a speech of welcome, saying he was "past all service, save only devotion". One of his sons was already dead, and the Crow feared for the rest. With good reason: four more perished within the next five years. When John, the most distinguished of them, died of his wounds in Ireland in 1597 the Queen wrote his mother a magnificent formal letter of condolence, adding in her own hand this postscript: "Mine own Crow, harm not thyself for bootless help; but show a good example, to comfort your dolorous yokefellow". The Crow died two years later, he in 1601.

The house was ruined by fire in 1745, not rebuilt, and most of it demolished in 1800. The stables, and a surviving fragment of one tower, were repaired early in the 20th century and pleasantly converted into the quite modest house that is there now. To the east of it, however, across a smooth green lawn, the chapel remains intact.

It is a medieval building, erected by Richard Quatremayne, who then owned the estate, in 1449 and dedicated to St Michael and All Angels, to serve as a chantry with three priests and as a private chapel. In plan it is a rectangle with a tower at the west end. But this plainness is set off by the ample windows, the decorated niche on the tower, and the north doorway, the entrance used by the family from the house. Externally, the building now looks very much as it did when it was new, the limestone fresh from the quarries at Taynton, west of Oxford.

Inside, things are different. The font, the seating in the nave, and the stalls in the chancel remain from the chapel as it was built, and so does the simple wooden roof; but very little else. Early in the 17th century great changes were made by the Norris family, to adapt the building to their own ideas of religion and social order. The gallery was built at the west end, a pulpit was introduced, and two capacious pews erected, one on either side of the nave. The one on the north side has an open loft above it for musicians, enclosed in an elaborate wooden frame. Its fellow is surmounted by a domed canopy. Inside, the ceilings of both are painted with stars on a blue background. The base of the medieval rood-screen forms part of their eastern walls. They are linked by a wooden arch, opening into the chancel.

Such pews were frequently inserted by the gentry into their churches at this time (as at *Stokesay*). But why, at Rycote, should there have been two? A highly credible tradition suggests an answer. The northern pew was erected first, for the Norris family. Then, in 1625, King Charles I came on a visit. Where could he be suitably seated? The awkward problem may have been solved by the construction of this pew, more stately than the first – especially when it was surmounted, as it then was, by carved figures at each corner

Rycote chapel: interior (Roy Nash)

and on the top. Once there the work stayed, commemorating the last of the royal visits paid to Rycote.

At the end of the 17th century another generation took a hand. The chancel was refurnished in 1682, when the present reredos was put up – much more refined in its carving than the pews. The altar-rails are of the same time, and so probably is the plain paving of black and white stones set diamond-wise. Above, in the north wall, is a monument to Edmund Bertie, Earl of Abingdon, who was also by descent Lord Norris of Rycote. He died in 1699, and the monument was put up by his family in 1767.

The chapel has now passed into the hands of the State, and under its direction the fabric has been faultlessly repaired; the harmony of timbers and low colouring inside is excellent. One thing alone is absent – and that because it never was here. The building tells us nothing at all of the most remarkable people who lived at Rycote, Lord Williams and the Black Crow, her husband and sons. Everyone else contributed something to the chapel – their obscure predecessor who built it, the undistinguished generations who succeeded them; they nothing. They are buried in a vault under the altar, but they have no monument. For that one must go to the north transept of Westminster Abbey. There they all are, magnificently commemorated: not in their own little chapel, but in the church of the nation.

Rye East Sussex 5B5

Hilltop towns are rare in this country – more common in Switzerland and France. Rye is one of the few. It stands in Romney Marsh, which lies between the low hills of the Weald and the sea: dead flat, drained by numerous dikes, and affording pasture for many thousands of sheep.

Though ancient, Rye was no considerable place before the 12th century. It was included in the confederation of the Cinque Ports, at first as a member of the Port of Hastings and then, early in the 14th century, as a Head Port in its own right. Rye benefited from a great storm in 1284, which diverted the course of the River Rother and put it on to the main stream, to the lasting detriment of New Romney. It was encircled with walls, guarded with gateways (one, the Landgate, survives); and in the south-east corner a little four-lobed fortress was built, also extant today and called the Ypres Tower. Such precautions were necessary. The friction with France that was a constant element in English history down to the 19th century spilled over into protracted conflict in the Hundred Years War from 1340, and Rye, as a port of increasing wealth, was exposed to assault from the sea. The defences were then strengthened, and though the town had savage attacks to endure – the worst of them in 1377, when a large part of it was destroyed – it weathered them: whereas its neighbour Winchelsea (founded on its present site in 1283) soon decayed.

When the Hundred Years War was over, though the south coast was still vulnerable, the danger was less great; and Rye settled down to a quiet prosperity. It was especially celebrated for its fish. The prosperity was both open and concealed: in the 18th century John Wesley had some severe things to say about Rye's addiction to smuggling. But it never became a big place. Though a comfortable town under the Georges, it stayed still, and then, by ceasing to go forward, declined. It acquired no industries; it ceased to be a port of much significance, though timber still comes in here, as you can see now on the quays, and fishing continues in Rye Bay. In 1901 its population was 3,900.

Among those enumerated here at that last census must have been one distinguished man – the most distinguished, by a long way, of all the inhabitants of Rye, ancient or modern. Henry James came to live in the town in 1898, at Lamb House, the former residence of one of the little dynasties that had dominated the borough in the quiet comfortable Georgian age. The first Hanoverian king, George I, had stayed in the house, driven ashore by a storm; his grandson the Duke of Cumberland too, in the course of an inspection of the town's defences in 1757. But Henry James was a greater man than either of those princes; and he did not merely visit Rye, he lived here for his last 18 years. "A kind of little becoming, high door'd, brass knockered *façade* to one's life", he called Lamb House. In its Garden Room he wrote all his final masterpieces: *The Ambassadors*, *The Wings of the Dove*, and *The Golden Bowl*. And if – a British citizen at last, and an O.M. – he died in London, his wallet contained a return ticket to Rye.

It is hard not to feel him here now. The Garden House was destroyed by a German bomb in August 1940, but the delightful walled garden remains (open, together with two rooms in the house, twice a week in summer). His greatness overshadows the place. One cannot walk out of the station without thinking of that bulky imposing figure meeting his friends, their luggage trundled after them on a barrow by his gardener. Yet his life is an accident in the long history of the place, even if it supplies its most august episode. The town as we see it is the creation of earlier centuries. It pivots on the church (St Mary), a large and noble building: deceptively large indeed, for its tower is squat and does not crown the hill as perhaps it might. If the church had a tower like those of its Kentish neighbours Ashford or Tenterden, or a spire like Playden's, only a mile away, what a spectacle it would make! The scale of the church is best appreciated from the west: from below, on the road to Rye Harbour. Van Dyck sketched the town from here about 1633 – no doubt passing through, to take ship at Rye, on his way to or from the Netherlands. There you will see the whole ancient place spread out along the back of its hill, with the long low church at the top.

The streets of Rye are surprisingly steep. The most remarkable of them are still cobbled, as they were when cobbling was a boon to horses, climbing and descending them. Red is the prevailing colour everywhere, but red of many shades and degrees of brightness: from the hard, vermilion tiling with which the houses are often faced – a wise expedient for confronting the winter gales on this hilltop – to mellow brick, in all gradations from pink to plum; and everywhere above (it is almost the sole uniformity) the flowing red of

Rye: Mermaid Street (A. F. Kersting)

the roof-tiles. But these reds, which might elsewhere be too powerful, are tempered by other colours: by white plaster here and there, and the black-and-white of half-timbering; by mauve wistaria, by daffodils and wallflowers and the whole spectrum of roses.

In its years of greatest enterprise, merchant townsmen made and defended Rye; the close Corporation of the Georgian age guarded it jealously (close indeed, for power rested almost continuously in the hands of four families); although in Queen Victoria's reign it slowly decayed, it has recovered much of its prosperity in our own time under the watchful eye of the middle class, through catering for many thousands of visitors, including a marked influx from America and France. If you despise the *bourgeoisie*, go and look at Rye without prejudice. You may detect a few little snobberies and follies, but you will see how delightful a town, a *bourg*, these *bourgeois* – never here under any aristocratic dominance – have been capable of making.

Some other buildings: the elliptical brick water tower (about 1735) at the east end of the church, a piece of elegant craftsmanship; some nice shop fronts (Ashbee the butcher, Dewe's "apothecary's shop"); the old Grammar School in the High Street, erected in 1636, an early example of the use of Dutch gables in England; the timber-built warehouses by the river, not elegant at all but an impressive indication of the town's commerce.

St Mawes Castle Cornwall 3A5

St Mawes is one of a series of castles and forts built under Henry VIII to protect the country against a threatened invasion from the Continent. This was the biggest single defensive operation undertaken in England before the 19th century, and concentrated into a short period of seven years (1539–45). The whole plan comprised the construction of strong points (in some cases the reconstruction of existing ones), irregularly spaced along the coast from Hull round to Milford Haven in Wales. The 15 castles on the south coast are the most important of these defences. St Mawes is one of a pair, with Pendennis Castle opposite, guarding the entrance to Carrick Roads, the natural harbour formed by the estuary of the River Fal.

Nearly all these south-coast castles survive today. They were not built at the direction of one designer, to any standard pattern. Most of them show the influence of German thinking about fortification, which had been the most advanced in Europe in the first quarter of the 16th century. But the last of the series, Southsea, is expressly stated to have been "of His Majesty's own devising", and it displays newer ideas then emerging from Italy.

Like all these castles except Southsea, Pendennis and St Mawes are circular. But they are not identical twins. Although the heart of them both is a circular stone keep, at Pendennis this stands alone, surrounded at a distance by a 16-sided wall, whilst at St Mawes it rises out of a cluster of three semicircular bastions, designed to hold guns, on the pattern of a clover-leaf. On the landward side it is protected by a ditch, approached through a hexagonal gatehouse and crossed by a drawbridge. That is a traditional device, the application of a medieval form of defence (see *Bodiam*, *Warkworth*). For the rest, St Mawes belongs wholly to the world of guns.

The castle is built of shale quarried in the neighbourhood, with dressings of granite and other stone here and there.

St Mawes Castle: the Keep (D.o.E.)

It is four storeys high. The entrance is on the first floor, from which there is immediate access to every part of the fort, including the bastions: down to the mess-room and the kitchen in the basement below it, upwards to the octagonal gun-room and so out on to the roof, with its little domed watch-tower. The whole building is compact, its plan determined by the guns and the needs of the men who served them.

In a work so strongly functional, decoration would have been out of place. There is little here in any of the rooms: a pair of carved doorways, a few small sculptured heads, and that is all. But outside the building bears four carvings of the royal arms (unfinished, except for the one over the main entrance), and a set of Latin inscriptions in hexameter verse, written expressly for this purpose by John Leland, the King's Antiquary. "Henry, thy honour and praises will remain for ever" are the words that greet the visitor still.

The planning of the castle was begun in 1540 with a visit to the site by the King's clerk of works, Thomas Treffry. The first Governor, Michael Vyvyan, was nominated in 1544. Very soon afterwards the threat of invasion passed, and the castle was never tested in warfare at all. It was held for the King in the Civil War, but surrendered to the Parliament peacefully in 1646. Though small garrisons continued to be maintained here, there was little for them to do. The appointment of Governor was abolished in 1849. The War Office continued to occupy the castle, however, and made some use of it for coastal defence in the first World War. In 1920 it was handed over to the Office of Works to be treated as an historic building. It has been excellently maintained by that Department and its successors ever since: the fabric well tended, its history investigated and explained, the green slopes that fall down to the water below it delightfully laid out and planted.

The diminutive town of St Mawes was formerly a borough, returning Members to Parliament from 1562 to 1832. It once had a thriving pilchard fishery. Its chief bustle now arises from the visitors who come here in summer.

Salisbury Wiltshire 4E3
Church spires are among the special distinctions of English architecture; and the king of them is at Salisbury.

Nearly all medieval towers and spires look better from some angles than others. It is part of the supremacy of this one that it is equally fine from any point of view. Make a circle round it, at some distance. There is no weak element here, no imbalance. It is one of those rare things: a work on a very large scale that achieves perfection.

This is all the more remarkable because it formed no part of the original design. The cathedral was begun in 1220 and completed about 50 years later. The central crossing may then have been surmounted by a low lead pyramid; or perhaps it had nothing but a flat cap, like the one still at Westminster Abbey. The bells were housed in a separate tower, north-west of the cathedral, which was demolished in 1789. The tower and spire as we see them were not begun until 1334. We do not know just when they were finished.

The cathedral is seen best from the north-east corner of the Close. The entire building rises in majestic and precise geometry to the spire that seems its inevitable crown. The interplay between horizontal and vertical is wonderfully managed. Look at the treatment of the buttresses, at what appear to be the sets of grooves incised into them. They take the eye laterally along the building, helping to anchor it firmly to the ground, to counteract its dizzy thrust into the sky. And what of the ground itself? The cathedral stands now on an open lawn: intersected by a path or two, enriched by one glorious cedar, but for the rest a smooth green plain. This vital contribution was made by the 18th century, by Bishop Barrington and his architect James Wyatt.

The cathedral close is something peculiar to England. Elsewhere, great churches either stand surrounded by houses or – as at Antwerp and Reims and Santiago de Compostella – they preside magnificently over urban squares. The English alone created green gardens as their setting. Salisbury's is the finest close of them all. The houses show wide diversity in form and scale, and in colour too: creamy limestone, much red brick, a little flint, their gardens filled with roses, a vivid splash of petunias in August. The cathedral rises from the lawn in an endless gradation of grey and brown. Yet "grey" and "brown" are clumsy terms. Much depends on the light. In sunshine the limestone of which the whole cathedral is built – quarried at Chilmark, a dozen miles away to the west – is shot through with yellow and pink, and notably with green, whilst the lead roof can turn nearly to silver.

Like nearly all buildings, the cathedral has its faults. It is perfect only when seen from the north-east. The west front is a dismal failure: a flat screen, broad and heavy in its proportions, merely applied to the building behind it, not growing out of it in any organic way. Unfortunately almost every photograph chooses to make this front prominent and therefore shows the whole composition at its greatest disadvantage.

Inside, the building has one inherent fault, and it has suffered two great misfortunes. The fault is its lack of height, which makes it perhaps rather tame; it is quite without the electric tension of Reims and Amiens, its contemporaries in France. That defect is accentuated by the hard clear light that fills it almost everywhere. Most of the ancient glass in the cathedral was smashed by detestable religious fanatics. The fabric is excellently maintained, the walls and vaults a plain white. Against this background, one decoration stands out in strong contrast: the Purbeck marble shafts, dark green and brown, clustering round the tall piers of the arcades and patterning the arches above. All this was once played over by many other colours, from glass that has now gone. Finally – to conclude criticism – the arrangement of the nave is too completely symmetrical. That is due to Wyatt, who took monuments from a pair of chapels he demolished at the eastern end and placed them here in rows, one to each bay.

Over page: Salisbury cathedral from the north-east

(A. F. Kersting)

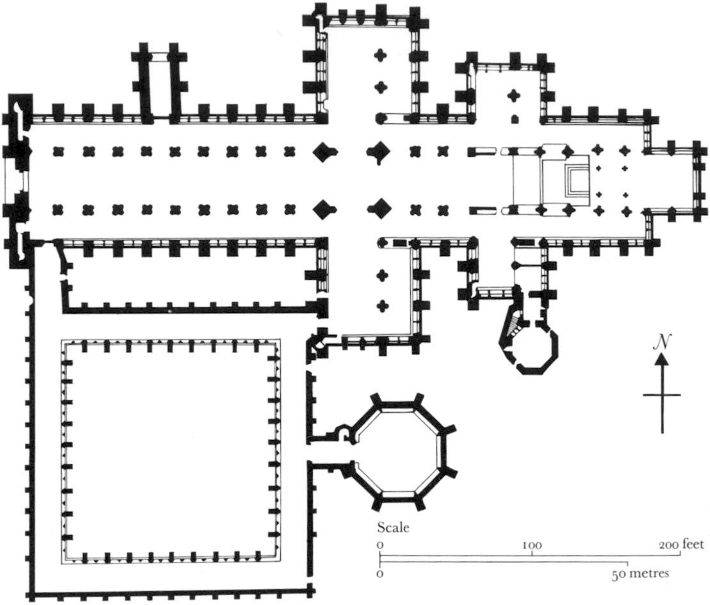

Allowing all these drawbacks their due weight, however, what beauties remain! If the building lacks tension, it has a serene harmony. Salisbury is the only medieval cathedral in England that represents one design. The whole interior was executed within the span of two generations. So it has a concentrated unity. When the spire was added 100 years afterwards it placed a formidable new burden on the structure below. The crossing space was therefore vaulted, and strainer arches were built over the transepts in the 15th century; but the work was discreetly done and involved no intrusion on the western arch, seen from the nave, as unhappily occurred for the same reason at *Wells*.

If most of the ancient glass has gone, a little remains, in the west window, in the third window from the west in the north aisle, and in the east window of St Anne's chapel. There and in other places what survives is chiefly the grisaille glass, grey tinged with green, which must have escaped destruction because it contained no human figures.

There are some exceptionally fine monuments. Two are in the nave: the 12th-century Bishop Roger's and that of William Longespee, Earl of Salisbury (d. 1226), the earliest military effigy in England. Bishop Bridport's monument in the south chancel aisle is outstanding, for all the disgusting mutilation of its sculpture. Nowhere are the properties of Purbeck marble shown so clearly to advantage, the range of its colours and the delicacy of carving it allows. Both chancel aisles are terminated to the east by grand post-Reformation monuments: to the Earl of Hertford (south), to Sir Thomas Gorges, builder of Longford Castle, a few miles away (north). In the south-east transept the west wall is occupied by the beautiful remains of the original rood-screen, only a little mutilated and scarcely at all restored.

The Chapter House is octagonal, one of the fine series that begins at *Lincoln* and ends at *Wells*. The cloisters are complete, and there is a splendid view of the spire looking across them.

Wyatt's work at Salisbury has been much criticised, and often unjustly. His destruction of the detached bell-tower may be allowed to be a mistake. Perhaps he valued symmetry too highly; but he revered the cathedral as a work of the greatest age of Gothic architecture. That was what led him to remove two chantry chapels, added more than 200 years later, which flanked the Lady Chapel on either side. Here it can be argued that he was right. Good though they may have been in themselves, they were alien excrescences on the original building, and their removal allows us to see it in its full purity.

The close was protected in the 14th century by a wall, which was pierced by two gateways. The buildings inside are of all ages from that century to the 20th. If Georgian red brick supplies the prevailing tone, it is only one tone of many. Mompesson House on the Choristers' Green – the finest of them all architecturally – is faced in Chilmark stone. That house, and Malmesbury House by the eastern gate, have notable interiors, and they are regularly open. No. 21

shows an Elizabethan front in flint. No. 19, the Salisbury and Wells Theological College, is a big house of the late 17th century, marred by Butterfield's arrogantly discordant flint Gothic chapel appended to it. Those are some of the grander houses. There are smaller ones worth looking at besides: Nos. 33–5, for example, mild intruders on to the grassy space. And then, by the north gate, there is the College of Matrons founded by Bishop Ward in 1682, low, with a hipped roof and a cupola: an almshouse characteristic of the charity of that age and of the next.

Salisbury is unusual among English towns in that it was founded at one moment by a conscious act. A bishopric had been established about 1075, uniting two previous smaller ones and covering approximately what are now Wiltshire and Dorset. Its seat was at Old Sarum, a fortified place one and a half miles north of the Salisbury we know today. A cathedral was built there, and a town grew up; but it was inadequately supplied with water and there were frequent disputes between the clergy and the garrison of the castle. Bishop Richard Poore, who was elected in 1217, decided to move his cathedral down on to a virgin site in the valley below, at the meeting-point of three rivers. A new town was laid out north of the new cathedral, with its streets on a grid pattern, and its centre has kept that shape ever since. The High Street runs straight on from the north gate of the close; to the east of it the streets form a chequer-board. At its far end is the civic church of St Thomas of Canterbury, a fine 15th-century building with good roofs inside and large paintings, of the Day of Judgment over the chancel arch and, in the south chapel, of the Annunciation. They are not great works of art, but they help us to realise something of what the interior of medieval churches was like (see *Kempley*) – quite different from the clear white walls of the cathedral today.

Close to the church is the 15th-century Poultry Cross, one of the four market crosses that formerly stood in the city. The Market Place has two handsome public buildings: the Guildhall at the south-east corner (Sir Robert Taylor,

1788-95) and the Market House at the diagonally opposite point with three very large glazed windows, well in the Georgian tradition but not erected until 1859. It has been ingeniously converted into a public library. There are two other medieval churches (one now an arts centre); five more

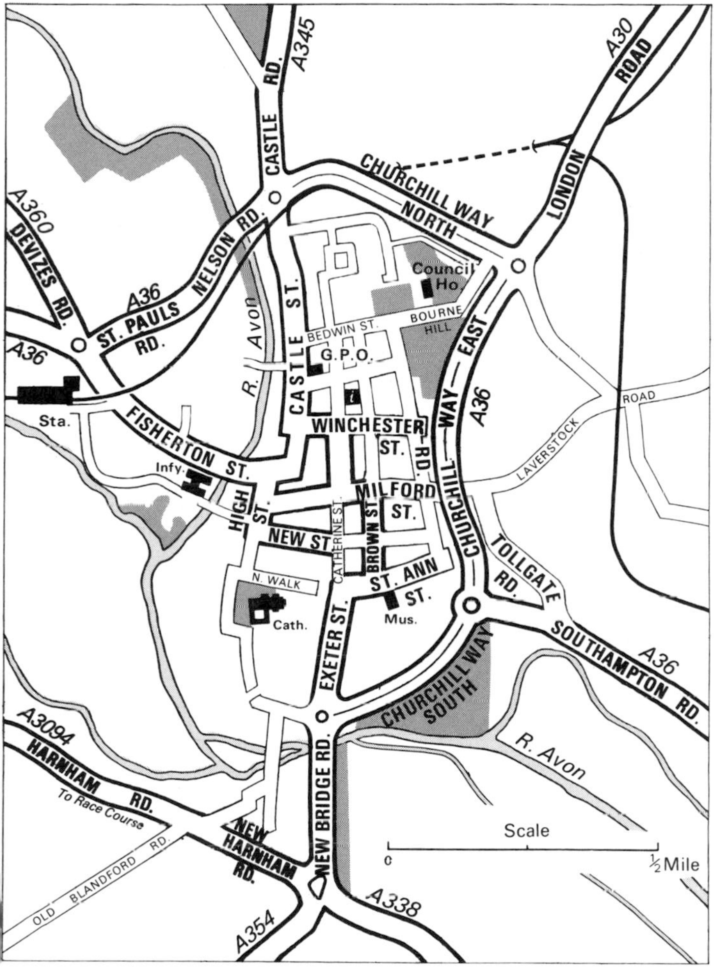

sets of almshouses, of which St Nicholas's Hospital may be the one in Trollope's novel *The Warden*; a good museum, with unusually rich and diverse collections; and numerous small and charming brick houses.

Three short excursions outside can be easily made. One is to Old Sarum, the original town on the chalk hills to the north. Only earthworks are to be seen there now, but they are themselves striking, showing clearly the military strength of the site, which was occupied successively by Romans, Saxons, and Normans, and then deserted in favour of the quiet ecclesiastical city below. Stonehenge lies only 10 miles to the north of Salisbury: the most spectacular monument of standing stones in Britain, and perhaps in Europe. The other excursion is to Wilton, three miles west. The church is a distinguished Italianate building of the 1840s. Wilton House is of outstanding interest, with a splendid collection of pictures. Its Double Cube Room (about 1650) is one of the finest rooms in the country.

Salisbury is an excellent centre, for a day or two or as much more time as can be spared. There is a special pleasure in staying there, returning to it in the summer evenings,* walking in the water-meadows as Turner and Constable did again and again. They drew and painted it more than any other building, of any kind. No wonder. Salisbury cathedral has been well called the Parthenon of England.

Sall: church of St Peter and St Paul Norfolk 5C1

A building memorable both for itself and for its place in the landscape.

The church dates entirely from the 15th century. It is built of local flint and rubble, with dressings of limestone brought round, as to so many Norfolk churches, by water from Barnack in Northamptonshire. The west tower is flanked

* The floodlighting of the spire at night – managed with subtlety and restraint – is an experience not to be missed.

by two large porches, matching each other, with rooms above reached by staircases within octagonal turrets. Taken together with the tower they form a coherent composition, a true west front – something uncommon in England.

The interior is a study in just proportion: the arcades are lofty, but the aisles are broad and the chancel is exactly in scale. Moreover, the font stands raised up on its pedestal, in an ample space that has never been cluttered with seating. It is itself a fine piece with the names of its donors on the base, its eight sides having panels – much damaged by vandals after the Reformation – representing the seven sacraments and the Crucifixion. Such "seven sacrament fonts" are found mainly in East Anglia. This one has moreover its original canopy, tall and fragile, complete with the crane for lifting it, on a beam above.

The church shows a range of medieval woodwork that

Sall church, looking west (N.M.R.)

is rare even for East Anglia: a complete set of roofs to nave, aisles, transepts, and chancel; six doors, some with their old ironwork; much seating in the nave, and stalls in the chancel with well-carved misericords; the base (though unhappily no more) of the rood-screen; a slender painted pulpit of the 15th century, with a sounding-board and reading desk added to it early in the 17th. The roofs of the transepts are pitched flat and finely panelled. The nave roof is sharply pointed, and remarkable in its construction, the thrust of its timbers being borne by posts between the windows of the clerestory, which terminate in brackets that are themselves the rafters of the aisles. A device more frequently adopted in East Anglia for taking the thrust of the roof is that of the hammerbeam, magnificently exemplified in the next parish at Cawston, and at Swaffham, not far to the west.

The colour of all this woodwork is now varying gradations of brown, blending harmoniously with the white of the walls, and the pale yellows, reds, and greys of the paved floor, all played on by the clear light streaming in through the large windows. But traces of colour remain in the nave roof, and there is some medieval glass in the east window and in the south transept. In the north transept there is pleasing glass of the 19th century. There are also two intruders here: elegant grey and white marble monuments of the Georgian age (one signed by John Ivory of Norwich). The larger of them occupies the blocked-up window that filled the north wall; but it carries off this impertinence acceptably. A number of brasses are to be discovered under mats on the floor of the nave; the most notable perhaps the bracket brass to Thomas Rose (d. 1441) and his wife, with their 12 children, and (opposite the third pier from the west) that of Thomas Hagham, priest, with four exquisite little roundels showing the symbols of the Evangelists. The room above the south porch may have been the Lady Chapel. Like its companion on the north side it is vaulted, with carved bosses.

The church has lost some things: most of its screen and glass, much of its original seating. But it has been touched very lightly by restoration. A hundred years ago it was said to be "in a state of disgraceful neglect". Since then it has been tenderly repaired.

There is nothing to be described as a village of Sall: only a few little modern houses in the by-road leading up to the church, a number of scattered farms, and a big house, Sall Park, concealed from view. So the church stands virtually alone, partly enclosed in trees, on a knob of hill. This detachment is enhanced by the low wall of flint and dark-red brick that surrounds the graveyard, making almost a plinth for the church itself. The tower is lofty, and different from most of its fellows in Norfolk (e.g. its noble neighbour at Cawston) in that it is slender, its height accentuated by tall pinnacles. It is far seen on every side.

This is well-wooded country, a rolling land of low hills. You can drive round the church in a circuit of five miles or so, sometimes glimpsing only the top of the tower, at other times the whole length of the building, emerging from its screen of trees. In summer it rises out of cornfields, and its lead roofs glisten brilliantly in the sun. It reigns over the whole of this tract of country, drawing it up to itself without any over-assertive domination. No building could sit in a landscape more serenely.

Scarborough North Yorkshire 1D3

Among the big seaside resorts of England – Blackpool, Bournemouth, Brighton, Scarborough, Southend, and Torbay – Scarborough enjoys supremacy on two counts. Its coastline is magnificent, both in scale and in sculpture. That certainly cannot be said of any of the others except Torbay; and there, though the coast all around is fine, the part immediately visible from the town is distant and much less exciting. Then, whereas the other five were nothing more than small fishing villages 200 years ago, if that, Scarborough has a very long history as a town, with a good deal to show from the distant past.

Its Headland is a natural point of defence. Not only does it rise sheer out of the sea; it also forms a steep hill on the landward side. A camp was established on it in the Bronze Age; and within that the Romans built a signal station about A.D. 370, when raids were expected from the German shore, to enable warnings of them to be transmitted to York. Within the same site again a tiny chapel was erected about the year 1000, which was subsequently rebuilt twice.

The Castle, within which all these things stand, dates mainly from about 1160. The medieval walls still encircle its enclosure and protect the Headland. The only part of the buildings to survive in an impressive form – and it certainly *is* impressive – is the four-storeyed Keep, of which the eastern face, looking out to sea, is more or less intact. To the south-east of the Keep, built into the wall, stood Mosdale Hall, erected in the 14th century and destroyed by other German raiders in the 20th: when the Kaiser's fleet bombarded Scarborough in December 1914 it directed some of its fire against this building, apparently on the mistaken supposition that it still served as barracks.

For all the strength of its site, the Castle was taken more than once: in 1312 when the defenders were starved out and Piers Gaveston was captured there; twice during the Civil War, when it was held for the King, in 1645 and 1648.

The town grew up below the Castle, on the southern face of the hill where it tumbles down to the bay, at the head of which is one of the infrequent natural harbours on this rugged coast. St Mary's church stands here: a big building mainly of the 12th century, which has lost its chancel and south transept but has double aisles. The most striking element in the building is the outer south aisle, which has four chapels covered by transverse ribbed vaults. A large number of 18th-century memorials have been assembled here, hanging almost like pictures, and below them are ranged the small oval brass plates that formerly stood on graves in the churchyard.

Now descend the steep hill to the Harbour. Scarborough is an active fishing port, though in summer its energies are directed chiefly towards catering for visitors. The harbour itself is a busy cheerful place, enclosed with quays and guarded by a lighthouse. But the buildings that surround it have now given themselves up to entertainment, to bingo and fish and chips, and there is nothing here that is much worth looking at now.

To get to the modern centre of the town, turn out of Sandside, the street that skirts the Harbour, into Eastborough, the beginning of what under a succession of names is in fact the main thoroughfare of the place. It too has been reshaped almost entirely by modern commercial development, though there are things worth seeking out on either side of it here and there. Bar Street, for example, has a terrace of houses with shallow bow windows, and the old shop-window frames below. Like much of what is interesting in Scarborough, it has been mauled quite lately, and it may not long survive. There were 12 houses in the terrace: there are now no more than nine.

In Cross Street, just north of Newborough, is the Market Hall (J. Irvine, 1853), a big handsome brick building with stone dressings, quite one of the best things in the town. Another public building nearly as good is the railway station, a stone structure by G. T. Andrews dating from 1845, though unhappily saddled with a facetious clock tower in 1882.

The most agreeable part of Regency and Early Victorian Scarborough lies south of the station. You reach it by York Place, with a set of 15 houses (about 1835), six in stone and nine in white brick, having fully rounded bay windows three storeys high. At the far end York Place splits what is really one terrace into two: Belvoir Terrace on the left and The Crescent on the right (R. H. and S. Sharp, 1835–57), all ashlar-faced and decorated with elaborate cast-iron balconies. They look on to gardens, on the other side of which is Wood End, now the Natural History Museum. For nearly 50 years this was the seaside home of the Sitwell family. It figures as such in Sir Osbert Sitwell's autobiography, and Edith Sitwell was born in it.

Below is the Valley, crossed by the high bridge of 1865 (widened in 1926–7) and dominated to the north-east by the Grand Hotel. That lives up to its name: it is surely

(Walkers Studios Ltd)

the grandest purpose-built hotel in the country, with the possible exception of St Pancras in *London*, and that is now disused as such. The architect was Cuthbert Brodrick, who designed the Town Hall in *Leeds*, and it was completed in 1867. It is a magnificent building, proudly self-assertive yet not strident, its rich decoration kept firmly in the service of the building as a whole. For example the red moulded brick, which might so easily have become fussily over-prominent in another Victorian's hands, is subordinated to its purpose of setting off the yellow brick used everywhere else. The scale of the building, its triangular shape, and its site high above Scarborough Bay are deeply impressive. Long may it continue to serve its original purpose!

Far below – you can make use of a cliff railway if you wish – the Valley comes down to the shore. In it are two elegant things: the domed Museum of 1829 (again by R. H. Sharp) and the slender cast-iron Spa Bridge, which spans the whole width of the Valley, over 400 ft long. The southern slopes are agreeably laid out with gardens, and on the sea is the Spa building. This dates from 1877–80, but it reminds us that Scarborough had a history as a watering place, offering cures to the sick, long before it became a popular seaside resort. The springs were discovered early in the 17th century, and by the 1660s they were widely known. Today the name of this building is all that directly recalls an important element in the history of the place. Here is a good point at which to end one's first exploration of Scarborough: looking across the bay to the Harbour, the red roofs of the old town, the church and Castle, and the Headland, where settlement began.

Scotney Castle Kent 5B4

The drive from London to Hastings by the A21 is agreeable, except at the week-end in summer, and one of its pleasantest stretches begins at Lamberhurst. The road rises up the side of a hill through trees, to come out on to an open ridge. That pattern repeats itself all over the Weald of Kent and Sussex and affords one of its many pleasures. But here, on the left of the road and hidden from sight, is a landscape not repeated anywhere else. It is both natural and contrived, partly old and partly quite recent, made by successive owners of the estate of Scotney.

Roger Ashburnham fortified his house here about 1380, giving it a polygonal wall and four towers, within a moat fed by the tiny River Bewl. One of these towers remains, resembling those at *Bodiam*, not far away, where a true castle was erected in 1386–8. Both works were undertaken for the same reason: for defence against the pressing danger of French invasion (see *Bodiam*, *Rye*).

That danger passed, and three of the towers were allowed to decay. The estate came to the Darell family, who lived here very quietly – more quietly still after the Reformation, for they remained Roman Catholics and concealed priests in their house. The old building was substantially modified in 1580, and then, some 50 years later, a bigger reconstruction took place on the site of the medieval hall. This Caroline house was altered in its turn in the 18th century, and then the Darells, broken by debt and by quarrelling among themselves, sold the estate. It was bought by Edward Hussey. His grandson, another Edward, decided to abandon the old house altogether and to build a new one on the hill above. Two things moved him to take this decision. The existing castle, improved though it had been to suit the ideas of succeeding generations, lay in a damp hollow. His mother thought it unhealthy, no doubt with good reason, and left it for the brisk air of St Leonard's-on-Sea, where Edward had been brought up. He now wanted a drier and more cheerful house. That anybody could have got easily enough. But he seized the chance of getting something more too, much rarer. He saw the opportunity to give the old castle a new setting beneath the steep hillside: a setting for itself, and a vision from the house he proposed to build above.

He entrusted that building to Anthony Salvin, then a young man making his name as a picturesque architect. His plans were drawn up in 1835, and the work was completed in 1843. The house was built of brown and grey Wealden sandstone quarried on the site. So although by its position, its character and comparative newness, it stands up boldly, it does not domineer with any aggression: rather it seems to be an outcrop of the place itself.

Edward Hussey took expert opinion in laying out the hillside below; but his sure taste allowed him both to accept and to reject the advice he was given. He enjoyed a long life, dying only in 1894. His son then continued here until 1952, carrying on his father's work through all the adversity and discouragement of the 20th century. He left no son; but, by one more blessed turn of fate, his heir was his nephew Christopher Hussey, a writer whose work is known and loved by everyone interested in the history of English building. It could have come to nobody better able to value and cherish it. On his death in 1970 he bequeathed it to the National Trust.

Scotney is a place of trees, of hill and water and shade. For 10 months in the year the landscape is predominantly green, from the trees, the grass in the hillside, and the very moat itself, which is sprinkled with water-lilies. It is brilliantly lighted up in June with rhododendrons and azaleas, and variegated when the leaves of the deciduous trees turn in October.

The old castle is a perfect blend of survival and refashioning. The first Edward Hussey pulled down most of the Caroline house; but he knew exactly where to stop the demolition. He intended to make it a picturesque ruin, and that is what it now is. It forms the left-hand side of an entirely new composition, when seen from across the moat. In front is a fragment of the medieval gatehouse, to the right part of the Tudor building (one of its gables, with an empty window, punctuating the skyline), and then, beside that, the sole remaining tower. Most ruins are the result of natural decay, which

Scotney: looking down to the old Castle (B.T.A.)

can make them sharply affecting. Here is one whose decay has itself been a creative act, and then deliberately arrested – for example, by the iron tie-bars, on the left-hand side of the house.

So the original castle has become a thing of great beauty in itself. And, even so, it is only one element in this complex landscape. The round tower is the pivot of it all. It is the focal point of the view carefully maintained through a clearing in the trees, from the terrace and the house above. Between the two castles the trees reign, an exactly calculated mixture of the deciduous with the conifers – tall sequoia, cedar, and cypress. Below, here and there, the hillside is planted with flowers and shrubs, showing their colours in succession, from daffodils to roses.

All this in the strictest seclusion, unguessed at by the travellers on the Hastings road. In the 18th century the old house was thought to present "a gloomy and recluse appearance". There is nothing gloomy about Scotney now; but it remains a most distinguished recluse.

Seaton Delaval Hall Northumberland 1C2

No house described in this book is more singularly situated than Seaton Delaval, or has gone through more poignant vicissitudes. There is something dramatic in everything Vanbrugh designed – in early life he was, after all, a playwright. The drama is an integral part of his architecture. It extends sometimes to the history of his buildings themselves: blazing rows with the Duchess of Marlborough at Blenheim, blazes of another kind that gutted the Italian Opera House in the Haymarket, and in 1940 Castle Howard; most of his garden buildings at Stowe ruthlessly destroyed. And drama is the very stuff of Seaton Delaval.

The Delavals were an ancient family, established in the country north of Newcastle not long after the Norman Conquest. They kept their estates intact in the Civil War, tending prudently towards the Parliamentarian side yet achieving pardon and favour under the restored monarchy after 1660.

The troubles of the family came not from politics but from internecine quarrelling, which nearly lost them their estate here altogether. In the end it was acquired by a remote cousin, Captain George Delaval, in 1717. He was a naval man. He determined to build himself a grand house in Northumberland, inviting Vanbrugh to design it in 1718. Neither he nor his architect lived to see its completion. He died in 1723, Vanbrugh less than three years later. His successor was another naval captain, and under him the house was completed in 1729. Later in the 18th century the estate passed by marriage to a Norfolk family, the Astleys. It remains with them still.

The chief event in the modern history of the house was a fire in 1822, which reduced the whole central block to a shell. For a time the place was left uninhabited. It was maltreated by soldiers billeted in it during the first World War; at the end of the second it seemed almost inevitable that the great pile would be demolished. But no such thing. Its owner Lord Hastings valiantly determined to repair it and to live there, and he and his son, aided by government grants, attained that end with a tenacity greatly to be admired. The task is not completed, as we shall see; but externally the whole building is now in good order, the west wing – a sizeable house on its own – now fully lived in.

Seaton Delaval lies in a dead flat plain north of Newcastle, heavily mined for coal. The house faces north and south. You approach it from the west, by an avenue of trees nearly a mile long. To the east, a mile away, lies the sea – invisible from the house, however, carefully screened by trees. This accords with 18th-century ideas that the sea was a rugged, repulsive element; and also with common sense, in protecting those who lived in the house from the bitter North Sea winds.

Looked at from the house, the landscape is therefore quite featureless. An accent is provided to the south by an obelisk in the park. To the north, three miles away, are the industrial buildings of Blyth – once among the busiest coal ports of England. The smoke from the surrounding coal mines has now disappeared. A whole world of wealth and fierce poverty has come and gone (of tragedy too, for Hartley pit, where one of the most appalling disasters in the history of mining occurred in 1862, lay little more than a mile from the house); but Vanbrugh's work still survives. In style and character it is, in one sense, a weird alien here in Northumberland; in another not so, for it is all built of gritstone quarried not far away, blackened by time, by coal smoke and the salt sea gales of the place. The history of Vanbrugh's houses being what it is, Seaton Delaval is the most perfect of them today, the most nearly complete.

The plan is simple, and unchanged. It comprises a tall central block, with two long and lower wings terminated by small pavilions, still lower, enclosing a gravelled courtyard. You visit the west, or right-hand, wing first, starting with the kitchen, a noble room, vaulted and lit by a big Venetian window, now given over to "medieval banquets". They represent the price that has to be paid, in the 1970s, to keep the house going. Besides, think of the sardonic entertainment they would have afforded to Vanbrugh. What a comedy he might have written about the business!

There are no other gimmicks at Seaton Delaval: nothing is evident but the serious, extended attempt that has been made to refurbish the house worthily and to maintain it in that state. The rooms on the first floor open out of a corridor, which faces on to the courtyard and has been made into a picture gallery, where family portraits have been assembled. Most of the rooms here are private, and not shown.

Now you cross the courtyard to move up the very broad staircase to the centre of the house. The front here is formidable – more menacing than perhaps Vanbrugh intended, through the blackening of the stone. The skyline is romantically varied with turrets and massive chimney stacks; the stonework plain and very precise, yet enlivened with a frieze and richly-carved pediment. If this is perhaps a grim front, it has the grimness of a giant who can be playful too.

Inside, however, there is nothing playful to confront us now: only the gaunt and tragic magnificence of the Great Hall, roofed in and partly repaired but otherwise unrestored

Seaton Delaval: the north front (A. F. Kersting)

since the fire of 1822. Its proportions are not Vanbrugh's, since it is now open to the roof, whereas originally the top storey comprised a separate room. If only one day the ceiling could be restored, and the room brought back to its old formality! It is, after all, the centre-piece of the whole house.

Spiral staircases with delicate iron balustrades, partly restored, lead to the rooms in the turrets, one of which now contains an interesting collection of documents relating to the Delaval family and the building of the house. Beyond the Great Hall you reach the Saloon, an even sadder shadow of itself. Here, facing south, were the principal living rooms. Except one, they are now empty and forlorn. But step out of the door, down the staircase, look back, and you will regain a happier mood. The south front of the house is by no means uniform with the north. It is altogether calmer and more gentle, offering for example the amenity of a portico bornc on fluted Ionic columns – whereas the approach to the front door of the house on the north is unsheltered, bare and blunt. From here you can make you way round to the gardens on the west side of the house. Well protected from the winds off the sea, they are a delightful and surprising element in this very unadorned landscape, the roses answering gaily to the sombre yellow and black stone.

There is one more thing still to see, of great note: the stables in the east wing. It has been jestingly observed that the Englishman often thought as much of his horses as of his household, even of his family. Judging the Delavals by their stables, that may well have been true. They are indeed superb, a suite of three noble vaulted apartments, the stalls divided from one another by partitions of ashlar masonry, the hay served to the horses in iron baskets set in alcoves in the walls. There are their names still written up above: Zephyrus and Tartar, Regulus and Prince and Pilot. What horses were ever more handsomely housed?

And so one emerges into the cold north-eastern light in the ample courtyard, looking away to industrial Blyth. One thinks of the excitement of the building of the house – compared with many of its size, a task completed rapidly, which must have called for a large force of labour; of the two visits (only two so far as we know, and those brief) paid by Vanbrugh himself to the site; of the life of the house in its prime, its dinners and theatricals; of the economic enterprise of the Delavals too, which helped to support all this expense, their coal mines and glass works, their harbour close by at Seaton Sluice; then of the fire, and of the melancholy desolation that followed, the house unoccupied for 40 years, hemmed in more and more closely by industrial development; and finally since the second World War, of its reclamation.

Selborne Hampshire 4F3
This is a place associated with one man, and one book: the Rev. Gilbert White and his *Natural History of Selborne.*

White was born in the village in 1720 and spent most of his life there at a house called The Wakes, where he died in 1793. The *Natural History* was published in 1789 by his brother, a London bookseller. It is composed of letters written to two distinguished friends, the earliest of them dating back over more than 20 years. In them he recorded, simply and with the utmost precision, the observations he had made of the life of the parish: not the human life alone, or even primarily, but the life of every sort of creature in it, birds and mammals and reptiles, plants and trees.

The task that White undertook was in large measure a new one. The great naturalists who preceded him, like Ray in England and Linnaeus in Sweden, had devoted themselves chiefly to the work of classification, of identifying species and explaining where they belonged in the system of Nature. White was one of the earliest field naturalists, intent on observing the behaviour of plants and animals in life. When he came to write he had no literary experience, beyond that of composing sermons, but his patient direct observation expressed itself easily and plainly, and his deeply humane character informs everything he wrote. The result is one of those rare masterpieces, the work of an unprofessional writer who published no other book.

The house he lived in at Selborne has been turned into a delightful museum, simple and unpretending like himself. This is no elaborate literary shrine. It contains a few pieces of his furniture, some of his letters and other writings in his graceful firm hand, portraits of members of his family – but none of himself, save a pair of artless sketches: it is characteristic of this retiring man that he seems never to have been painted. There is a plain monument to him in the church, on the south side of the altar, and he is buried in the churchyard.

His true memorial is not indoors at all: it is in the open air. The Wakes garden is still very much as he planned it, with the ha-ha or sunk fence at the foot of the lawn and the brick path, laid to ease his constant passage across the sodden grass in winter to the little wooden alcove he

Selborne: the village from the Hanger (A. F. Kersting)

constructed for watching the birds, and to the Hanger, the cliff beyond. For climbing this hill he and one of his brothers constructed in 1753 a path composed of 15 zig-zags. It provides a steep but easy access to Selborne Common.

Though rising up only some 200 ft, this commands an extensive tract of central southern England: Woolmer Forest and the hills of Hindhead to the east, the chalk downs of Sussex and Hampshire in a great arc to the south and west. The north-eastern face of the hill, the Hanger, is thickly clad in beeches. Through them you look sharply down on to Selborne itself, with White's house immediately below. This is a view that has changed little in the last 200 years. The *Natural History* opens with an account of the landscape and of the geology that determines it: especially of these beeches, descending the hill just as far as the limits of the chalk, and of the clays and malms in the valley below.

Selborne is not a picturesque village; it boasts no house of distinction, and several that one might wish away. It still, in White's expression, "consists of one single straggling street" – narrow, and choked at times with a far too dense traffic, pounding through. Yet it would be physically awkward to by-pass it on the east side, and intolerable on the west, in the space between the village and the Hanger, for that would rip to pieces the quiet green tract that White made especially his own. There is no artificial "preservation" here – only the salutary, unobtrusive presence of the National Trust on both sides of the valley. On the whole the village's fate has been kind.

Few men can ever have been more intimately conversant with a small tract of country than White, and he felt assured in the strength that this gave him. "Men that undertake only one district", he wrote, "are much more likely to advance natural knowledge than those that grasp at more than they can possibly be acquainted with". His book, indeed his life, was devoted to this one district. The vagaries of the seasons, the habits of birds, the growth of plants – he considered and recorded them all minutely; and so he did as much as any man in his time to "advance natural knowledge".

Severn Bridge Gloucestershire 4D2
The Severn is the longest of English rivers, and in its estuary the broadest. The lowest ancient bridge over it was just outside Gloucester. Travellers between Bristol and South Wales had therefore to make a 60-mile detour to cross that bridge, or else use the ferry from Aust to Beachley, close to Chepstow: the Old Passage as it was called, slow, inconvenient, and often dangerous. A railway was opened in 1863, connecting with another ferry lower down, the New Passage; a railway bridge was completed higher up at Sharpness in 1879, and the Severn Tunnel – an heroic Mid-Victorian achievement – in 1886. The 20th-century motorist had to use the archaic ferries or put his car on to one of the rather infrequent trains through the tunnel. Otherwise, as in the past, he had to go round by Gloucester. This inconvenience became serious, removable only by the construction of a new bridge, formidably long and high enough to allow ships of substantial size to pass underneath it.

Having advanced the art of bridge-building in the 18th and 19th centuries (see *Bristol*, *Coalbrookdale*, *Maidenhead*), the English grew timid for a time in the 20th. Their early use of reinforced concrete was hesitant and clumsy (see *Berwick-on-Tweed*), and they showed no disposition, in situations like this one, to follow the example set by the Americans in their great suspension bridges of the 1930s in New York and San Francisco. Their caution was reasonable, for those bridges were not always successful. The destruction of the Tacoma Narrows Bridge in a gale in 1942 was a warning they were obliged to heed. However, after the war plans began to be worked out for structures of this kind to span the Tamar, the Severn, and the Humber, and in Scotland the Forth and the Tay. The Tamar and Forth Bridges were the first to be completed, in 1961 and 1964. The Severn Bridge came next, in 1966. It was designed by a team led by Sir Gilbert Roberts.

The length of the bridge across water is almost exactly a mile. The two pylons are 400 ft high. It represented a great economic advance. The tubular construction of its

The Severn Bridge from the west (B.T.A.)

streamlined deck allowed the total weight of the steelwork to be substantially reduced, by comparison with that in the corresponding American bridges, lowering the cost by 20 per cent.

The scale of the structure, and its implied but invisible

strength, are apparent to anyone standing on the adjacent shore. The stone slipway of the Old Passage ferry is still in place at Beachley on the western side. At this point you are almost underneath the bridge. Its height, its lightness and grace are all evident, but so is something of its solidity, to withstand the pressure of the winds and the exceptional tides of the Severn.

Above, on the bridge itself, you are chiefly conscious of the height of the two great pylons towering over you and the strength of the steel cables and ties. From a distance they look ethereally slender: crazily so, they would have seemed to the builders of the old Severn railway bridge or to those of the Forth Bridge of 1890. But aerodynamics was then a science hardly born. This bridge – so light, so rapidly built, and so relatively cheap – is a triumph for that branch of science and for all the others that contributed to it.

A full view of the bridge is to be had downstream on the Gloucestershire bank at the New Passage Hotel. From this point it is all in sight – the main bridge itself over the river and the long additional section, on which there are no tall pylons, carrying it over the mouth of the Wye into Wales.

Sledmere Humberside 2D4

The landscape of East Yorkshire is a very subtle one. Elsewhere in small England one sometimes finds a great sense of space – in Northumberland, for instance (see *Cheviot*); but that is generally in wild tracts. Here, whilst there is the same amplitude, the chalk landscape is fertile, well cultivated, man-made. The characteristic forms are long steady slopes, towards the sea, with occasional shallow valleys. There are no great heights, still less steep declivities, and yet the scale is impressively large. The landscape is clean-cut, and the sweeps are diversified by careful, often generous planting.

At Sledmere, 450 ft up to the north of Driffield, the Sykes family created everything. One's first impression is of the noble beeches that greet one on every side. It is obviously an estate village, with all the trimness that goes with that; dominated by most capacious stables, for the Sykes have been notable breeders of race-horses.

By origin they were Leeds merchants; they acquired the Sledmere estate through marriage with the Kirbys in 1748. Richard Sykes began to build the existing house in 1751. What he put up forms the centre of the house today, though encased in another skin. The whole place was transformed by Richard Sykes's nephew Sir Christopher, who came into the property in 1776.

He gave his attention first to the landscape, and with Capability Brown's advice replanned it drastically. The village of Sledmere stood to the south of the house, in full view; it was now moved to a new position, tucked away entirely out of sight. In its place there emerged an unbroken expanse of green, diversified only with single trees, and with woods in the distance up the hill on the opposite side of the valley. Then in 1781 he set to work on the house.

He appears to have been his own architect. For the internal decoration he employed Joseph Rose, who worked with Adam at *Syon* and elsewhere; but even here he knew what he wanted, and he did not give Rose an entirely free hand.

The *clou* of the house was to be its Library, designed to occupy the whole of the first floor of the south front, looking out over the newly-made landscape. Sir Christopher's south and north wings projected beyond the earlier building. A large part of the centre of the old house was now occupied by a staircase, with two branches leading to a gallery. Architecturally, the style was the most modern in England at the time, the style of the young James Wyatt, with very large triple windows set in segmental or semicircular arches: calm, dignified, almost – yet not quite – austere; the perfect counterpart to the landscape, both natural and artificially created, around.

Inside, two influences can be seen. They might have been antagonistic, but they have been fused into well-bred conversation. Rose's plasterwork appears at its most delicate and elegant in the Drawing Room, above all in the ceiling; the

Sledmere: the Library (A. F. Kersting)

giltwood furniture was made for this room, by John Robbins in 1792. It stands now side by side with Chinese Chippendale chairs.

This is the one room in which one might say that Rose is allowed to prevail. In the Music Room opposite his voice is a little muted; and in the Dining Room, though he made designs for a new ceiling in 1787, Sir Christopher finally decided to keep the much plainer one from the earlier house, allowing Rose to enrich the walls, no more.

The next thing to enjoy is the ascent of the staircase, with its large oval skylight. Having looked at the bedrooms that are shown, go on into the Library, the house's masterpiece. As a library it has few rivals in England. It is 100 ft long and comprises three groin-vaulted bays, square on plan, with a semi-circular entrance; the decoration, in pale blue, gold, and white, is elaborate and yet chaste. Sir Christopher and his son Sir Mark Masterman Sykes assembled here a collection of books worthy of the room, including illuminated manuscripts and important incunabula; but alas 2,700 of them had to be sold in 1824, in the hard times that many English landowners experienced after the long wars with France. Much remains, however, of beauty and value still.

Sir Tatton Sykes, who sold those books, did much for his estate. He is commemorated by a curious spiky monument on the road to Garton, and inside the house by a fine portrait painted of him when he was 80 by Sir Francis Grant. In his successor's time, in 1911, the house was damaged seriously by a fire; the front entrance hall dates from the reconstruction that followed. On the north side of it is a curiosity: a small room decorated wholly in blue Turkish tiles, to the designs of an Armenian architect employed by the sixth Baronet, Sir Mark Sykes, who played an important part in shaping British policy in the Near East during the first World War and died, under 40, while attending the Peace Conference in 1919.

This then is a family of varied interests, intellectual, sporting, aesthetic, and practical. It is just to single out among them the first Sir Christopher, who gave the house its present form. He seems to have inspired everything he touched – including Romney, whose portrait of him and his wife, which hangs in the Music Room, rises high above the standard that painter usually attained. House and landscape together – they are one, the product of one mind, one eye – embody to perfection a single moment of history: the eve of the French Revolution, which both for ill and for good wrought decisive change in the world.

Slindon West Sussex 5A5
Most of the best walking in England is to be had, naturally, in open country, the southern downlands, the fells and dales of the north; country that is either pasture for sheep or uncultivated altogether. The Slindon estate provides a delight-

Slindon: looking northwards to the Downs from above the village
(A. F. Kersting)

ful exception. Its chalk lands are heavily ploughed to grow wheat and potatoes, with here and there a brilliant patch of mustard. But it is traversed by a series of bridleways, from which motor traffic is excluded, very well signed and delightful to walk on, often in the shade of tall beeches; to reach a climax at Bignor Hill on the open Downs.

"Climax" is indeed the right word, for this is a dramatic landscape, changing completely in the course of a five-mile walk (and 700 ft ascent) northwards from the coastal plain.

That plain is physically uninteresting. It exemplifies the least attractive features of 20th-century life, and is intersected by A27, the rowdy highway from Brighton to Portsmouth. To turn away from that into Slindon village is a happy relief. Not that the village is totally sequestered, or in itself picturesque. It is a pleasant place, centred on a large Victorian house (now given over to education) and having only two curiosities: a remarkable wooden effigy of the early 16th century in the church, and an exceptionally long sequence of dated houses, from 1693 to 1929.

You are already 100 ft and more above the plain, on the first of what are really a series of terraces. In Paleolithic times the sea ran up to this point; the shore stretched from Arundel to Goodwood. In its retreat it has left an extraordinary legacy: a shingle and pebble beach, high and dry.

To the north it is all open country. A shallow valley cuts into it, overlooked on the western side by Nore Hill, with an 18th-century sham ruin among its woods. The ground falls away, and then begins its final steady climb up to Burton Down and Bignor Hill. Across the top of the ridge runs a long stretch of the Roman Stane Street, in its direct line from London to Chichester. There it is still, essentially as the Romans made it, the raised causeway in the middle, of chalk and flint, bordered by ditches on either side. Beyond, and far below, in Bignor itself is the site of a Roman villa, with a series of mosaic pavements.

The Slindon estate was once a possession of the archbishops of Canterbury; it was here that one of the most notable of them, Stephen Langton, died in 1228. In our own time it has come into the hands of the National Trust – 3,500 acres of it. Its peace is therefore as secure as it can be made, in a part of England very vulnerable to "development". And it is secure in the best possible way: not as a reservation, an open-air museum, but as a prosperous working estate. To the walker it offers, in a very small compass, something of the essence of Sussex: the high Downs and their valleys, magnificent beech trees, simple building in flint and brick; and, everywhere to the south, the glitter of the sea.

South Dalton: church of St Mary Humberside 2D4
There are two reasons for going to South Dalton: for its landscape and for the spire of its church. The Yorkshire Wolds are seen at their full extent at *Sledmere*. At this point, much lower down on the edge of the coastal plain, they are heavily planted with trees, from which the spire, looked at from any direction and far seen because of its great height, seems to rise.

The Victorian architect J. L. Pearson did a great deal of work, especially in his earlier years, in this neighbourhood. He built his first church, Ellerker, down by the Humber in 1843–4; and over the next 30 years or so he designed or restored at least 16 others in East Yorkshire. The third Lord Hotham commissioned him to build two churches on his estates. This was one of them, erected between 1858 and 1861.

With a rich patron, the architect could do much of what he liked – though money did not run here to the stone vaulting that Pearson loved and came to handle so well (see *Brighton*). Inside the effect is sumptuous, the chancel decorated perhaps to excess: there is something almost Spanish in the riot of stone-carving in the sanctuary. On the south side of the chancel is the Hotham chapel, which contains a striking monument from the earlier church commemorating Sir John Hotham (d. 1689). It is perhaps by John Bushnell and is modelled on the Salisbury monument at *Hatfield*.

The stonework inside has failed to acquire, as yet, any

SOUTH DALTON: CHURCH OF ST MARY

(A. F. Kersting)

texture with age; the pointing is over-precise, unsympathetically hard. Outside, however, things are different. The whole composition is seen best from the south-east corner of the churchyard, with its complications of transept and mortuary chapel and the external enrichment of the chancel. The glory of the church is its spire, which shoots up to a height of

200 ft. It is exceptionally delicate and slender, the corners of the tower knife-sharp, the belfry windows very tall, the spire itself soaring and yet free of any suggestion of thinness: a powerful direct assertion of faith, made at a critical time in the Victorian age – at the moment when *The Origin of Species* was published, and the Church was agitated by the controversy over *Essays and Reviews*.

As you turn down the village street to the south there is a glimpse of the rich Yorkshire cornfields, framed in a cut between the trees. Again it is the Victorian setting that one thinks of: the blessed years for English agriculture just before the depression that began in the seventies. South Dalton seems to embody the spirit of England at the height of its peaceful power.

Speke Hall Merseyside 2B5

Although *Liverpool* is built on a striking site, rising in terraces from the Mersey, the countryside around it is uninteresting. What is unplifting is the sight of the Welsh mountains – and their nearest foothills are 15 miles away. In between are the two estuaries of the Mersey and the Dee, divided by the low-lying peninsula of the Wirral. North of Liverpool along the coast there are sand dunes; eastwards the Lancashire plain, heavily industrialised for miles. When the city grew in the 19th century it came to engulf all the surrounding villages. A few tiny pockets were left, however, of open land and older buildings; notably at Speke, eight miles south-east of the city centre.

The house lies almost on the shore of the Mersey, hedged in on one side by an industrial estate, on the other by Liverpool Airport: so that as you approach your hair is almost brushed by the little aircraft on their descent, and a loud whirring noise tells you a larger one is coming down to land just beyond. You must make your way, undeterred by all this, along half a mile of dreary unsheltered road to the Hall gates. Inside them is an avenue of trees and to the left, over grass, the house itself.

Speke Hall: the south front (B.T.A.)

It is one of the most complete half-timbered structures, on a large scale, in England. *Little Moreton* is lofty and fantastic. Speke is low, broad, a pre-eminently sensible building. It is constructed round a courtyard centering on a pair of yew trees, much older than the house. A sandstone plinth is the base of it with a timber erection above; it is roofed for the most part with sandstone slabs, quarried probably near Woolton, four or five miles away. The building has suffered little from vexatious restoration.

It is entirely the work of the Norris family, who had acquired the manor of Speke by the end of the 13th century. The present house seems to have been begun about 1490 and completed a little more than 200 years later. It is therefore now predominantly a work of the Elizabethan age. The south range, with the entrance, seems to be the oldest part, erected by Sir William Norris, a staunch supporter of Henry VII. His building probably comprised a simple rectangle. The chief room in it, the Great Hall, was remodelled by his grandson, who put into it the screen at the east end and the chimney-piece in the Great Chamber next door, its carved overmantel depicting three generations of the family. That carving is crude. The Elizabethan plasterwork in the ceiling, on the other hand, is not crude at all but charmingly delicate. It may date from about 1600, when there was evidently a good deal of alteration to the house. The doorway at the main entrance bears an inscription stating that "this work 25 yards long was wholly built" by Edward Norris in 1598. "This work" appears to mean the entrance itself and the stone bridge leading to it, together with much of the eastern range. Edward's son Sir William fell into financial trouble, and then no further important additions were made to the house by him; nor have there been any since.

After the Reformation the Norris family, like many of the gentry of Lancashire and Cheshire, remained Catholics. Edward Norris conformed to the extent of attending services of the Church of England; but he maintained priests secretly – they are known to have been at Speke in 1586 and 1598. They were concealed in "priest holes", no bigger than large cupboards, attached to the upstairs rooms. Three of those holes can still be seen. Edward's son Sir William would have none of his father's compromise. He refused to conform, even outwardly, and was therefore subjected to constant heavy fines, which impoverished him and his estate.

The Norrises were Royalists in the Civil War, and that brought them into further financial trouble. But they then moved over to the Church of England, and after the Restoration, though far from rich, they were able to take their natural place in the government and society of their county. In the 18th century the estate passed out of their hands through the failure of male heirs. The house became neglected; but its subsequent owners and occupiers – Liverpool merchants and shipping magnates – rescued and repaired it. The property came to the National Trust in 1943, for which, by a rather uncommon arrangement, it is administered now by the Merseyside Museums.

Speke is a house with a strong character of its own: low-built, tucked away by the water, hardly less secret now than it was when it kept its priests hidden in the 16th century, a very perfect reflection of the life of north-western England – remote and then little touched by industry – under the Tudors.

Standen East Grinstead West Sussex 5A4

There are several pleasures in visiting Standen. The house is worth seeing, for itself alone and even more for its setting: physically, in the delectable Sussex landscape, historically at a particular moment in time.

It was planned and built in 1891–5 for a solicitor practising in London, James Beale, and his wife Margaret. They wanted a sizeable country home for weekends and holidays, adequate for a family of seven children, though not for lavish hospitality. Their architect was Philip Webb, an old friend and associate of William Morris. The house reflects a good deal of both those men.

Beale bought the land in 1890, and his wife quickly started laying out the garden, with the advice of G. B. Simpson, a conventional landscape designer of the time. The placing of the house was decided on with Simpson, but Webb insisted on a different site for it, to face due south and to group with a set of old farm buildings and cottages that were already there. Webb appreciated vernacular building in all its shapes. He had been, with Morris, one of the founders of the Society for the Protection of Ancient Buildings.

The relationship that developed between this architect and client was friendly. Beale felt obliged to disappoint Webb by scaling down his first designs, which would have run him into more money than he wished to spend. But once the reduced plan had been agreed, Webb was the dominant partner, persuaded only with difficulty to make changes in what had been settled.

The house that resulted is highly informal; essentially a rectangular structure on two storeys with attics above and a small service wing splayed out at one end, the whole pivoting on a low tower capped by a pyramid. The exterior is well

Standen, from the front lawn (A. F. Kersting)

seen from the summer-house at the corner of the front lawn. Here the disposition of the main building can be appreciated, and the varied materials that went into it: Wealden stone quarried on the spot, yellow and grey; Horsham brick; bright vermilion tiles, sensible Georgian windows; weatherboarding, some of it white. Nothing is alien (i.e. not of this district of Sussex) except the rather harsh glass-and-iron conservatory and the pebble-dash used on the tower. This was originally washed white but is now a dingy brown. Will it presently be white again?

The house is approached from the back, past the older buildings that Webb liked and treated with so much respect. The entrance courtyard cuts into the hillside quite deeply, to require a high stone retaining wall on one side. Part of the main building – the Beales' living quarters – is shown to visitors. None of the rooms is large. The hall indeed is distinctly poky. No wonder that when it had been in use for a little while as a sitting-room, as intended, Webb was asked to enlarge and lighten it with a bay window. He agreed reluctantly, insisting however that the bay should proclaim itself frankly as an afterthought. So it projects as an oddly-placed excrescence, destroying the balance of the entrance front. The rooms on the other side, looking south, are delightful, especially the Drawing Room and Dining Room. The Drawing Room has a lovely carpet, designed by Morris and hand-made at his Merton workshops. The panelling of the Dining Room, in a dull sage green, is picked out with blue and white Chinese porcelain: a charming device first hit on by Rossetti. Almost everywhere else the woodwork is painted white, though the staircase (a chastened Jacobean design) is in natural oak. A bedroom and its dressing-room are shown upstairs, with a rich set of marquetry furniture purchased in 1896. The little Willow Bedroom next door is also shown sometimes, particularly charming for its Morris furnishings: Willow Bough wallpaper, Tulip chintz curtains, and again a fine carpet.

Throughout the house the wallpapers are of Morris's design, though a number of them have had to be replaced with new papers reprinted from the original blocks. Most of the pictures and other things on the walls did not belong to the Beales but have been lent. One group may be singled out: the splendid tiles by William de Morgan that adorn the Billiard Room.

Webb did all he could to give the occupants of the house

the full pleasure of its gardens. The pleasure might have been more complete if they had been designed by him, or by someone he worked with closely. Still, in outline they realise his own idea. The siting of the house was his, and that is the *clou*: facing south for warmth and steady light, over steeply falling lawns. Another architect might have made the house face south-east, for the view into the far distance, down the valley of the infant Medway. Webb knew better, allowing that pleasure to be had sideways on and putting windows into the eastern wall for the purpose, but keeping back the full view to be had from the garden or the hills behind. It is one of the delights of Standen that this beautiful countryside – green, hilly, forested with small trees, dotted here and there with roofs of mellow red and brown – unfolds itself gradually, changing with the levels and one's angle of vision. The garden is extensive, steep, and varied. It is a place to walk in for an hour, or a whole afternoon.

The house was lived in by two generations of Beales only. James Beale's youngest daughter Helen died in 1972, bequeathing it to the National Trust.

Standen is a very English creation: English in its landscape and the treatment of it; in its seeming casualness that yet is not unstudied; in its romanticism, the intense feeling it shows for the past – not the Mediterranean past of the Renaissance and the 18th century, but the Northern past, of the country itself. Everything here is exactly of its time, even poignantly. Not that the house is "Victorian": nothing about it is that except the technology. It was designed to be lighted electrically from the start, and it would never have been built where it is – over 30 miles out of London, for a busy man who worked there – but for railways, and especially the direct line to East Grinstead, opened in 1884.

The house is romantic in another way too. Here the Beales turned their backs most deliberately on the world they belonged to, in London and the Birmingham in which they had both been bred. A century earlier or more a man like James Beale would have built himself a very different house: not retiring like this one, but composed, serene, and bold

– looking out foursquare, with confidence. By this time the confidence has been shaken. Here is England at the beginning of its retreat, with Kipling's "Recessional" for its warning and 1914 ahead. There are such moments in history, and sometimes on the very edge of whirlpools they develop special perfections of their own. The 1630s in England had been one such age, the 1780s in France and in Mozart's Austria another. At Standen perhaps, looking back over the past 80 years, we feel in the presence of that spirit again.

Stanford-on-Avon Northamptonshire 4E1

The A50 between Northampton and Leicester is a delightful quiet road, lined frequently with feathery ash trees. A side-turning to the west leads to Stanford, through the ample park of its Hall: a charming red-brick house of 1697–1700, open three days a week.

The church (St Nicholas) is a large-limbed building, almost all dating, as it now stands, from the early 14th century and distinguished in the first place for its colouring. Outside, three stones are used, the limestone and ironstone so frequent in Northamptonshire with the red sandstone of Warwickshire, making a harmonious texture of grey, tawny, pale yellow, and rose pink. Inside, the harmony is a different one: white walls, a smooth floor of grey stone slabs, limestone and ironstone again, decoratively combined in the arcades; and much light old oak, above all in the excellent 15th-century roofs. The woodwork in the chancel is darker, with some medieval seating and 16th-century linenfold panelling. These colours are all neutral. They are played upon by others, more positive: from the glass, from the monuments that stand in every part of the church, and from the sumptuous organ case.

The glass varies in quality and age. The big east window is a hotchpotch, with some panels that must have been there since the church was built, a Crucifixion and a small figure of the Virgin for example; then, low down, some 16th-century figures with bold, coarse heraldic devices, and 19th-century portraits, much coarser, of Henry VII and his Queen, Elizabeth of York. Perhaps the 14th-century glass that affords the purest pleasure here – because it is unmixed with anything less good – is that in the top lights of the east windows of the nave aisles, especially the southern one with its strong accent of green – a colour not often prominent in medieval glass (though see *Wells*).

Then everywhere the monuments. Let us content ourselves here with seven. They all relate to the family of Cave and others connected with it. The Caves acquired the manor of Stanford in 1540, at the Dissolution, from Selby Abbey. The first of them to be commemorated here is Sir Thomas Cave (d. 1558), whose alabaster monument faces the choir screen on the north side. His brother Sir Ambrose (with a plainer monument in the north aisle) was Chancellor of the Duchy of Lancaster at the beginning of Elizabeth's reign. The Caves made many prudent marriages: one to the sister of the great Lord Burghley, others to a Knollys, a St John, a Bromley, and a Verney. The grandest, and also the finest, of these monuments is the one on the north side of the altar to Sir Thomas Cave, who died in 1613. It is the very ideal of a Jacobean monument, quite free of all vulgar ostentation. The colouring is rich but temperate: pink alabaster set off by much black, with a little gilding and heraldry. Semi-attached to it is a miniature figure of a boy kneeling under a canopy: the eldest son of the family, Richard, who died at Padua in his father's life-time, aged 18. Next to it is the memorial of Dorothy St John, just as characteristic of the Caroline age: a plain polished black slab, elegantly lettered and bearing no effigy. Then at the back of the church come three interesting monuments of the 19th century: two in white marble, each blocking the west window of one of the aisles – less sympathetic perhaps in their hard brightness but both well carved in their fashion; and the last of the series, to Edmund Verney, killed at Ulundi in the Zulu War of 1879 – a late survival of the old tradition of the soldier's monument, with a medallion portrait, a mourning military figure, and weapons and equipment cast to the ground.

Under the tower, between the two white monuments just

Stanford-on-Avon church, looking west (N.M.R.)

mentioned, stands what for some people is the church's principal treasure: the 17th-century organ case, most delicately carved and gilded. It is said (though it has not been proved) that it came from the King's chapel in the Palace of Whitehall, thrown out at the revolution in 1649.

The church has escaped all harsh restoration. It is totally unencumbered with superfluous furniture; an admirable vessel for the distinguished things it holds.

Stapleford Leicestershire 2D6

Although the Gothic manner of building ceased to be fashionable at the Reformation in the 16th century, it continued to be practised, as at St John's in *Leeds* and at *Staunton Harold.* The traditional form was never wholly displaced. In the 18th century a few people, like Horace Walpole, turned back to Gothic modes with enthusiasm. Some beautiful works

(B.T.A.)

resulted, including this little-known church. It was erected to the orders of the fourth Earl of Harborough and the design of George Richardson (who worked with Adam, in a different manner, at *Kedleston*) in 1783.

The church (St Mary Magdalen) stands in the clearing of a wood. The best time to see it is in the spring when the daffodils are out all around. It is a simple building, rectangular with a west tower, and the masons' work in ashlar, like all the other craftsmanship embodied in it, is of high quality. It is furnished like a College chapel, with the seats facing inwards, apart from the west gallery, the Earl's pew, which looks down the length of the church to the altar and is fitted with every convenience including a fireplace. The seating is chastely plain. The reredos has another reference to Kedleston, for Richard Brown of Derby, who made it, had supplied a pair of "purple obelisks" to that house, of the fluorspar called Blue John also used here.

A series of monuments commemorates members of the Earl's family, the Sherards, from 1440 (a brass) to the fourth Earl himself, who died in 1799. Two of them are outstanding. One is Caroline: to Lord Sherard of Leitrim (d. 1640), with two fine white effigies resting on a tomb covered in polished marble, jet black. The other is Georgian, a splendid work of Rysbrack to the first Earl of Harborough (d. 1732), Roman and truly patrician.

The colours are as cool as can be: pale brown woodwork, a black and white floor, white marble monuments, and the green of the trees outside.

The big house, close by, is also worth visiting. (There are lions in the park, a strange importation into Leicestershire.) Its most notable element is the wing prominently dated 1633, built by the Lord Sherard commemorated in the church. This displays on its outer walls a range of statues, some of that time and some dating from about 1500. Sir Nikolaus Pevsner observed in 1960 that this part of the house "defies description and dating": a remark that can only challenge effort.

Staunton Harold Leicestershire 2C6

Staunton Harold is the creation of a single family, the Shirleys, who acquired the estate in 1423 and held it until 1954. They threw up a succession of masterful eccentrics, from whom the place took an indelible stamp. Sir Robert Shirley – a grandson of Queen Elizabeth's Earl of Essex – succeeding very young at the outbreak of the Civil War, threw himself into the King's cause and was imprisoned again and again during the Commonwealth. (A portrait of him is to be seen in the long gallery at *Sudbury*.) In 1653 he began to erect a new Anglican chapel on his estate. Here it is: in form a building of the late 15th century; inside, planned entirely for the worship of Laud's Anglican Church. It is the proudest monument erected anywhere in defiance of the Republican

government. Sir Robert himself died in the Tower of London in 1656, aged 27. The building was not completed until about 1665, when a noble inscription was placed over the west door: "When all things sacred were throughout the nation either demolished or profaned, Sir Robert Shirley Baronet founded this church; whose singular praise it is to have done the best things in the worst times and hoped them in the

(A. F. Kersting)

most calamitous". The chapel is dedicated to the Holy Trinity and remains today almost unaltered, save for the addition of an organ of the early 18th century, singularly sweet-toned in its wooden pipes, and a splendid iron screen of the same time, probably by Robert Bakewell.

Sir Robert's great-nephew was created Earl Ferrers in 1711, and the fifth Earl refronted the house from 1763 onwards.

He seems to have been his own architect. His design was austere, his material red brick: a good complement to the stone chapel, with its pinnacles and elaborate balustrade. Set informally at an acute angle to each other, linked by the cedars and the lake in front, the composition the two buildings make is perfect.

The chapel was given to the National Trust by the twelfth Earl Ferrers in 1954 and is open to the public. The house became at the same time one of the Cheshire Homes, and the interior is not shown.

It should be added that Staunton Harold lies within the parish of Breedon-on-the-Hill, whose church (St Mary) is a very notable one, standing on a dramatic site within an Iron-Age camp and containing a series of important sculptures of the 8th century.

Stockport: church of St George Greater Manchester 2B5
A magnificent church, ennobling the drab and crowded Buxton Road, just before it plunges down into the centre of Stockport. It is beautifully placed in relation to the road, right on it but set at a diagonal, withdrawn between two little avenues of lime trees.

The church was built in 1893–7, a late work of Hubert Austin of Lancaster. He was a partner in the firm of Paley & Austin, which produced many fine churches throughout north-western England. Here he had money at his disposal in abundance. The site was given by Wakefield Christie-Miller, and the cost of the building was defrayed by George Fearn. Money has often corrupted architecture, but here (as with Bodley at *Hoar Cross*) it enabled a patron and architect, both exacting, to realise their own vision of what they were working for.

The church is cruciform, with a broad, big nave and aisles, slender transepts, and a very short chancel. The material throughout is the pinkish-buff sandstone of Cheshire. The steeple is distinguished in its proportions and boldly ribbed and panelled.

Stockport: St George's church, looking west (N.M.R.)

Inside, the nave and its aisles are broad, but tall enough to carry off their breadth to perfection. The nave has an oak roof of a modified local character. Everything here is unadorned, the glass nearly all clear. The crossing – rendered octagonal by little galleries placed across the corners – has a pretty painted ceiling, and provides the transition to the sumptuous chancel. Here there is an alabaster reredos (but the stone chosen is so delicate that from the far end of the church it has almost the quality of ivory) and a fine east window, in which gold and ruby-red provide the highlights. The corresponding west window is quite different, and perhaps even better. Blue prevails here, against a grisaille background, with a strong pattern made by curving scrolls.

The workmanship throughout the building is excellent. It is not, like so many of the finest Victorian churches, an alien in its place. Rather, in materials and design, it belongs here, and would be a foreigner anywhere else. The medieval churches of Cheshire – *Astbury*, for example – have been greatly admired and beloved; this building of the 1890s has its natural place in their evolution.

The whole building, from conception to completion, is a work of the nineties, a decade to which we have attached in our minds very different associations: with the raffishness of the Prince of Wales and Oscar Wilde, with the increasing uneasiness of Englishmen at their country's place in the world, and in artistic terms with the gaieties of *art nouveau*. Not one of these things is in evidence here. The building is serious and quietly self-confident; the ideas of *art nouveau* have not touched it. Like *Standen*, it shows how much was going on in these years that had little to do with the modes fashionable in the capital.

Stockport has a few other good things. Its Town Hall, very proud of itself in Portland stone (Sir Alfred Thomas, 1908), faces the Georgian Infirmary of 1832, and at the foot of the hill, where the Mersey flows through, its deep valley is spanned by a tremendous brick viaduct built by the Manchester & Birmingham Railway to the design of its engineer, G. W. Buck, in 1842. It was illustrated in a famous early print, showing the industrial town crouching beneath it, wreathed in smoke. Though the smoke has gone, the viaduct remains, widened (unobtrusively) on the west side and now disfigured by the electric railway's clutter of wires and standards. Like St George's church, the work is massive but not ponderous; cyclopean in its magnitude and power.

Stokesay Salop 2B6
The landscape here is notable. To the north the distance is closed by the high green and purple range of the Long Mynd. Immediately southward is a modest gorge cut by the River Onny between wooded hills about 1,000 ft high. The western of these two has been defaced by felling and replanting with scrubby conifers; but the eastern, Nortoncamp Wood, is clothed in a big sweep of deciduous trees, the hill topped by an Iron-Age camp. Stokesay Castle stands right at the entrance to the gorge.

It is really a fortified manor-house – one of the most complete of its time that survives anywhere in the country. A moat (now dry) surrounds it. The earliest part of the building is the tower at the north end, whose lower part dates from the 12th century, with a timber superstructure added very

Stokesay Castle from the west; behind the trees, the church
(A. F. Kersting)

much later. Immediately adjoining it is the Great Hall, built about 1275, lighted by four big gabled windows with bold tracery, and covered with fine timber roofs. Then to the south comes the Solar building, and finally the polygonal South Tower, now the most "fortified" part of the whole structure, which was probably built in 1291. This range of buildings faces north-west. Across the courtyard stands the Gatehouse, which was probably erected about 1620 – it shows some affinities with the Council House Gateway in Shrewsbury, put up in that year. The Gatehouse here is a quite perfect timber building, lovely in shape and in colour – the timber a silvery grey and the plaster a pale ochre. It contrasts delightfully with the Castle, which except for the top stage of the North Tower is built of sandstone, yellow tinged faintly with green.

Though the Gatehouse is still lived in, the Castle itself has been empty for very many years. Its floors and walls are pretty complete inside, however. There is a notable 13th-century fireplace in the upper part of the North Tower. The Solar is panelled and contains a splendidly elaborate chimney-piece, perhaps dating from the same time as the Gatehouse. It fits imperfectly, and was probably brought here from somewhere else.

The Castle never had to stand attack, so far as we know, in the Middle Ages. But there was fighting here in the Civil War, in 1646, when the Royalist horsemen occupying the church were driven out of it by Parliamentarian troops, who had seized the Castle. In this operation the church (St John Baptist) was seriously damaged. The nave was rebuilt in 1654, the chancel 10 years later. The medieval tower survives. The nave is rectangular, with a flat ceiling: modest and utilitarian work, much plainer than its contemporaries at *Berwick-on-Tweed* and *Staunton Harold*. The only piece of ostentation is the squire's pew at the entrance to the chancel. This, the pulpit, and the pews in the nave all seem to date from 1664–5. The west gallery is later, of the early 18th century; perhaps at the same time, texts were painted on the walls, in a simple architectural framework.

Stourhead Wiltshire 4D3
The Stourhead estate was sold by the Stourton family (ruined by an entailed preference for losing causes) in 1714 and acquired three years later by Henry Hoare, a member of a family of London goldsmith-bankers. He pulled down the house at once and built a new one, to the designs of Colen Campbell. It was completed in 1724, one of the first works in the new Palladian style.

Campbell's house still stands, with two important modifications. Sir Richard Colt Hoare added the wings in 1790–1804, for a library and a picture gallery. He was a considerable scholar, a pioneer of modern archaeology, and he compiled here his huge *History of Wiltshire*, one of the grandest devoted to any county in England. Appropriately, the Library is the outstanding room in the house, splendidly ample, a cool green in colour, enlivened by painted glass and still provided with the magnificent furniture made for it by the younger Chippendale.

The stamp of this distinguished owner is firmly imprinted everywhere in the house. The pictures – apart from the numerous portraits – are mainly of his choosing, and they reflect the cultivated taste of his time. By an odd irony, those likely to be most enjoyed today are a pair of Flemish altar-pieces, which Colt Hoare himself can scarcely have valued as we do. Chippendale's furniture is all over the house. It can be documented, piece by piece, in the family's accounts.

About 1840 a second alteration was made to the building, which was (most surprisingly) an improvement. The big portico was put on: an element that was in Campbell's original design, but for some reason not executed by him.

Since that happy time the house and estate have endured adversity. The extravagance of Sir Henry Ainslie Hoare, M.P., demanded the selling of Sir Richard's splendid library of books and of the most evidently valuable pictures in 1883. The depleted estate came in 1894 to his son Sir Henry, who struggled valiantly against further misfortune. In 1902 there was a fire, which gutted the centre of the house. With the aid of meticulous photographs (some of them taken, by good luck, only two years earlier) the destroyed rooms were sensitively reconstructed. In 1917 his only son died of wounds in France, and at the close of his life in 1946 he determined to make over the estate to the National Trust. It was the happiest possible decision.

The house therefore is a fine one, with a strongly-marked character of its own. Yet the fame of the place does not rest on the house at all, but on the landscape, made by succeeding generations of Hoares and reflecting their taste. It owes most to the second Henry Hoare, who inherited in 1725 and devoted himself to it for 40 years, from 1744 to 1783. For all his wealth, his life was a succession of griefs.

Stourhead: looking across the lake to the Pantheon

(A. F. Kersting)

He lost his two wives, his only son, and one of his two daughters. He was a strong, quiet patriot, who rejoiced in his country's triumphs in the Seven Years War and then saw it tumble, as it seemed to him, to ruin in the War of American Independence. Through it all he was sustained by his absorption in the Stourhead estate. His work there was the great passion of his life, and it stands as his enduring monument.

The landscaped garden lies well away from the house, invisible from it. Here is one of the subtleties of Stourhead. The main front of the house faces east, out to the bare chalk downs; on the west side it has a conventional pleasure garden. Henry Hoare's activity went on below, in the steep-sided valley of the Stour, which rises near by. From it and from two other small streams he created a triangular lake, whose banks he adorned with a series of buildings, most of them designed by Henry Flitcroft. The first was the Grotto on the western side, with a statue of the river god; a magical place still, cool and silent except for the splashing of the water from the springs and offering an exquisite view across the lake. Then came the Pantheon, on the same side, and the Temple of Flora opposite, both set against the background of the existing woodlands. The first stage of the plan was realised by about 1755. What Hoare aimed at here, in very general terms, was to re-create in Wiltshire the classical landscape of Italy, of the Lakes of Nemi and Avernus and the paintings of Claude Lorrain.

That attempt succeeded perfectly; but something more remarkable lay beyond. For Hoare was not content with any mere importation, a piece of Italy translated into England. He set himself to fuse Italy and England into one. The lake he had created lay immediately below the little village of Stourton, with its medieval church. It would have been quite within his power to sweep it all away, as many masterful landlords, re-shaping the country to their taste, did in his time. Instead he kept it, and made it part of his landscape. The English Gothic was to contribute to the final achievement, as well as the art of classical Rome. He went here far outside the common taste of his time, and that too brought him advantage: for in 1764 he was able to acquire the Bristol High Cross (condemned by the townspeople as "a public nuisance") and re-erect it at Stourhead. It is a magnificent piece, of 1373: a slender, lofty spire, which punctuates the valley precisely, in conjunction with the church and the village buildings, seen from across the lake.

Hoare's last additional adornments were up on the heights: the Temple of Apollo to the south and – two miles off, away from the lake altogether – Alfred's Tower, a triangular erection of brick, designed to commemorate King Alfred's victory over the Danes and George III's triumphs over France. It is one of the most striking landmarks in England, well seen by the traveller from London to Plymouth as he passes in the train two or three miles to the north.

But though the buildings give the landscape much of its character, they are only incidents in it. The trees are the chief thing, and the water. Henry Hoare and his successors had firm ideas about planting, all of them visible to us still. To begin with his own words: "The greens should be ranged in large masses as the shades are in painting, to contrast the *dark* masses with the *light* ones". He did much to increase the dark masses by the introduction of Scotch firs and spruce trees, in clumps by the lake and on the hillside, using them here and there to point the skyline. Richard Colt Hoare did not care for this simple mixture, and he began a much more elaborate diversification, adding numerous trees from Europe and across the Atlantic. It is to him that the woods of Stourhead owe most, in variety and distinction. Not everything he did is perhaps congenial to us now. He was fond of laurel, for example, and planted it extensively to form an undergrowth. In the 20th century most of it has been removed. On the other hand, at the very beginning of this large operation he introduced one new element that has had marvellous consequences since. In 1791 he planted his first rhododendron. By 1828 there were 200. They could not be counted now.

The Victorian Hoares, as we should expect, added greatly

to the number of the conifers, and to their variety, with monkey puzzle, sequoia, Douglas fir. Except under the spendthrift Sir Henry Ainslie Hoare, the work is all recorded in a continuous series of Annals, supplemented for Sir Richard's time by his nurserymen's bills. Each owner planted for posterity, and we enjoy the fulfilment of what in many cases they never saw themselves. Moreover, by the natural process of decay and death as well as by further planting, the landscape is constantly changing still. It is not the same now as it was when the National Trust acquired the estate in 1946, or as it will be in the year 2000. A house and its contents can be frozen, kept static as they were at some moment in the past. A garden, still more a landscape like this, is a living thing, which takes on its own momentum, to change beyond human control.

Stourhead is a place for all seasons, and the gardens are liberally open. You can walk right round the lake – an hour's leisurely stroll – on any day in the year. The highest points come perhaps in June with the rhododendrons and in October, when the beeches, which still set the fine tone to the landscape, are turning, the maples and the other exotics too. No man-made landscape in England excels it in beauty; to many people it stands quite alone, at the top. Even more, it is a work of European importance. On that, take the opinion not of an Englishman but of a German-born scholar, Sir Nikolaus Pevsner. His final reflection on Stourhead is that "English picturesque landscaping of the 18th century is the most beautiful form of gardening ever created, superior in variety and subtlety to the Italy of Frascati and the France of Versailles".

Stow: church of St Mary Lincolnshire 2D5

Perhaps the only Anglo-Saxon work surviving in England that can truly be called magnificent.

It is not clear why so large a church should have been built here. Romantic notions that it was the cathedral of the diocese of Lindsey, the predecessor of Lincoln, are un-

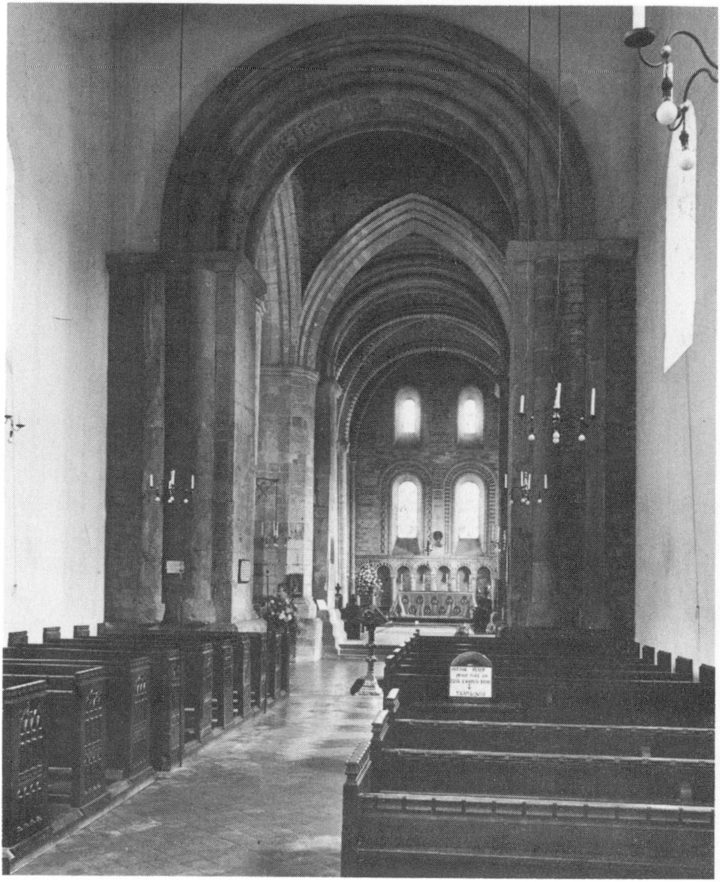

Stow church, looking east (Janet & Colin Bord)

founded. A Benedictine abbey was established at Stow, but that was after the church had been built on its present scale; and it was quickly removed, apparently after no more than five years. So the early history of the building remains obscure.

The interior is inspiring. The structure of the crossing, with its four great arches 30 ft high, and of the transepts is entirely Saxon. The lower part of the walls, reddened by a fire, seems to date back to the 10th century; the rest to the first half of the 11th. The nave was rebuilt to its present form not long after the Norman Conquest, and after that the chancel was rebuilt too, in the richest late-Romanesque manner. Its stone vault is of about 1860, put in by J. L. Pearson, who restored the building with great care and respect; he had good evidence that it had been part of the original design. In the north transept there is a fragment of a large figure of St Thomas Becket, of fine quality, painted on the east wall. It is among the earliest representations of the saint to be seen in England, dating probably from within 30 years of his martyrdom in 1170. In the 14th century a new tower was built (perhaps in place of a previous timber structure), and this unfortunately required the crossing to be strengthened by the insertion of four additional pointed arches, which do something to mask the splendid Saxon originals.

For the rest the church remains, in essentials, much as it was in the 12th century. It presents a severe face to the world outside; bulky and high-shouldered, presiding over the dead flat plain that stretches from Lincoln Edge to the Trent.

Styal: Quarry Bank Mill Cheshire 2B5

It is not easy for us to put ourselves back into the world of the Industrial Revolution. Much is now known about its technology and economic history; there have been good accounts of individual firms, and some investigations of social consequences. But its physical setting has been largely destroyed, or overlaid, or changed beyond recognition. Thirty years ago in Nottingham or Birmingham the small-scale processes of manufacture were still to be seen by anyone who walked the streets with his eyes open. Now in those towns they have been almost entirely swept away, and in that respect we have moved backwards, to become dependent for our understanding of early industrial history on written evidence almost alone.

It is a rule that the buildings and sites chosen for description in this book shall all be open regularly to the public. That makes it difficult to find industrial monuments that are not ruinous or preserved out of context in museums. Fortunately there are some, like *Coalbrookdale*. Here is another: a textile mill building, quite intact, 10 miles south of Manchester.

It stands in a deep wooded valley, with a road leading down into it steeply from the Cheshire plain. The earliest part of it was erected by Samuel Greg, an Ulsterman from Belfast, in 1784. It was then enlarged in successive stages; the date of one, 1810, is carved on a sandstone arch over a leat into the river at the back.

Greg's were, and still are, spinners of yarn – cotton, wool, and man-made fibres. They now occupy only a small part of the south end of the building (their main business being in Wilmslow), and the property at Styal belongs to the National Trust. The manager's office is open, furnished with a desk and chair and some relics from the past, such as a set of blunderbusses for defence against machine-breakers and a very well-chosen series of documents, including photocopies from the firm's older records now in Manchester Central Library. They are chiefly concerned with the management of the business, showing for example the stringent instructions given to secure the observance of the Factory Act of 1833, with its requirements for the education of apprentices. Here also is a plain statement by an apprentice of his history and his decision to run away, not on account of ill-usage but in order to see his mother, who had been ill, in 1806. The apprentices (he says he was one of 90) lived in a brick building at the top of the hill, still known today as the Apprentice House.

One section of the main mill building is shown (not the oldest). This part is a structure of brick and iron, and a variety of spinning machines is displayed here. To see the building as a whole it is necessary to cross the little river, by a path on the left of the entrance road and below it. This leads into a meadow, underneath a beech-clad hill. The building is large, 31 bays long in all and four storeys high. The oldest part is at the north end, with the chimney and the little cupola over the bell that summoned the hands to their work. The owner's house is beyond, to the north; to the south is the manager's, with a few outbuildings; and that is all.

Everything is very quiet here now. The mill wheels no longer turn to provide power, the apprentices and the workers

Styal: Quarry Bank Mill (B.T.A.)

have all gone. There is no need to romanticise the life that was lived here. There must often have been misery in it, much harshness and petty tyranny, even more boredom. But every kind of group employment, ancient or modern, is likely to involve some or all of those things. There were many mills like this one in the hilly country north of the Trent up to the Pennines, where the swiftly-running rivers provided water power; the complement of the bigger ones – no doubt much more often dark and satanic – in the towns. Those others are disappearing fast, and before long few if any of the older mills will survive. Here at any rate is one, kept for us, which embodies a long history of life and labour.

Sudbury Derbyshire 2C6
Great houses of the late 17th century are now very few in England. Some of the most notable have gone, from Clarendon House in London, pulled down in 1683, to Coleshill – perhaps the greatest loss of all – which was burnt out in 1952. Others, like Chevening in Kent, have been altered, inside or out, beyond recognition. This is one of the best to survive unchanged.

The Sudbury estate was acquired by the Vernons in 1513. A hundred years later they began to build a house here, probably not on the present site. The whole of the present house appears to be a work of the late 17th century and due to George Vernon, who started the building about 1660 and took more than 30 years to complete it. It is all very evidently of a piece, and the little touches of Jacobean character to be seen outside – some strapwork, for example, in the window frames – can be accounted for by the timelag usually found in provincial building compared with that of London. Sudbury shows some close affinities with other buildings that are certainly of this time, in the towns of Derby and Warwick and in Leicestershire.

George Vernon may well have designed the house himself. The copious surviving accounts mention a number of the artists and craftsmen concerned with the decorative work.

The plan is in the shape of the letter E, the wings and porch forming the projecting members. The left-hand side of the house, as one looks at it from the front, is a Victorian addition; the date 1884 appears above the small entrance door. The porch is two-storeyed and decorated with elaborately carved stonework, ponderous yet engaging. The hipped roof, tall panelled chimney-stacks, and cupola are all characteristic of the years after 1650. There has however been one change. The openwork balustrade was put into its present position, immediately below the dormer windows, by E. M. Barry in 1870. Originally it was smaller, placed above the dormers, and of wood painted white, not of stone – in exactly the fashion still to be seen at *Ashdown*. The brickwork is a subdued but rich dark red, diapered with blue in a manner that looks backwards to the Tudor age.

Inside, three things are outstanding: the staircase, the plasterwork and wood-carving, and the Long Gallery. This is one of the finest staircases of its time in any country house in England (but compare *Durham*: Castle), magnificently rich yet superb in its proportions. The balustrade is of pine. It used all to be painted brown, and heavily gilt. This has now given place to white, which is believed to be the original colour. The plasterwork around and above it in the ceiling is of equally high quality. It is the work of James Pettifer in 1675. The paintings are a little later, by Louis Laguerre, who worked for George Vernon from 1691 to 1694. His work is to be seen in many great houses, like Hampton Court and Chatsworth. Here, working within the frames of the plasterwork designed earlier – not intended indeed to hold paintings at all – a conciseness has been forced upon him, and the result has a crisp brilliance.

The Saloon is now unfurnished, and yet in that bare state made very rich by its plaster and woodwork. Look for example at the single rectangular panel over the window, where it can be appreciated in the strong light. The portraits that line the room are contained in a uniform set of frames made for them in the 18th century. George Vernon, the builder of the house, is to be seen above the door. The wood-carving here is by Edward Pierce, who did a great deal of work in the City churches in London when they were rebuilt after the Fire. Next door in the Drawing Room the glorious carving above the chimney-piece is by Grinling Gibbons, who received £40 for it in 1678.

Sudbury Hall: the Long Gallery. The book-cases have now been removed, and the furnishing altered (A. F. Kersting)

A corridor at the end of the series of rooms on the ground floor is hung with interesting paintings of the house in the 18th century. Upstairs in the Porch Room are a few prints and other relics relating to Admiral Edward Vernon (1684–1757), the best-known member of the family – "Vernon the fellow who took Portobello". In the Queen's Room (the reference is to Queen Adelaide, William IV's widow, who lived here for a time in the 1840s) the chimney-piece is of alabaster carved in 1670 by William Wilson, remembered as the architect of St Mary's church, Warwick.

You now cross a landing at the head of the staircase. The charming little Talbot Room, fitted up as a library, is of the Early Victorian age. Next to it is the Long Gallery. When it was completed in 1676 it was very old-fashioned: for long galleries are essentially a feature of Elizabethan and Jacobean houses (as at *Little Moreton* and *Hatfield*) and were by this time quite out of date. The one at Sudbury may well be the last of all to be constructed. George Vernon knew what he wanted, and got it: an ample, splendid apartment facing south, generously lighted on three sides, and decorated in a way never seen in any long gallery before. His plasterer here was Robert Bradbury, whose luscious work on the ceiling, in swirling curves disciplined with rectangles and diagonals, prevents any feeling that the very long room is a tunnel. Among the portraits, note the set of four in more elaborate frames than the rest, of members of the Shirley family. They include (no. 72) the madcap Royalist Sir Robert, who built the chapel at *Staunton Harold*. His daughter was George Vernon's second wife.

The Vernon monuments are in the church (All Saints), close by, and worth a brief visit. The church itself can give one little pleasure, from its harsh restoration; if you value your eyes, keep them away from the garish east window, presented by Queen Victoria and the Prince Consort.

Away to the north over the fields, the castellated brick edifice is a deer-cote, for sheltering the animals (there were over 600 of them here at one time) in winter. The village is all built of dark red brick like the house, including its handsome inn the Vernon Arms. It lies along the old main road from Derby to the Potteries and was a nightmare of traffic until 1972, when it was released from torment by a bypass.

The country in which Sudbury stands is pleasant but unemphatic. There are interesting places within reach all round. To the south, in a clearing in Needwood Forest, is the remarkable Victorian church of *Hoar Cross*; due north Ashbourne, and the Peak District beyond. North-eastwards, the church of Norbury contains the splendid Fitzherbert tombs, and the adjoining parish of Ellastone has three improbable associations. Handel stayed here; Rousseau spent a year at Wootton Hall in 1766–7, and began there to write his *Confessions*; and the village is the setting of George Eliot's first novel *Adam Bede*. The road leads on to Alton Towers, in a romantic landscape, natural and man-made, partly debased now but still dramatic and compelling.

Swaledale see **Richmond**

Tattershall Lincolnshire 2D5

There are few large tracts of quite flat country in England. The biggest of them lies to the west and south of the Wash. Here you can travel for 30 or 40 miles without rising 20 ft above the sea-level. It is like that all the way if you go from *Boston* to Tattershall. Thirty years ago the skyline was almost unbroken, its one landmark the tower of the church at Boston until the line of the Lincolnshire Wolds came into sight to the north. Now things are different. Electricity has invaded this landscape, and spread its clutter of wires everywhere: on lines of tall pylons and – more disfiguring – little brown poles. The emptiness of the air has now been encroached on, and with that the main visual charm of this country has been impaired. Nor is that all. You pick out the tower of the castle at Tattershall, shouldering its way up among trees; but what lies in front? It is the big R.A.F. station of Coningsby, with its sheds and a village of attendant houses. In fact the castle is now surrounded on three sides, at no great distance, by that installation and by extensive gravel workings.

But all that said, the journey to Tattershall is handsomely rewarding, from *Boston* or *Lincoln* or from much further afield. The castle and church stand close to one another. Both are notable buildings, and their histories interlock.

The first castle on this site was licensed in 1231. It had a wall with circular towers, but no keep. The bases of two of the towers remain immediately north and south of the present building, which was erected by Ralph Lord Cromwell between 1430 and 1450. For 10 of those years (1433–43) Cromwell was Lord Treasurer to Henry VI. He was an able politician, and successful at least to this extent, that at a time of exceptional instability and violence he died in his bed in 1456. His castle at Tattershall exemplifies all the tendencies of its time. Formidable as it looks, and protected by a double moat, it could never have stood up long to a concentrated assault, especially with artillery, which was then coming into general use. Its entrance is placed on the ground floor, unlike those of earlier keeps, which were true military works (see *Conisbrough*, *Portchester*).

The building comprises five floors, beginning with a basement, each with one large room in the centre and four small ones in the turrets. The whole structure is of brick, of a rich dark red in the external walls. It was all made locally; much, if not most of it on Edlington Moor, nine miles away near Horncastle. The rooms are now almost entirely unfurnished; but each has its original fireplace with heraldic carving, made of limestone from Ancaster. On the second floor the eastern passage has a good brick vault. The top floor comprises an open court, with a gallery running round it. The view from it northward is striking, still little touched by modern changes.

To the east you look down on the church (Holy Trinity): a building of Ancaster stone, dressed smooth throughout. It was the church of a college of canons established by Lord

(A. F. Kersting)

Cromwell about 1440. His castle must by then have been well advanced, and he could turn his mind to a complementary undertaking. The church was finished in the 1480s, long after his death, and then under the supervision of William of Waynflete, Bishop of Winchester (founder of Magdalen College, Oxford), who was one of his executors. The building is large, expensive, and as it now stands rather empty. Only in the east window is any painted glass left, and that is set confusedly. Some of the glass that was in the church was taken away and is now to be seen in St Martin's church at Stamford, and in Burghley House near by. The parishioners rioted in protest, but to no purpose.

As usual in collegiate churches, the nave is divided from the choir by a solid screen, creating in effect two churches enclosed in a single building. With its windows unglazed, the nave fell into disrepair and passed out of use in the 19th century. Everything is now in good order again. In the north transept the surviving brasses have been assembled; Lord Cromwell's is here, now headless, and those of three priests of the college. All the collegiate buildings have gone. So have the wooden almshouses erected to Lord Cromwell's order; but they have been replaced by a pretty row on the north side of the church, dating perhaps from the 17th century.

The modern history of the castle is curious. It has not been lived in since the 1690s; it was last put to any practical use during the Napoleonic wars, when a beacon was prepared on the top stage, to be lighted in case of a French invasion. By 1911 the fabric was decaying fast. The floors had fallen in, and the fireplaces were removed, to be sold in the United States. Lord Curzon (see *Bodiam*, *Kedleston*) succeeded in preventing their export, and purchased the castle. He then set about its repair and bequeathed it to the National Trust on his death in 1925.

The Test Valley and Mottisfont Abbey Hampshire 4E4
The chalk landscape of southern England is consistently delightful. One thinks of it first in terms of downland, in Sussex for instance, and in the cliffs that confront the English Channel from *Dover* to Dorset (see *Golden Cap*). But those are the conspicuous outcrop of the chalk. It appears more intimately, and no less happily, in the rivers and the valleys that fall away from the Downs to the sea. Among these the Test is one of the pre-eminent trout streams of England. It rises on Ashe Down west of Basingstoke and takes a gently sinuous course to Southampton Water. The river is shallow and not navigable. It has its economic importance. In the parish of Overton, where it rises, it provided power for nine mills in the 12th century. Next door, at Laverstoke, for 250

(Gerd Franklin)

years past its water has proved particularly well suited to paper making; the paper used in bank-notes is made here. The value of the fishing rights in the Test is extravagantly high, which has helped to ensure that the water is kept quite pure. It is a special pleasure to watch this pellucid stream, flowing over its chalk bed.

The Test valley is generally a broad one, filled with water meadows, sometimes with beds of cress. Towards its lower end, a little above Romsey, stands Mottisfont Abbey. To be exact, it was a Priory, given its grander designation by a romantic owner in the 18th century: a small house of Austin canons, founded probably in 1201. The "font" is still to be seen: a spring rising in a clear chalk bowl, just south-west of the present house. At the Dissolution it was acquired by Lord Sandys of *The Vyne*. He decided to make himself a house from the Priory buildings, based on a conversion of the church. Its nave survives as the main part of the present house. On to it he added two long projecting wings, to frame courtyards to the south. Early in the 18th century most of these wings was swept away. The stumps of the Tudor wings were moulded into a new south front, making the house far more compact; with minor differences the house we see now. It has fared very well in our own century, at the hands of a succession of owners of elegant taste. The estate passed away from Lord Sandys's descendants in 1934 when it was sold to Gilbert Russell. Two years later Geoffrey Jellicoe was commissioned to remodel the gardens to the north of the house, and in 1938–9 Rex Whistler redecorated one of the principal rooms, to a most charming result. Mrs Russell gave the property to the National Trust in 1957 after her husband's death, and she continued to live there until 1972.

The contrast between the north and south fronts is fascinating. The north front is really no more than the north wall

Mottisfont Abbey: the Rex Whistler room (A. F. Kersting)

of the church, tricked out with 18th-century sash windows; all in plain grey stone. The south front is mainly of brick, with stone dressings: a complicated sequence of half-octagons, the remains of the Tudor building clearly visible where they have been incorporated into the 18th-century composition.

The Rex Whistler room is a delightful piece of gaiety, with *trompe-l'œil* painting that does indeed deceive the eye. A beautiful 18th-century Chinese mirror hangs over the fire-place, brought here from Wardour Castle. Do not miss the reflection in it of Whistler's painting on the opposite wall. Alas, he had time to carry through the decoration only, not to design the furniture that was intended to fill the room. It was 10 months' work, finished in the summer of 1939. He then went off to the war and was killed in 1944 in Normandy.

The stable block of 1836 is distinguished both for its delicate brickwork and for the curved sweep of its eaves. It is a more regularly finished piece of architecture than the house itself.

But delightful as man's craftsmanship has been, the ultimate triumph at Mottisfont is Nature's. The first things of all here are the trees. Although there is a walled garden, given over largely to roses, it lies away from the house. There is a pretty parterre on the south front, but the whole building stands in a green landscape, in which flowers play only a small part. The trees are superb; best of all perhaps the enormous planes, reaching up to 100 ft high, beeches and oaks and cedars too, of exceptional magnificence. Beneath them flows the Test, smooth and as clear as glass.

Totnes Devon 3C5

It is right to open with a warning. Alone among the towns described here, Totnes has given itself up to the summer tourist. Every Tuesday from May to September the place "goes Elizabethan". The narrow main street is almost impassable then with cars, prams, and shop-gazers. There have been some efforts to brighten it up; some of them – at least to some people's taste – unhappy. Unless you like such things, go there between October and April, or early in the day; or stay there and walk round it quietly in the evening.

For behind this innocent playing to the gallery of the modern world, Totnes remains what it always was, one of the outstanding historic towns of the West of England, with a continuous life of well over 1,000 years. Not content with that, it claims in legend an origin far older. A little way up Fore Street, on the right-hand side, you will see a stone commemorating the arrival here of Brutus, prince of Troy. So Totnes has its place in English mythology too.

Its real history begins as an Anglo-Saxon borough in the 10th century (it had a mint then for 70 years at least) and with the building of a castle not long after the Norman Conquest. The site is eminently defensible, a steep hill rising up from the River Dart, and here the town developed: dominated by the castle, with its noble church below, enclosed by its walls, and at the river, a bridge. Bridgetown, the suburb on the far side, was not part of the borough but owned wholly by the rich Seymour family. Hence the Seymour Arms over there, with the big town coaching inn, the Seven Stars, facing it: the headquarters, in borough-mongering days, of the two parties, the Whigs in Bridgetown, the Tories at the Seven Stars.

The main street (Fore Street below the gateway, High Street above it) has always been the town's spinal cord. No perambulation is offered here (that is well provided in a free leaflet to be obtained from the Information Office on the Plains). Instead, some comments follow on a few notable things. The scale is very small, and everything easily found.

To begin with the three chief public buildings: the Castle, the church, and the Guildhall. The Castle mound (or motte) is one of the biggest in England. It was protected by two ditches, one immediately at its foot, the other below the bailey, the courtyard by which one enters. Gaps in the wall on the north side give views down on to it and the steep valley below – and also, far away, to the hills of Dartmoor.

Up above is the circular keep: not Norman, but dating from the 14th century. The site of a small rectangular Norman tower is indicated in the grass. There are no other buildings.

The castle seems never to have had to withstand attack. The history of its ownership is complicated, from Judhael, to whom Totnes was granted by William the Conqueror, through Nonants and Braoses, Cantelupes and Zouches and Edgcumbes, to the Seymours, who acquired it by purchase about 1559. With them it remained, until the Duke of Somerset placed it in the keeping of the Government in 1949.

The town was walled, under a licence granted in 1256, in a rough oval, with North, East, and West Gates. The West Gate spanned the High Street near its top and has now gone; the other two still stand. The walls remain in part, and their line is clear on the north side of the churchyard and along South Street. There was a Benedictine priory, established by Judhael. Its church became the parish church of the town (St Mary). It is a splendid one, among the finest in Devon.

It is built partly of the sandstone quarried in this district; here an intense, almost glowing dark red, heightened by dressings of white limestone sparingly applied. The tower is lofty, its height accentuated by tall pinnacles. The placing of the spiral staircase needed for access to the bells and the roof was always a difficulty. Here it is managed admirably by putting the stair-turret into the centre of the south face and treating it as part of the composition, with the buttresses that flank it.

The interior of the church was restored in the 19th century, and altered. The window tracery belongs to that age, all the glass, nearly all the indifferent woodwork. But it has kept its great glory: one of the best stone screens in any parish church in the country. The Devon churches have very lavish carved wooden screens – like those at Ipplepen and Dartmouth, not far away. Here, about 1450, the design and craftsmanship that went into them were applied to stone. The effect is of an extraordinary richness, given by the depth, the traces of original colouring that remain, the play of light through the whole screen and over its face. Part of the rood-loft remained until the restoration of the 1860s. It was reached, oddly, not from a staircase adjoining it but from one half-way up the chancel, by a gallery on the north side.

The monuments have little to do with art, but much with history. At the north-west corner is a tablet to commemorate Walter Venning, founder of the Prison Society of Russia, who died at St Petersburg of gaol fever, aged 40, in 1821: one of the English humanitarians who made their mark in the world. Close by there is a memorial to John Prince (1643–1723), author of *The Worthies of Devon*, a biographical dictionary very remarkable as the work of one man, recording the contribution made by a single county to the life of England. He was vicar of Berry Pomeroy, the adjoining parish across the river.

The worthies of Totnes are indeed a striking company: among them W. J. Wills, a young explorer who crossed Australia from south to north for the first time in 1861 and died on the return journey; and Charles Babbage, who was known when he was a boy living in the town for his astonishing powers of calculation and went on to develop the first computer. Another, William Brockedon, is depicted in a self-portrait over the door in the Guildhall. As a painter he perhaps never fulfilled himself, but his book *The Passes of the Alps* did much to inspire Englishmen to travel in Switzerland.

The Guildhall is immediately north of the church: a very small building, approached now through a rather rustic granite colonnade, two of its piers inscribed RYC (for Richard) LEE. These piers were brought here in 1897 from a Jacobean building then being demolished on the opposite side of the church. The Guildhall contains the court of the borough magistrates (used as such until 1974) and up a flight of steps the Council Room, originally furnished in 1624 and still used for meetings of the Council. Beyond it lies the tiny Mayor's Parlour. These rooms, and the pictures and other relics in them, commemorate a municipal history reaching back over more than 600 years.

The houses of Fore Street and High Street are a study

Totnes: site of the west gate; the Castle Keep above (A. F. Kersting)

in themselves. Many of them have slate-hung fronts; the best are close to the church, where the slates are the pale-grey Cornish ones, not the Welsh purple. Towards the top of the High Street the houses are built on arcades supported on granite pillars: an admirable arrangement in this rainy western climate, which the planners might have attended to with advantage when Plymouth was rebuilt after the war. There are some good merchants' houses here of the 16th century. Opposite the church is a fine one (marked by a tablet referring to Sir Thomas Bodley's wife). It is privately owned, but the fine plaster ceiling of its first-floor front room can be seen from the pavement below. Such plasterwork is a speciality of Devon. Another merchant's house, lower down, is now the Museum: an Elizabethan town house, filled with things connected with Totnes and its neighbourhood, including a well-presented display to illustrate the work of Babbage and what it led to.

There are many other small things to be enjoyed here. Some of the shops have nice fronts: a couple for instance with pretty Victorian ironwork (64 and 69 High Street). Side lanes, alleys, or courts lead off the main street. There is a long one, boring its way beside houses and even through them, starting at No. 20 High Street and going through to South Street at the other end; Atherton Lane, a *cul-de-sac* of cottages with a little garden down the middle, leads off opposite the Brutus Stone. Close by, an 18th-century house with an uncommonly exuberant porch (covered in no less exuberant ivy) housed the Totnes Grammar School for many years; it is still given over to education. And at the foot of the hill the Seven Stars has a capacious two-storeyed porch, projecting out on pillars right on to the pavement. What spying-out, what gossip has gone on in its ample windows, facing three ways, above!

Totnes is a good centre for exploring a delectable countryside. Every yard of the Dart is beautiful: its curving, thickly-wooded lower course down to Dartmouth, the stretch above (best seen in summer, if you enjoy such things, from a steam train operating from Buckfastleigh), the wild uppermost part of all, along the two valleys of the divided river, to be followed to its sources on Dartmoor.

Trelissick Cornwall 3A5

The gardens of south-west Cornwall form a unique group. Nowhere else in Britain (indeed, where else in the world?) is there such a cluster of notable gardens so close together.

The celebrated series in Scotland are distributed down the west coast, over 300 miles. In Cornwall most of them lie within about 40. The soft, mild climate here allows an exceptionally wide range of plants to grow, from northern daffodils to palms and other things usually associated with the Mediterranean.

Nearly all of them lie on or close to the sea. The sea forms an essential element in their landscape, arising from the very nature of the coast of south Cornwall, where its rivers have long estuaries, the water stretching fingers far up into the land. The biggest and finest of these is the estuary of the Fal, into which five small rivers flow, in addition to the Fal itself. Together they come to form a huge expanse of water: about six square miles of it, 12–18 fathoms deep,

Trelissick: looking south-west to Carrick Roads (A. F. Kersting)

known as Carrick Roads. The Roads are said to have been big enough at one time to hold the entire British battle fleet; they certainly accommodated 300 ships that took shelter here from a great storm in 1815. The Trelissick estate straddles a peninsula between the Fal and another arm of the estuary. It owes a large part of its character to its cross-visions of water.

The estate was bought in 1800 by Ralph Allen Daniell, one of the wealthiest men in Cornwall. (His nickname was "Guinea-a-minute Daniell", alluding to his reputed income from one single mine at St Agnes alone.) His son, who succeeded him in 1823, enlarged the house and laid out rides and carriage drives towards the Fal; but he overreached himself financially, and was obliged to sell up in 1832. He lived on abroad in poverty, to die in 1866 at Boulogne. Trelissick was in the hands of the Gilbert family from 1844 to 1928. In 1937 Mrs Ida Copeland succeeded to it. She and her husband (managing director of the Spode china factory) devoted themselves to the planting of the garden as we now see it. She gave the property to the National Trust in 1955.

The approach is a work of art itself: by a gently curving road, looking down over grassland towards the sea. This drive leads to the back of the house. The entrance, through the Trust's shop, gives access immediately to the three divisions of the gardens, each different and affording its own pleasure. The path to the left, down a steep slope, leads to the Dell, a sheltered little valley, planted largely for late spring and summer. Then, by a bridge across the road down to the ferry at King Harry Passage, you come to Carcadden, a steep slope of rough grass, formerly an orchard, dominated by great conifers, like Monterey pines from California. New planting, undertaken about 15 years ago, will presently diversify and enrich the whole of this steep side of the valley.

The centre of the gardens, directly in front of the entrance, is presided over by a magnificent series of rhododendrons, some shooting up to a great height, in every gradation of colour from white to scarlet and crimson. From a broad semi-circular clearing there is a memorable view across the river to Tregothnan, Lord Falmouth's house. You can then make your way right down to the water's edge or upwards, to come out into the open beside Trelissick House, facing south-westwards away to Carrick Roads.

The garden is rich in all the flowering trees and shrubs of spring, azaleas, camellias, magnolias, with daffodils everywhere in March and April. It has now a great variety of hydrangeas, flowering much later. Trelissick is by no means a spring garden only, though that is perhaps the season when it is at its best. Spring in Cornwall, in an ordinary year, comes much earlier than it does further east. Yet here, as everywhere in England, the climate is quite unfixed. In winter there will often be no snow at all. Sometimes, however (as in 1978), it may come as late as April. The gardens here can now give pleasures throughout the months in which they are open, from March to October. The pleasures are diverse, variable according to weather, mood, inclination; and as planting continues – in the tradition of the best landscape art – there will be changes to note here successively, from one visit to another.

Trerice Cornwall 3A5

A small Elizabethan house of great charm; a notable example too of careful restoration and improvement. It is close to Newquay, a resort packed out with visitors in summer; deeply sequestered, looking sideways on to the slope of a hill, which protects it from the traffic of the highroad to St Austell. There was formerly a railway half a mile away on the other side. It has gone, and there is now no noise here at all.

The Trerice estate passed by marriage into the Arundell family in the 14th century. Under the Tudors they became powerful in Cornwall, a clan with several branches, each with its separate house; one of them was at Lanherne, in a delightful valley north of Newquay. In the Civil War they were notable Royalists and suffered much loss in consequence. But Charles II rewarded their fidelity with a peerage, making

Sir Richard Arundell Lord Arundell of Trerice. The estate continued in the family until 1768, when it passed to a Wentworth, and then in 1802 to the Aclands. They sold it in 1915. The National Trust purchased it in 1953.

The house at Trerice was given its present form in 1573 by Sir John Arundell, who became Sheriff of Cornwall the next year; no doubt it pleased him to exercise the accustomed hospitality of the office here when his work was new. It faces east and comprises an E-shaped block (the porch forming the short central projection), with north and south wings that run backwards from it at right angles. The central block is entirely due to him. Part of the south wing is older, though he inserted the half-turret into it and rebuilt the upper floor. The gables of the east front are unusual, perhaps reflecting some Flemish influence. Their curvaceous shapes contrast effectively with the very big rectangular window. This fills most of one side of the Great Hall. It has nearly 600 panes, many of them containing their original glass – though somewhat fewer now since the Concorde aircraft was tested down this coast, wreaking considerable damage among them.

The Hall is entered in the medieval way, through a screens passage from the porch. Above that passage is a little Musicians' Gallery. The plaster ceiling is good, restored in the 1840s. The table exemplifies fine traditional craftsmanship in oak, of the early 19th century. It is all that belongs historically to the house. The rest of the furniture has been either lent or brought here from the National Trust's other possessions. Notice, for example, the Georgian travelling case standing below the tapestry, fitted snugly with bottles for the owner's refreshment on his long and tedious journeys.

The Library, next door, is a charming room entered down some steps and graced by Sir John Arundell's semi-circular bay; facing south, yet kept cool even in summer by its green Donegal carpet and its view over the grass to the stream below. There is a Gothic bookcase here of outstanding quality. The crisply-coloured banner, painted on silk, was made for an Arundell when he was Sheriff of Cornwall in 1817.

Upstairs is the grand Drawing Room, with another plaster

Trerice: the Drawing Room (A. F. Kersting)

ceiling, more richly decorated than that in the Hall, and a good frieze. Above the over-mantel is the date 1573 – quaintly rendered in Roman characters with the final digit in Arabic. The heraldry here displays the matrimonial connections of the Arundells; that on the west wall (at right angles to it) the specially distinguished marriage of one of them to Henry Fitzalan, Earl of Arundel, in 1557. The Chippendale armchairs in this room came from Coleshill, the lovely 17th-century house in Berkshire whose destruction by fire in 1952 was a disaster. A door in the corner gives on to a narrow tunnel-like passage, which in turn leads to the Musicians' Gallery above the Hall.

A well-planned garden has been laid out around the house, to give changing views of it from different levels. A fine barn has been restored, to accommodate a shop and restaurant.

It is just over 25 years since the National Trust acquired Trerice, the shell of a house with 20 acres around it. Steadily throughout that time it has cherished and improved the property. If one knew it then and goes back there now, the experience is heartening.

Turville see **Fingest**

The Tweed see **Cheviot**

Uffington and Ashdown Oxfordshire 4E3

The Berkshire Downs – for so we may still call them, though they have been partly within Oxfordshire since 1974 – form a large tract of chalk. They are unlike the Sussex Downs (see *Slindon*, *Uppark*) in that they nowhere consist of a single ridge. They are, at their greatest extent, about 20 miles broad and seven miles deep, bounded roughly by Swindon, Newbury, and the Goring Gap (see *Fingest and Turville*). Only two major roads run across them, north and south, from Oxford to Salisbury and Southampton; none at all from east to west. Their one town is Lambourn, which is tiny, given up chiefly to the training of race-horses. That and sheep-farming are the traditional occupations. There are no areas sealed off by military activities, as there are on the Wiltshire Downs and on Dartmoor. Everything is open to anyone. These things, and the springing turf, and the sense of remoteness from cities – London is only some 60 miles away, but here it might not exist – make the Berkshire Downs a walkers' country indeed.

This excursion begins at Uffington, in the Vale of the White Horse. It has a large church (St Mary): a 13th-century cruciform building with an octagonal tower and a good many windows that have subsequently been given strange shapes – especially some in the transepts, whose heads are triangular. But the church is not merely curious, it is beautiful, for its south porch and its refined chancel. Many of the older houses in the village, including the little 17th-century school on the south side of the churchyard, are built of chalk.

The Downs are very close, with Uffington Castle and the White Horse itself not much more than two miles away. To see them properly, and particularly the Horse, you need to go a little to the west, along the road towards Compton Beauchamp. The horse is stylised, not natural, and leaping splendidly. It probably dates from the 1st century B.C. – horses like it are to be seen on coins of that time – and it is much the finest work of its sort in England. There are other white horses, but they are not prehistoric; among figures cut in the chalk, only the Cerne Giant in Dorset can rival it, in scale and power. The White Horse has always been held in reverence; its cleaning, to remove turf and weeds periodically, was an obligation laid on people in the Vale, and used to be the occasion of a lively festival.

The slope of the Downs on which it is cut is surmounted by Uffington Castle: not a stone building of the Middle Ages, but an Iron-Age fort. We do not know much about it, for it has been little examined archaeologically. It comprises a single huge enclosure, surrounded by a ditch and a turf rampart strengthened with sarsens, the rough grey sandstone

Uffington: the White Horse (Aerofilms Ltd)

boulders that lie plentifully about everywhere. The Downs rise here to their highest point, 856 ft.

The entrance to the Castle was from the Ridge Way, a track that is usable still nearly all the way to Goring. In the Vale below the modern road, running along the foot of the hills from Swindon to Wantage, is the ancient Icknield Way, which is similarly continued, to cross the Thames and then go on by the Chilterns to end in Norfolk. So here at Uffington Castle, with the numerous barrows and tumuli about, there is a strong sense of the continuity of the prehistoric world with our own. The Romans provided the connection; and traces of them are here too, in the sites of villas below at Compton Beauchamp and Challow and of a substantial building of some kind in the heart of the Downs, two or three miles north-east of Lambourn.

If you are on foot, you now walk west along the Ridge Way, past Wayland Smith's Cave, a megalithic chambered tomb, and then south to the Lambourn road; by car you make a little circuit through Ashbury. As the road descends southwards there are big trees on the right and then at a break in them, suddenly, you see Ashdown House, narrow and tall, with a lantern on top crowned by a cupola. It is one of the most improbable sights in England.

The house was built soon after 1660 by Lord Craven, a Royalist returned from exile, with a devoted attachment to Charles I's sister Elizabeth, the widowed Queen of Bohemia. The old tradition was that he intended Ashdown to be a refuge for her when London should be infected with the plague. If so, it was to no purpose: for she died in London, of just that disease, in 1662. It really seems likelier that the house was a hunting lodge, with the lantern and the balustraded platform round it affording a high point from which the course of the hunt could be observed.

The building is square, with two small detached oblong pavilions. It looks to the four points of the compass, and each front faces an avenue of trees. The house is a rich creamy white, built of chalk with Bath stone dressings. There is only one other chalk building in England (Sawston Hall in Cambridgeshire) comparable in size and architectural pretensions.

Inside, a broad oak staircase – massive, plain and handsome – leads up to the roof. It is now hung very happily with portraits, largely from Lord Craven's own collection, of himself, his Queen, and his friends, including a conversation piece of the Civil War, by Dobson, on the first landing. There is no elaborate plaster or woodwork. The house is lived in, but none of the rooms is shown. What really matters is the ascent, to stand on the platform by the lantern and survey the country around. The trees are splendid here – the beeches above all, which love the chalk; the air crisp,

Ashdown House from the west (A. F. Kersting)

delightful on the hottest summer day; the whole experience unique and intriguing. Why did Lord Craven choose this remote site? Who was his architect? Perhaps William Winde, but it is by no means certain.

Ashdown House and Uffington Castle are less than five miles apart in distance, and perhaps 1,700 years in time. They are both human habitations; but they could scarcely be more remote from each other, in spirit and function.

Ullswater Cumbria 1A3

"Perhaps, upon the whole, the happiest combination of beauty and grandeur, which any of the Lakes affords". So Wordsworth on Ullswater: a judgment without partiality, for it was never his own lake, as at various times *Esthwaite* was, and Windermere and Grasmere. It does indeed show nearly all the elements that distinguish the landscape of the English Lakes; and, except at its northern end, it has scarcely been marred at all by any building development.

Ullswater is the second largest of the Lakes, after Windermere: 10 miles long and at its broadest, opposite Glencoyne, about three-quarters of a mile across. It has three arms making a reverse curve, and they are markedly different. There is a road (A592) all along the north and west side of the lake, with a corresponding smaller one for about half the way on the opposite shore. The circuit can be made on foot, keeping close to the water, though walking along A592, a narrow road, is no great pleasure, and there is not always an alternative footpath. Anyone who does not propose to walk the whole distance will see the lake best by taking the little steamer *Raven* (a steam yacht built 90 years ago, dieselised in 1935, and still going strong). It is desirable to pick it up at the north end, so sailing towards the head of the lake, set into the mountains. Here, at Pooley Bridge, the Eamont flows in, a substantial river running down from the Pennines.

The pier is at the foot of a conical hill, with an Iron-Age fort concealed in the trees at the top. Otherwise the scene is a placid pastoral one, the slopes very low. The water is dotted with small boats, for there is a sailing centre at Sharrow Bay. Ahead is Hallin Fell, tall and rounded, with the much higher Place Fell behind it. Hallin Fell juts out boldly, forming the entrance to a deep bay, into which the steamer sails to call at the pier of Howtown. To the left are the very striking slopes of Fusedale, steep and clean-cut. On the right a zig-zagging road climbs up into Martindale. There is a good walk into Boardale, around the slopes of Place Fell and down into Patterdale. Another, very much longer and involving some stiffer climbing, leads up on to High Street, with the Roman road striding over the mountains from a fort near Troutbeck towards Carlisle.

As you come out of Howtown Bay, glance backwards. If the weather is right, beyond Pooley Bridge you will see a long range of blue hills: the Pennines, 15 miles away.

The lake now narrows between Hallin Fell and a low green promontory opposite. It then expands to its greatest breadth. This is the second of its three divisions. The mountains to the north and west now become much grander, crowned by Helvellyn, which soon comes into sight ahead. It comprises a long even ridge (Striding Edge), with a peak at the right. There may be snow here still as late as May. Much of the western shore of the lake is cultivated and planted, notably the grounds of Lyulph's Tower, a Gothic house of 1780. Gowbarrow Park is above, from which there is a superb view over the whole lake. On the shore below, Wordsworth and his sister Dorothy, walking from Pooley Bridge to Gras-

Ullswater: above Howtown, looking south-west from the first to the second reach (Geoffrey Berry)

mere in 1802, saw the vision of daffodils that she described so perfectly in her journal and he later in his poem "I wandered lonely as a cloud". Aira Beck comes tumbling down here over two celebrated little waterfalls, High Force and Aira Force, to run out into the lake gently through a level green field.

Again the lake narrows. The tiny Norfolk Island in the middle is the pivot on which the whole scene turns southwards into the final section, closed in by mountain walls. Glencoynedale comes down at this point from the west, with a delectable walk up to the shapely saddle at its lower end, leading to steeper climbs above. The next valley on the same side, Glenridding, is a little scarred with quarrying and lead-mining. There is a village at its foot, with a pier at which the steamer terminates its voyage.

The final 10 minutes on the water, or on the road as it curves round north of Glencoynedale, are magnificent. Helvellyn is now out of sight, hidden behind the nearer masses. You are looking straight up into Patterdale, and beyond that towards the Kirkstone Pass, in the narrow gap between Hart Crag and Raven Crag. The main road toils up the pass steeply (a good bit of it at 1 in 4). It is the only way out of the valley, except for climbers and walkers, to the south.

Ullswater affords a perfect introduction to the English Lakes. Others surpass it in wildness, notably Wastwater far to the west; Windermere and some quite small ones have been more richly celebrated in poetry. But none offers a greater abundance of different pleasures; and none is more beautiful in its own right.

Uppark West Sussex 5A5

In site and architecture and furnishing, in the personalities that twist through its story, this is a house of beguiling charm.

It stands alone among the great houses of Sussex in being placed on the top of the Downs, right out on the open turf and chalk. It was built about 1690 and probably designed by William Talman, whose work is to be seen also at Chatsworth and Dyrham: a four-square house, of a red brick now slightly subdued by grey, with a strong cornice and pediment, it confronts the storms with total self-assurance.

Its builder was an elusive, rather ignoble politician: Ford, Lord Grey of Werk, a vehement Whig who played a shifty part in the 1680s, the inefficient commander of Monmouth's horse in his rebellion. After that defeat he managed to buy off his own life, and he eventually did well enough under William III to become Earl of Tankerville and, briefly at the end, Lord Privy Seal. We can appreciate his taste here without much liking his conduct.

The estate was sold in the middle of the 18th century to Sir Matthew Fetherstonhaugh, who adapted the house to the fashion of his time, plastered the ceilings, and, in particular, made the Saloon as we see it now. His son Harry succeeded him in 1774: another man of fine taste, gaily extravagant in horse-racing as well as in buying furniture, and a member of the circle of the Prince Regent, who came to Uppark again and again from 1785 onwards. For a year Sir Harry kept Emma Hart here as his mistress – and then sent her packing, to become in later years Nelson's Lady Hamilton. He was eventually estranged from the Regent, and retired from society about 1810, to lead a very quiet life at Uppark. He made one or two changes there at the instigation of his friend Humphrey Repton – the most conspicuous the addition of the heavy *porte-cochère* by which the visitor enters the house today, and the garish stained glass that indirectly illuminates the dining room. But this was by no means the end of Sir Harry's life. At the age of 70 he married his head dairymaid, Mary Ann Bullock, and having had her well educated in Paris lived happily with her until his death, at an age not far from 92. His wife succeeded him, and then his wife's sister, who lived there with a companion until 1895. Under them for 13 years the housekeeper was Mrs Wells, whose son H. G. Wells described the life of the house astringently in *Tono Bungay* and in his autobiography. The estate was then left successively to the

Uppark: the Red Drawing Room (A. F. Kersting)

sons of two neighbouring peers. The second was a distinguished Admiral, Sir Herbert Meade-Fetherstonhaugh, and he and his son gave the house to the National Trust in 1954.

There are some great treasures here. The mirrors form one of the finest series in England. The carpets include a lovely crimson Axminster in the Red Drawing Room and a noble Wilton, on a dark-blue ground, in the Saloon. The best furniture in that splendid room is French, but it also contains two sumptuous book-cases by Repton, a massive architectural framework for the gilt bindings of the books they hold.

Nearly all the most interesting pictures in the house were commissioned or bought by Sir Matthew Fetherstonhaugh. They include, at one end of the scale, six big formal works by Luca Giordano, the 17th-century Neapolitan, and at the other the set of eight little family portraits by Arthur Devis hung on the staircase. Sir Matthew himself is here, in the Red Drawing Room, painted by Pompeo Batoni in Rome at the close of his Grand Tour in 1751; and next to him the young Sir Harry, done by the same painter in 1776. They are both excellently characterised: Sir Matthew decisive, perhaps peremptory, very sure of himself yet not pompous; his son sensitive, refined, with a hint of the dilettante of the second generation.

But what many people will remember most about the rooms of Uppark is the way they are drenched with light. Nothing breaks it anywhere, except trees at the back of the house. On all other sides everything is open to the sun and the winds. The corner rooms, the Red Drawing Room and the Little Parlour, have a cross-light, from windows set at right angles to one another. So each enjoys two views of the Downs, sweeping away into the distance. Everything here has been kept wonderfully fresh; and for that it owes much to its last owners, Sir Herbert and Lady Meade-Fetherstonhaugh, who bestowed endless care upon the whole place in their time. It is a house that has always been much loved; and rightly.

The Vyne Hampshire 4E3

The Vyne lies only four miles north of Basingstoke, but in deep agricultural country. There is nothing to suggest the near presence of a town. You come out from there by Sherborne St John, and then along an undulating by-road shaded by big oaks, passing a tiny brick building – circular, with a tiled dome – which is the south lodge of The Vyne. Almost immediately afterwards the front of the house comes into sight.

It was built by William Sandys, a notably successful politician under Henry VIII, ennobled in 1523 with the title Lord Sandys of The Vyne. He was Lord Chamberlain from 1526 until his death in 1540, but though he evidently disliked some parts of his master's policy during the later years of his life, he kept his head, in both senses. Latterly he seems to have turned his attention away from The Vyne to another house, *Mottisfont*. When, a century later, the sixth Lord Sandys fell into financial trouble in the Civil War, he kept Mottisfont and sold this estate in 1653 to Chaloner Chute, a successful and prudent lawyer, who was Speaker of Richard Cromwell's Parliament and died while it was sitting in 1659. There were now Chutes at The Vyne for about 300 years, though the estate descended twice through women, with the family name being adopted by the male successor. Chaloner Chute's great-grandson John did much to alter the house during his tenure from 1754 to 1776. When Sir Charles Chute died in 1956 he bequeathed the estate to the National Trust.

The Vyne is a house that is equally delightful inside and out. The entrance today is on the west side straight into the Stone Gallery. This seems originally to have been used as a dormitory for visitors' servants; then it became a green-house; now it serves for the display of sculpture.

A series of rooms leads out of it, stretching across the north front. The first three have a unity, from their hangings of crimson damask, and the rococo plasterwork of the ceilings. These decorations were due to John Chute, who was a man of exquisite taste, rising at one moment as we shall see towards genius. He was a close friend of Horace Walpole and much associated with him in the Gothic work at Strawberry Hill. Two portraits of him hang in these rooms. In one of them he holds a sketch of his ideas of giving The Vyne a Gothic exterior. We must be glad, on the whole, that he did not realise them. The Ante-Room contains a Florentine jewel-casket encrusted with semi-precious stones, on a gilt stand probably made for it by William Vile, and in the Large Drawing Room there is a highly-finished portrait by Rosalba Carriera of Francis Whithed, a relation of John Chute's who was adopted by him and died young in 1751.

The Dining Room is predominantly not of the 18th century but of the 16th. This is the first place at which the oak panelling, so characteristic of the Tudor age, appears. Here it is fairly plain, and Elizabethan. The Tudor panelling is one of the outstanding distinctions of the Vyne. It varies considerably in colour according to the treatment it has received over the years. Here for example it was painted blue and patterned with stars in the 18th century; and then the paint was stripped off in the 20th. Next door, in the Chapel Parlour, the panelling is earlier, of Lord Sandys's time, and it is more beautiful in texture and in its variegated colour (partly owing to the insertion of some pine here and there), which ranges from the palest buff through all the gradations of brown.

John Chute's taste could go awry; and that duly appears in the Ante-Chapel, where his panelling, gimcrack, perfunctory, and painted a dark chocolate brown, is deplorable. It is best disposed of as a frivolous experiment he never troubled to undo. It need not disturb one now, however, for the room is small and leads straight into the Chapel, which is one of the most striking things in the house. It belongs to the extreme end of the medieval world and was erected in 1518–27. In those very years Luther began to challenge much of the faith it represented in Germany; and within a short time of its completion the foundations of that faith were undermined in England. The stalls of the chapel are richly carved. The glass of the east window is Flemish, and excellent of its kind. Scriptural scenes are placed above figures of royalty, Katherine of Aragon, Henry VIII and his sister, with their patron saints. At the top of each window stand the armorial bearings of the royal person represented below: a neat summary of Lord Sandys's views – his public views, anyway – of the religious and social order. Above the entrance is a gallery, at the back of which can be seen part of the interesting paintings done by Spiridone Roma, an artist from Corfu, for the walls of the chapel above the stalls. They show the fan vaults and reticulated tracery of Gothic architecture in a gay 18th-century manner.

To the south of the altar the Tomb Chamber opens out, erected by John Chute to contain a monument to his great-grandfather, Richard Cromwell's Speaker, the founder of the family here. The whole *ensemble* was planned by Chute himself, and we can be sure that he wrote the inscriptions, referring to the Speaker's services. The figure on the top is extraordinarily fine, contemplative, without any touch of the theatrical. It is the work of a little-known sculptor, Thomas Carter. The material is white Carrara marble. So often that is glaring and unsympathetic; here its properties appear at their best.

From the Ante-Chapel, turning left and then right, one reaches the staircase, the most brilliant thing in the house and due to John Chute himself. The staircase breaks into two at a half-landing and then leads up into a gallery running round the well. The heavily coffered ceiling is supported on slender Corinthian columns. With a skill worthy of Wren in his City churches, Chute has contrived not merely to overcome the limitations of this space but actually to turn them to advantage. The whole area is only 18 ft wide, but it is 44 ft long, and that has allowed him to make the rise of his staircase gentle and to give a sense of great height, long distance, even of mystery, subtly accentuated by the colonnade.

Ascending this lovely staircase slowly one comes to the Library, the Tapestry Room, with delightful small Mortlake tapestries on a very dark blue ground, and finally the Oak Gallery, which runs the whole length of the west side of the house and retains its original panelling of about 1525 complete, carved with the heraldic bearings of William Sandys, his master, and his friends. This is one of the finest displays of such woodwork in England.

Looked at from outside the house is essentially Tudor, unchanged. Its red brick (patterned a little with blue) has mellowed, to turn rose-pink in some lights. The original mullioned windows have been replaced by the white-painted sash windows of the 18th century. The north front was very materially altered by the addition of a classical portico, designed by John Webb to the orders of Speaker Chute. It has no function, but it provides a splendid accent to that front, which must always have been wanted, and if you cross the lake to the meadow on the far side you can see it is exactly right.

The Vyne is a house to visit for much of a day. It needs

(A. F. Kersting)

to be taken slowly, savoured for its strong idiosyncrasy. To the west of the house there is a notable herbaceous border – large, contrived with art, a fine addition of the 20th century. And all around it are magnificent trees: limes in front, with the king of them all, an enormous oak, south-west of the house towards the road.

Walpole St Peter: church of St Peter Norfolk 5B1
The country at the southern end of the Wash is divided between the Fenland and the Marshland. The Fenland is drained by rivers, and often flooded by them; the Marshland, to the west of it, by salt water from the sea. Both represent, like the Netherlands, a triumph of tenacity and patience in the endless battle with the waters. Both have had their reward in the wealth of the agriculture that resulted: corn and fruit-growing especially in the Fenland, whilst the Marshland became a splendid pasture for sheep. This wealth is reflected in the churches built here in the Middle Ages. The greatest of them is *Ely* cathedral in the Fens. The Marshland has no cathedral; but its parish churches constitute a group unsurpassed in England. This is one of them.

Walpole St Peter lies tucked away, reached by crooked little roads. The church stands in a big graveyard, planted with roses and shaded on the south side by one glorious beech tree. The fabric as we see it dates almost entirely from the second half of the 14th century. The exterior of the building is distinguished by its delicately panelled battlements, the sanctus bell-cote over the chancel arch, and the south porch, lavishly decorated and unusually long. There is a vaulted passage underneath the chancel, perhaps used for processions, certainly as a right of way. The west tower is a little too small and plain for the rest of the building. There was a terrible flood here in 1337, as a result of which it was decided to reconstruct the church, on a much larger scale befitting the parish's wealth. But enough remained of the tower to allow its lower part to be kept, and all that was done was to heighten it, in general conformity with the new work.

The interior offers no disappointments. In the richness and variety of its furnishings this one of the most fortunate churches in England. The building is big, with broad aisles, and uplifted by the raising of the chancel, above the passage just mentioned. Across the whole breadth of the nave runs a plain screen of the 17th century. Beyond that is much good medieval seating, a beautiful parclose screen in the south aisle, and

(N.M.R.)

well-carved stalls in the chancel. There are some pleasing fragments of medieval glass in the north aisle; otherwise the whole of the nave is flooded with light through clear glass of the 18th century. There is a noble brass chandelier, of Dutch origin, bought in 1701; six smaller modern ones have been added in the chancel. The fine brass lectern is of the early 16th century, and the pulpit of 1620. Among the minor fittings are the 18th-century wooden shelter for the clergyman reading the burial service – a sensible piece of equipment in the fiercely cold winters of the Marshland; a poor box of 1639; and a notice requiring the congregation to remove its pattens (muddy, no doubt, from these lanes) before coming into church.

The whole here is greater than its parts. Stone, wood, glass, metalwork, all combine together to produce a richness that reflects both the late-medieval Catholic Church and the Church of England that displaced it. There is nothing here of grandeur or ostentation. The chancel is due to the monastery of Ely, which then had the rectory in its hands; the rest, including the furniture, came from the parishioners. A community could not wish for a finer memorial of itself.

No other church, even in the Marshland, is furnished as this one. But to appreciate the architectural wealth of the district one should see at least two of Walpole's neighbours, more splendid externally though not inside: Gedney and Terrington St Clement. And away to the south, near Wisbech, are two others, of an earlier time: Walsoken, mainly of the late 12th century, and West Walton, in the purest manner of the 13th.

Warkworth Northumberland 1C1

Castles are works of military engineering. Their sites often render them spectacular, and the tall stone keeps of the 12th century, as at *Conisbrough* and *Portchester*, are magnificent symbols of power; but their designers were engineers, not architects. The special distinction of Warkworth Castle is that it is a fortification that is also, in some of its parts, a major work of architecture.

It stands at the lowest crossing-point of the River Coquet, two miles inland from its mouth. The village comprises one steep street rising up from the bridge (a medieval structure fortified with a tower, the main traffic carried by a modern bridge adjoining it). The church lies at the foot of the street, the castle at the top. Approach Warkworth if you can this way, or up the river from its mouth at Amble.

The place had had a long history before the first castle arose. St Lawrence's church, founded by Ceolwulf, King of Northumbria, was conferred by him on the abbey of Lindisfarne (see *Holy Island*) in 737. It is a handsome Norman building now, surprisingly lofty when one enters it, with a chancel vaulted in stone and decorated in the manner of *Durham* cathedral. The large south aisle, divided from the nave by a fine arcade, is an addition of the 15th century. At its west end is the effigy of a knight of about 1330, incisively sculptured and exceptionally well preserved.

Castle Street is pleasant, though not exciting in itself. The road skirts the east side of the Castle, and you enter by the Great Gate on the south.

There was probably a castle here early in the 12th century; certainly one by 1158, when Henry II made a grant of it and the manor of Warkworth to "Roger son of Richard". His son Robert, who succeeded him in 1177, ordered the building of some parts of the present castle, the Gatehouse and the wall lying west of it up to and including the Carrickfergus Tower at the south-west corner. Warkworth remained with this family (who were subsequently known as Clavering, from the estate they held in Essex) until 1332, when the last of them died without male heirs. It was then granted to Henry, second Lord Percy of Alnwick; and it has rested with that family, with intermissions of forfeiture, ever since. Warkworth was their second capital, preferred by some of them to Alnwick, and as such it figures repeatedly in Shakespeare's *Henry IV*. The Second Part of the play opens in front of it, in 1405, with Rumour addressing the audience at "this worm eaten hold of ragged stone".

That is poetically memorable, but it does not reflect historical truth: for the castle was still very much in commission, and indeed the plans may by then have been laid for what is now its most splendid element, the remodelled Keep. The first Earl of Northumberland – the old Earl in Shakespeare's play – determined to establish a college of secular canons within the castle, like Edward III's at Windsor. Its church, lying across the walled enclosure roughly at its centre, was begun by the second Earl, but it seems not to have been completed before his death at St Albans (fighting on behalf of Henry IV's grandson) in 1455. Thereafter the castle reflected the stormy and on the whole unsuccessful fortunes of the Percy family under the Yorkists and Tudors. By the 17th century it was gravely out of repair, damaged by the Scots and Parliamentarian soldiers who occupied it in 1644–9,

Warkworth Castle: the Keep (A. F. Kersting)

and finally dismantled in 1672 when the auditor of the Percy estates was permitted to remove 272 cartloads of its stone to build a house for himself. There was talk of rebuilding it in the next generation. But it was Alnwick that was repaired instead; lavishly in the 19th century, under the direction of Salvin. Salvin was engaged at Warkworth too, and he made a set of rooms in the Keep inhabitable for the fourth Duke in 1853–8. They are occupied occasionally still.

The outstanding parts of the castle now are the Gatehouse, two of the polygonal towers on the walls, the Lion Tower, and the Keep. Of these the Gatehouse is the earliest: the lower part of it was built soon after 1205, and its upper stage before the end of the 13th century. It was the focal point of the outward defences of the castle, which were strengthened on this side by a ditch – unnecessary anywhere else because of the river and the steep hill falling away to the north. The Carrickfergus Tower (named after an Irish property of the Claverings), at the south-west corner of the castle, belongs to the same age. So does the Grey Mare's Tail Tower, a fine five-sided structure on the eastern wall. The Lion Tower is later, dating perhaps from about 1400. It stands at the north-east corner of the Great Hall (now almost vanished), distinguished by the sculpture in high relief of the Percy Lion on its southern face, and two shields of arms set in a rectangular frame. The tower was designed to form a nobly impressive entrance porch to the hall and to the collegiate church – every trace of which has now gone, above ground.

But fine as these are, they are all eclipsed by the Keep. This stands at the highest point of the rock, at the north end of the castle enclosure. Though it evidently incorporates fragments of an older keep, it belongs now in essence to the early 15th century. It is a splendid symbol of the Percy family's power. Unmistakably it is still a work of military fortification: a square building with its corners sawn off. But there is a projection from each face, which makes the whole structure in effect cruciform, and it is crowned by a tall thin tower. It stands up proudly, instantly recognisable from miles around: there is nothing quite like it, in England or anywhere else. From the windows on its eastern side you look straight down the Coquet to the sea. Ahead to the north is the village of Warkworth, the castle's dependency. Here, even more insistently than at Alnwick, you are in the presence of the Percies, the greatest of northern magnates, when their troubled dominion was at its height in the national politics of England.

Wells Somerset 4D3

Wells is the most complete ecclesiastical city in England, and among the most perfect anywhere. It was not a political or military capital, like *Durham*. It never became a centre of manufacture, like *Norwich* and *Lincoln*, or of railways like *Ely*, or Laon in France. It was a place of the Church and nothing else, from its Saxon foundation down to the 20th century, when the influx of tourists gave it, for the first time, a substantial industry. In physical terms, it was little affected by the Reformation. Its cathedral had always been served by priests, who lived in the world, not by monks. Whilst Glastonbury, near by, was ruined by the dissolution of its great Benedictine monastery in 1539 and has been casting about ever since for an occupation it has not found, Wells has continued to be the chief administrative centre of its diocese. By a curious arrangement that diocese is a dual one, of Bath and Wells; but though Bath is much the bigger town, Wells has always been the cathedral city.

The distant view of Wells is enchanting, whether it is seen from across the plain to the west, or descending from the Mendips, or suddenly round a corner on the road from Shepton Mallet. The cathedral is not a very large building, but it is compact, and coherent throughout. Though the present structure dates almost entirely from two periods, there is no striking discordance of style between them. Speaking roughly, everything west of the central tower is of the late 12th century and the early 13th; the tower itself and all to the east of it 100 years later. That statement needs two qualifications. The towers that surmount the west front were added between about 1390 and 1430; the cloisters rebuilt later, about 1425–1510.

The west front is the most famous element in the cathedral. It tells the story of the Christian church in sculpture on a very large scale. There were 340 figures originally, nearly half of them life-size. Though many have been damaged or destroyed, there is still more 13th-century sculpture to be seen here than anywhere else in England. In quality it bears no comparison with contemporary French work, any more than the whole broad screen itself can rival the tautly-organised, soaring fronts at Reims or Amiens. Its impression of squat breadth is increased by the addition of the two towers. They demanded pinnacles, answering to those of the central tower; but those were never built. The west front of Wells, for all its celebrity, is a good deal less than perfect, in composition and in detail. But it stands beautifully now, above the expanse of the Cathedral Green: a setting to which there is nothing comparable in France.

It is best to enter the building by the north porch: a lofty and beautiful structure in itself, decorated with fine carving, in the stiff-leaf designs in which the English showed their mastery. Inside, the arcades of the nave are exceptionally good, rising from their clustered columns, and enriched by the small sculptures on the capitals and in panels set high above. This and the transepts of Wells are among the earliest surviving works of true Gothic in England or France (i.e. Gothic freed from all traces of the Romanesque style, in which the capitals derived from the ancient world), and it has all the charm of freshness upon it, enhanced by the colour of the limestone, quarried at Doulting, nine miles to the east.

Between the nave and the choir stands a set of great stone arches, unique in their design and arrangement. These vast scissors were inserted about 1340 to shore up the new tower, which was in danger of falling in. Visually, they mar the nave, and most people are happier with their backs turned on them. But they are a superb piece of medieval engineering – no substantial new work to support the tower has ever been called for since. They are also very powerful, with their heavy mouldings and huge round eyes. They have the full courage of strong conviction.

The eastern arm of the church is as fascinating inside as out, one of the supreme achievements of the 14th century in England, coming between the great work at *Bristol* cathedral and the triumph of the new Perpendicular style at *Gloucester*. Three elements in it may be mentioned here. All are visible at once by standing inside the choir, at the back. First, the treatment of the stonework: the canopies of the stalls (they have finely-carved wooden misericord seats), the complex panelling above the arches and the lovely lierne vault

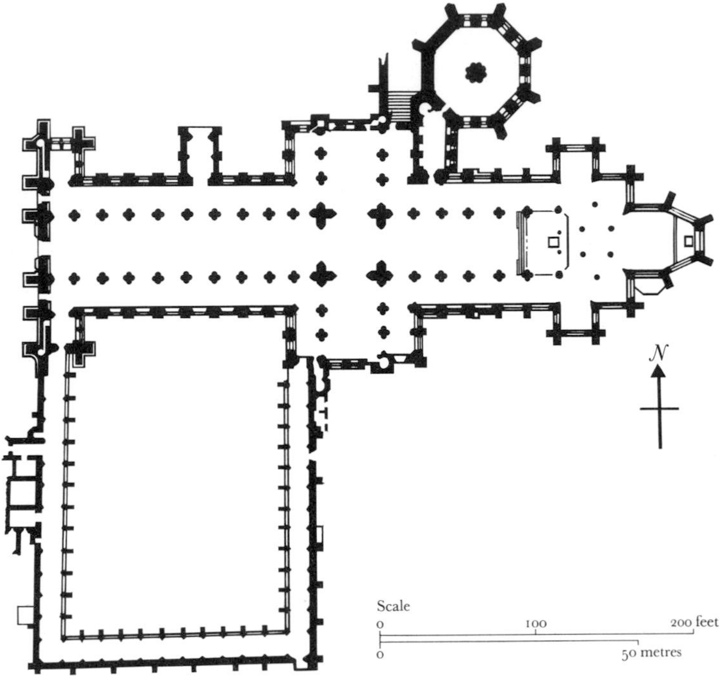

(see p. 188). Second, the glass in the high east window, some of the most beautiful that survives of the 14th century. The finest glass in any English cathedral is surely in the choir of Canterbury. That is of the 12th and 13th centuries, and the predominant colour in it is blue. Here there is scarcely any blue at all; it is yellow and green that stand out, supported by a little ruby red. The subject is the Tree of Jesse, tracing Christ's ancestry back to him. A vine issues from Jesse's side; Solomon and David flank the Virgin and Child; Christ appears in the centre of the window, crucified, between St Mary and St John.

Below it, behind the high altar, is the retrochoir, with the Lady Chapel beyond. Even from this distance the complexity of the design is apparent. That becomes plainer as one

(A. F. Kersting)

Wells cathedral: the retrochoir, looking to the Lady Chapel

walks through it and behind on both sides, stopping every few paces to take in the fresh vista of changing shapes, the exquisitely slender piers and the vaults they support. Finally the Lady Chapel, a five-sided projection, the windows producing a diagonal cross-light. Unhappily the glass here is mutilated in the side windows, and confused, though a series of fine figures survives under canopies in the south-east window. The east window is virtually the work of Thomas Willement in 1845. He was among the best 19th-century glass-painters, but he cannot hold a candle to what surrounds him here.

From the north aisle a broad stone staircase leads up to the Chapter House. It is slightly skewed, with a branch sweeping out of it into a doorway full of light. Originally it led to the Chapter House alone, but late in the 15th century the second branch was added, leading to a bridge (to be mentioned later), and the present effect appeared.

The Chapter House is octagonal, large and lofty, covered with a splendid stone vault of 32 ribs. Some of its original glass survives, red and white. The small sculptures all around are delightful (and so are the pair on the wall of the staircase). The Chapter House was the meeting-place, the business room, of the chapter, affording 31 seats for the purpose. Its construction was under way in 1300; it was probably complete by 1307, certainly by 1319. Polygonal chapter houses were a speciality of England, unknown in France or elsewhere. Together with the one at York, this is the latest of the series. It may well be thought the finest.

On the opposite side of the cathedral, reached from the south transept, are the cloisters, a work mainly of the 15th century, but given a faint Georgian flavour by the monuments on their walls. There was another Lady Chapel opening out of the east walk, rebuilt in 1478–88. It was demolished in 1552; excavations now in progress may tell us more about it. Above the east walk is the Library, erected under the terms of a bequest of 1424 and furnished as it is now from 1670 onwards. A few of its medieval books survive, some of them chained.

Leaving the cathedral by the north porch and turning right, you see a bridge over the road. The second branch of the Chapter House staircase was built to give access to it. Passing under it through a gateway to the left you are in a medieval street: the Vicars' Close. The vicars were subordinate priests who deputised for the prebendaries; they were established as a body in 1348, and these quarters were then built for them, forming a self-contained unit, like an Oxford or Cambridge College. There are 42 houses, with their own tiny chapel at the north end and a hall, reached by stairs, at the south. The Vicars then occupied a complete unit of their own, linked comfortably to the cathedral, in which their duties lay. They continued in existence as a body until 1931.

Most of the houses have been somewhat altered, notably through the insertion of Georgian sash windows; one of them, No. 16, has been reconstructed to make a five-bay Georgian house. But at the bottom on the left, and again higher up on the same side, a few present the original appearance with small Gothic windows. The chimneys stand up boldly, accenting the whole street. The houses are private and not open; but the interior of the chapel and hall can generally be seen, and both are worth visiting.

The bridge from the cathedral is known as the Chain Gate. It was erected as such, as a gateway to the cathedral close, shutting it in and protecting it if necessary. Along the street westwards, past the Deanery on the right (a 15th-century square building disguised by sash windows), is Brown's Gate. Turn left into Sadler Street and then right through the High Street. This brings you to the parish church, St Cuthbert's. Like *Beverley*, Wells enjoys the distinction of a great collegiate church at one end of the town and a very good parish church at the other.

St Cuthbert's has one of the most splendid of all Somerset towers (see *Ile Abbots*): nearly the highest (122 ft), and that height emphasised by the pairs of very tall arches on each face, and the lofty pinnacles at the corners. The church is an enlargement of a 13th-century building, light, ample, and spacious. It is defaced by blatant Victorian glass at the east end. The roof, a very fine one, has lately been repainted and looks garish. Most unhappily the tower arch and the space inside it have now been enclosed by a glass and metal screen, blocking up one of the best parts of the church, even intruding on the panelling of the arch itself. On the

(Iris Hardwick Library)

Wells cathedral: east end, from the foot of Tor Hill

other hand, the south aisle has now been cleared to make a space round the font, producing a diagonal view of the aisle itself and the chapel beyond.

Return now up the High Street to the Market Place. At the entrance to it is an 18th-century fountain replacing the medieval conduit, for the town's water supply. The row of houses on the left, all shops now, are a set, built about 1450 and altered only with Georgian windows. Opposite them is the Town Hall of 1779, in golden Ham Hill stone. The third gate leading to the cathedral, Penniless Porch, is tucked into the corner. Much more impressive is the fortified gatehouse to the Bishop's Palace.

The Palace is protected by a moat, high walls, and a drawbridge guarded by a second gatehouse. The walls were built under a licence of 1341. There was much disorder then, up and down the country. At that very time a political struggle between the King and Archbishop Stratford of Canterbury was taking place, which looked as if it might end in violence, like the murder of Archbishop Thomas Becket in 1170. The desire of the bishop to fortify himself here at Wells is easily understood.

Inside, the chapel and the hall of the palace were already standing as now (built about 1280). The chapel is complete, a most satisfying design inside; but the hall is ruined, presenting no more than a screen formed by one of its walls. Yet what a screen! The whole court as we now see it, inside the second gatehouse, is exquisite, the medieval building, in its pink stone, perfectly offset by the lawns and cedars of the 18th century.

You can now complete your visit to Wells by walking round two sides of the moat until you come to a road. In front of you is the wooded Tor Hill. From the foot of it you have by far the most remarkable external view of the cathedral. For all the celebrity of the west front, the east end is the finest. Here you can see its polygonal shapes, linked by the diagonals of the flying buttresses of the choir, the whole surmounted by the calm, majestic tower. Every element combines perfectly, even to the willows rising from the garden below: the garden that contains the springs, the wells from which the place takes its name.

West Bromwich: Oak House West Midlands 4D1
West Bromwich is one of the chief towns of the Black Country. But it is rather different from what that statement suggests. It is no longer black. The air is now clean, allowing a distant view of the hills behind Dudley; many daffodils are about in spring. The town has a main street, long and straight, much of it now pedestrianised. It also has a recognisable centre, with parish church, Town Hall, Library, and Post Office all together. There are hints of civic pride, not to be submerged one hopes now that it has become part of the new Metropolitan Borough of Sandwell. Nobody would be likely to visit West Bromwich expecting to find an ancient

building of note there. The greater the surprise and pleasure, then, to come upon this one.

It stands within five minutes' walk of the Town Hall in a garden (most carefully tended), overlooked by neat little modern houses: a perfectly authentic piece of timber construction of the 16th century, with a 17th-century brick addition behind. It has one feature that is very unusual: a tall timber erection in the centre under two small gables, with a window in it. This was designed as a lantern – an Elizabethan light-house, one might call it – to guide travellers approaching from the north and west. It can hardly have retained that function for long, for one of the chimney-stacks of the 17th-century extension masks it on the side where it had previously been most useful, facing down the valley.

Nothing seems to be known of the history of the house. It came into the possession of the Turton family, well-to-do

Oak House: the entrance front, surmounted by the lantern
(Sandwell District Council)

nail manufacturers, before 1634. It may be that the brick addition at the back was due to them and erected at this time. The Turtons continued there (latterly in an illegitimate branch, and indirectly) until 1837. In 1894 it was purchased by a public-spirited citizen, Alderman Reuben Farley. He gave it to the town to serve as a museum and generously paid for its restoration by a local firm of architects, Wood & Kendrick. The work was completed in 1898, and the house then opened to the public. It is no longer a general museum. Since 1951 it has been furnished as far as possible in the style appropriate to the house itself – i.e. largely of the 17th century.

The furnishing is on the sparse side, which is excellent, since Tudor and Stuart rooms were, by our standards, rather bare. The chief rooms are the Parlour and Dining Room to the right of the entrance, with the more intimate little Morning Room behind, the Kitchen on the other side of the house, and upstairs two bedrooms. An internal view of the lantern can now be got from the landing.

Of the furniture perhaps these pieces may be specially mentioned: the early-18th-century long-case clock in the parlour; the Jacobean dining-room table – extendible to nearly 11 ft and the armchair at the head of it; the small William and Mary bureau in the Morning Room; in the front bedroom the big four-poster bed with its Jacobean cover and curtains, and the little movable "baby-cage". There are also some fine massive chests of drawers and presses.

Oak House has been fortunate. When its landscape, near and far, filled with industry and a large town grew up around it, the chances must have been that it would be destroyed, or altered beyond recognition, or heavily restored in the late-Victorian age, to make it like so much black-and-white building (in Chester, for example) a caricature of itself. But it survived intact, and at last fell into the hands of sensitive architects, who did their work knowledgeably, and with affectionate restraint. It is admirably cared for now; a true piece of the historic timber building of the West Midlands, handed down to us in an enjoyable form.

Wreay: church of St Mary Cumbria 1A2
Nothing stranger than the church of Wreay* is described elsewhere in this book. It is strange in itself and in the story that lies behind its erection. It is the only building treated here that was designed by a woman. She was Sara Losh, and her own story needs to be understood before one addresses oneself to her church.

Her father John Losh was an ironmaster with a flourishing business in Northumberland. He was a Cumberland man by birth and built himself a house, Woodside, in the northern part of the parish of Wreay. His family comprised one son, mentally defective, and two daughters, Sara (b. 1785) and Catherine. Because of their brother's condition, the two daughters were the heiresses to John Losh's considerable wealth. In character they were rather like Elinor and Marianne in *Sense and Sensibility* – though Sara was much more of an intellectual than Elinor, and Catherine was free of Marianne's romantic follies. They travelled together on the Continent, in Italy for example in 1817. When Catherine died in 1835 Sara, in her grief, decided to rebuild the little Georgian parish church of Wreay in her sister's memory. She did so to her own designs, consulting so far as we are aware no architect at all, employing only a local mason, whom she is said to have sent to Italy to improve himself in his craft.

The building she erected was consecrated in 1842. It is like nothing else of its date in England. In so far as there are parallels to it in Europe, it seems impossible that Sara Losh can have known of them. Plainly she had been impressed by the Romanesque churches she had seen in France and in Lombardy, and they furnish the chief influence on what she built. But it is an influence, no more. There is no exact model anywhere for the church of Wreay.

It is a small stone building, nicely placed by the village

* Pronounced so as to rhyme with "fear".

Wreay church: the chancel (A. F. Kersting)

cross-roads: an almost square nave with a semi-circular apse, very large in proportion to it. What first arrests the attention is the carving of animals and leaves on the outside: powerful yet delicate, closely observed in a naturalist's sense. This is even more apparent inside. Here it takes on some bizarre shapes. The conventional furniture of lectern and reading-desk is in the form of rough-hewn tree trunks, of black bog oak found in a neighbouring peat moss. But the delicacy appears here too, at its most original and delightful. The east wall of the apse is pierced by a series of small round-headed windows. These are filled with yellow glass and with iron tracery in the form of fossilised plants: more beautiful than anything in the acres of Gothic tracery that were being produced in stone and metalwork to the orders of professional architects all over England at the time. In the nave Sara Losh had the opportunity, like many other church builders and restorers, to work in some fragments of medieval glass – bought for her by a cousin from the palace of the Archbishop of Paris, wrecked in the Revolution of 1830. But her treatment of it is disciplined and individual. She allows the old glass to form a jumble, a jewelled kaleidoscope, round the edges of the windows, with a severe standard pattern of modern glass in the centre, imposing a coherence upon the whole glazing scheme.

From photographs and descriptions one may expect something interesting indeed at Wreay, but not at all beautiful. The reality is more complex. There is some harshness, an occasional crudity, but also a strange beauty, which is independent of the building's touching story. The eastern limb of the church is genuinely impressive, monumental on the smallest scale.

But there is more to be looked at and thought about yet. In the north-east corner of the churchyard is a small hut, built of irregular blocks of hewn stone. It is Catherine Losh's mausoleum. She is seated inside, in white marble; on the walls are medallion portraits of the sisters' parents and their uncle. No ornament whatever. It is a stark commemoration: that is all.

Outside the mausoleum stands a free version of the Bewcastle Cross, put up by both sisters to the memory of their parents; and in the cemetery to the north a replica of St Piran's oratory, discovered in the sands of Perranzabuloe in Cornwall in 1835.

Another riddle remains. Close to the west door of the church is a tiny enclosure, like a well-head, with an iron fence in the form of arrows; and inside, at the north-west corner, an arrow is poised, entering the wall. What do these arrows signify? The answer seems to be that they commemorate a close friend, with whom one or other of the sisters was in love, Major John Thain, who was killed by a poisoned arrow on the Khyber Pass in 1842. It is one more addition, the most remote of all, to the amalgam of allusion, from stored-up memories, that Sara Losh fused together in this secluded Cumbrian church.

Writtle Essex 5B3

The village green is one of the best-known elements in the English landscape. It is found most commonly in the north-east, and in the south-east from Suffolk to Sussex. The green usually forms the centre of the village, the equivalent of the market-place in a town; the focus of its everyday communal life, of its sports (one thinks most of all of cricket) and its occasional celebrations.

Some of these greens may well have originated with a defensive intention, to provide a secure enclosure into which cattle could be driven at night to keep them safe from beasts of prey.

Those in the south-east are commonly triangular. Here at Writtle is a highly characteristic example. The Church Green is a large space lined with houses, mostly of two storeys, clad in plaster or red brick. A pond lies at the eastern apex of the triangle, overhung with willows. The green itself is bordered with limes. It is not secluded: busy with the traffic of the main road from Chelmsford to Ongar, running along its north side.

Writtle: the Church Green, with its pond (A. F. Kersting)

There is one tall and handsome house on that road. But the best houses are on the south, screening the church. Close to the pond is Motts, a 17th-century building with the bold chimney-stacks that appear frequently in Essex, behind a Georgian *façade*. Church Lane is flanked by two very different houses. On the left is the half-timbered Aubyns, of about 1500 (notice the blocked-up windows in the side wall, which may have been those of a Tudor shop); on the right Mundays, 17th-century, low, with square windows and pretty Georgian iron railings.

The church (All Saints) has been much rebuilt. The chancel contains a curious monument by Nicholas Stone to Sir Edward Pinchon (1629), not very happily repainted in recent years; and beside it a charming small alabaster memorial to Edward Eliott (d. 1595). Facing them is the bust of Sir John Comyns (d. 1740), by Henry Cheere, excellently set on a richly-carved pedestal. He was the builder of Hylands Park, a big house (now shut down) two miles away to the south.

There is another way to leave the church, to the east by Romans Place, with a trio of delightful 18th-century houses. The parish is a large one, and includes some scattered settlements; among them Newney Green, to the west, with a fine house, Benedict Otes, of 1644.

This tract of country, north of the A12, remains sequestered. It stretches across unbroken from Chelmsford to the delightful Epping Forest. The London tube gives access to the Forest (at Loughton and Theydon Bois stations) and continues to Ongar, at the very heart of this quiet district. But when you are driving or walking here, you forget London. It is only 20 or 30 miles away; it might be 100.

THE PLAN OF A CHURCH

Some of the technical terms used in describing churches in this book are shown on the accompanying plan. It was usual to lay them out with the altar at the east end, though this custom was not followed invariably. All descriptions in the text assume this alignment, the north being on the left-hand side of the altar, the south on the right.

The majority of parish churches – particularly those built from the 14th century onwards, e.g. *Astbury*, *Walpole St Peter* – are without transepts and have towers placed at the west end, not centrally over the crossing. In many (like Astbury again, and St Andrew Undershaft in *London*) there is no structural division between the nave and the chancel. In most parts of the country the screens have been removed, though many survive in East Anglia and the West Country (see for example *Hartland*).

The plan shown here was subject to many variations. In some churches the eastern arm was rounded with an apse, perhaps even (as in the cathedral at *Norwich*) a group of them, in the fashion almost universal in France. In many churches smaller chapels have been added, sometimes a Lady Chapel leading out of one of the transepts or beyond the altar at the east end. Some very opulent churches (e.g. *Patrington*) have double aisles, on one side of the nave or both. In larger churches there was often a processional path, or ambulatory, behind the altar, and a Lady Chapel beyond (see *Abbey Dore*). And so on. The plan given here is simple and basic; it should enable the variations to be appreciated and understood.

The reasons for adopting them were not so often aesthetic as functional: to provide for a larger congregation or for more elaborate ritual, or after the Reformation to adapt the medieval building to new forms of worship. These matters are admirably explained in two books, one old and the other more recent: for the medieval buildings A. H. Thompson, *The Ground Plan of the Medieval Parish Church* (1911), for their conversion and replacement after the Reformation G. W. O. Addleshaw and F. Etchells, *The Architectural Setting of Anglican Worship* (1948).

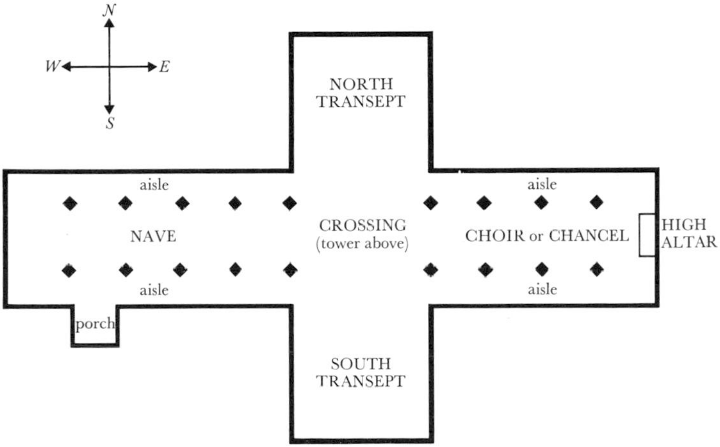

BOOKS AND MAPS

No guidebook can be self-sufficient, providing all the information and comment that its reader needs in order to appreciate fully what he is looking at. This book, from its very nature, is an introduction and no more. It should be used in conjunction with other books. The *Blue Guides* to England and to London are invaluable. Almost all the buildings discussed here have their own guides, to be bought on the spot. Those published by the Department of the Environment, to monuments in the care of the State, and by the National Trust to its properties usually reach a very high standard. The whole country is now surveyed in Sir Nikolaus Pevsner's splendid series *The Buildings of England* (45 vols., 1951–74). Each volume covers one, occasionally two, of the old pre-1974 counties. New and revised editions are being steadily produced. Lengthier accounts will be found in two very large series, by no means complete: the *Reports of the Royal Commission on Historical Monuments* and the *Victoria History of the Counties of England*. Among works on archaeology E. S. Wood, *Collins Field Guide to Archaeology* (1963 and subsequent editions), and R. J. A. Wilson, *Guide to the Roman Remains in Britain* (1974), are very helpful.

Four general books concerned with England as a whole may be mentioned: Sir George Clark, *English History: a Survey* (1971), the best one-volume history now available; W. G. Hoskins, *The Making of the English Landscape* (1955); Alec Clifton-Taylor, *The Pattern of English Building* (revised edition, 1972), and *English Parish Churches as Works of Art* (1974).

Finally, maps. Two series are of particular importance. The Ordnance Survey covers England in 186 sheets on a scale of 1:50,000. This is the modern successor of the one-inch map, which had been in course of production and then of continuous revision since 1805. Bartholomew's 36-sheet map on a smaller scale (1:100,000) has the great advantage that it shows heights in different colours, making it easier to appreciate the configuration of the country. For long-distance motoring the Ordnance Survey *Route Planning Map of Great Britain* (scale 1:625,000), published in a new edition every year, is excellent.

Other good maps are the *National Trust Atlas*, the Ordnance Survey's *Geological Map of Great Britain* (two sheets), and its series of historical maps, depicting the country at different periods.

There is no entirely satisfactory map of London. All the detailed street-plans currently available are in need of revision. Bartholomew's *London Plan* and the Ordnance Survey's *Greater London Map* are both clear and well designed.

NOTES ON TRAVELLING

The places described in this book vary greatly in size and importance. Nobody should have any difficulty in finding his way to Liverpool or Leeds. But many of the other places are more difficult to get to, by car or public transport. The following list (to be used of course in conjunction with the maps on pp. 23–9) gives the minimum directions that seem to be required. Places marked with an asterisk (*) have railway stations of their own, appearing in the index to British Rail timetables. Otherwise the railhead is indicated, together with the distance. The addresses of the larger bus operators are given in the British Rail timetables; those of others can be obtained from Tourist Information Centres, which are listed on the Tourist Boards' *Britain Tourist Map*.

The London entries are listed at the end.

Days and times of admission to buildings are not given; they are apt to be altered from year to year. They are to be found in two publications issued annually by ABC Historic Publications Ltd: *Historic Houses, Castles, and Gardens* and *Museums and Galleries*. These also indicate the means of public transport available. Many houses belonging to the National Trust are closed to visitors on Fridays.

In the second column a small number of additional places are listed that are in the vicinity of each place discussed – usually within a radius of 20 miles. Their outstanding features are indicated by the number attached to them.

Symbols used:

‡ Owned by the Government; in the care of the Department of the Environment

† Owned by the National Trust

* Railway station

NOTES ON TRAVELLING

1 Prehistoric or Roman antiquity
2 Castle
3 Cathedral
4 Church
5 House
6 Landscape
7 Town
8 Village

The places in italics in col. 2 are described in this book.

Place and Nearest Rly Stn	*Vicinity*
Abbey Dore [Hereford, 11m.]	Hereford 3, 4; Kilpeck 4
‡Abingdon [Oxford, 6m.]	Dorchester 4; Milton 5; Oxford 3, 7; *Uffington*
*Appleby [Penrith, 13m.; rly service infrequent]	Brougham 2, 4; Eden Valley 6; *Ullswater*
‡Appuldurcombe [Shanklin, 3m.]	Godshill 4; St Boniface Down 6
Astbury & †Little Moreton [Congleton, 2m.]	Gawsworth 5; Jodrell Bank Radio Telescope
Astley Hall [Chorley, 2m.]	Hoghton Tower 5; Preston (Harris Lib., Victn chs.); Rivington Pike 6
‡Avebury [Swindon, 12m.]	Barbury Cas. 1; Devizes 7; Marlborough 7; Mildenhall 4
Barfreston [Shepherdswell, 2m.]	Canterbury 3, 7; *Dover*
*Bedford	Elstow 8; Kimbolton 5; Old Warden (Shuttleworth Coll., old aircraft etc.)
Berkeley [Gloucester, 16m.]	*Bristol*; *Gloucester*; *Severn Bdg.*
†Berrington [Leominster, 4m.]	Croft 5; Eye 5; Ludlow 4, 7

Place and Nearest Rly Stn	*Vicinity*
*Berwick-on-Tweed	*Holy Island*; Norham 2, 4; Tweed 6 (see *Cheviot*)
*Beverley	*Burton Agnes*; Hull 7; *Patrington*; *S. Dalton*; *Sledmere*
*Bingley	*Haworth*; *Leeds*; Saltaire 7
Blanchland [Hexham, 10m.]	Hexham 4, 7; Weardale 6
†Bodiam [Robertsbridge, 4m.]	*Rye*; *Scotney*
*Boston	Heckington 4; *Tattershall*
*Brighton	Ditchling Beacon 6; Lancing Coll. chapel 4; Lewes 7
*Bristol	Badminton 5; Bath 7; *Berkeley*; Dyrham 5; *Wells*
Brympton d'Evercy & †Montacute [Yeovil, 3m.]	Sherborne 4, 7; Stoke-sub-Hamdon 4; Tintinhull 5
Burton Agnes [Bridlington, 6m.]	*Beverley*; *Sledmere*; *S. Dalton*
†Castle Drogo [Exeter, 14m.]	Dartmoor 6
Cheviot and the Tweed [Berwick-on-Tweed, 20m. to Cheviot]	*Berwick-on-Tweed*; *Holy Island*
Chipping Campden & †Hidcote [Evesham, 8m.]	Broadway 8; Stratford-upon-Avon 7; Kiftsgate Court 6
Clunbury [Broome, 3m.]	Clun 7; Ludlow 7; *Stokesay*
Coalbrookdale & Ironbridge [Wellington, 6m.]	Bridgnorth 7; Morville Hall 5; Much Wenlock 7
†Coggeshall [Kelvedon, 3m.]	Colchester 7; Layer Marney 5
*‡Conisbrough	Rotherham 4; Tickhill 2, 4
†Cotehele [Calstock, 2m.]	Plymouth 7; River Tamar 6
†Coughton [Redditch, 6m.]	Ragley Hall 5; Stratford-upon-Avon 7

Place and Nearest Rly Stn	*Vicinity*
*Dorchester & ‡Maiden Castle	Athelhampton 5; Cerne Abbas 8; Weymouth 7
*Dover (Castle‡)	*Barfreston*; Canterbury 3, 7; Deal 2
*Durham	Newcastle 7; *Penshaw*; Sedgefield 4
*Ely	Cambridge 7; *Mildenhall*
Esthwaite [Windermere, 5m.]	Coniston 6; Grasmere 6; Windermere 6
*Farnham	Chawton (Jane Austen's house); *Selborne*
Fingest & Turville [Marlow, 5m.]	Marlow 7; W. Wycombe 5
†Gibside [Newcastle, 7m.]	*Blanchland*; Newcastle 7
*Gloucester	Cheltenham 7; Painswick 8
†Golden Cap [Axminster, 9m.]	Bridport 7; Lyme Regis 7
Great Amwell [St Margaret's, 1m.]	Broxbourne 4; Hertford 7
†Great Chalfield [Bradford-on-Avon, 3m.]	Bath 7; Bradford-on-Avon 7; Lacock 5, 8
Hartland & Clovelly [Barnstaple, 25m.]	*Launcells*; Morwenstow 4
*Hatfield	*Great Amwell*; Hertford 7; St Albans 3, 7
*Haworth	*Bingley*; E. Riddlesden 5
‡Heveningham [Halesworth, 6m.]	Framlingham 2, 7; Southwold 4, 7
Hoar Cross [Burton-on-Trent, 7m.]	*Sudbury*; Tutbury 2
‡Holy Island [Berwick-on-Tweed, 12m.]	Bamburgh 2; *Berwick*; *Cheviot*; Farne Is. 6

Place and Nearest Rly Stn	*Vicinity*
Houghton [Kings Lynn, 13m.]	Castle Acre 2; Castle Rising 2; Kings Lynn 7
‡†Housesteads [Bardon Mill, 3m.]	Hexham 4; *Lanercost*
Ile Abbots [Taunton, 9m.]	Ilminster 4; Quantock Hills 6; Stocklinch Ottersey 6
Kedleston [Derby, 4m.]	Ashbourne 4, 7; Derby 7
Kempley [Ledbury, 7m.]	Ledbury 4, 7; Ross-on-Wye 7; Wye Valley 6
Kirkleatham [Redcar, 2m.]	Cleveland Hills 6; Ormesby 5; Guisborough 7
†Knightshayes [Exeter, 17m.]	Cullompton 4; Exmoor 6; Tiverton 2, 4
‡Lanercost [Brampton, 3m.]	Roman Wall 1 (see *Housesteads*)
Launcells [Bude; Exeter, 51m., or Barnstaple, 35m.]	Crackington Haven 6; *Hartland*; Morwenstow 4
*Leeds	*Bingley*; Bradford 7; Bramham 5; Harewood 5; Nostell 5
*Lincoln	*Boston*; *Newark*; *Stow*; *Tattershall*
*Liverpool	Chester 3, 7; *Speke*
†Lytes Cary [Yeovil, 8m.]	*Brympton d'Evercy*; *Montacute*; Tintinhull 5
*Maidenhead	Cliveden 6; *Fingest*; Marlow 7; Windsor 2, 7
Mildenhall [Newmarket, 8m.]	Bury St Edmunds 7; Cambridge 7; *Ely*
Molland [Barnstaple, 18m.]	Chittlehampton 4; Exmoor 6
*Newark	*Lincoln*; Southwell 3
*Norwich	Blickling 5; Felbrigg 5

Place and Nearest Rly Stn	*Vicinity*
Patrington [Hull, 16m.]	*Beverley*; Hull 7
†Penshaw [Sunderland, 5m.]	*Durham*; Jarrow 4; Monkwearmouth 4; Newcastle 7
‡Plaxtol [Wrotham, 3m.]	Knole 5; Tonbridge 2
*Portchester (Castle‡)	Portsmouth 7 (Southsea Cas. 2); Titchfield 4; *Uppark*
Richmond (Castle‡) & Swaledale [Darlington, 12m.]	Barnard Castle 7; Greta Bridge 6; Wensleydale 6
‡Rievaulx [Thirsk, 13m.]	Byland 4; Coxwold 8; Helmsley 2; Sutton Bank 6
‡Rycote [Oxford, 10m.]	*Fingest*; Oxford 3, 7; Thame 7
*Rye (Lamb Ho.†)	*Bodiam*; *Scotney*; Winchelsea 7
‡St Mawes [Truro, 10m.]	Pendennis 2; *Trelissick*; Truro 3
*Salisbury	Stonehenge 1; Wilton 5
Sall [Norwich, 13m.]	Swanton Morley 4; Blickling 5
*Scarborough (Castle‡)	*Burton Agnes*; Castle Howard 5; *Sledmere*; Whitby 4, 7
†Scotney [Tunbridge Wells, 10m.]	*Bodiam*; *Rye*; Sissinghurst 5; Tunbridge Wells 7
Seaton Delaval [Newcastle, 10m.]	Newcastle 7; Tynemouth 4
†Selborne [Alton, 5m.]	Chawton (Jane Austen's house); *Farnham*
Severn Bridge [Chepstow, 2m., or Bristol, 15m.]	*Berkeley*; *Bristol*; Wye Valley 6
Sledmere [Driffield, 8m.]	*Burton Agnes*; Castle Howard 5
†Slindon [Barnham, 4m.]	Bignor 1; Chichester 3, 7
South Dalton [Beverley, 5m.]	*Beverley*; *Burton Agnes*; Hull 7; *Sledmere*

Place and Nearest Rly Stn	*Vicinity*
†Speke [Liverpool, 8m.]	*Liverpool*
†Standen [E. Grinstead, 3m.]	Ashdown Forest 6; E. Grinstead 7; Sheffield Park 6
Stanford-on-Avon [Rugby, 6m.]	Althorp 5; Naseby 6
Stapleford [Melton Mowbray, 4m.]	Brooke 4; Gaddesby 4; Oakham 7
†Staunton Harold [Derby, 11m.]	Ashby-de-la-Zouch 2, 7; Appleby Magna School; Melbourne 4
*Stockport	Lyme Hall 5; Marple canal locks & viaduct
Stokesay [Craven Arms, 1m.]	*Clunbury*; Ludlow 4, 7; Wenlock Edge 6
†Stourhead [Gillingham, Dorset, 6m.]	Bruton 4, 7; Cadbury Castle 1; Longleat 5
Stow [Gainsborough, 7m.]	Gainsborough (Old Hall); *Lincoln*; *Newark*
*†Styal	Bramall 5; Tatton Park 5
†Sudbury [Uttoxeter, 5m.]	See entry
†Tattershall [Sleaford, 13m.]	*Boston*; Heckington 4; *Lincoln*; Sleaford 4, 7
Test Valley & †Mottisfont [Romsey, 4m. to Mottisfont]	Romsey 4; Southampton 7; Winchester 3, 7
*Totnes	Dartmouth 7; and see entry
†Trelissick [Truro, 5m.]	Pendennis 2; *St Mawes*; Truro 3
†Trerice [Newquay, 4m.]	Lanhydrock 5; St Columb Major 4; Truro 3
Uffington (Castle & White Horse‡) & †Ashdown [Swindon, 8m.]	Great Coxwell Barn; Lydiard Tregoze 4, 5; Swindon Rly Museum

Place and Nearest Rly Stn	*Vicinity*
Ullswater [Penrith, 4m.]	Brougham 2, 4; and see entry
†Uppark [Petersfield, 5m.]	Butser Hill 6; Midhurst 7; Petworth 5
†The Vyne [Basingstoke, 4m.]	Silchester 1; Stratfield Saye 5
Walpole St Peter [Kings Lynn, 10m.]	Kings Lynn 7; Terrington St Clement 4; Walsoken 4; W. Walton 4; Wisbech 7
Warkworth (Castle‡) [Alnmouth, 4m.]	Alnwick 2; Cragside (Rothbury) 5
Wells [Bath or Bristol, 21m.]	Bath 7; *Bristol*; Chewton Mendip 4; Croscombe 4; Nunney 2
*West Bromwich	Dudley 2; Wightwick Manor 5
Wreay [Carlisle, 5m.]	Carlisle 3, 7; Corby & Wetheral 6; *Lanercost*
Writtle [Chelmsford, 3m.]	Blackmore 4; Epping Forest 6; Margaretting 4

LONDON

Place	*Nearest Underground Station (where none, British Rail (BR) shown)*
Church of St Andrew Undershaft	Mansion House or Aldgate
Church of St Mary Abchurch	Cannon St
*Greenwich	See entry
†Hampstead: Fenton House	Hampstead
Harefield	Denham stn (BR) 2m.; thence bus 247
Monument & church of St Magnus the Martyr	Monument

Place	*Nearest Underground Station*
Museum of London	St Pauls or Barbican
St James's Park	St James's Park
St Pancras Station	Kings Cross
Syon Park	Gunnersbury (2m.), thence bus 117, 267; BR Syon Lane (1m.)

INDEX

I. PERSONS, PLACES, AND SUBJECTS

*architects and engineers
†artists and craftsmen
descriptions in the text are indicated by italics

INDEX

INDEX

II. CHRONOLOGICAL

For buildings and events before the Norman Conquest see the entries "Prehistory" and "Romans" in the previous index.

INDEX